LifeCode

PERSONALIZED FORECAST FOR 2023

A General Look at Your Whole Life Karmas

- ❖ Your mind is running at a thousand miles an hour.
- ❖ You are constantly thinking and analyzing everything.
- ❖ Sometimes you keep most of your thoughts to yourself.
- ❖ You do not tell your plans very easily to others.
- ❖ You feel you are right in everything 33% of the time.
- ❖ Sometimes you think everyone is against you.
- ❖ You are very beautiful, or handsome in the case of males.
- ❖ You attract the opposite sex very easily.
- ❖ Your need for love and romance is very high.
- ❖ You experience many difficulties in your marriage.
- ❖ A sure key to happiness for you is meditation and music.
- ❖ You are very kindhearted and are sometimes deceived easily by your lovers.

*Chakra Square Healing Center * Miami, FL 33186*

*(305) 253 – 5410 * swamicharran@gmail.com*

Lifecode Series™
presents

LIFECODE #7
THE CONSCIOUSNESS OF TIME & SPIRITUALITY

BIRTHDAYS FOR LIFECODE #7					
06-January	22-March	20-May	27-July	15-October	31-December
15-January	31- March	29-May	08-August	24-October	
24-January	03-Apr	01-June	17-August	05-November	
05-February	12-Apr	10-June	26-August	14-November	
14-February	21-Apr	19-June	07-September	23-November	
23-February	30-Apr	28-June	16- September	04-December	
04-March	02-May	09-July	25-September	13-December	
13-March	11-May	18-July	06-October	22-December	

We use the Sun as a measurement that makes the day, the Moon as a measurement that makes the Month, the year is created by the movement of the Earth around the Sun in the solar system.

Using Vedic Mathematical methods of calculation, the day of the Month plus the Month of the Year can be used as real number in the above equation. Let's say the baby was born on February 12, 1956 then the equation for birth will be: SUN + MOON = 12 (day) + 2 (Month) = Moment of Birth = 14 = 1 + 4 = 5

In this case the numbers above 9 are repetitions of the real numbers so in Vedic mathematics the higher numbers are reduced to real numbers so in this case 14 is really 5. This final number from the above equation is then referred to as your **LifeCode**.

Please Note: For Eastern countries, it is important that you check the book also with the day after the above day shown in the table if the Birth was in the evening in the Eastern Time zones of the world. The reason why is because the forecasts measurements in this book were calculated based on North American and South American time zones and dates. For places such as those located in Africa, Europe, Asia and the Far East, and the birth occurred in the evening local time, then the LifeCode number after the above one should be consulted also.

Swami Ram Charran

COPYRIGHT INFORMATION

Author Credits:

Editor in Chief:	LURESA RAMCHARRAN
Designed by:	SWAMI RAM CHARRAN
Cover Design by:	LUANA RAMCHARRAN
Printed by:	CHAKRA SQUARE HEALING CENTER

Section 1

LifeCode #7– Vedic Deity Shiva

General Look at Your Whole Life Karmas

❖ Your mind is running at a thousand miles an hour.

❖ You are constantly thinking and analyzing everything.

❖ Sometimes you keep most of your thoughts to yourself.

❖ You do not tell your plans very easily to others.

❖ You feel you are right in everything 33% of the time.

❖ Sometimes you think everyone is against you.

❖ You are very beautiful, or handsome in the case of males.

❖ You attract the opposite sex very easily.

❖ Your need for love and romance is very high.

❖ You experience many difficulties in your marriage.

❖ A sure key to happiness for you is meditation and music.

❖ You are very kind hearted and are sometimes deceived easily by your lovers.

❖ You should avoid the color black...wear light colors.

Seven is the most significant and magical of the numbers. It has long been held sacred, as is shown by the extraordinary frequency of seven in mythology, the Bible, and classifications of all kinds: there are seven notes in the musical scale, seven phases of the Moon, seven seas, seven heavenly bodies in the old Ptolemaic system, seven wonders of the world, seven hills of Rome, seven virtues, seven deadly sins, seven days of creation, seven plagues of Egypt, seven sentences in the Lord's Prayer, seven trumpets in the Apocalypse, and many more. The seventh son of a seventh son is believed to possess great magical powers. People who are Sevens are sometimes great thinkers and may have an occult or psychic side. They may be researchers, investigators, or inventors. They have an affinity with the sea and often travel widely. But they must use their powers wisely, avoiding pride and cynicism, and accepting that their talents will never make them materially rich.

You have a secretive and sometimes very private personality. You hardly speak about what you are thinking but your mind is running at 100 miles per hour. However, when you do speak your words are like fire ready to destroy the person you are directing it at. People around you see you as an egg shell ready to break with the slightest intimidation so your partner or lover feels like he or she is always walking on eggshells because he or she never knows when you are going to find something wrong with him or her. Your criticism of others can be very high and may prevent others from getting very close to you. You tend to hold back a lot of your personal feelings about others. Even your beloved one will ask you when you are going to say "I love you." It is very important that you do not analyze others too much for there are no such persons who are perfect in everything. The first lesson you must learn in life is that no one can be perfect. Once you have learnt this your love life and your marriage life will be much happier. You possess a very high temper and may sometimes speak very harshly to others. If this is a quality that is carried into your marriage it may surely end in divorce. Out of all others in this astrological analysis you possess the highest ego there is. You will never admit when you are wrong. You will never admit when you feel weak inside and you will always put up an outward appearance much different from the one that is inner. Your true feelings never seem to come out, even though your true feelings given to the other person will solve all the problems. If you are an extremely negative individual you may be addicted to drugs, alcohol or smoking. You may also be constantly complaining over petty or unnecessary matters. A small matter may worry you a great deal. You are constantly studying or reading if you are not sleeping or relaxing watching TV. You are very slow in your movements and may experience many delays in your life as a result of this. You may get married very late in life. If you do get married early there may be a possibility of separation. Late marriages are usually more successful. Your interests may lie in the field of medicine and if you study medical sciences you will be successful in a career associated with it. If you are a positive individual you may become a priest, a yogi or saint. If you are religious you may experience inner encounters with God and other divine manifestations of the universal deities. If you happen to find yourself a GURU you may experience a divine connection through that personality. If this path is followed most of your wishes will be fulfilled in life and your desires may become a reality. You may encounter many religious individuals in your life. You are advised to pay much attention to what they say for their advice may be very beneficial to you. Respect must be given to all holy people or elders in the family. Christians are advised to say the Lord's Prayer 11 times every day.

POSSIBLE HEALTH PROBLEMS

❖ Heart problems, addiction to drugs and alcohol
❖ Insanity, possession by spirits and physical disabilities
❖ Children may be born retarded or disabled.
❖ Can be given false medicine by doctors

MEDITATION RECOMMENDATIONS

❖ Your primary meditation focus is love and godly things.
❖ I recommend that you meditate for at least 30 minutes, to slow your thoughts.
❖ While meditating you should always be in the lotus position of sitting with folded feet, with your thumb and forefinger touching.
❖ You should always close your eyes during meditation, as you are always looking at your inner self.
❖ A holy location, temple, mountain or place of worship is your best place for meditation

CAREER RECOMMENDATIONS

Amusements, artist, communication, electrical, journalist, management, printing, publishing, sculptor, expert, clothes, sales, athlete, cowherd, leader, textiles, paper press, writer, literature, stenographer

Section 2

Love & Marriage Life Code Compatibility

The compatibility of a marriage or love union can determine the level of happiness and understanding the couple will enjoy throughout their lives together. It can also alert the couple of what are the most likely issues or tests they will have to confront together and there are some suggestions about what tendencies come with a particular energy and how to avoid them to have a better and happier marriage. Regardless of a match people and couples go through different periods in life when they are tested and Swami Ram Charran can help you to make the journey a little lighter.

Table 2.1 - COMPATIBILITY QUALITY OF LOVE MATCH OR MARRIAGE									
YOUR LIFE CODE	PARTNER'S LIFE CODE								
7	1	2	3	4	5	6	7	8	9
7	Excellent	Very Bad	Neutral	Excellent	Good	Neutral	Excellent	Very Bad	Good

Section 3

LifeCode #7 Predictions for the Year 2023

Forecasts by the Vedic Deity Lord Narayan

The key word is **change**. Movement, travel, sexuality, freedom, romance, greed and excessiveness are the influences this year. This is the year to improve on your old operations or plans. This is a good year to fix up the old dwelling or perhaps buy a new home. Personal freedom will be at its peak, take advantage of it. If you seek personal change, it will not be hard to find this year. The personal vibrations are very good. Many changes will come into your life now. Any move you make at this time may lead to another change in every respect including, perhaps business, travel, sex, parties, or a new romance. However, BE CAUTIOUS...The vibrations are a little shaky. Things started in this year are not going to be of a permanent nature. Married people must guard against becoming involved in outside love affairs. For those who have run into problems in the past four years, and for those who have met with adversity because of negative actions, now is the time to try to salvage what is left of your good karmas. Take advantage of this year's vibration; you must change everything that is negative in your life that has to be changed. For those who have lived the past four years in a positive manner, this year will be a period of happy changes, travel, sexual enjoyment and romance. I advise those who have been positive not to make unnecessary changes this year with regard to either their home or job. To do so would be to court disaster, for one change will lead to other negative changes. The good will turn into bad. Start nothing new this year, as it will not last, instead use this period for expressing changes within that, which is already in progress. For those who have been negative, if you will treat this year as an independent year, and seek change in all that is spiritual, the bad will turn into good. You will realize gains from your investments now in two years. There will be no misuse of personal freedom tolerated this year. All must watch the sex life. If you are married, you must avoid having an illicit affair at all cost, as you will be unable to face the many difficulties that will come up in the next year. Over indulgence in the wrong kind of sex will bring many problems in your marriage as well as your reputation. Enjoy all the sex you care to, but do not hurt any individual, or make promises without the intention of keeping same. All sexual relations with your spouse will be very pleasurable this year if both of you are positive. However, the misuse of sexual freedom will guarantee the individual loneliness and misery for the next two years after this year ends. I warn all of you: this could be the year when someone close to you may also betray you. Any betrayal by you or your lover will definitely end in separation or in divorce in the next year. Any newfound love or romantic relationship will be of a physical and sexual nature. Usually the relationship starts with sexual motivations. If you are cheating on the person you met two years ago, you will definitely end up in losses in the next year. You will consider marriage in the next year if both of you are very physically compatible.

Negative people who plan marriages this year usually end up separated any time within the next four years, and usually the marriage is short-lived.

Those who are experiencing problems this year are those who have been dishonest in their intentions and must do a RAMAYAN POOJA. Christians are required to upkeep the festival of LENT and fast for 40 days this year.

Section 4

LifeCode #7 Money, Health, Love, Career and Other Predictions in 2023

Your Life Will Be Affected By: Venus Known As Shukra in Vedic Science

MONEY THIS YEAR

The money situation will be much better than last year. You may even have some extra money for a vacation go for it! You will spend much of your money on parties, traveling, opposite sex and fraudulent salespersons who will try to offer you dreams of riches. Do not get involved in get rich quick schemes. Do not lend money; you will not get it back.

HEALTH THIS YEAR

Health will be excellent and your energy will be high this year. However, be careful of sexual diseases, infections or pain around the hip area. Exercise as much as you can and pay attention to your diet. You will feel wonderful in the middle of the year.

LOVE THIS YEAR

Sex and love will be the focus of your life this year. Romance will be surely important in your life this year. However, be careful if you are cheating on someone, they will catch you next year, but if you are single, you will have fun and pleasure. Do not commit yourself too much to that great person too quickly as you could get hurt. If you deceive your lover, you will have to pay next year, so be honest and sincere with your lover as much as possible. Any marriage this year may have problems next year.

CAREER THIS YEAR

You will have a lot less work this year than last year. Prepare your vacation or to move this year which is overdue. You will be spending more time at home rather than at the job. You coworkers will like you this year. This is a good time to change jobs. You will meet new friends at your workplace. Expect to do a lot of driving this year.

LEGAL, GOVERNMENT AND COURTS IN THIS YEAR

You must watch out for problems with the IRS and audits. Most of your legal problems may be related to this institution this year. You may have the feeling that no one is watching you, but do not be surprised if you are caught in an illegal act or stopped for a traffic violation. Any fraudulent schemes will definitely be exposed. Any lawyers you have may not be genuine. Keep your taxes up to date and file early.

ROBBERY BURGLARY AND LOSSES IN THIS YEAR

Robbery may come from people around you and those you trust. Watch out for who you trust as the people around you are not genuine. Be careful of get rich quick schemes. You could be accused falsely of doing something you did not do. Do not get involved in any partnerships or secret affairs.

ACCIDENTS, CONFRONTATIONS AND CONFLICTS IN THIS YEAR

There are some possible accidents while driving with someone else in the car. You may be taking a long trip. If so, be careful of who is driving. If you are driving there is no possibility of accidents. Most of your confrontations will result because you feel deceived. Avoid conflicts with government officials as this could result in penalties next year.

FAMILY, FRIENDS AND RELATIVES IN THIS YEAR

You may be accused falsely by family members. Anything you do for your family will not be appreciated. Do not expect any gratitude for your efforts. Your blessings will come from above. Be careful of lending money to family members or relatives as you possibly will not get it back.

CHILDREN IN THIS YEAR

Children will find you very exciting and friendly. You will enjoy the energy of young people around you. Be playful and helpful to the children.

SEXUALITY AND ENERGY IN THIS YEAR

Your levels of sexuality and energy will be very high. This is the most energetic year you have had in the last three years. You will experience many good changes because of your energy. Exercising will be beneficial and sex will come to you easily. Be careful of having illicit affairs as you will be caught next year. Sexual contact this year should not involve commitment as the relationship will end next year. Those starting a relationship and who wish to marry their partner must abstain from sexual contact or the relationship will end. Romantic energy is also very high, but after September this energy will diminish so enjoy it while you can.

PRAYERS, MEDITATION AND YOGA THIS YEAR

You are a very materialistic person, but Hatha Yoga is very good for you because you worry about your looks and appearance; however, prana yoga and chanting will help you with everything else. Meditation will help you control the racing of the mind that you will be experiencing during this period. Although you are materially inclined, you need to realize the material comes from the spiritual.

TRAVEL, MOVING AND MAJOR CAREER CHANGES THIS YEAR

Your traveling plans are highly exciting this year. You will enjoy pleasurable vacations and journeys. You may find you are moving to a new location or new job at this time. You may enjoy new locations and new environments. All career changes are positive this year. Be prepared for a lot more responsibility and promotions next year.

OPENING A BUSINESS, PROFITS. NEW PRODUCTS, MARKETING, AGREEMENTS AND CONTRACTS IN THIS YEAR

It is a good year to open a new business but you must be cautious about your spending. The next year may present a backlash to your business and you must be prepared for that. Try not to overspend on administrative costs. If this is a partnership, you will experience conflicts next year. Do all your marketing, new products and presentations before September because after that for a period of 12 months it will be very difficult to be successful with any of those endeavors.

REAL ESTATE BUYING AND SELLING IN THIS YEAR

It is an excellent year to buy and sell real estate; however, everything must be done before September as that will be very difficult next year. Be careful of fraudulent deals, false attorneys or false real estate agents. Any property you purchase this year must be checked very carefully as there may be hidden violations or foundation problems.

GAMBLING IN THIS YEAR

It is an average year for gambling. You must be very cautious as you could lose more than you think. Watch out for risks that are unexpected that may produce losses.

How to Avoid Negative Effects from the Planets This Year

1. Try to avoid gossip or telling people about other people's affairs. Any secret affairs will get you into trouble next year. Avoid deceiving anyone or lying to those people close to you. Any lies or false statements will result in punishment, frustrations and quarrels later. You think GOD is not watching you...WELL, HE IS!!!

2. Be religious, helpful to the temple and assist women in distress by advising them properly. Purchase gifts for women and donate to female children in the temple. Worship the images of KRISHNA & RADHA, Chant "Govinda Jai, Gopala Jai Jai...." and eat many milk products.

3. Mix Panch Amrit (Milk, Yogurt, Milk Cream, Coconut Water, and Honey) and drink it twice every month.

4. Fast every Thursday, Participate in singing groups, take a vacation to an extravagant location, and avoid all meat products if possible, if not just eat seafood if you can. This will help you to avoid sickness and health problems the next year

Section 5
The Vedic Code of Science
The Science Of Karma And Your Life

The Law of Action and Reaction

The Patra is not astrology as we know it in the Western World today. It is not like your psychic line advertised on radio and television. It is a very advanced science that teaches how to change and control YOUR destiny and future so that YOU and YOUR children will be assured a proper future and a better universe. It does not just accurately tell you about your future but also offers instructions on what type of remedies can be used to correct any unwanted or negative situations in your life. People are of the impression that VEDICs perform a lot of magic ceremonies and worship a lot of gods. THIS IS NOT TRUE!!! On the contrary it is a very profound and deep science that encompasses all of physics, mathematics, chemistry, biology and more.

YOUR NAME Determines Your Death, Your Wealth, Your Health and Your Success in Life

A NAME CAN NEVER BE WRITTEN CORRECTLY no matter which way you look at it! Do you realize that the name you have is really a group of letters that forms a sound? Do you realize that your name is really a sound bit on a musical scale? Did you know that every time your name is verbalized and pronounced it creates a vibration in the universe?

EACH LETTER OF YOUR BUSINESS NAME HAS A PROSPERITY LEVEL LOOK AT THE FOLLOWING GRAPH

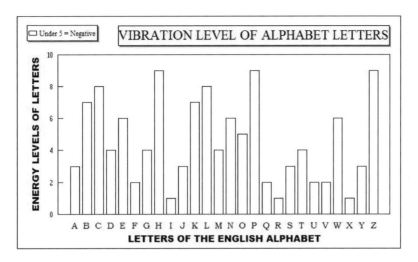

Each letter controls 9 years of the life of your business; so insert the name in the following box and you can know how the name affects your business prosperity during its life from creation (time of incorporation) until the present time and onto the future. Insert the name into the following worksheet and then find the prosperity level of your business. A high prosperity period brings all wealth and positive relationships with employees, customers and suppliers. If you are in a low prosperity period pray, give charity and fast until the next prosperity level. If all prosperity is low, then you need to change the spelling of the company name.

Because of the creation of music, the sounds of the animals and birds, and the names of things, songs were created, prayers were created from mantras or groups of words and soon NAMES became very important to all people.

YOUR BIRTH FREQUENCY SOUND OR JANAM NAAM CHARRAN
(Also known as NAVAMSA)

The 28 stars are further divided into 108 divisions, each division representing a specific sound in the universe According to the position of the Moon at the time of birth. This sound is used as the first syllable (sound) of the name for the newborn child or person. Usually the sound consists of two or three letters. This sound is used throughout your life and will forecast exactly when in your life will experience danger or happiness each name sound measures 3.333 degrees. For more information about your Hindu birth name or the Hindu birth name of others', you may purchase the CHARRAN MALA HANDBOOK available by contacting Chakra Square Healing Center at (305) 253 – 5410 or via email swamicharran@gmail.com

YOUR BIRTH FREQUENCY SOUND OR JANAM NAAM CHARRAN
(Also known as NAVAMSA)

The 28 stars are further divided into 108 divisions, each division representing a specific sound in the universe According to the position of the *Moon* at the time of birth. This sound is used as the first syllable (sound) of the name for the newborn child or person. Usually the sound consists of two or Three Letters This sound is used throughout your life and will forecast exactly when in your life will experience danger or happiness each name sound measures 3.333 degrees. For more information about your Hindu birth name, you may purchase the *CHARRAN MALA HANDBOOK* available by contacting Chakra Square Healing Center at (305) 253 – 5410 or via email swamicharran@gmail.com

FORECAST YOUR LIFE BASED ON THE NAME GIVEN TO YOU

For example, The first letter controls the experience for 9 years as shown in a previous chapter, and the second letter controls the next 9 years; however, when the two letter are combined they both determine other events in your life that occur within the 9 years and so it forms a matrix of your life experiences.

WHY DO I HAVE UNHAPPINESS? WHY AM I SUFFERING AND STRUGGLING? WHY AM I MARRIED TO THIS PERSON IN THIS LIFE? WHAT MADE ME CHOOSE THIS PERSON FOR MYSELF? WHY DID THIS PERSON ROB ME? WHY AM I HURT OR WHY AM I SICK THIS WAY? WILL I EVER HAVE HAPPINESS...?

BUSINESS NAMES AND THEIR RATINGS

MORE INFORMATION AND GREATER DETAILS ON OPENING YOUR OWN SUCCESSFUL BUSINESS, READ "THE BUSINESS LIFECODE" BY SWAMI RAM CHARRAN AVAILABLE FOR THE LOW PRICE OF $29.99

Now available in Spanish

Section 6

What are the Best Days for Love & Romance?

EQUATION TO FIND DAY CODE BY USING YOUR LIFE CODE:

MONTH OF BIRTH: = _____   e.g. for February = 2

DAY OF BIRTH: = _____   e.g. 12th = 3

DAY OF INQUIRY: = _____   e.g. 5th of any month

****TOTAL ****   = _____   e.g. total here is 10

REDUCE TO SINGLE DIGIT: + _____   e.g. 10 = 1 + 0= 1

NOW READ THE FORECAST FOR THAT LOVE MAKING DAY IN THE FOLLOWING PARAGRAPHS

VEDIC LOVE DAY CODE # 1
o A fair day for love making
o If there are no ego and feelings of rejection lovemaking will go well today
o You will feel aggressive and dominating in your sexual needs and desires
o You may not be able to concentrate fully as you will worry about things
o Avoid being too dominant, do not rush the lovemaking session today

VEDIC LOVE DAY CODE # 2
o Excellent and positive day for lovemaking
o If male you will find that you are having an erection almost all day
o Your feelings of love are strong and may want to go more than once
o The opposite sex will look beautiful and attractive to you today
o You may meet many friends of the opposite sex today

VEDIC LOVE DAY CODE # 3

- Not such a great day for lovemaking but good for playing with each other
- You may enjoy good sex if your partner is running a good day
- You may find yourself losing interest in the middle of the session
- You may find yourself getting too excited so that you finish too quick
- More foreplay should be done and a massage to your partner is suggested first
- If you are looking to get pregnant, this is a good day – fertility is high
- Looking at x-rated movies with your partner will help a lot today
- You love to hear sexy talking and funky words from your partner

VEDIC LOVE DAY CODE # 4

- A difficult day to make love, lots of effort will be needed
- Tempers can flare and stop the desire for love, do not get angry
- Lots of effort will be needed by you to please your partner
- Your mind could be on your work instead of sex today
- If you have to make love today, relax first , avoid stress and then do it

VEDIC LOVE DAY CODE # 5

- EXCELLENT DAY for lovemaking and great sex
- You will be feeling very sexy and ready today
- Provided you partner is on a good day, you will have fun in lovemaking
- Try to make it last as long as you can as it will be fulfilling
- If male your erection will be coming often, fantasies will be good for you
- If male all the women will look sexy to you, if female vice versa
- You will come into contact with attractive people of the opposite sex

VEDIC LOVE DAY CODE # 6

- A NEGATIVE DAY for lovemaking and partnership fun
- You find yourself frustrated by the opposite sex today
- You may lose the desire for sex quickly while making love
- Your partner may not be ready when you are and you may be disappointed
- If your partner refuses to be with you in the morning,, try again later
- There may be interruptions from family members causing no sex for today
- Interruptions can come from phone calls etc causing a lack of concentration
- You and your partner may have a fight or a quarrel thus killing the desire for sex
- Usually lovemaking after a fight today may make the session more passionate

VEDIC LOVE DAY CODE # 7

o   Deep Lovemaking full of desire and fantasies today
o   As a female, being naked and or scantily clad for your partner is good
o   You may wish to do a striptease dance for you partner today , it will help
o   Sexual desire is strong and lovemaking should be slow and sure
o   Looking at sex or love movies will help you fantasize more with your lover
o   Short dresses and tight clothes will stimulate your partner very quickly

VEDIC LOVE DAY CODE # 8

o   An excellent day for lovemaking and for enjoying each other's body
o   Dress up sexy today as your partner is looking for beauty and poise
o   Spend some money with your partner, go to dinner, give a gift
o   You are looking to go out today around the town and then a sexy night
o   You will feel good if you make money today, you will want to make love
o   You enjoy a clean and luxurious environment, a hotel is good for sex today
o   Pamper yourself , you will meet attractive and sexy looking individual
o   You could meet prostitutes, strippers or actresses today
o   If sex is in your karma today, it will be after you spend some money

VEDIC LOVE DAY CODE # 9

o   A CONFLICTING DAY for sex and love, Good if it happens…good if it don't
o   This can be an extremely enjoyable day for sex or a negative day for it
o   You will be feeling very sexy today or very exhausted also if negative
o   If lovemaking is done, it will be very passionate, if not its also good
o   You may be feeling sexy but your partner will not be, you will have to try hard
o   If the marriage is negative you could find yourself sleeping in another room
o   Try to avoid being tense or stressed out during love making …pray or meditate

Section 7

Investments & Monetary Advice

WHAT IS THE BEST WAY FOR ME TO INVEST MY MONEY ACCORDING TO MY LIFECODE?

LIFE CODE #1 - INVESTMENT ADVICE

- You must do it all by yourself – having a partner is trouble.
- To make this investment profitable you need to maintain and research all information about it.
- Try to seek leadership and creativity in this investment, as this helps you improve profits.
- Avoid becoming too dominant.

LIFE CODE #2 - INVESTMENT ADVICE

- A good business doing a partnership with your spouse, friend or family member (If LifeCodes are compatible).
- You will always make profits as long as your relationship with the people involved is positive.
- Learn to be very cooperative with the people you meet in this investment and watch what you say, as this can cause you losses.
- Learn to say "no" and do not let people take advantage of your kindness. Do not be too giving.

LIFE CODE #3 - INVESTMENT ADVICE

- Many opportunities present themselves in business for you.
- Always maintain constant knowledge about your investments, then your profits will always be high.
- Try to maintain a good sense of humor as it brings profits.
- Avoid childishness or immature controlling of others.

LIFE CODE #4 - INVESTMENT ADVICE

- Your investments will require that you work very hard.

- No matter how hard you work, you must work harder to make any profits with any investment.

LIFE CODE #5 - INVESTMENT ADVICE

- A constant changing investor, which requires rapid thinking and action before you can become successful.
- Constant change and new ideas are needed to make any investment profitable.
- Watch out for fraudulent and deceptive people.

LIFE CODE #6 - INVESTMENT ADVICE

- All investments require research, responsibility, and power.
- This investor should never have a partnership.
- Avoid confrontation, conflicts, and disagreements in as you may lose your investments.
- Watch out for thieves and robbers.

LIFE CODE #7 - INVESTMENT ADVICE

- Investments must be done with the utmost discretion and secrecy.
- All transactions in any investment should be done with caution, and profits will come to you slowly but surely.
- Research into the background of any investment, as there may be secret pitfalls awaiting you.

LIFE CODE #8 - INVESTMENT ADVICE

- A very lucrative and profitable investor.
- Invest as much as you can and with good timing your sales will become profitable.
- Most of the people you contact regarding any investment will want to be paid their fair share.

LIFE CODE #9 - INVESTMENT ADVICE

- You should avoid any type of investment.
- Extreme caution is needed with any investment or else you will lose a great deal of money.
- Try to invest as little as you can and do not spend too much money on improvements, as this will create very little profit.
- Buying and selling quickly is better as a short-term investment.
- Consult with a priest regarding any investment.

Section 8

How Will My House or Apartment Affect My Life?

Add up the digits of the building or home number to get a single digit as the Vedic Building Code. For example, if your house address is 3149 Macabee Drive, add the 3+1+4+9 and then reduce the results (17) to a single digit to get the Vedic Building Code, 1+7=8.

The #8 is the Vedic Building Code for this address. The name of the street is not important. If the address were 3993, the Vedic Building Code would be #6. If You have an apartment do NOT add the building number, only use the apartment number. Now add up your address number on your home (or apartment) and then read the interpretation of your house code below.

How Will your Home Affect You?

Match your life code on top row with building number on left row

TABLE OF VEDIC HOME CODES									
BUILDING CODE:	**YOUR LIFECODE**								
	1	*2*	*3*	*4*	*5*	*6*	*7*	*8*	*9*
BldgCd#1	2	3	4	5	6	7	8	9	1
BldgCd#2	3	4	5	6	7	8	9	1	2
BldgCd#3	4	5	6	7	8	9	1	2	3
BldgCd#4	5	6	7	8	9	1	2	3	4
BldgCd#5	6	7	8	9	1	2	3	4	5
BldgCd#6	7	8	9	1	2	3	4	5	6
BldgCd#7	8	9	1	2	3	4	5	6	7
BldgCd#8	9	1	2	3	4	5	6	7	8
BldgCd#9	1	2	3	4	5	6	7	8	9

Match your LifeCode on the top row to your Building or House Code in the left column then cross them to find your Vedic Home Code #. For example if your LifeCode is #2 and your House Location Code is #5, the Vedic Home Code is #7. Now check below for the forecast about how the house affects you.

Vedic Home Code #1 - Life in This Home

- You will feel independent, lonely sometimes and be bossy at home.
- You will achieve high status in career and position in life.
- You should be very spiritual in your thinking or you worry a lot.
- You love to advise others; people will listen to your advice.
- You will have a lonely child or you will feel pressured.
- You always feel that others leave you alone a great deal.
- Marriage partners are cautioned not to be too dominant.
- You may become too independent for your partner's feelings.
- You may worry a great deal; this may result in mental nervousness.

Vedic Home Code #2 – Life in This Home

- You like to shop a great deal and look for bargains.
- You cook tasty foods and food will always be in this house.
- You may have a job that involves cooking while living here.
- Make sure you serve all those who come here to reap good karma.
- Anyone who visits you and is fed will bless you with prosperity.
- You hate when your peace and quiet is disturbed in this house.
- People see you as kindhearted and too helpful to others.
- Others in the home will take advantage of your kindness.
- You will be involved in religious activities while living here.
- You will be involved in singing or may become a famous singer.
- Your partner in marriage makes a lot of demands for attention.
- You hate when anyone shouts at you here; it makes you angry.
- You will receive a lot of romance; too much for you sometimes.

Vedic Home Code #3 – Life in This Home

- Here you are usually skinny, small in stature and have a thin waist.
- You are argumentative and usually think you are always right.
- You may experience loss of children or have abortions in your life.
- Women here experience problems regarding their uterus.
- They may also experience cramps, lower back pain or bleeding.

- You are childish in your ways; people think you are immature.
- You hesitate to accept responsibility but are forced to do it.
- You interact with the children a great deal.
- You may be involved in publishing, writing or selling books.
- Your career may involve some form of telephone communication.
- You have many telephone lines or sets in this home.
- There will be many computers or television sets in the home.
- You will be involved with videos, television and music publishing.
- You may lose weight while living here; you will look 10 years younger.
- You may have dental or plastic surgery done while living here.
- You will feel very comfortable and lazy while living here.

Vedic Home Code #4 – Life in This Home

- You will be very hardworking and conscientious while living here.
- You may have a high temper because of many stressful moments.
- You will be determined in your attitude and will not admit defeat easily.
- If you want something done, you'll pressure others to do it immediately.
- Too much work and overtime will affect your health.
- It may take you a long time to buy a home, as you save money slowly.
- Your income and expenses will most of the time be equal; try hard to save.
- You are always busy doing something in this home; rest a little.
- Your mortgage may be high and your bills may be too stressful.
- Back pain and stomach problems will affect you from working.
- See the doctor regularly make sure your follow a spiritual life.

Vedic Home Code #5 – Life in This Home

- You will change your mind a great deal and quickly in this home.
- You love to travel and will travel to many places in the world.
- Because your thinking is fickle it's hard for others to know your thinking.
- You have intuitive powers and usually know things ahead of time.
- You will be able to tell if others are telling false things to you.
- You may be able know what others think about you by watching them.
- You will be helpful to others by self-sacrifice, forgiving enemies easily.
- You will help others without asking for compensation or money.
- You will have a psychic and profound connection with the universe.
- You will counsel and advise friends and family in their business.
- You are not very lucky with relatives; family members have no appreciation.

- You will make friends easily; friends will help you the most in life.
- The more good actions in life, the more beneficial it will be for you.
- Being a vegetarian while living here will give you no health problems.
- You may experience problems with the government, IRS or immigration.
- While living here you will encounter many great spiritual personalities.
- You will own more than one vehicle while living here.
- Your job may involve traveling or driving long distances or using public transportation.
- You will receive many long distance telephone calls or contacts from overseas.

Vedic Home Code #6 - Life in This Home

- In this home you like to be in charge; you have a very strong ego.
- Your job will thrust many responsibilities upon you.
- If you fail to handle responsibilities while here, you will experience misery.
- You may experience a lower or upper back pain, headaches or migraines.
- Eating red meat in this home may lead to high blood pressure problems.
- If not working for the government, you may have government problems.
- Credit card problems, high mortgages and loans affect you here.
- Make sure you pay all bills by cash while living here; avoid credit.
- You may be able to have a business while living here; avoid loans.
- You refuse to accept astrology, the occult or God very easily. Pray.
- You feel very frustrated when you cannot have things your way.
- You will experience inner fears and may think there is no help from God.
- Avoid the color red or black as it brings surgery and health problems.
- You may experience police or court problems while living in this house.
- You could have many traffic tickets also while living here.
- Your marriage will experience family problems while living here.
- There will be fears of divorce or separation while living in this house.
- You could experience robbery or burglary while living here.

Vedic Home Code #7 - Life in This Home

- Your mind is running a thousand miles an hour while living here.
- Your mind constantly thinks and analyzes everything.
- You keep most of your thoughts to yourself; you hardly ever talk.
- You will not tell your plans to other members of the household.
- You feel you are right most of the time; you have a strong ego.
- You will experience jealousy; you may think everyone is against you.

- You appear very beautiful or handsome in the case of males.
- You appear very sexy and attract the opposite sex very easily.
- You have strong urges for love, sex and romance; you are very passionate.
- If your spouse is negative you will ignore him or her a great deal.
- A sure key to happiness for you is meditation, chanting and music.
- You will make a good radio announcer, singer or religious leader.
- You may become too kind hearted and will feel deceived by your lovers.
- You should avoid the colors black and red; wear light colors.
- You will become critical of others and gossip while living here.
- You may have a fear of spirits while living here in this home. Pray.
- You will meet many religious priests, psychics and astrologers while here.

Vedic Home Code #8 – Life in This Home
- You love money and constantly think or quarrel about it.
- You will have a business of your own at some point in this home.
- Money flows through your hands very easily; try to save some.
- If you are spiritual and conservative, the money will stay with you.
- You may purchase expensive items and will be attracted to luxury items.
- You will suffer from constipation problems and shortage of money.
- You may become involved in fashions, modeling or designing.
- You may have a strong ego and will feel that you are above others.
- Investments in the stock market may prove to be profitable.
- You will have money and will have people working for you always.
- You love jewelry and may own of lot of it. Silver and pearls are good.
- Avoid wearing anything black; this will kill your prosperity in life.
- You will be attracted to movies, yoga, stock market, etc.

Vedic Home Code #9 – Life According to Indra
- You may have a high temper or a suspicious mind while living here.
- You will experience the death of older family members.
- Be careful of accidents and traffic violations while living here.
- Alcohol will be very damaging to your life; avoid it in this home.
- You may think very deeply about life and may become religious.
- If you are positive person you could become popular or famous.
- You may become involved in politics or become a leader.
- You will become confused and will sometimes have many doubts.
- Working for the government will be very beneficial for you.

- You will struggle to fulfill your desires while living in this home.
- You will spend more than you earn and bring financial problems.
- You will be very fickle and impulsive in your actions in these houses.
- Negative husbands may abuse their wives physically and mentally.
- You will have a loud voice and will shout at others sometimes here.
- The key to your happiness – donate yourself to work for charity.
- You may spend your money without keeping some for the bills.

WHAT ARE THE FORCASTS FOR MY HOME THIS YEAR
How will my home be affected in 2022-2023
Matching the Year Code to the Building Code

Every year your home goes through a cycle of influence that harmonizes with the universe. The position of the sun, moon, planets and the gravitational effects of other bodies in the universe can create the vibration that can make your location positive or negative. The number or Vedic Location Code can be used to identify this vibration. In the following table the years are indicated in the rows above, which will cross the Vedic Location code as it matches with your Vedic Building Code. This Vedic Location Code for the year in question will describe the influences for the location that year.

YOUR VEDIC BUILDING CODE	YEAR	
	2022	2023
1	7	8
2	8	9
3	9	1
4	1	2
5	2	3
6	3	4
7	4	5
8	5	6
9	6	7

VEDIC LOCATION YEAR CODE # 1
- People in this house will experience Loneliness, separation and worry in this year
- Promotions and progress may affect the people living here
- Some people could experience rejecting from others while living here at this time
- Avoid being too bossy or dominating, you may get into trouble
- Any new projects or business should be started at this time

VEDIC LOCATION YEAR CODE # 2
- Weddings, marriages, romance may take place at this location
- Lots of visitors and guests at this location
- People in this house will be enjoying good food, lots of shopping and a rewarding love life during this year
- A good time for this house to be cleaned, decorated, repaired, remodeled and enjoyed.
- Lots of dressing up, new clothes and eating of sweets will be some of the activities in this house now

VEDIC LOCATION YEAR CODE # 3
- Lots of children visiting this home now
- Possible pregnancy or news of birth
- Menstrual cycle or uterus problems
- Lots of studies, writing and reading of books
- Too much watching of television and computer activities
- Childishness, immaturity, and irresponsibility at this time
- There will be many social parties and engagements this year
- The year will bring problems of children, schools, or abortions to this home if the inhabitants are negative
- Problem with telephone equipments and billing

VEDIC LOCATION YEAR CODE # 4
- Possible job problems, hard work, overtime, low pay and more career problems will affect the people in this home at this time
- Tension, high-blood pressure, and high temper will affect the people
- Gossip will create lots of arguments and negative feelings
- This home may experience construction and repairs which will improve the value of your house

VEDIC LOCATION YEAR CODE # 5
- People in this house will be traveling or taking vacations at this time
- During this year, there will be many visitors to this home, some of them may not be genuine

- Long distance calls and long-distance relationships may be popular during this time
- It is possible that some inhabitants may be having illicit affairs or some fraudulent deals or transactions
- People in this house will be conscious of their physical appearance and most of the women living or visiting here will appear beautiful
- Common ailments in this house will affect the feet or sexual organs at this time

VEDIC LOCATION YEAR CODE # 6

- Conflicts, disagreements and power struggle will affect the people living in this home now
- Frustration and responsibility will be the experience of people living here
- Be careful of disturbing visits from family members who will have an attitude towards the inhabitants
- Possible police, court, or collection agencies will be communicating with the people living here
- There may be suggestions of divorce or separation among the couples
- One or more of the people living in this house may experience accidents or surgical operations
- Possible problems from in-laws

VEDIC LOCATION YEAR CODE # 7

- The inhabitants of this house may feel tired or sleepy during this year
- Inhabitants will worry at this time about their life path, their goals, their objectives, and their future
- They will feel that they need to meet with astrologers, psychics, Hindu priests and swamis
- people in this house will become very secretive at this time
- this house will be visited by lots of snakes this year

VEDIC LOCATION YEAR CODE # 8

- Inhabitants will be receiving or spending a lot of money
- This house may experience a change in furniture or fixtures which may be more expensive
- It is a good time to do reconstruction or renovations in this house
- Starting a business will become very profitable in this house
- People in this house will look more beautiful and presentable this year
- Expensive parties or purchases may affect inhabitants of this house

VEDIC LOCATION YEAR CODE # 9

- Possible sewer, flooding, boiler, or water Problems
- Possible Death or news of death Sickness or operations

- Government, city, or state problems
- Accidents where only the vehicle was damaged
- Money spent unexpectedly
- Husbands and wives will find themselves sleeping separately
- Any business started at this time will fail Any selling or houses will be delayed
- Frustrations with your job Do not do any construction or rebuilding at this time

Section 9

What Are the Best Days for Traveling?

What will happen if I travel on certain days?
Planning a successful Journey by date

All machinery, vehicles or mechanical devices have a lifeline from the day its completed. Just like how a baby is born, so also a car is born after the last part is completed and it gets delivered from the factory. That year of delivery or its identification number is now used to find its life code. If all planes, rockets, cars, and other machinery are checked by their equation of life codes, then we may be able to avoid the fatalistic and disastrous accidents in the world. Tests have been conducted on thousands of cars and the results have always proved true to the equations presented here. We as humans are subjected to the security and safety of machines. What greater safety can there be more than the knowledge ahead of time that a piece of machinery can be subjected to negative energy on a certain day, month or day. If this equation serves to save even one person's life from danger , then Swami Ram Charran's book "The Equations of Life "is worth reading.

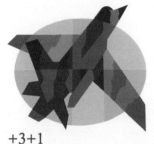

INTERESTING NUMBERS ON FRENCH AIRLINE CRASH!
In June 2009, French Airbus 330 left Brazil as Flight 447 headed for Paris, it never reached. Notice the LifeCode #6 of the airbus itself . (3+3+0 = 6) and the flight number (4+4+7 = 15 then 1+5=6). In addition to that it took off on May 31, which when added is a 9 (5 +3+1 =9). A #6 flight taking off on a #9 day with 216 passengers, a #9 also (2+1+6 =9). Note also that the missing flight was recorded as 6/1/2009 which when added comes out to #9 (6 + 1 + 2 + 0+9) = 18 then 1+8=9 ➔ same as 666).
In addition to that The last Air France airplane crash took place when it was flight 4590 which is a #9 (4+5+9+0=18 then 1+8=9). That crash took place in July 2000. Previous to that there was another airline incident which happen on June 3, 1962, which is also a #9 (6+3+ 1+9+6+2 = 27 = 9)   For your information, these were the only plane crashes that France have had in its history. No other. Other interesting airline crashes are …Austria flight 2553 which is LifeCode #6 (2+5+5+3) and the date was October 1997.
More can be read on this topic later in Swami Ram's new upcoming book "Equations of life"

When we travel we move from one set of space to another set of space in the Universe. As we travel we replace the energy that was in the space previous to the one that we are presently occupying. Sometimes we can move into a positive space or a negative one, and our own energy can conflict with that location or space. Difficulties in travel can occur when we enter a space that conflicts with our own.

To find a proper time for traveling you must be able to use the table below. The table is divided into Vedic Birth Codes on the left columns and days of the month on the top row. To find your good or bad day for traveling, look or the day of the month when you plan to travel and cross it with the number next in line with your Vedic Birth Code.

VEDIC TRAVEL CODES

YOUR VEDIC BIRTH CODE	DAY OF THE MONTH YOU ARE TRAVELING								
	1 10 19 28	2 11 20 29	3 12 21 30	4 13 22 31	5 14 23	6 15 24	7 16 25	8 17 26	9 18 27
1	2	3	4	5	6	7	8	9	1
2	3	4	5	6	7	8	9	1	2
3	4	5	6	7	8	9	1	2	3
4	5	6	7	8	9	1	2	3	4
5	6	7	8	9	1	2	3	4	5
6	7	8	9	1	2	3	4	5	6
7	8	9	1	2	3	4	5	6	7
8	9	1	2	3	4	5	6	7	8
9	1	2	3	4	5	6	7	8	9

For example, if your Vedic Birth Code is #5 and you're traveling on the 1st of the month or the 10th of the month, the Vedic Travel Code will be #6. Now look up the meaning of the #6 Travel Code in the paragraphs that follow the Table. You may notice that such a day may be negative for traveling. You can either try to change the date to a positive one or at least plan to expect many delays, frustration, and tedious moments during your travel, so prepare to leave early and pray that you avoid any serious mishaps.

Vedic Travel Code # 1

- A *fair* day for traveling.
- Most likely you'll be traveling alone.
- You'll have lots of time to think and meditate.
- You may spend most of your time worrying about things in your life.
- Take a book; you may need it while traveling.

Vedic Travel Code # 2

- An *excellent* day for traveling.
- You may be traveling with a partner or family.
- You will enjoy the company that you are traveling with.
- Prepare to be talking or listening to music with someone.
- Dress well as you may be meeting people on your trip.

Vedic Travel Code # 3

- An *excellent* day for traveling.
- You may be traveling with children or young people.
- This may be an educational trip to a seminar or school project.
- You may be watching a lot of television or entertainment media.
- Take a notepad and book as you may be spending time writing or reading.
- Prepare to go to a party or social event on this trip.

Vedic Travel Code # 4

- A *negative* day for traveling.
- A hard and stressful day lies ahead.
- This trip may be job related or a business trip.
- If not job related, prepare to be tired at the end of your trip.
- You may be carrying extra luggage today.
- Make sure you take extra lunch and snacks as you may need them.
- Try to rest as much as you can after this trip.

Vedic Travel Code # 5

- An *excellent* day for traveling.
- This will be a fun trip or a vacation journey.
- Whether you're traveling alone or with others you will enjoy yourself.
- This may be a long distance trip or one out of state or country.
- You will return from this trip very satisfied and rejuvenated.

- Be careful of fraudulent contacts and deceptive agents.

Vedic Travel Code # 6

- A *negative* day for traveling.
- Whichever way you look at it, the trip ahead is rough.
- You may experience delays, additional costs and losses.
- Be careful of accidents if you're driving or of thieves if you're shopping.
- Prepare to leave home early so as to avoid delays.
- You may get frustrated and angry during the trip.
- A good advice is to accept all delays without arguments as this may be in your best interest; acceptance may save you from disaster.
- If you're visiting your family, prepare to have family disagreements after your trip
- Try to change your date to a good day for travel; it will help.

Vedic Travel Code # 7

- A *fair* day for traveling.
- Nothing exciting or interesting will happen on this trip.
- You will be doing a lot of inner analysis of yourself and your life.
- Take time off to meditate and plan your future well.
- Avoid getting drunk or intoxicated on this trip.
- You may encounter religious individuals or astrologers.
- Prepare to fall asleep sometime on your journey.
- Enjoy this quiet moment by yourself; you will feel rested at the end.

Vedic Travel Code # 8

- An *excellent* day for traveling.
- If this is not a business trip, it must be for pleasure indeed.
- Prepare to spend lots of money on this trip.
- If you're visiting casinos or gambling you may win.
- You may encounter beautiful and handsome individuals in your journey.
- Prepare to watch TV, look at fashions or enjoy great scenery.
- Business meetings and partnerships will be successful on this trip.
- Prepare to bring back lots of good stuff when you return.

Vedic Travel Code # 9

- A *negative* day for traveling.
- Whichever way you look at it, the trip ahead is rough.

- You may experience delays, additional costs, and losses.
- Be careful of accidents if you're driving or of thieves if you're shopping.
- This could be a journey to a funeral or hospital or a court.
- If you're traveling to a government center, prepare for delays.
- If your trip is changed without your control, do not protest as it may be for your own good.
- The location that you are leaving will demand you return to it soon.
- You may definitely have baggage problems, and additional expenses, so make sure you walk with extra money.

I hope that the above travel codes will guide you to make travel plans that will take you and bring you back safe from your journeys. Vedic Code of Science is recognized for its potential in preventing unfortunate and lucky occurrences in a person's life. Armed with the knowledge of this science, people can learn to travel safely.

*****

The flight number of the Airline is very important. If the flight number adds up to 9, then there will be delays in the flight schedule, however there is no danger to the passengers on that flight, everyone will arrive safely.

If the flight number is #6 then there is a possibility of some danger of a breakdown, turbulence, or accident. However other factors must be taken into consideration when assessing the #6 flight. The best way to avoid all airline accidents is to get airline companies to avoid booking certain flight numbers on certain dates. If only they will listen to this knowledge many lives could be saved.

Section 10

How to Find Missing Person &

Lost/Stolen Articles

To know where a missing or stolen article is, you must know where it was last and when it was pronounced missing exactly. The type of article is important also.

Let's say that A = LifeCode number of the person

And   B = LifeCode # of the date the article was last seen

And   C = The Location Code # of the place where it was

Then the Equations for locating the article would be as follows:

A + DAY CODE number will determine whether the article was stolen or not as well as what relationship the person have with the thief. It will also determine if the article is with someone.

B = the LifeCode number of the date the item was last seen or stolen. This number when added to the DAY CODE will determine whether it is in possession with the thief and what type of thief he or she is. Adding the PRESENT DAY CODE number to B will also tell in which direction the article is located.

B + C determines where determines where in the house it is located if it was not stolen.

A + C will determine if the thief is a family member or not, and if it will return to you by police or by others.

Using The Following List Of Codes, You Can Interpret The Results Of The Equations

For answers to A + DAY CODE NUMBER they are as follows

1. The article might e with someone elder, it could be your boss
2. The article is not stolen , it is with someone you know & love
3. It is with the Children or it is in the location where toys are
4. It is at your workplace or it is below the ground at home
5. The article is traveling or moving in a vehicle or car or truck
6. It has been stolen and may never be recovered, get police
7. It is hidden in a dark place, or it fell into a hole, near water
8. It has been sold , or it has been placed in a better location
9. Most likely it is still there, but will not be found now. Later.

For answers to B & C they are as follows

1. It was by itself and is not being taken care of by anyone, thieves might have worked alone
2. It is with someone and it is well taken care of in love. More than one person were involved.
3. He or she or it is very happy there, and it is with young ones. A child or young person may be the thief.
4. The article is being used and it is being harassed or stressed
5. The article is on the move, it is not in its original location. It may be returned after along time.
6. It was stolen by Criminals who stole from others also. A family member may be involved.
7. It has been hidden and the person forgot where. May have to consult with astrologers. Alcohol or drugs are involved
8. The thief is well dressed and like expensive things like jewelry etc. Lots of money is involved. People like it
9. The missing article or person is located next to water or under water. It will be recovered possibly in two days or two months or two years

There is more to these equations. If applied to missing persons, it can tell with some precision where exactly that person is and what he or she is doing, whether he or she is dead or live. Take an example. Let's say the person is born March 14, and then he or she has a LifeCode number of #8. If this is added to the day he or she left the home or the day it was found that that person is missing. And the result calculated, it can be determined from the list below what is the person doing, and whether he or she will return, is happy or sad.

1. The person is alone, perhaps kidnapped or imprisoned
2. The person is with someone else, possible a friend
3. The person is in a school, or is in a group
4. The person is at work or in a farm or underground
5. He or she is traveling or is in transit
6. He or she is among enemies, or thieves or in a hospital
7. He or she is depressed or in a bar or in a religious place
8. He or she is enjoying himself, getting paid for his services
9. Drowned, imprisoned, sick or wounded, or died accidentally

If our subject with LifeCode 8 left his home on a DAY code of 9, then he is enjoying himself wherever he is. If that date was not known but he did not return on a DAY CODE 1, he is delayed by water, accident, or sickness. As you can see the day code will decide a lot of the factor involved. Sometimes someone could be dead if the resulting code is 6 or 9 or 1.

Section 11

Your Name & Your Karmic Cycles

How Your Life Changes According to Your Name and When You Should Expect Major Changes.

THE NAME OF A BABY IS CHOOSEN CAREFULLY FOR KARMIC PURPOSES.

USING YOUR FIRST AND SECOND NAME ENTER THE LETTERS IN YOUR NAME USING THE TABLE OF LETTERS

WORKSHEET TO DETERMINE YOUR KARMIC CYCLES IN VEDIC SCIENCE		
ENTER THE IST LETTER OF YOUR NAME HERE....		Cycle 1 begins from BIRTH to AGE 9
ENTER THE 2ND LETTER OF YOUR NAME HERE....		Cycle 2 begins from AGE 9 to AGE 18
ENTER THE 3RD LETTER OF YOUR NAME HERE....		Cycle 3 begins from AGE 18 to AGE 27
ENTER THE 4TH LETTER OF YOUR NAME HERE....		Cycle 3 begins from AGE 27 to AGE 36
ENTER THE 5TH LETTER OF YOUR NAME HERE....		Cycle 4 begins from AGE 36 to AGE 45
ENTER THE 6TH LETTER OF YOUR NAME HERE....		Cycle 5 begins from AGE45 to AGE 54
ENTER THE 7TH LETTER OF YOUR NAME HERE....		Cycle 6 begins from AGE 54 to AGE 63
ENTER THE 8TH LETTER OF YOUR NAME HERE....		Cycle 2 begins from AGE 63 to AGE 72
ENTER THE 9TH LETTER OF YOUR NAME HERE....		Cycle 2 begins from AGE 72 to AGE 81

TABLE – 2											
A	Sun	*Surya*	I	Saturn	*Shanee*	Q	Sun	*Surya*	Y	Sun	*Surya*
B	Moon	*Chandra*	J	Sun	*Surya*	R	Saturn	*Shanee*	Z	Jupiter	*Guru*
C	Mercury	*Budh*	K	Moon	*Chandra*	S	Moon	*Chandra*			
D	Pluto	*Rudra*	L	Mercury	*Budh*	T	Pluto	*Rudra*			
E	Venus	*Shukra*	M	Pluto	*Rudra*	U	Mars	*Mangal*			
F	Mars	*Mangal*	N	Venus	*Shukra*	V	Mars	*Mangal*			
G	Pluto	*Rudra*	O	Neptune	*Varuna*	W	Uranus	*Indra*			
H	Jupiter	*Guru*	P	Jupiter	*Guru*	X	Venus	*Shukra*			

Now check the cycle that you are in now under the planetary name shown against the letter.

THE VEDIC CYCLES OF LIFE

CYCLE OF THE SUN – SURYA DEVTA

You'll feel strong. You'll enjoy power and authority for 6 years. During these 6 years, you'll get lots of favors from older people, your boss, and your government. You'll succeed in most of your undertakings, and you'll bring luck to your father or your spouse, who will enjoy some prosperity. Your health will be excellent now and you may have to travel as a result of your job. At this time, you may acquire land or properties. Your health will improve slowly. If you are eating red meat, or if you have a bad diet, you could acquire cancerous diseases. You must be careful of fire. The government will be very favorable to you. You'll be able to overcome many of your enemies at this time. And you may form many new friendships as well. You'll enjoy a very happy home life for the next five years and you will earn much money as a result of promotions, businesses and spiritual contacts. If you had a loss of love in the last cycle, you will regain that love again in this cycle. You could get stressed out with children or with the loss of opportunities that you may miss without realizing it. You must try to eat well. Avoid being too dominant and be religious. If not, you could face separation from family and relatives or lovers. If you are negative, you will face the wrath of the Gods in the second half of your nine-year cycle where you could face imprisonment, deception by dishonest people and you may even face scandals.

You are advised not to get high-tempers and during this time, you must learn to spend time discovering who you are, what your objectives are in this life. Be willing to perform helpful tasks and do not accuse anyone falsely and you must be careful of friends who will envy you and will become your enemies later. If not very independent, you will find this cycle a worrisome one and you may feel cheated by others. You must conduct your behavior by showing gratitude to the elements of the universe, which will in turn bless you with happiness by showing appreciation for all that you have.

CYCLE OF THE MOON- CHANDRA DEVTA

A happy and vigorous mental condition that could bring facial luster to your life, you'll gain heavily thru the opposite sex. Your spouse/lover will bring a lot of happiness. There will be many sexual pleasures, gain of wealth, romance, attendance to religious locations, attendance of seminars, lectures, and other speech-forums. You will feel very happy with reading, writing, music, and sweet foods. You may buy a new vehicle, attend weddings, get married yourself and find happiness with mother or mother-in law; you may buy a new home, get a better job, or be loved by the people you work with. You'll be very successful in any business started now or any requests you may have in a court case or the government. You will meet many friends and form new friendships and love connections. You will be invited to attend many parties and religious functions and may travel with your partner to very luxurious places. The only way you will not enjoy this period is if you have given disrespect to your sisters, aunts, mother, mother-in-law and all the female relationships that are connected with you. Because the mother principle is governing your life at this time, you must treat all women with great respect, love, and care. Failure to do so will result in abuse by women, conflicts with your marriage life, high blood pressure, heart problems and quarrels with the women-folk. A female could become responsible for you losing your job or losing your money in the later part of this period. You could have a problem with your stomach and indigestion illnesses will affect you during the last four years of this period. You may find yourself having to go to the dentist often during this period and you could experience diabetes or throat problems. You'll find yourself acquiring lots of material possessions by shopping, finding bargains; desire to decorate the house and storing food for later consumption. If you are involved in the use of alcohol, drugs, and cigarettes, this will affect your love life and your sexual strength very seriously. You must place a special emphasis on what you consume as food poisoning is possible.

At this time, you are advised to not indulge excessively in your eating habits; try to do fasting, eat more fruits and juices and use mostly cholesterol-free foods to overcome your health problems in this period.

CYCLE OF THE PLANET MERCURY – BUDH DEVTA

Children, education, pregnancy, hip problems, sexual weakness, menstrual illness, abortion miscarriages, television and so on are the keywords for this period. You may find yourself involved in training, going to college, attending special schools, or having problems with your studies. You may also have a hard time concentrating or focusing on your courses and teachers. This is a learning cycle. It is what you do now, that will decide the amount of knowledge that you will acquire that will help you make your life prosperous later. Seeking a Guru or teacher at this time will help you progress faster in life. The first half of this period will involve you seeking comfortable environments such as an extravagant home, a luxury car, high tech television and music sets, new and comfortable furniture, and so on. If you have children, you will enjoy their company as well as their love and attention. You will become particularly worried about your sons and if your wife is pregnant at this time, she will surely give birth to a great son. You may get many visits from your parents, or they will be in touch with you frequently. At this time, worshipping your parents as your Gods will bring lots of blessings to you and your children.

Gossiping, criticizing others, proving complaints, talking bad about others, egotistical attitudes are all viruses that can affect the happiness of your life in this period. You may feel like acting childish sometimes. You will enjoy comedy and jokes of others but not of yourself. You will discover many opportunities waiting for you in career and business. You may enjoy lots of sexuality if you eat healthy, but this period could be filled with lots of sexual weaknesses, impotence and inability to perform your duties of love. This could be a period of great financial gain if you are sensitive to authority and elders. Avoid traveling in northeast directions. Check your location before you buy a house, and do not listen to friends who encourage you to commit evil acts or sins against God. You will be invited to many social functions and parties. You might find yourself attending many concerts and shows or going to the movies a great deal. If you make these too much of a distraction, it could affect your education and your ability to save money. It is advisable to perform many charitable programs; volunteer your services at the temple and think about your spouse's and children's feelings more than your own. Avoid quarrels with young people. If all actions of yours are positive at this time you will gain in business, you will have peace of mind in the family and you will enjoy the gains of real-estate and fame. Keep all your business out of the public's ears and your knowledge will increase, your children will prosper, and business will prosper. You will dream of winning the lottery at this time, try to realize that these get-rich-quick schemes will only go to people obsess with money only and not the serious things in life. You could win the lottery if you are dutiful to your parents.

CYCLE OF THE PLANET PLUTO – RUDRA DEVTA

Stress, hard work, low pay, high temper, overtime at work, high blood pressure, back problems, slow progress, problems with co-workers, loss of job position, employee or employer problems, fear of spirits, domestic list, enemies who are jealous, scandals are all the influences of this cycle period. Frequent domestic quarrels, sicknesses, body pain, and expenses will affect you quite a lot in the first 5 years of this cycle. You may find that your spouse will act coldly toward you. Your family will accuse you of not helping them out sometimes. You should try to eat well this period as you can get sick and drained of your strength. Your progress in life will be slowed for the next 7 years but will be sure. Avoid getting too close with people at the job and do not let your co-workers know too much about your private life. You may find that many may become jealous of you and your bosses may seem to be working against you. Stress and high blood pressure can become the cause of your sickness during this cycle. To avoid this, you should visit the beaches, relax, and spend time with your family in open park areas on weekends. Your high temper can get you into a lot of trouble with those who are close to you. You could become lonely and rejected. Unemployment problems may step into your life, and you may find yourself working or visiting a farm or getting a career in manufacturing or even be working in a factory. You may have problems sleeping and may suffer from insomnia. There will be many disappointments and lots of mental agony as a result of problems with marriage life, in-laws and government obstacles. Feeding elephants or worshipping the elephant God, Lord Ganesh, will help you to overcome some of the karma of this period. If you are positive and religious in your life, you will experience great happiness and promotions in your career at the end of the period. You could inherit a large amount of money or property and you may find yourself in a leadership position in a new department at your place of employment. You may travel to the southeast and may attend career oriented lectures and teachings. A move to the south will benefit you at this time. Be careful of moving into an area where there might be earthquakes or land problems.

CYCLE OF THE PLANET VENUS – SHUKRA DEVTA

Tremendous changes in your life will take place at this time. You may experience moving to new locations, loss of old friends, meeting with new friends, traveling to far-away locations, taking long journeys by land and air or simply finding a new job at a distant location. You must be very careful of being deceived by lovers or new friendships. You may become attracted to someone very romantic, but the relationship may not become permanent. You may meet a lover or a special friend while attending social functions or gatherings. You could meet that special someone while visiting a foreign state or country.

If you are married, temptations will be strong to cheat on your spouse. You must make an effort not to do this, as the karma of this will react against you in the second half of this nine-year cycle. Any business partnership or marriage that takes place in this cycle will be subjected to the test of trust and fidelity. Men may be tempted by pornography, prostitutes, and loose members of the opposite sex. During the cycle, you may be tempted to participate in get-rich-quick schemes and fraudulent projects that can place you in conflict with your partner, the government, and the revenue services. It is important that you keep your finance and taxes up to date as you may be investigated by revenue officers such as the IRS or state department. If you have been very positive and religious in your life, you may experience a successful move to a wonderful home or new business location. You will be blessed by the Goddess of Prosperity, and you will enjoy lots of romance and sexuality. Many parties, functions, pleasures with spouse and children, learning in art and sciences, purchase of new car and/or home, income from foreign locations will all be your blessings at this time. If you are negative, you may be infected with sexual diseases, experience severe menstrual cramps, and your body may be short of Vitamin E. You may hear news or meet with homosexuals at this time. You may be in the company of criminals or false individuals. Your feet may become sick or be affected by circulation and skin problems. It is important that you realize at this time that you cannot hide from God, and you cannot feel that you are free to break any rules of The Universe because if you do, you will be severely punished by the universe. You should find yourself a great Guru or teacher who will provide you with proper knowledge on how to deal with some of the psychic and mental gifts that you have. You should learn to eat very little meat, avoid alcohol and cigarettes, and eat mostly a fish diet. A wicked lover will deceive you. You will be sensitive to your appearance and so you will get involved in exercise and other physical projects that involve making you appearance better. You should wear a pearl or diamond ring to avoid negative energy. Eat low fat diets to avoid sickness. Take up yoga and meditation to help you with your body and mind and take holy baths at the sea.

CYCLE OF THE PLANET MARS – MANGAL DEVTA

Be very careful of accidents and injury in this nine-year period. If you end up in an accident, you could suffer loss of blood and pain in your body for a long time. During this nine-year period if you do not attend to your diet your health will suffer. And if you do not perform strict religious fasts and prayers, your enemies will overcome you and you can even end up having a lot of disagreements at the place you work. A family member may become sick, or you can end up facing some type of hospitalization for medical treatment, or surgery. During this period, you may become separated from your family and will have difficulty moving or traveling. You will feel very much rejected and empty in your life. You will feel crippled without family support and love. Learn to meditate and clam your mind through yoga exercise as this will help you to deal with these difficulties in love life and family relationships. Do not try to impress anyone right now, as this is going to reverse against you. You could end up in courts, get traffic tickets and meet with lawyers or police. Real estate foreclosures, losses of land and property, loss or change of career, injury through weapons, repairs at home, sex scandals or divorces will become to your life in the last half of this cycle. If you are living a positive life then any moves, temporary separations, acceptance of all responsibilities will result in more power, higher status, and success in the first 6 years of this period. If you work for the government, you will receive honor, fame, and power. If you conduct charitable acts, you will be promoted to a new leadership and you will be able to defeat your enemies and secure high positions in your career. Do not try to conclude any disagreements or large issues with family at this time. You'll find that most of the projects and tasks that you work on may have failed the first time but it will succeed in the second effort, so do not give up too easily.

CYCLE OF THE PLANET NEPTUNE – VARUNA DEVTA

Spirituality, religion, meeting with psychics, holy people, priests, astrologers, and fortune tellers is the influence of this cycle. You may find yourself studying spirituality, researching the existence of God in your life, or searching for your purpose and identity for being on earth. Deep thoughts about the truth of reincarnation, the afterlife, and so on. It is very important that you find yourself a spiritual teacher or Guru who can lead you to some type of enlightenment of your life. He/she will answer the question of who you are, why are you here, where are you going, and what is your purpose. You may also find yourself during this cycle taking a pilgrimage or a religious journey, getting involved in ritualistic prayers, joining psychic clubs, or being involved in medium séance groups. During this whole cycle, you will be involved in the search for your objectives and goals in life. You will be dealing with your inner soul, your subconsciousness, and your emotions. These qualities can become so negative, that it can lead you into a period of depression. If it becomes negative, to a point where drugs and tranquilizers must be used, you may find yourself being admitted at the psychiatric ward of the hospital. It is important to avoid alcohol, drugs, and smoking of all kinds, and highly medicated sleep aids. If you do get involved in alcoholic and drug habits, you may become more and more addicted as the cycle progresses. If this continues into the 9th cycle, you could find yourself health-related problems.

Trips to the temple will occur more often in this cycle, and you are advised to get involve in charity as this will help you to overcome the questions about your goals and objective which may be realized at the end of the period. Time will appear to be slow, and your life will progress slowly, but if you get involved in meditation, yoga, and prayer groups, you will find that your inner self will experience a sense of self-fulfillment and satisfaction. Try to attend congregational worship so that you don't spend too much time alone. The mind will be deeply affected by all things and people around you. You should get involved in intelligent discussion with others and stay away from arguments and criticism. You'll be tested greatly in your dedication to the one you love and if you are married, you will go through many tests with your spouse. Connecting with the planet Venus and the Hindu Goddess Durga will help you to withstand these tests of love. Reading and consulting with people who are involved in astrology and the occult will help you to understand your purpose and your objectives. Very little career problems will come up at this time, and generally people will leave you alone. Your dreams may become spiritual; you may be invited to participate in evil sacrifices to so-called devilish gods. You may be invited to participate in magical rituals which may result in you being hurt spiritually, financially and health—wise. Avoid getting involved in these negative types of worship, as they will only destroy you and your family in the end. If you are feeling negative energies around you as well as in your dream, you should consult a priest immediately. If positive you will find success happiness, favors from the government, gain wealth, and fame.

CYCLE OF THE PLANET JUPITER – BRHASPATI DEVTA

 Money, investments, luxury, extravagance, meeting with models and fashion designers getting involved in the movie industry, going to the movies, buying a luxury home and a luxury car are all the key influences of this period. Opening businesses, dealing with Wall Street brokers, investment in stocks, bonds, and real estate. Your knowledge will increase, your children will prosper, and you'll benefit from partnership and government deals. Loans and mortgages will come to you very easily and you'll enjoy going on luxurious locations and long-distance travel. During this period, you could inherit money, win in gambling, gain from the lottery and other casino-type activities. Your assets may increase, and you may find your life will be more sensuous. Someone in your family may give birth to a female child. If you're in business, your income and your sales will increase, and you'll attend meeting with wealthy professionals. Your popularity will increase, and you may even develop a new marketing technique that will bring you a windfall of profit. You will gain the respect of associates of the opposite sex; you will enjoy a very happy sexual lifestyle and will be invited to many parties and social activities. You will find yourself enjoying many comforts and luxuries that have had a desire for in the past. You'll gain the respect of community leaders and may even get involved in artistic and fashionable careers such as modeling, graphic design, yoga, interior design, and other art-related fields.

Money spending and financial instructions will be part of your life this cycle. You must learn all the lessons of dealing with money on a personal basis. You must avoid treating money as more important than God and you must realize that nothing in the world is owned by you, but it is only lent to you by God for a short time. The Goddess of Prosperity can leave you very easily if you don't treat Her with respect. Think of money as being like a fish, that the more you squeeze it, the faster it will slip out of your grasp. If you do not think of money as a gift from God, then you might find that you will lose it all at the end of the period and may find yourself in the same position you were at the beginning of the cycle.

CYCLE OF THE PLANET SATURN – SHANEE DEVTA

A cycle that will bring you into contact with old friends, old rules, ancient ideas and far away locations. The government, the courts, the police will all be part of this period. You could experience the death of close family members and a serious illness during this period. You may find yourself suffering financial, legal and health problems for over 7 years in this cycle. If you have forgotten to go to the temple or forgotten to perform your prayers and gratitude to God, this will be the year where you will be reminded throughout your suffering that God *really does* exist. It is recommended to go to the beach and spend time around water or oceans. You will enjoy taking long shower and may even spend extra time in the pool and Jacuzzi. This is the cycle where you should perform lots of prayers, attend many temples and churches, and get involved in meditation, yoga, and other types of congregational worship. Most of the projects and plans you put into practice this year may fail by the end of the period. You could find yourself financially ruined and completely broke as a result of some financial disasters. Be careful of accidents. Even though you may not get a serious injury, your vehicle can still become completely totaled. Friends, associates, and family are all people who could create problems for you or become your greatest helpers later in this cycle. You may be caught up by hurricanes, floods, thunderstorms and bad weather as well as earthquakes. Prayers to the sea will become very important for you at this time, as well as feeding the poor/homeless, and doing charitable services.

EXPLANATION OF MONTHLY FORECAST FOR THE YEAR

DAILY INFLUENCE: (NEGATIVE, POSITIVE or NEUTRAL)
This tells you how the month is going to be in General. Some months are more negative than some, and some months are more positive than some others. You can enjoy the neutral months by doing activities that have been left back or those that do not require too much effort, as in neutral months your energy is on a middle level. It is good to pray more on your negative months. Do more meditation or Chanting of the Mantras. Perform Charity or spiritual work as this will make you more connected to the universe. On Positive months you will be able to relax more and you will have more energy to do what you want. It's good to set up interviews and important projects for those months. Court cases are postponed usually on negative months.

FORECAST AND ADVICE FOR THE MONTH:
This is a generally close description of the month. It helps you to assess your month accordingly and lets you have an idea of some of the things that may show up in your life that month.

KEYWORDS:
These are suggested words that will mostly affect you life that month. All may not apply, only some will apply. This is to let you know that some of these things may affect you. It prepares you to expect these.

They may be positive or negative according to the influence of the month.

BIBLE VERSES: (Proverbs)
These have been taken from the Book of Proverbs in the Christian St James Bible.

READ PSALMS #'s:
More than Five Psalms have been recommended, but you only need to read at least two of those given.

VEDIC MANTRAS FOR THE month:
These are special words which are designed to produce certain sounds and vibrations that will create positive changes in your life. Just like the bible says that "In the beginning it was the word, and the word was God and the word became one" so also the Hindus have the word "OM" which is known as the first word of Creation and is known as the vibration of birth. Dr. OZ on OPRAH recommends the Chanting of "OM" for relieving stress change mental energy- good or bad.

RULING PLANET:
The Planets acts as Timers in our life. Like the Moon controls the ovulation cycle in women, the planets affect our emotions and Moods, and our reaction to the Universal forces. SUN, MOON, MERCURY, VENUS and JUPITER are all Positive effects. The Negative ones are SATURN, RAHU, KETU, NEPTUNE, URANUS and PLUTO.

RULING DEITY:
Each of us is influences by cosmic forces and elements constantly in the Universe. The Deities are these forces and elements that affect our life every minute, hours, months, months and years. For example when there is a predominance of Salt in our body, then our energy is hyper and when there is a lot of sugar, our nerves become itchy. The deities which are all the elements in the periodic table such as odium, etc. can affect our health, money and more by they way our brains and bodies handle them.

PUJAS & CHARITABLE SUGGESTIONS FOR THE MONTH:
These are suggested charitable actions that will create good reactions in your life, as well as payoff your Karmic debts. Everything we do is a ritual in life. Puja simple means holy or Karmic rituals.

Jan-2023	Shiva	This is considered a POSITIVE month for you	Planet: Jupiter

ADVICE & DETAILS

LIFECODE FORECAST: Money is the main issue in your life this month. All aspects of your life connected with money may be affected such as your job, your mortgage, your prestige, your income and so on. Love and romance may be expensive but pleasurable if you are positive. Marriage this month may be very profitable to the female partner. You may be tempted to buy yourself that expensive item you have wanted to buy for a long time but never had the money. On the other hand if you have been negative this month may bring delay, disappointment, deception or trickery pertaining to finance. It is a good time to request a promotion from your superiors and also a good time to play the lottery. Try to save some of the money that will come your way this month as you will need it in emergency next month. Real estate opportunities may seem attractive for investment purposes. It is a good time to invest in the stock market, but very little. This is a positive month for money matters and for purchasing that expensive item that is needed. Income should be high now and money will be coming from unusual quarters. If you are negative expect unforeseen expenses this month. Save some of your money for next month as you will need it. Avoid extravagance or over spending.

MONEY	LOVE	CAREER	FAMILY	TRAVEL	WEDDING	MOVE	BUSINESS	HEALTH	Lotto #'s	play 3 #s
Excellent	Good	Excellent	Good	Good	Excellent	Good	Excellent	Excellent	1,6,20,18,1,60,57	958

SHOPPING	GAMBLE	SEX	KEYWORD	KEYWORD					
Excellent	Excellent	is excellent	MONEY	Business,Major Expense,Money - Profits,Income,Investments,Power,Promotion,Fame - TV					

STRESS LEVEL	LUCKY COLORS	JEWELERY	MOONS EFFECT	GRAHA EFFECT	MONTHLY DEITY
Low	Yellow/Silver	Diamonds/Gold/Pearls	Secretive	Money Graha	LAXMI

MONTHLY PUJA	MONTHLY PSALMS
Decorate Land, Feed the poor, Donate milk /products to all, Feed holy guests,	, 35 ,44, 53, 62, 80,

BODY PARTS	DISEASE /sickness	POSSIBLE HEALTH PROBLEMS	MONTHLY EFFECT ON…Intestines
Intestines	Disease of the colon	Constipation problems	Laxmi Affects You This Month – Your Wealth

MANTRA FOR MONTH
Om Hareem Nama Swaha..Shri Maha Laxmi Aye Namah swaha 12 times

SPECIAL MESSAGE FOR THIS MONTH:
RULES FOR SUCCESS ; Avoid spending so much. Control expenses - always keep track. You must have a specific amount consistantly every day, week, or month. Avoid being extravagant unless you can afford it. Play lotto with your head not over it. Do not create debts - avoid credit . Always use cash - you will be more successful.

NEGATIVE DAYS:.............	2*8*11*17*20*26*29	January

Feb-2023	Shiva	This is considered a NEGATIVE month for you	Planet: Saturn

ADVICE & DETAILS

LIFECODE FORECAST: Be careful of accidents, conflict with police officers, negative involvement with the court and worrisome problems from all sides. At all cost you are advised to keep a low profile this month and avoid confrontations with others who are negative. Your income may be low, expenses may be high and money may be short. You may also receive sad news from afar, or news of an illness. Your personal affairs may be delayed and opportunities that may seem great at first may not be attained successfully if started this month. Of course if you are religious and charitable most of these problems may be minimized. Control your temper. Do not speak harshly and avoid conflicts with co-workers. You must go to the temple as much as you can and meditate a great deal as all these will assist you safely through this month. Any activity this month should involve spirituality, or learning. Tension may be very high and sexual feelings may be very strong. If you are having an illicit affair, you must be careful of scandal. The key word is finish. Take care of unfinished business this month. Write your ideas down and keep it for next month. Don't think of changing jobs at this time. You may be prone to accidents or have worrisome problems from all sides. Keep a low profile and avoid confrontations of a negative nature with others. Income will be low and money may be short. There is possible sad news. Delay or deception in personal affairs and opportunities will not be attained successfully. If you are religious most of these problems will be minimized.

MONEY	LOVE	CAREER	FAMILY	TRAVEL	WEDDING	MOVE	BUSINESS	HEALTH	Lotto #'s	play 3 #s
Bad	Bad	Bad	Fair	Bad	Bad	Bad	Bad	Bad	41,36,37,40,74,2,18	301

SHOPPING	GAMBLE	SEX	KEYWORD	KEYWORD					
Bad	Bad	is very bad	KARMA	Destruction,Losses,Death,Sickness - cold,Legal matter,Abusive,Karmic debts,God - Karma					

STRESS LEVEL	LUCKY COLORS	JEWELERY	MOONS EFFECT	GRAHA EFFECT	MONTHLY DEITY
High	Gold/Brown//Green	Saphire/Hessonite	Ivestments	Evil Graha	PITREES

MONTHLY PUJA	MONTHLY PSALMS
Remembrance of family members who died, worship of older people. gifts to grand parents	9, 18, 36 63, 81,

BODY PARTS	DISEASE /sickness	POSSIBLE HEALTH PROBLEMS	MONTHLY EFFECT ON…Circulation
Circulation	Disease all kinds	General health is weak	Pitrees Affects You This Month – Your Problems

MANTRA FOR MONTH
Om Ganga mataye nama swaha Om Varuna Devta aye Pahimam 11 times

SPECIAL MESSAGE FOR THIS MONTH:
RULES FOR SUCCESS ; Become a student of the Universe Respect elder people and authority Follow all government laws and regulations Attend religious functions regularly Read and learn from others Avoid commanding others impulsively Seek advise for religious teachers Follow astrology and occult science Stop denying or doubting when facts are presented to you Avoid suspicion of loved ones Do not help others unless you are in a position to do so. Never! Never! Fight the government Always give to charity Avoid alcohol, drugs and cigarrettes

NEGATIVE DAYS:.............	2*8*11*17*20*26*29	February

Mar-2023		Shiva		This is considered a **NEUTRAL** month for you				Planet: Sun			

ADVICE & DETAILS

LIFECODE FORECAST: You may be feeling quite independent this month and possibly lonely. You may be very busy attending to a lot of your projects, your career or your business. You may find yourself in conflict with others as a result of your becoming too commanding or too dominating. If you are married, tension may arise at the beginning of the month where you may be denied attention from your spouse or lover. Some of your personal projects or dreams may become a reality at this time. Your inventive abilities are extremely high and you may be congratulated or honored by persons in authority. A promotion may come about at your place of employment. Your health may be affected on the 8th or 17th of the month. Quarrels may occur on the 5th, 14th and 23rd of the month. A few opportunities for promotions and advancements in your ambitions may present themselves. Take advantage of these. If you are experiencing negative feelings of loneliness, perform meditative Puja. Concentrate on yourself this month and try to do everything that you have to do on your own without requesting help from others. People will not be as cooperative as you want them to be. You may feel lonely at times. However, any new opportunities presented will make you feel good about yourself. Do not be over-confident or too competitive with others. Do not expect many invitations until next month.

MONEY	LOVE	CAREER	FAMILY	TRAVEL	WEDDING	MOVE	BUSINESS	HEALTH	*Lotto #'s*		*play 3 #'s*
Fair	Bad	Good	Bad	Fair	Bad	Fair	Fair	Fair	75,17,64,19,3,6,14		532

SHOPPING	GAMBLE	SEX	KEYWORD	KEYWORD							
Fair	Fair	is fair	MIND	Independence,Loneliness,Meditative,Worry,Dominating,Illness - Cold,On Your Own,Commanding							

STRESS LEVEL	LUCKY COLORS	JEWELERY	MOONS EFFECT	GRAHA EFFECT	MONTHLY DEITY
High	White/Yellow/	Pearl/Quartz	Arrogance	Status Graha	GURU

MONTHLY PUJA	MONTHLY PSALMS
Give Gifts to Priests, Invite holy ones to your home, Feed Swamis and Yogis, Do Shiva Puja.	1, 28 ,46, 73,,

BODY PARTS	DISEASE /sickness	POSSIBLE HEALTH PROBLEMS	MONTHLY EFFECT ON...Head
Head	Disease of the head	Nervousness caused by worrying	Guru Affects You This Month – Your Mind

MANTRA FOR MONTH
Om Namo Bhagawate Mukhtanandaya, 108 times

SPECIAL MESSAGE FOR THIS MONTH:
RULES FOR SUCCESS: Do not let your mind idle. Always try to be a leader. Meditate to slow down your mind. Do not be dominating or bossy to others. Only give advise when asked for it... When left alone by partner do not fight - pray instead. Avoid depression moments - meditate when feeling lonely. When accused of anything - rise above it When offered a leadership position at work - accept it

NEGATIVE DAYS:.............	2*8*11*17*20*26*29	March

Apr-2023		Shiva		This is considered a **POSITIVE** month for you				Planet: Moon			

ADVICE & DETAILS

LIFECODE FORECAST: Romance and love may be predominant in your mind this month. If married you will be enjoying the pleasures of the opposite sex this month. If single you may be dating that favorite person you wanted to date for a while now. Expect quite a few visitors at home or through the telephone. Your emotion may be high and you may be asked to perform good deeds. If your partner is not properly matched astrologically with you then expect a great deal of disagreements this month. Your popularity may rise now so expect quite a few requests for service from others. That invitation you have been looking forward to may come now. Expect many friends to call you or visit you this month. You may meet some new contacts or some new interests in your love affairs. That special someone, you have been thinking about may enter your life now. Married couples will be spending much more time with each other this month. Business partnerships will be profitable.

MONEY	LOVE	CAREER	FAMILY	TRAVEL	WEDDING	MOVE	BUSINESS	HEALTH	*Lotto #'s*		*play 3 #'s*
Good	Excellent	Good	Good	Excellent	Good	Good	Good	Good	68,67,29,34,6,60,13		570

SHOPPING	GAMBLE	SEX	KEYWORD	KEYWORD							
Good	Good	is good	LOVE	Romance,Popularity,Visitors,Shopping,Food, Drinks,Co-operation,Friendships,Affection							

STRESS LEVEL	LUCKY COLORS	JEWELERY	MOONS EFFECT	GRAHA EFFECT	MONTHLY DEITY
Low	Red/Yellow/Pink	Topaz/Diamonds	Conservative	Love Graha	KRISHNA

MONTHLY PUJA	MONTHLY PSALMS
Give Gifts to females andnMother, Serve milk Products, Worship Durga forms	, 29 ,38, 47, 56,

BODY PARTS	DISEASE /sickness	POSSIBLE HEALTH PROBLEMS	MONTHLY EFFECT ON...Speech
Speech	Disease of the mouth	Food poisoning problems	Krishna Affects You This Month – Love Life

MANTRA FOR MONTH
Kali Durge Namo Nama Om Durge aye nama swaha 108 times

SPECIAL MESSAGE FOR THIS MONTH:
RULES FOR SUCCESS;   Control your speech or words. Always be cooperative to others. learn to cook - you will be great. The more people you feed the more success in your life. Always offer guests something to drink or eat. Never! Never! Have an affair - it will ruin you. Learn to be religious - it will help. Listen to music when you are sad. Learn to sing - you have a great voice Always be well dressed and neat. Hug and embrace all close people - you will find peace quickly. Do not speak if your heart does not say it. Love for one person is your karmic test. Be diplomatic in business - do not let out all your plans or secrets. Your words can really becom reality so watch what you say.

NEGATIVE DAYS:.............	2*8*11*17*20*26*29	April

| May-2023 | | Shiva | | This is considered a POSITIVE month for you | | | | | Planet: Mercury | |

ADVICE & DETAILS

LIFECODE FORECAST: If you are a female and not pregnant at this time then you may surely hear news of pregnancy from someone related to the family. Children may need your attention this month and may demand that you spend more time with them. You may find yourself studying or reading a great deal now and if you are a student you will be successful in your exams or courses at school. You may be spending a great deal of time on the telephone and may receive lots of calls from old friends who may surprise you. If you are in business for yourself expect a great deal of profits coming to you through the telephone and an increase in clientele, but be aware that is not how much money you make, but how much you get to keep. If you are negative then expect some distress through younger individuals. You should be doing a lot of entertaining or you are being entertained a great deal this month. Your creativity is high and you will be successful with many of your undertakings. Most of your wishes will be realized. Old friends will show up at your home. Enjoy the month.

MONEY	LOVE	CAREER	FAMILY	TRAVEL	WEDDING	MOVE	BUSINESS	HEALTH	Lotto #'s	play 3 #s
Good	Fair	Good	Good	Excellent	Good	Good	Good	Excellent	54,47,24,2,47,22,34	752

SHOPPING	GAMBLE	SEX	KEYWORD	KEYWORD						
Good	Good	is great	SOCIAL	Children,Education,Astrology,Bargains,Social Functions,Childishness,Groups - Parties,Teacher						

STRESS LEVEL		LUCKY COLORS	JEWELERY	MOONS EFFECT	GRAHA EFFECT	MONTHLY DEITY
Low		Green/Sky Blue/	Diamonds/Silver	Enthusiastic	Social Graha	GAUREE

MONTHLY PUJA	MONTHLY PSALMS
Wash the feet of Children, Do Satnarayan Pooja, Read & chant Geeta	57, 75, 102, 120

BODY PARTS	DISEASE /sickness	POSSIBLE HEALTH PROBLEMS	MONTHLY EFFECT ON...Hips
Hips	Disease of sexual organs	Menstrual cycle problems (females)	Gauree Affects You This Month – Social Life

MANTRA FOR MONTH
Om hareem Kleem Hreem Aem Saraswataye namaha 21 times

SPECIAL MESSAGE FOR THIS MONTH:
RULES FOR SUCCESS; Avoid too much Television. Accept and love children always. Do not seat around too much. Avoid demanding too much attention from parents. Read a great deal - books will answer all questions. Never drop out of school or quit classes. Respect your teachers. Do not be too playful or immature. Be careful of abortions and miscarriages.

NEGATIVE DAYS:.............. 2*8*11*17*20*26*29   May

| Jun-2023 | | Shiva | | This is considered a NEGATIVE month for you | | | | | Planet: Pluto | |

ADVICE & DETAILS

LIFECODE FORECAST: Repairs in the home, pains in the joints, overwork, tiredness, sleepiness are the influences of this month. You may be feeling very lazy and may have to put in extra time at the job for your boss. It may be a very busy time in your business or occupation. Now is the time when you may be able to fix that broken appliance or wall in your home. If you are looking for a job this month you may not find one because wherever you go the salary may not be to your satisfaction. If you are employed presently you may feel at this time that the payment received does not compensate for the work you are performing. Owners of real estate or rental properties may experience difficulty with tenants this month. In the beginning of this month your car may also require some maintenance. Contact with your mother or a female mother figure may be expected soon. Purchase of antiques or articles of those who have died may come into your possession. This is a good time for constructive activities, exercise, diet and hard work. Expect to participate in community affairs. Accept all overtime given to you at your place of employment and put in extra hours to complete your personal duties. Cut down on expenses as money is low at this time. Watch your health. This is a good time to visit the doctor.

MONEY	LOVE	CAREER	FAMILY	TRAVEL	WEDDING	MOVE	BUSINESS	HEALTH	Lotto #'s	play 3 #s
Bad	Fair	Bad	Fair	Bad	Good	Bad	Bad	Bad	57,13,5,24,20,69,44	176

SHOPPING	GAMBLE	SEX	KEYWORD	KEYWORD						
Bad	Bad	is tough	CAREER	Career,Hard Work,Co-workers,Low Payment,Job Problems,High Temper,Low Pay,Laziness						

STRESS LEVEL		LUCKY COLORS	JEWELERY	MOONS EFFECT	GRAHA EFFECT	MONTHLY DEITY
High		Dark Blue/ Purple/	Amethyst/Gold	Emotional	Job Graha	GANAPATI

MONTHLY PUJA	MONTHLY PSALMS
Worship Ganesh, Give gifts to father, and co -workers, Plant gardens, farms	4, 13, 31 ,40,

BODY PARTS	DISEASE /sickness	POSSIBLE HEALTH PROBLEMS	MONTHLY EFFECT ON...Stomach
Stomach	Disease of the belly	Bone problems and stomach problems	Ganapati Affects You This Month – Your Career

MANTRA FOR MONTH
Om Jai Viganeshwaraya.. Lambodaraya Namo Namaha 21 times

SPECIAL MESSAGE FOR THIS MONTH:
RULES FOR SUCCESS; Always work hard at your job Never demand a raise - it will come. Rest yourself well after a day's work. Keep an open mind - Don't be annoyant. Do not get angry at everybody.

NEGATIVE DAYS:.............. 2*8*11*17*20*26*29   June

Jul-2023	Shiva	This is considered a POSITIVE month for you	Planet: Venus

ADVICE & DETAILS

LIFECODE FORECAST: Short travel or driving to a distant location is forecasted for you this month. If you are not taking a vacation, then you may be traveling as a result of your employment or personal business. Your romantic feelings may be extremely high at this time and single individuals may encounter an exciting month and find new romance. If married you will be enjoying the pleasures of the opposite sex this month. If single you may be dating that favorite person you wanted to date for a while now. You may be involved in a false situation where you may be accused of insincerity or you may be deceived by somebody close to you. All telephone calls coming to you from long distances should not be taken seriously. It is possible that the situation may not be as somber as you think it is. If you are negative be careful of affliction to the private organs. You must also be careful of loss of reputation. If you are making a trip you will enjoy meeting some interesting people. Your appearance may be a major topic this month. Sex, love and romance are prevalent in your mind this month. Also travel and long distance communications occupy most of your time now. You will be meeting with strangers or attractive members of the opposite sex. New changes or a possible move is the highlight of this month. Avoid impulsiveness, trickery, or dishonesty from others.

MONEY	LOVE	CAREER	FAMILY	TRAVEL	WEDDING	MOVE	BUSINESS	HEALTH	Lotto #'s	play 3 #s
Bad	Excellent	Fair	Good	Excellent	Good	Excellent	Good	Excellent	51,63,3,6,15,62,8	722

SHOPPING	GAMBLE	SEX	KEYWORD	KEYWORD					
Good	Good	is good	CHANGE	Sexuality,Travel,Change,Distant, far,Travel delays,Deception,Excercise,Illicit Affairs					

STRESS LEVEL		LUCKY COLORS	JEWELERY	MOONS EFFECT	GRAHA EFFECT	MONTHLY DEITY
Fair		Tan/Green/ Beige	Pearl/Silver/quartz	Courageous	Travel Graha	NARADA

MONTHLY PUJA	MONTHLY PSALMS
Artistic gifts, Pray to Krishna, Do good deeds, do Spiritual trips	5, 32 , 50, 77, 122

BODY PARTS	DISEASE /sickness	POSSIBLE HEALTH PROBLEMS	MONTHLY EFFECT ON...Feet
Feet	Disease of the feet	Blood poisoning and muscle problems	Narada Affects You This Month – Your Pleasures

MANTRA FOR MONTH
Om Graam Greem Graum Sa Gurave namah swaha 21 times

SPECIAL MESSAGE FOR THIS MONTH:
RULES FOR SUCCESS; Avoid illicit affairs or cheating. Being false or lying is prohibited as it will be negative karma. Sex and consistancy is your karmic test. Avoid doubting the existence of God. Never fight the Revenue Service or Government You think God is not watching you sometimes..Are your sure? You must admit when you are wrong - keep an open mind

NEGATIVE DAYS:.............	2*8*11*17*20*26*29	July

Aug-2023	Shiva	This is considered a NEGATIVE month for you	Planet: Mars

ADVICE & DETAILS

LIFECODE FORECAST: Control your anger or your temper. It is a very tense month and you may experience some delays and difficulties at your place of employment as well as at home. Equipments may break down and traveling may be difficult. It is advisable for you to stay together with family and relatives. Do worship and meditate with them and last but not least attend services at the temple. All this will serve to assist you from having many difficulties now. Be careful of accidents and possible pain or injury to the lower back. If any disagreements develop between you and your partner, it surely is your fault for not being able to control your temper. If positive you may be promoted at your place of employment or be given more responsibility with more pay. Avoid conflicts with co-workers or being involved in discussions that are argumentative. Most of all admit when you are wrong, if you are. Avoid aggressiveness. Accept all responsibilities given to you. There is the possibility of association with negative people who will try to take advantage of you. Be calm and patient as you will be torn between your love life and your job. Be prepared for a possible quarrel with your partner or the end of a friendship. Do not cry or get angry over petty annoyances or younger individuals. Sexual activity is low.

MONEY	LOVE	CAREER	FAMILY	TRAVEL	WEDDING	MOVE	BUSINESS	HEALTH	Lotto #'s	play 3 #s
Bad	Bad	Bad	Bad	Bad	Bad	Bad	Fair	Bad	64,36,50,30,66,21,32	152

SHOPPING	GAMBLE	SEX	KEYWORD	KEYWORD					
Fair	Bad	is frustrating	POWER	Responsibilty,Disagreement,Family,Back Pain,Family Conflicts,Traffic Ticket,Quarrels,Jealousy					

STRESS LEVEL		LUCKY COLORS	JEWELERY	MOONS EFFECT	GRAHA EFFECT	MONTHLY DEITY
High		Purple/Blue/Rose	Emerald/Saphire	Educational	Family Graha	HANUMAN

MONTHLY PUJA	MONTHLY PSALMS
Meditate, Control temper, Pray to Hanuman, Chant Hanuman Chalisa	6, 15, 33 ,42,

BODY PARTS	DISEASE /sickness	POSSIBLE HEALTH PROBLEMS	MONTHLY EFFECT ON...Back/Spine
Back/Spine	Disease of the bones	Broken bones, back pain, migraine headaches	Hanuman Affects You This Month - Responsabilities

MANTRA FOR MONTH
Om Mana Swasti Shanti Kuru kuru Swaha Shivoham Shivoham 27 times

SPECIAL MESSAGE FOR THIS MONTH:
RULES FOR SUCCESS ; Avoid borrowing money or credit. Do not eat meat or fish everyday. Avoid red meat totally. Responsibility is your karmic test. obey all traffic laws - police sees you quickly. Respect your in-laws avoid conflict. Even if others are jealous - trust in God. Learn to be patient - you'll win. Do not command religious people. Avoid thinking that you know everything. Do not be hasty - you will loose in business. Respect Laxmi - do not waste your money.

NEGATIVE DAYS:.............	2*8*11*17*20*26*29	August

Sep-2023		Shiva	This is considered a NEUTRAL month for you				Planet: Uranus			

ADVICE & DETAILS

LIFECODE FORECAST: Avoid criticizing anyone or getting yourself involved in any gossip as this may become very damaging to your reputation this month. You may receive news of an older person dying far away or you may visit a sick person in the hospital or a prison. Income may be very low at this time. Do not start any business or project this month as it may be delayed. Admit your fault and apologize if necessary as this may prevent any serious confrontation with others. You may be feeling very sleepy or tired at this time. Rest and relax as much as you can as next month may be very hectic. Most of your money problems will disappear in a few weeks. If you are negative you may experience inner conflicts and worries. It is most important that you attend the temple or any religious functions this month as this will assist you in some of the problems you are experiencing. You may find the solution in those places. If you are positive you may find yourself among spiritual individuals who are very knowledgeable and who may be able to teach you a great deal about religion or spirituality. See an astrologer or Guru if you are having difficulties this month. Accept gracefully when others criticize you. Avoid being hasty or too secretive about your feelings. You may be feeling lonely. If so try to read or study or meditate. Write those letters that you had planned to write last month. Financial gains are low so avoid spending. Listen to religious people and be charitable to those in need of help. You will get into trouble because of gossip or criticism this month.

MONEY	LOVE	CAREER	FAMILY	TRAVEL	WEDDING	MOVE	BUSINESS	HEALTH	Lotto #'s	play 3 #s
Good	Good	Fair	Good	Good	Bad	Good	Bad	Fair	10,15,55,9,14,16,42	498

SHOPPING	GAMBLE	SEX	KEYWORD	KEYWORD				
Bad	Fair	is quiet	DIVINE	Spirituality,Religious,Astrology,Inner Conflicts,Religious ,Sleepiness,Advice given,Alcohol - drugs				

STRESS LEVEL	LUCKY COLORS	JEWELERY	MOONS EFFECT	GRAHA EFFECT	MONTHLY DEITY
Fair	Light Blue/Peach	Tiger's eye/Gold/Silver	Affectionate	God'S Graha	GANGA

MONTHLY PUJA	MONTHLY PSALMS
Chant Shiva Mantras, Take gifts to Ocean - Ganga Puja, Donate to Temple, Priests, etc.	61, 79, 106,

BODY PARTS	DISEASE /sickness	POSSIBLE HEALTH PROBLEMS	MONTHLY EFFECT ON...Emotions
Emotions	Disease of the blood	Heart problems, addiction to drugs and alcohol	Ganga Affects You This Month – Your Beliefs

MANTRA FOR MONTH
Jai Jai Shiva Shambo.(2) ...Mahadeva Shambo (2) 21 times 8

SPECIAL MESSAGE FOR THIS MONTH:
RULES FOR SUCCESS ; Avoid alcohol, drugs and smoking. you must learn to be religious Do Durga pooja Give respect to all women. Marriage is your karmic test. Too much sleep will be a drag in your life. Express your feelings without hurting others. Do not mix business with friendship. Pay respect to all religious people.

NEGATIVE DAYS:.............	2*8*11*17*20*26*29	September

Oct-2023		Shiva	This is considered a POSITIVE month for you				Planet: Jupiter			

ADVICE & DETAILS

LIFECODE FORECAST: Money is the main issue in your life this month. All aspects of your life connected with money may be affected such as your job, your mortgage, your prestige, your income and so on. Love and romance may be expensive but pleasurable if you are positive. Marriage this month may be very profitable to the female partner. You may be tempted to buy yourself that expensive item you have wanted to buy for a long time but never had the money. On the other hand if you have been negative this month may bring delay, disappointment, deception or trickery pertaining to finance. It is a good time to request a promotion from your superiors and also a good time to play the lottery. Try to save some of the money that will come your way this month as you will need it in emergency next month. Real estate opportunities may seem attractive for investment purposes. It is a good time to invest in the stock market, but very little. This is a positive month for money matters and for purchasing that expensive item that is needed. Income should be high now and money will be coming from unusual quarters. If you are negative expect unforeseen expenses this month. Save some of your money for next month as you will need it. Avoid extravagance or over spending.

MONEY	LOVE	CAREER	FAMILY	TRAVEL	WEDDING	MOVE	BUSINESS	HEALTH	Lotto #'s	play 3 #s
Excellent	Good	Excellent	Good	Good	Excellent	Good	Excellent	Excellent	37,2,17,34,57,7,64	858

SHOPPING	GAMBLE	SEX	KEYWORD	KEYWORD				
Excellent	Excellent	is excellent	MONEY	Business,Major Expense,Money - Profits,Income,Investments,Power,Promotion,Fame - TV				

STRESS LEVEL	LUCKY COLORS	JEWELERY	MOONS EFFECT	GRAHA EFFECT	MONTHLY DEITY
Low	Yellow/Silver	Diamonds/Gold/Pearls	Secretive	Money Graha	LAXMI

MONTHLY PUJA	MONTHLY PSALMS
Decorate Land, Feed the poor, Donate milk /products to all, Feed holy guests,	, 35 ,44, 53, 62, 80,

BODY PARTS	DISEASE /sickness	POSSIBLE HEALTH PROBLEMS	MONTHLY EFFECT ON...Intestines
Intestines	Disease of the colon	Constipation problems	Laxmi Affects You This Month – Your Wealth

MANTRA FOR MONTH
Om Hareem Nama Swaha..Shri Maha Laxmi Aye Namah swaha 12 times

SPECIAL MESSAGE FOR THIS MONTH:
RULES FOR SUCCESS ; Avoid spending so much. Control expenses - always keep track. You must have a specific amount consistantly every day, week, or month. Avoid being extravagant unless you can afford it. Play lotto with your head not over it. Do not create debts - avoid credit . Always use cash - you will be more successful.

NEGATIVE DAYS:.............	2*8*11*17*20*26*29	October

Nov-2023	Shiva	This is considered a NEGATIVE month for you	Planet: Saturn

ADVICE & DETAILS

LIFECODE FORECAST: Be careful of accidents, conflict with police officers, negative involvement with the court and worrisome problems from all sides. At all cost you are advised to keep a low profile this month and avoid confrontations with others who are negative. Your income may be low, expenses may be high and money may be short. You may also receive sad news from afar, or news of an illness. Your personal affairs may be delayed and opportunities that may seem great at first may not be attained successfully if started this month. Of course if you are religious and charitable most of these problems may be minimized. Control your temper. Do not speak harshly and avoid conflicts with co-workers. You must go to the temple as much as you can and meditate a great deal as all these will assist you safely through this month. Any activity this month should involve spirituality, or learning. Tension may be very high and sexual feelings may be very strong. If you are having an illicit affair, you must be careful of scandal. The key word is finish. Take care of unfinished business this month. Write your ideas down and keep it for next month. Don't think of changing jobs at this time. You may be prone to accidents or have worrisome problems from all sides. Keep a low profile and avoid confrontations of a negative nature with others. Income will be low and money may be short. There is possible sad news. Delay or deception in personal affairs and opportunities will not be attained successfully. If you are religious most of these problems will be minimized.

MONEY	LOVE	CAREER	FAMILY	TRAVEL	WEDDING	MOVE	BUSINESS	HEALTH	Lotto #'s	play 3 #s
Bad	Bad	Bad	Fair	Bad	Bad	Bad	Bad	Bad	40,20,9,75,26,59,47	927

SHOPPING	GAMBLE	SEX	KEYWORD	KEYWORD				
Bad	Bad	is very bad	KARMA	Destruction,Losses,Death,Sickness - cold,Legal matter,Abusive,Karmic debts,God - Karma				

STRESS LEVEL	LUCKY COLORS	JEWELERY	MOONS EFFECT	GRAHA EFFECT	MONTHLY DEITY
High	Gold/Brown//Green	Saphire/Hessonite	Ivestments	Evil Graha	PITREES

MONTHLY PUJA	MONTHLY PSALMS
Remembrance of family members who died, worship of older people. gifts to grand parents	9, 18, 36 63, 81,

BODY PARTS	DISEASE /sickness	POSSIBLE HEALTH PROBLEMS	MONTHLY EFFECT ON...Circulation
Circulation	Disease all kinds	General health is weak	Pitrees Affects You This Month – Your Problems

MANTRA FOR MONTH
Om Ganga mataye nama swaha Om Varuna Devta aye Pahimam 11 times

SPECIAL MESSAGE FOR THIS MONTH:
RULES FOR SUCCESS ; Become a student of the Universe Respect elder people and authority Follow all government laws and regulations Attend religious functions regularly Read and learn from others Avoid commanding others impulsively Seek advise for religious teachers Follow astrology and occult science Stop denying or doubting when facts are presented to you Avoid suspicion of loved ones Do not help others unless you are in a position to do so. Never! Never! Fight the government Always give to charity Avoid alcohol, drugs and cigarrettes

NEGATIVE DAYS:.............	2*8*11*17*20*26*29	November

Dec-2023	Shiva	This is considered a NEUTRAL month for you	Planet: Sun

ADVICE & DETAILS

LIFECODE FORECAST: You may be feeling quite independent this month and possibly lonely. You may be very busy attending to a lot of your projects, your career or your business. You may find yourself in conflict with others as a result of your becoming too commanding or too dominating. If you are married, tension may arise at the beginning of the month where you may be denied attention from your spouse or lover. Some of your personal projects or dreams may become a reality at this time. Your inventive abilities are extremely high and you may be congratulated or honored by persons in authority. A promotion may come about at your place of employment. Your health may be affected on the 8th or l7th of the month. Quarrels may occur on the 5th, 14th and 23rd of the month. A few opportunities for promotions and advancements in your ambitions may present themselves. Take advantage of these. If you are experiencing negative feelings of loneliness, perform meditative Puja. Concentrate on yourself this month and try to do everything that you have to do on your own without requesting help from others. People will not be as cooperative as you want them to be. You may feel lonely at times. However, any new opportunities presented will make you feel good about yourself. Do not be over-confident or too competitive with others. Do not expect many invitations until next month.

MONEY	LOVE	CAREER	FAMILY	TRAVEL	WEDDING	MOVE	BUSINESS	HEALTH	Lotto #'s	play 3 #s
Fair	Bad	Good	Bad	Fair	Bad	Fair	Fair	Fair	74,17,52,46,66,6,49	287

SHOPPING	GAMBLE	SEX	KEYWORD	KEYWORD				
Fair	Fair	is fair	MIND	Independence,Loneliness,Meditative,Worry,Dominating,Illness - Cold,On Your Own,Commanding				

STRESS LEVEL	LUCKY COLORS	JEWELERY	MOONS EFFECT	GRAHA EFFECT	MONTHLY DEITY
High	White/Yellow/	Pearl/Quartz	Arrogance	Status Graha	GURU

MONTHLY PUJA	MONTHLY PSALMS
Give Gifts to Priests, Invite holy ones to your home, Feed Swamis and Yogis, Do Shiva Puja.	1, 28 ,46, 73,,

BODY PARTS	DISEASE /sickness	POSSIBLE HEALTH PROBLEMS	MONTHLY EFFECT ON...Head
Head	Disease of the head	Nervousness caused by worrying	Guru Affects You This Month – Your Mind

MANTRA FOR MONTH
Om Namo Bhagawate Mukhtanandaya, 108 times

SPECIAL MESSAGE FOR THIS MONTH:
RULES FOR SUCCESS: Do not let your mind idle. Always try to be a leader. Meditate to slow down your mind. Do not be dominating or bossy to others. Only give advise when asked for it... When left alone by partner do not fight - pray instead. Avoid depression moments - meditate when feeling lonely. When accused of anything - rise above it When offered a leadership position at work - accept it

NEGATIVE DAYS:.............	2*8*11*17*20*26*29	December

Explanation Of Daily Forecast For The Year

DAILY INFLUENCE: (NEGATIVE, POSITIVE or NEUTRAL)

This tells you how the month is going to be in General. Some months are more negative than some, and some months are more positive than some others. You can enjoy the neutral months by doing activities that have been left back or those that do not require too much effort, as in neutral months your energy is on a middle level. It is good to pray more on your negative months. Do more meditation or Chanting of the Mantras. Perform Charity or spiritual work as this will make you more connected to the universe. On Positive months you will be able to relax more and you will have more energy to do what you want. It's good to set up interviews and important projects for those months. Court cases are postponed usually on negative months.

FORECAST AND ADVICE FOR THE MONTH:

This is a generally close description of the month. It helps you to assess your month accordingly and lets you have an idea of some of the things that may show up in your life that month.

KEYWORDS:

These are suggested words that will mostly affect your life that month. All may not apply, only some will apply. This is to let you know that some of these things may affect you. It prepares you to expect these.

They may be positive or negative according to the influence of the month.

BIBLE VERSES: (Proverbs)

These have been taken from the Book of Proverbs in the Christian St James Bible.

READ PSALMS #'s:

More than Five Psalms have been recommended, but you only need to read at least two of those given.

VEDIC MANTRAS:

These are special words which are designed to produce certain sounds and vibrations that will create positive changes in your life. Just like the bible says that "In the beginning it was the word, and the word was God and the word became one" so also the Hindus have the word "OM" which is known as the first word of Creation and is known as the vibration of birth. Dr. OZ on OPRAH recommends the Chanting of "OM" for relieving stress change mental energy- good or bad.

RULING PLANET:

The Planets acts as Timers in our life. Like the Moon controls the ovulation cycle in women, the planets affect our emotions and Moods, and our reaction to the Universal forces. SUN, MOON, MERCURY, VENUS and JUPITER are all Positive effects. The Negative ones are SATURN, RAHU, KETU, NEPTUNE, URANUS and PLUTO.

RULING DEITY:

Each of us is influences by cosmic forces and elements constantly in the Universe. The Deities are these forces and elements that affect our life every minute, hours, months, months and years. For example, when there is a predominance of Salt in our body, then our energy is hyper and when there is a lot of sugar, our nerves become itchy. The deities which are all the elements in the periodic table such as odium, etc. can affect our health, money and more by the way our brains and bodies handle them.

PUJAS & CHARITABLE SUGGESTIONS FOR THE MONTH:

These are suggested charitable actions that will create good reactions in your life, as well as payoff your Karmic debts. Everything we do is a ritual in life. Puja simple means holy or Karmic rituals.

LIFECODE 7 DAILY FORECASTS

Sunday, January 1, 2023 — This is considered a POSITIVE day for you — Planet: Jupiter

ADVICE & DETAILS

If you can, take short trips and enjoy high pleasure. There will be lots of moving today.

MANTRA FOR TODAY

Om Hareem Nama Swaha..Shri Maha Laxmi Aye Namah swaha 12 times

MONEY	LOVE	CAREER	FAMILY	TRAVEL	WEDDING	MOVE	BUSINESS	HEALTH	Lotto #'s	play 3 #s
Excellent	Good	Excellent	Good	Good	Excellent	Good	Excellent	Excellent	2,17,57,61,36,38,53	630

SHOPPING	GAMBLE	SEX	KEYWORD	KEYWORD						
Excellent	Excellent	is excellent	MONEY	Business,Major Expense,Money -						

STRESS LEVEL	LUCKY COLORS	JEWELERY	MOONS EFFECT	GRAHA EFFECT	DAILY DEITY
Low	Yellow/Silver	Diamonds/Gold/Pea	Secretive	Money Graha	Mahalaxmi

DAILY PUJA

Decorate Land, Feed the poor, Donate milk /products to all, Feed holy guests,

DAILY PSALMS

8, 17, 35 ,44, 53, 62, 80, 107, 125

Monday, January 2, 2023 — This is considered a NEGATIVE day for you — Planet: Saturn

ADVICE & DETAILS

Connect with the God within today so you can avoid the loneliness that can result from being boastful and criticizing others. Look at yourself first instead of trying to fix others.

MANTRA FOR TODAY

Om Ganga mataye nama swaha Om Varuna Devta aye Pahimam 11 times

MONEY	LOVE	CAREER	FAMILY	TRAVEL	WEDDING	MOVE	BUSINESS	HEALTH	Lotto #'s	play 3 #s
Bad	Bad	Bad	Fair	Bad	Bad	Bad	Bad	Bad	65,36,37,43,60,3,43	156

SHOPPING	GAMBLE	SEX	KEYWORD	KEYWORD						
Bad	Bad	is very bad	KARMA	Destruction,Losses,Death,Sickness - cold,Legal matter,Abusive,Karmic debts,God -						

STRESS LEVEL	LUCKY COLORS	JEWELERY	MOONS EFFECT	GRAHA EFFECT	DAILY DEITY
High	Gold/Brown//Green	Saphire/Hessonite	Ivestments	Evil Graha	Agnidev

DAILY PUJA

Remembrance of family members who died, worship of older people. gifts to grand parents

DAILY PSALMS

9, 18, 36 ,45, 54, 63, 81, 108, 126

Tuesday, January 3, 2023 — This is considered a NEUTRAL day for you — Planet: Sun

ADVICE & DETAILS

Today, you may be home alone, you may feel a bit confined, but at the same time you will have a sense of independence and the realization of your capabilities. This day may be influenced by dealings with the government, courts or legal institutions.

MANTRA FOR TODAY

Om Namo Bhagawate Mukhtanandaya, 108 times

MONEY	LOVE	CAREER	FAMILY	TRAVEL	WEDDING	MOVE	BUSINESS	HEALTH	Lotto #'s	play 3 #s
Fair	Bad	Good	Bad	Fair	Bad	Fair	Fair	Fair	13,16,29,45,46,47,3	669

SHOPPING	GAMBLE	SEX	KEYWORD	KEYWORD						
Fair	Fair	is fair	MIND	Independence,Loneliness,Meditative,Worry,Dominating,Illness - Cold,On Your						

STRESS LEVEL	LUCKY COLORS	JEWELERY	MOONS EFFECT	GRAHA EFFECT	DAILY DEITY
High	White/Yellow/	Pearl/Quartz	Arrogance	Status Graha	Saraswaty

DAILY PUJA

Give Gifts to Priests, Invite holy ones to your home, Feed Swamis and Yogis, Do Shiva Puja.

DAILY PSALMS

1, 10, 28 ,37, 46, 55, 73, 100, 118

Wednesday, January 4, 2023 — This is considered a POSITIVE day for you — Planet: Moon

ADVICE & DETAILS

There will be opportunity for romantic dates or encounters. You will make money today and get profits. There is a good chance of promotion.

MANTRA FOR TODAY

Kali Durge Namo Nama Om Durge aye nama swaha 108 times

MONEY	LOVE	CAREER	FAMILY	TRAVEL	WEDDING	MOVE	BUSINESS	HEALTH	Lotto #'s	play 3 #s
Good	Excellent	Good	Good	Excellen	Good	Good	Good	Good	58,53,5,27,12,5,9	87

SHOPPING	GAMBLE	SEX	KEYWORD	KEYWORD						
Good	Good	is good	LOVE	Romance,Popularity,Visitors,Shopping,Food, Drinks,Co-						

STRESS LEVEL	LUCKY COLORS	JEWELERY	MOONS EFFECT	GRAHA EFFECT	DAILY DEITY
Low	Red/Yellow/Pink	Topaz/Diamonds	Conservative	Love Graha	Gauri

DAILY PUJA

Give Gifts to females andnMother, Serve milk Products, Worship Durga forms

DAILY PSALMS

2, 11, 29 ,38, 47, 56, 74, 101, 119

Thursday, January 5, 2023 — This is considered a POSITIVE day for you — Planet: Mercury

ADVICE & DETAILS

This is slow and lazy day, but for your karma you are advised to work and to be industrious. Your accomplishments today will be important for your personal growth.

MANTRA FOR TODAY

Om hareem Kleem Hreem Aem Saraswataye namaha 21 times

MONEY	LOVE	CAREER	FAMILY	TRAVEL	WEDDING	MOVE	BUSINESS	HEALTH	Lotto #'s	play 3 #s
Good	Fair	Good	Good	Excellen	Good	Good	Good	Excellent	73,72,19,72,49,43,4	51

SHOPPING	GAMBLE	SEX	KEYWORD	KEYWORD
Good	Good	is great	SOCIAL	Children,Education,Astrology,Bargains,Social Functions,Childishness,Groups -

STRESS LEVEL	LUCKY COLORS	JEWELERY	MOONS EFFECT	GRAHA EFFECT	DAILY DEITY
Low	Green/Sky Blue/	Diamonds/Silver	Enthusiastic	Social Graha	Vishnu

DAILY PUJA	DAILY PSALMS
Wash the feet of Children, Do Satnarayan Pooja, Read & chant Geeta	3, 12, 30 ,39, 48, 57, 75, 102, 120

Friday, January 6, 2023 — This is considered a NEGATIVE day for you — Planet: Pluto

ADVICE & DETAILS

If you can, take short trips and enjoy high pleasure. There will be lots of moving today.

MANTRA FOR TODAY

Om Jai Viganeshwaraya.. Lambodaraya Namo Namaha 21 times

MONEY	LOVE	CAREER	FAMILY	TRAVEL	WEDDING	MOVE	BUSINESS	HEALTH	Lotto #'s	play 3 #s
Bad	Fair	Bad	Fair	Bad	Good	Bad	Bad	Bad	51,13,37,69,11,22,7	271

SHOPPING	GAMBLE	SEX	KEYWORD	KEYWORD
Bad	Bad	is tough	CAREER	Career,Hard Work,Co-workers,Low Payment,Job Problems,High Temper,Low

STRESS LEVEL	LUCKY COLORS	JEWELERY	MOONS EFFECT	GRAHA EFFECT	DAILY DEITY
High	Dark Blue/ Purple/	Amethyst/Gold	Emotional	Job Graha	Lingam

DAILY PUJA	DAILY PSALMS
Worship Ganesh, Give gifts to father, and co -workers, Plant gardens, farms	4, 13, 31 ,40, 49, 58, 76, 103, 121

Saturday, January 7, 2023 — This is considered a POSITIVE day for you — Planet: Venus

ADVICE & DETAILS

Today is a positive day to spend with others. You will be surrounded by partners, friends, associates and teachers. The exchange is beneficial, even if it is not what you expect.

MANTRA FOR TODAY

Om Graam Greem Graum Sa Gurave namah swaha 21 times

MONEY	LOVE	CAREER	FAMILY	TRAVEL	WEDDING	MOVE	BUSINESS	HEALTH	Lotto #'s	play 3 #s
Bad	Excellent	Fair	Good	Excellen	Good	Excellen	Good	Excellent	49,75,24,67,13,65,1	504

SHOPPING	GAMBLE	SEX	KEYWORD	KEYWORD
Good	Good	is good	CHANGE	Sexuality,Travel,Change,Distant, far,Travel delays,Deception,Excercise,Illicit

STRESS LEVEL	LUCKY COLORS	JEWELERY	MOONS EFFECT	GRAHA EFFECT	DAILY DEITY
Fair	Tan/Green/ Beige	Pearl/Silver/quartz	Courageous	Travel Graha	Nataraja

DAILY PUJA	DAILY PSALMS
Artistic gifts, Pray to Krishna, Do good deeds, do Spiritual trips	5, 14, 32 ,41, 50, 59, 77, 104, 122

Sunday, January 8, 2023 — This is considered a NEGATIVE day for you — Planet: Mars

ADVICE & DETAILS

You will feel in command of everything today, be careful not to be too bossy and to be careful with your expression. It is a good day for creative endeavors such as publishing or writing. You will have an opportunity to work or be in groups or to be invited to parties.

MANTRA FOR TODAY

Om Mana Swasti Shanti Kuru kuru Swaha Shivoham Shivoham 27 times

MONEY	LOVE	CAREER	FAMILY	TRAVEL	WEDDING	MOVE	BUSINESS	HEALTH	Lotto #'s	play 3 #s
Bad	Bad	Bad	Bad	Bad	Bad	Bad	Fair	Bad	42,22,18,54,71,34,7	662

SHOPPING	GAMBLE	SEX	KEYWORD	KEYWORD
Fair	Bad	is frustrating	POWER	Responsibilty,Disagreement,Family,Back Pain,Family Conflicts,Traffic

STRESS LEVEL	LUCKY COLORS	JEWELERY	MOONS EFFECT	GRAHA EFFECT	DAILY DEITY
High	Purple/Blue/Rose	Emerald/Saphire	Educational	Family Graha	Mahakali

DAILY PUJA	DAILY PSALMS
Meditate, Control temper, Pray to Hanuman, Chant Hanuman Chalisa	6, 15, 33 ,42, 51, 60, 78, 105, 123

Monday, January 9, 2023 — This is considered a NEUTRAL day for you — Planet: Uranus

ADVICE & DETAILS	MANTRA FOR TODAY
This is a day for expressing yourself in oral, visual or written form. Talk to others possibly in a group or at a gathering, paint or write a poem, book or article. This is also a day that if you are negative the use of alcohol or drugs will create danger for you, try to avoid it.	Jai Jai Shiva Shambo.(2) ...Mahadeva Shambo (2) 21 times 8

MONEY	LOVE	CAREER	FAMILY	TRAVEL	WEDDING	MOVE	BUSINESS	HEALTH	Lotto #'s	play 3 #s
Good	Good	Fair	Good	Good	Bad	Good	Bad	Fair	29,42,63,9,40,4,10	393

SHOPPING	GAMBLE	SEX	KEYWORD	KEYWORD
Bad	Fair	is quiet	DIVINE	Spirituality,Religious,Astrology,Inner Conflicts,Religious ,Sleepiness,Advice

STRESS LEVEL	LUCKY COLORS	JEWELERY	MOONS EFFECT	GRAHA EFFECT	DAILY DEITY
Fair	Light Blue/Peach	Tiger's eye/Gold/Sil	Affectionate	God'S Graha	Shesnaag

DAILY PUJA	DAILY PSALMS
Chant Shiva Mantras, Take gifts to Ocean - Ganga Puja, Donate to Temple, Priests, etc.	7, 16, 34 ,43, 52, 61, 79, 106, 124

Tuesday, January 10, 2023 — This is considered a POSITIVE day for you — Planet: Jupiter

ADVICE & DETAILS	MANTRA FOR TODAY
If you can, take short trips and enjoy high pleasure. There will be lots of moving today.	Om Hareem Nama Swaha..Shri Maha Laxmi Aye Namah swaha 12 times

MONEY	LOVE	CAREER	FAMILY	TRAVEL	WEDDING	MOVE	BUSINESS	HEALTH	Lotto #'s	play 3 #s
Excellent	Good	Excellent	Good	Good	Excellent	Good	Excellent	Excellent	40,65,34,19,51,20,1	932

SHOPPING	GAMBLE	SEX	KEYWORD	KEYWORD
Excellent	Excellent	is excellent	MONEY	Business,Major Expense,Money -

STRESS LEVEL	LUCKY COLORS	JEWELERY	MOONS EFFECT	GRAHA EFFECT	DAILY DEITY
Low	Yellow/Silver	Diamonds/Gold/Pea	Secretive	Money Graha	Mahalaxmi

DAILY PUJA	DAILY PSALMS
Decorate Land, Feed the poor, Donate milk /products to all, Feed holy guests,	8, 17, 35 ,44, 53, 62, 80, 107, 125

Wednesday, January 11, 2023 — This is considered a NEGATIVE day for you — Planet: Saturn

ADVICE & DETAILS	MANTRA FOR TODAY
Connect with the God within today so you can avoid the loneliness that can result from being boastful and criticizing others. Look at yourself first instead of trying to fix others.	Om Ganga mataye nama swaha Om Varuna Devta aye Pahimam 11 times

MONEY	LOVE	CAREER	FAMILY	TRAVEL	WEDDING	MOVE	BUSINESS	HEALTH	Lotto #'s	play 3 #s
Bad	Bad	Bad	Fair	Bad	Bad	Bad	Bad	Bad	25,68,30,44,38,50,6	188

SHOPPING	GAMBLE	SEX	KEYWORD	KEYWORD
Bad	Bad	is very bad	KARMA	Destruction,Losses,Death,Sickness - cold,Legal matter,Abusive,Karmic debts,God -

STRESS LEVEL	LUCKY COLORS	JEWELERY	MOONS EFFECT	GRAHA EFFECT	DAILY DEITY
High	Gold/Brown//Green	Saphire/Hessonite	Ivestments	Evil Graha	Agnidev

DAILY PUJA	DAILY PSALMS
Remembrance of family members who died, worship of older people. gifts to grand parents	9, 18, 36 ,45, 54, 63, 81, 108, 126

Thursday, January 12, 2023 — This is considered a NEUTRAL day for you — Planet: Sun

ADVICE & DETAILS	MANTRA FOR TODAY
Today, you may be home alone, you may feel a bit confined, but at the same time you will have a sense of independence and the realization of your capabilities. This day may be influenced by dealings with the government, courts or legal institutions.	Om Namo Bhagawate Mukhtanandaya, 108 times

MONEY	LOVE	CAREER	FAMILY	TRAVEL	WEDDING	MOVE	BUSINESS	HEALTH	Lotto #'s	play 3 #s
Fair	Bad	Good	Bad	Fair	Bad	Fair	Fair	Fair	22,22,51,31,15,44,2	394

SHOPPING	GAMBLE	SEX	KEYWORD	KEYWORD
Fair	Fair	is fair	MIND	Independence,Loneliness,Meditative,Worry,Dominating,Illness - Cold,On Your

STRESS LEVEL	LUCKY COLORS	JEWELERY	MOONS EFFECT	GRAHA EFFECT	DAILY DEITY
High	White/Yellow/	Pearl/Quartz	Arrogance	Status Graha	Saraswaty

DAILY PUJA	DAILY PSALMS
Give Gifts to Priests, Invite holy ones to your home, Feed Swamis and Yogis, Do Shiva Puja.	1, 10, 28 ,37, 46, 55, 73, 100, 118

Friday, January 13, 2023 — This is considered a POSITIVE day for you — Planet: Moon

ADVICE & DETAILS
There will be opportunity for romantic dates or encounters. You will make money today and get profits. There is a good chance of promotion.

MANTRA FOR TODAY
Kali Durge Namo Nama Om Durge aye nama swaha 108 times

MONEY	LOVE	CAREER	FAMILY	TRAVEL	WEDDING	MOVE	BUSINESS	HEALTH	Lotto #'s	play 3 #s
Good	Excellent	Good	Good	Excellen	Good	Good	Good	Good	75,14,28,74,17,34,2	41

SHOPPING	GAMBLE	SEX	KEYWORD	KEYWORD
Good	Good	is good	LOVE	Romance,Popularity,Visitors,Shopping,Food, Drinks,Co-

STRESS LEVEL	LUCKY COLORS	JEWELERY	MOONS EFFECT	GRAHA EFFECT	DAILY DEITY
Low	Red/Yellow/Pink	Topaz/Diamonds	Conservative	Love Graha	Gauri

DAILY PUJA: Give Gifts to females andnMother, Serve milk Products, Worship Durga forms

DAILY PSALMS: 2, 11, 29 ,38, 47, 56, 74, 101, 119

Saturday, January 14, 2023 — This is considered a POSITIVE day for you — Planet: Mercury

ADVICE & DETAILS
This is slow and lazy day, but for your karma you are advised to work and to be industrious. Your accomplishments today will be important for your personal growth.

MANTRA FOR TODAY
Om hareem Kleem Hreem Aem Saraswataye namaha 21 times

MONEY	LOVE	CAREER	FAMILY	TRAVEL	WEDDING	MOVE	BUSINESS	HEALTH	Lotto #'s	play 3 #s
Good	Fair	Good	Good	Excellen	Good	Good	Good	Excellent	70,54,6,11,9,53,64	690

SHOPPING	GAMBLE	SEX	KEYWORD	KEYWORD
Good	Good	is great	SOCIAL	Children,Education,Astrology,Bargains,Social Functions,Childishness,Groups -

STRESS LEVEL	LUCKY COLORS	JEWELERY	MOONS EFFECT	GRAHA EFFECT	DAILY DEITY
Low	Green/Sky Blue/	Diamonds/Silver	Enthusiastic	Social Graha	Vishnu

DAILY PUJA: Wash the feet of Children, Do Satnarayan Pooja, Read & chant Geeta

DAILY PSALMS: 3, 12, 30 ,39, 48, 57, 75, 102, 120

Sunday, January 15, 2023 — This is considered a NEGATIVE day for you — Planet: Pluto

ADVICE & DETAILS
If you can, take short trips and enjoy high pleasure. There will be lots of moving today.

MANTRA FOR TODAY
Om Jai Viganeshwaraya.. Lambodaraya Namo Namaha 21 times

MONEY	LOVE	CAREER	FAMILY	TRAVEL	WEDDING	MOVE	BUSINESS	HEALTH	Lotto #'s	play 3 #s
Bad	Fair	Bad	Fair	Bad	Good	Bad	Bad	Bad	21,11,58,54,67,47,3	443

SHOPPING	GAMBLE	SEX	KEYWORD	KEYWORD
Bad	Bad	is tough	CAREER	Career,Hard Work,Co-workers,Low Payment,Job Problems,High Temper,Low

STRESS LEVEL	LUCKY COLORS	JEWELERY	MOONS EFFECT	GRAHA EFFECT	DAILY DEITY
High	Dark Blue/ Purple/	Amethyst/Gold	Emotional	Job Graha	Lingam

DAILY PUJA: Worship Ganesh, Give gifts to father, and co -workers, Plant gardens, farms

DAILY PSALMS: 4, 13, 31 ,40, 49, 58, 76, 103, 121

Monday, January 16, 2023 — This is considered a POSITIVE day for you — Planet: Venus

ADVICE & DETAILS
Today is a positive day to spend with others. You will be surrounded by partners, friends, associates and teachers. The exchange is beneficial, even if it is not what you expect.

MANTRA FOR TODAY
Om Graam Greem Graum Sa Gurave namah swaha 21 times

MONEY	LOVE	CAREER	FAMILY	TRAVEL	WEDDING	MOVE	BUSINESS	HEALTH	Lotto #'s	play 3 #s
Bad	Excellent	Fair	Good	Excellen	Good	Excellen	Good	Excellent	66,66,64,60,20,64,5	337

SHOPPING	GAMBLE	SEX	KEYWORD	KEYWORD
Good	Good	is good	CHANGE	Sexuality,Travel,Change,Distant, far,Travel delays,Deception,Excercise,Illicit

STRESS LEVEL	LUCKY COLORS	JEWELERY	MOONS EFFECT	GRAHA EFFECT	DAILY DEITY
Fair	Tan/Green/ Beige	Pearl/Silver/quartz	Courageous	Travel Graha	Nataraja

DAILY PUJA: Artistic gifts, Pray to Krishna, Do good deeds, do Spiritual trips

DAILY PSALMS: 5, 14, 32 ,41, 50, 59, 77, 104, 122

Tuesday, January 17, 2023 — This is considered a NEGATIVE day for you — Planet: Mars

ADVICE & DETAILS

You will feel in command of everything today, be careful not to be too bossy and to be careful with your expression. It is a good day for creative endeavors such as publishing or writing. You will have an opportunity to work or be in groups or to be invited to parties.

MANTRA FOR TODAY

Om Mana Swasti Shanti Kuru kuru Swaha Shivoham Shivoham 27 times

MONEY	LOVE	CAREER	FAMILY	TRAVEL	WEDDING	MOVE	BUSINESS	HEALTH	Lotto #'s	play 3 #s
Bad	Bad	Bad	Bad	Bad	Bad	Bad	Fair	Bad	49,63,51,37,30,63,7	349

SHOPPING	GAMBLE	SEX	KEYWORD	KEYWORD
Fair	Bad	is frustrating	POWER	Responsibilty,Disagreement,Family,Back Pain,Family Conflicts,Traffic

STRESS LEVEL	LUCKY COLORS	JEWELERY	MOONS EFFECT	GRAHA EFFECT	DAILY DEITY
High	Purple/Blue/Rose	Emerald/Saphire	Educational	Family Graha	Mahakali

DAILY PUJA	DAILY PSALMS
Meditate, Control temper, Pray to Hanuman, Chant Hanuman Chalisa	6, 15, 33 ,42, 51, 60, 78, 105, 123

Wednesday, January 18, 2023 — This is considered a NEUTRAL day for you — Planet: Uranus

ADVICE & DETAILS

This is a day for expressing yourself in oral, visual or written form. Talk to others possibly in a group or at a gathering, paint or write a poem, book or article. This is also a day that if you are negative the use of alcohol or drugs will create danger for you, try to avoid it.

MANTRA FOR TODAY

Jai Jai Shiva Shambo.(2) ...Mahadeva Shambo (2) 21 times 8

MONEY	LOVE	CAREER	FAMILY	TRAVEL	WEDDING	MOVE	BUSINESS	HEALTH	Lotto #'s	play 3 #s
Good	Good	Fair	Good	Good	Bad	Good	Bad	Fair	4,2,34,18,18,28,30	723

SHOPPING	GAMBLE	SEX	KEYWORD	KEYWORD
Bad	Fair	is quiet	DIVINE	Spirituality,Religious,Astrology,Inner Conflicts,Religious ,Sleepiness,Advice

STRESS LEVEL	LUCKY COLORS	JEWELERY	MOONS EFFECT	GRAHA EFFECT	DAILY DEITY
Fair	Light Blue/Peach	Tiger's eye/Gold/Sil	Affectionate	God'S Graha	Shesnaag

DAILY PUJA	DAILY PSALMS
Chant Shiva Mantras, Take gifts to Ocean - Ganga Puja, Donate to Temple, Priests, etc.	7, 16, 34 ,43, 52, 61, 79, 106, 124

Thursday, January 19, 2023 — This is considered a POSITIVE day for you — Planet: Jupiter

ADVICE & DETAILS

If you can, take short trips and enjoy high pleasure. There will be lots of moving today.

MANTRA FOR TODAY

Om Hareem Nama Swaha..Shri Maha Laxmi Aye Namah swaha 12 times

MONEY	LOVE	CAREER	FAMILY	TRAVEL	WEDDING	MOVE	BUSINESS	HEALTH	Lotto #'s	play 3 #s
Excellent	Good	Excellent	Good	Good	Excellent	Good	Excellent	Excellent	26,7,1,22,11,30,25	336

SHOPPING	GAMBLE	SEX	KEYWORD	KEYWORD
Excellent	Excellent	is excellent	MONEY	Business,Major Expense,Money -

STRESS LEVEL	LUCKY COLORS	JEWELERY	MOONS EFFECT	GRAHA EFFECT	DAILY DEITY
Low	Yellow/Silver	Diamonds/Gold/Pea	Secretive	Money Graha	Mahalaxmi

DAILY PUJA	DAILY PSALMS
Decorate Land, Feed the poor, Donate milk /products to all, Feed holy guests,	8, 17, 35 ,44, 53, 62, 80, 107, 125

Friday, January 20, 2023 — This is considered a NEGATIVE day for you — Planet: Saturn

ADVICE & DETAILS

Connect with the God within today so you can avoid the loneliness that can result from being boastful and criticizing others. Look at yourself first instead of trying to fix others.

MANTRA FOR TODAY

Om Ganga mataye nama swaha Om Varuna Devta aye Pahimam 11 times

MONEY	LOVE	CAREER	FAMILY	TRAVEL	WEDDING	MOVE	BUSINESS	HEALTH	Lotto #'s	play 3 #s
Bad	Bad	Bad	Fair	Bad	Bad	Bad	Bad	Bad	1,17,37,39,19,75,34	361

SHOPPING	GAMBLE	SEX	KEYWORD	KEYWORD
Bad	Bad	is very bad	KARMA	Destruction,Losses,Death,Sickness - cold,Legal matter,Abusive,Karmic debts,God -

STRESS LEVEL	LUCKY COLORS	JEWELERY	MOONS EFFECT	GRAHA EFFECT	DAILY DEITY
High	Gold/Brown//Green	Saphire/Hessonite	Ivestments	Evil Graha	Agnidev

DAILY PUJA	DAILY PSALMS
Remembrance of family members who died, worship of older people. gifts to grand parents	9, 18, 36 ,45, 54, 63, 81, 108, 126

Saturday, January 21, 2023 — This is considered a NEUTRAL day for you — Planet: Sun

ADVICE & DETAILS

Today, you may be home alone, you may feel a bit confined, but at the same time you will have a sense of independence and the realization of your capabilities. This day may be influenced by dealings with the government, courts or legal institutions.

MANTRA FOR TODAY: Om Namo Bhagawate Mukhtanandaya, 108 times

MONEY	LOVE	CAREER	FAMILY	TRAVEL	WEDDING	MOVE	BUSINESS	HEALTH	Lotto #'s	play 3 #s
Fair	Bad	Good	Bad	Fair	Bad	Fair	Fair	Fair	34,14,6,54,4,18,54	415

SHOPPING	GAMBLE	SEX	KEYWORD	KEYWORD
Fair	Fair	is fair	MIND	Independence,Loneliness,Meditative,Worry,Dominating,Illness - Cold,On Your

STRESS LEVEL	LUCKY COLORS	JEWELERY	MOONS EFFECT	GRAHA EFFECT	DAILY DEITY
High	White/Yellow/	Pearl/Quartz	Arrogance	Status Graha	Saraswaty

DAILY PUJA: Give Gifts to Priests, Invite holy ones to your home, Feed Swamis and Yogis, Do Shiva Puja.

DAILY PSALMS: 1, 10, 28 ,37, 46, 55, 73, 100, 118

Sunday, January 22, 2023 — This is considered a POSITIVE day for you — Planet: Moon

ADVICE & DETAILS

There will be opportunity for romantic dates or encounters. You will make money today and get profits. There is a good chance of promotion.

MANTRA FOR TODAY: Kali Durge Namo Nama Om Durge aye nama swaha 108 times

MONEY	LOVE	CAREER	FAMILY	TRAVEL	WEDDING	MOVE	BUSINESS	HEALTH	Lotto #'s	play 3 #s
Good	Excellent	Good	Good	Excellen	Good	Good	Good	Good	11,17,51,72,31,48,5	661

SHOPPING	GAMBLE	SEX	KEYWORD	KEYWORD
Good	Good	is good	LOVE	Romance,Popularity,Visitors,Shopping,Food, Drinks,Co-

STRESS LEVEL	LUCKY COLORS	JEWELERY	MOONS EFFECT	GRAHA EFFECT	DAILY DEITY
Low	Red/Yellow/Pink	Topaz/Diamonds	Conservative	Love Graha	Gauri

DAILY PUJA: Give Gifts to females andnMother, Serve milk Products, Worship Durga forms

DAILY PSALMS: 2, 11, 29 ,38, 47, 56, 74, 101, 119

Monday, January 23, 2023 — This is considered a POSITIVE day for you — Planet: Mercury

ADVICE & DETAILS

This is slow and lazy day, but for your karma you are advised to work and to be industrious. Your accomplishments today will be important for your personal growth.

MANTRA FOR TODAY: Om hareem Kleem Hreem Aem Saraswataye namaha 21 times

MONEY	LOVE	CAREER	FAMILY	TRAVEL	WEDDING	MOVE	BUSINESS	HEALTH	Lotto #'s	play 3 #s
Good	Fair	Good	Good	Excellen	Good	Good	Good	Excellent	32,43,71,23,34,29,4	978

SHOPPING	GAMBLE	SEX	KEYWORD	KEYWORD
Good	Good	is great	SOCIAL	Children,Education,Astrology,Bargains,Social Functions,Childishness,Groups -

STRESS LEVEL	LUCKY COLORS	JEWELERY	MOONS EFFECT	GRAHA EFFECT	DAILY DEITY
Low	Green/Sky Blue/	Diamonds/Silver	Enthusiastic	Social Graha	Vishnu

DAILY PUJA: Wash the feet of Children, Do Satnarayan Pooja, Read & chant Geeta

DAILY PSALMS: 3, 12, 30 ,39, 48, 57, 75, 102, 120

Tuesday, January 24, 2023 — This is considered a NEGATIVE day for you — Planet: Pluto

ADVICE & DETAILS

If you can, take short trips and enjoy high pleasure. There will be lots of moving today.

MANTRA FOR TODAY: Om Jai Viganeshwaraya.. Lambodaraya Namo Namaha 21 times

MONEY	LOVE	CAREER	FAMILY	TRAVEL	WEDDING	MOVE	BUSINESS	HEALTH	Lotto #'s	play 3 #s
Bad	Fair	Bad	Fair	Bad	Good	Bad	Bad	Bad	18,35,38,13,35,27,6	881

SHOPPING	GAMBLE	SEX	KEYWORD	KEYWORD
Bad	Bad	is tough	CAREER	Career,Hard Work,Co-workers,Low Payment,Job Problems,High Temper,Low

STRESS LEVEL	LUCKY COLORS	JEWELERY	MOONS EFFECT	GRAHA EFFECT	DAILY DEITY
High	Dark Blue/ Purple/	Amethyst/Gold	Emotional	Job Graha	Lingam

DAILY PUJA: Worship Ganesh, Give gifts to father, and co -workers, Plant gardens, farms

DAILY PSALMS: 4, 13, 31 ,40, 49, 58, 76, 103, 121

Wednesday, January 25, 2023 — This is considered a POSITIVE day for you — Planet: Venus

ADVICE & DETAILS

Today is a positive day to spend with others. You will be surrounded by partners, friends, associates and teachers. The exchange is beneficial, even if it is not what you expect.

MANTRA FOR TODAY

Om Graam Greem Graum Sa Gurave namah swaha 21 times

MONEY	LOVE	CAREER	FAMILY	TRAVEL	WEDDING	MOVE	BUSINESS	HEALTH	Lotto #'s	play 3 #s
Bad	Excellent	Fair	Good	Excellen	Good	Excellen	Good	Excellent	55,54,13,57,14,63,2	279

SHOPPING	GAMBLE	SEX	KEYWORD	KEYWORD				
Good	Good	is good	CHANGE	Sexuality,Travel,Change,Distant, far,Travel delays,Deception,Excercise,Illicit				

STRESS LEVEL	LUCKY COLORS	JEWELERY	MOONS EFFECT	GRAHA EFFECT	DAILY DEITY
Fair	Tan/Green/ Beige	Pearl/Silver/quartz	Courageous	Travel Graha	Nataraja

DAILY PUJA	DAILY PSALMS
Artistic gifts, Pray to Krishna, Do good deeds, do Spiritual trips	5, 14, 32 ,41, 50, 59, 77, 104, 122

Thursday, January 26, 2023 — This is considered a NEGATIVE day for you — Planet: Mars

ADVICE & DETAILS

You will feel in command of everything today, be careful not to be too bossy and to be careful with your expression. It is a good day for creative endeavors such as publishing or writing. You will have an opportunity to work or be in groups or to be invited to parties.

MANTRA FOR TODAY

Om Mana Swasti Shanti Kuru kuru Swaha Shivoham Shivoham 27 times

MONEY	LOVE	CAREER	FAMILY	TRAVEL	WEDDING	MOVE	BUSINESS	HEALTH	Lotto #'s	play 3 #s
Bad	Bad	Bad	Bad	Bad	Bad	Bad	Fair	Bad	52,19,15,70,6,5,42	249

SHOPPING	GAMBLE	SEX	KEYWORD	KEYWORD				
Fair	Bad	is frustrating	POWER	Responsibilty,Disagreement,Family,Back Pain,Family Conflicts,Traffic				

STRESS LEVEL	LUCKY COLORS	JEWELERY	MOONS EFFECT	GRAHA EFFECT	DAILY DEITY
High	Purple/Blue/Rose	Emerald/Saphire	Educational	Family Graha	Mahakali

DAILY PUJA	DAILY PSALMS
Meditate, Control temper, Pray to Hanuman, Chant Hanuman Chalisa	6, 15, 33 ,42, 51, 60, 78, 105, 123

Friday, January 27, 2023 — This is considered a NEUTRAL day for you — Planet: Uranus

ADVICE & DETAILS

This is a day for expressing yourself in oral, visual or written form. Talk to others possibly in a group or at a gathering, paint or write a poem, book or article. This is also a day that if you are negative the use of alcohol or drugs will create danger for you, try to avoid it.

MANTRA FOR TODAY

Jai Jai Shiva Shambo.(2) ...Mahadeva Shambo (2) 21 times 8

MONEY	LOVE	CAREER	FAMILY	TRAVEL	WEDDING	MOVE	BUSINESS	HEALTH	Lotto #'s	play 3 #s
Good	Good	Fair	Good	Good	Bad	Good	Bad	Fair	12,8,6,58,63,52,12	620

SHOPPING	GAMBLE	SEX	KEYWORD	KEYWORD				
Bad	Fair	is quiet	DIVINE	Spirituality,Religious,Astrology,Inner Conflicts,Religious ,Sleepiness,Advice				

STRESS LEVEL	LUCKY COLORS	JEWELERY	MOONS EFFECT	GRAHA EFFECT	DAILY DEITY
Fair	Light Blue/Peach	Tiger's eye/Gold/Sil	Affectionate	God'S Graha	Shesnaag

DAILY PUJA	DAILY PSALMS
Chant Shiva Mantras, Take gifts to Ocean - Ganga Puja, Donate to Temple, Priests, etc.	7, 16, 34 ,43, 52, 61, 79, 106, 124

Saturday, January 28, 2023 — This is considered a POSITIVE day for you — Planet: Jupiter

ADVICE & DETAILS

If you can, take short trips and enjoy high pleasure. There will be lots of moving today.

MANTRA FOR TODAY

Om Hareem Nama Swaha..Shri Maha Laxmi Aye Namah swaha 12 times

MONEY	LOVE	CAREER	FAMILY	TRAVEL	WEDDING	MOVE	BUSINESS	HEALTH	Lotto #'s	play 3 #s
Excellent	Good	Excellent	Good	Good	Excellent	Good	Excellent	Excellent	23,39,12,19,38,21,2	647

SHOPPING	GAMBLE	SEX	KEYWORD	KEYWORD				
Excellent	Excellent	is excellent	MONEY	Business,Major Expense,Money -				

STRESS LEVEL	LUCKY COLORS	JEWELERY	MOONS EFFECT	GRAHA EFFECT	DAILY DEITY
Low	Yellow/Silver	Diamonds/Gold/Pea	Secretive	Money Graha	Mahalaxmi

DAILY PUJA	DAILY PSALMS
Decorate Land, Feed the poor, Donate milk /products to all, Feed holy guests,	8, 17, 35 ,44, 53, 62, 80, 107, 125

Sunday, January 29, 2023 — This is considered a NEGATIVE day for you — Planet: Saturn

ADVICE & DETAILS

Connect with the God within today so you can avoid the loneliness that can result from being boastful and criticizing others. Look at yourself first instead of trying to fix others.

MANTRA FOR TODAY

Om Ganga mataye nama swaha Om Varuna Devta aye Pahimam 11 times

MONEY	LOVE	CAREER	FAMILY	TRAVEL	WEDDING	MOVE	BUSINESS	HEALTH	Lotto #'s	play 3 #s
Bad	Bad	Bad	Fair	Bad	Bad	Bad	Bad	Bad	73,59,14,56,70,68,4	533

SHOPPING	GAMBLE	SEX	KEYWORD	KEYWORD
Bad	Bad	is very bad	KARMA	Destruction,Losses,Death,Sickness - cold,Legal matter,Abusive,Karmic debts,God -

STRESS LEVEL	LUCKY COLORS	JEWELERY	MOONS EFFECT	GRAHA EFFECT	DAILY DEITY
High	Gold/Brown//Green	Saphire/Hessonite	Ivestments	Evil Graha	Agnidev

DAILY PUJA	DAILY PSALMS
Remembrance of family members who died, worship of older people. gifts to grand parents	9, 18, 36 ,45, 54, 63, 81, 108, 126

Monday, January 30, 2023 — This is considered a NEUTRAL day for you — Planet: Sun

ADVICE & DETAILS

Today, you may be home alone, you may feel a bit confined, but at the same time you will have a sense of independence and the realization of your capabilities. This day may be influenced by dealings with the government, courts or legal institutions.

MANTRA FOR TODAY

Om Namo Bhagawate Mukhtanandaya, 108 times

MONEY	LOVE	CAREER	FAMILY	TRAVEL	WEDDING	MOVE	BUSINESS	HEALTH	Lotto #'s	play 3 #s
Fair	Bad	Good	Bad	Fair	Bad	Fair	Fair	Fair	32,14,2,35,19,14,34	648

SHOPPING	GAMBLE	SEX	KEYWORD	KEYWORD
Fair	Fair	is fair	MIND	Independence,Loneliness,Meditative,Worry,Dominating,Illness - Cold,On Your

STRESS LEVEL	LUCKY COLORS	JEWELERY	MOONS EFFECT	GRAHA EFFECT	DAILY DEITY
High	White/Yellow/	Pearl/Quartz	Arrogance	Status Graha	Saraswaty

DAILY PUJA	DAILY PSALMS
Give Gifts to Priests, Invite holy ones to your home, Feed Swamis and Yogis, Do Shiva Puja.	1, 10, 28 ,37, 46, 55, 73, 100, 118

Tuesday, January 31, 2023 — This is considered a POSITIVE day for you — Planet: Moon

ADVICE & DETAILS

There will be opportunity for romantic dates or encounters. You will make money today and get profits. There is a good chance of promotion.

MANTRA FOR TODAY

Kali Durge Namo Nama Om Durge aye nama swaha 108 times

MONEY	LOVE	CAREER	FAMILY	TRAVEL	WEDDING	MOVE	BUSINESS	HEALTH	Lotto #'s	play 3 #s
Good	Excellent	Good	Good	Excellen	Good	Good	Good	Good	54,55,28,4,57,1,46	936

SHOPPING	GAMBLE	SEX	KEYWORD	KEYWORD
Good	Good	is good	LOVE	Romance,Popularity,Visitors,Shopping,Food, Drinks,Co-

STRESS LEVEL	LUCKY COLORS	JEWELERY	MOONS EFFECT	GRAHA EFFECT	DAILY DEITY
Low	Red/Yellow/Pink	Topaz/Diamonds	Conservative	Love Graha	Gauri

DAILY PUJA	DAILY PSALMS
Give Gifts to females andnMother, Serve milk Products, Worship Durga forms	2, 11, 29 ,38, 47, 56, 74, 101, 119

Wednesday, February 1, 2023 — This is considered a POSITIVE day for you — Planet: Jupiter

ADVICE & DETAILS

You will probably be taking short trips today or you will be moving. You will feel like moving and exercising and you should do it! There will be opportunity for illicit affairs, stay aware of how this affects you and others around you.

MANTRA FOR TODAY

Om Hareem Nama Swaha..Shri Maha Laxmi Aye Namah swaha 12 times

MONEY	LOVE	CAREER	FAMILY	TRAVEL	WEDDING	MOVE	BUSINESS	HEALTH	Lotto #'s	play 3 #s
Excellent	Good	Excellent	Good	Good	Excellent	Good	Excellent	Excellent	53,52,8,17,36,27,56	39

SHOPPING	GAMBLE	SEX	KEYWORD	KEYWORD
Excellent	Excellent	is excellent	MONEY	Business,Major Expense,Money -

STRESS LEVEL	LUCKY COLORS	JEWELERY	MOONS EFFECT	GRAHA EFFECT	DAILY DEITY
Low	Yellow/Silver	Diamonds/Gold/Pea	Secretive	Money Graha	Mahalaxmi

DAILY PUJA	DAILY PSALMS
Decorate Land, Feed the poor, Donate milk /products to all, Feed holy guests,	8, 17, 35 ,44, 53, 62, 80, 107, 125

Thursday, February 2, 2023 — This is considered a NEGATIVE day for you — Planet: Saturn

ADVICE & DETAILS

Try to remember that when you criticize others, you are seeing in others what you think you are missing, be kind and concentrate on the positive characteristics of others not in what you perceive are negatives. The influence of this day will make you introspective and thoughts about your spiritual self will arise. Remember that loves heals all, try to have loving, healing thoughts as much as possible. Rest today if you

MANTRA FOR TODAY

Om Ganga mataye nama swaha Om Varuna Devta aye Pahimam 11 times

MONEY	LOVE	CAREER	FAMILY	TRAVEL	WEDDING	MOVE	BUSINESS	HEALTH	Lotto #'s	play 3 #s
Bad	Bad	Bad	Fair	Bad	Bad	Bad	Bad	Bad	57,2,44,19,19,18,34	77

SHOPPING	GAMBLE	SEX	KEYWORD	KEYWORD
Bad	Bad	is very bad	KARMA	Destruction,Losses,Death,Sickness - cold,Legal matter,Abusive,Karmic debts,God -

STRESS LEVEL	LUCKY COLORS	JEWELERY	MOONS EFFECT	GRAHA EFFECT	DAILY DEITY
High	Gold/Brown//Green	Saphire/Hessonite	Ivestments	Evil Graha	Agnidev

DAILY PUJA	DAILY PSALMS
Remembrance of family members who died, worship of older people. gifts to grand parents	9, 18, 36 ,45, 54, 63, 81, 108, 126

Friday, February 3, 2023 — This is considered a NEUTRAL day for you — Planet: Sun

ADVICE & DETAILS

The only obstacle to this very positive day is your speech. If you are careful and kind with your words expect money, romance and positive outlook for partnerships in any area.

MANTRA FOR TODAY

Om Namo Bhagawate Mukhtanandaya, 108 times

MONEY	LOVE	CAREER	FAMILY	TRAVEL	WEDDING	MOVE	BUSINESS	HEALTH	Lotto #'s	play 3 #s
Fair	Bad	Good	Bad	Fair	Bad	Fair	Fair	Fair	43,68,69,2,8,14,45	666

SHOPPING	GAMBLE	SEX	KEYWORD	KEYWORD
Fair	Fair	is fair	MIND	Independence,Loneliness,Meditative,Worry,Dominating,Illness - Cold,On Your

STRESS LEVEL	LUCKY COLORS	JEWELERY	MOONS EFFECT	GRAHA EFFECT	DAILY DEITY
High	White/Yellow/	Pearl/Quartz	Arrogance	Status Graha	Saraswaty

DAILY PUJA	DAILY PSALMS
Give Gifts to Priests, Invite holy ones to your home, Feed Swamis and Yogis, Do Shiva Puja.	1, 10, 28 ,37, 46, 55, 73, 100, 118

Saturday, February 4, 2023 — This is considered a POSITIVE day for you — Planet: Moon

ADVICE & DETAILS

Every word your lips utter today have great power and they must be used with love and positive intention to avoid conflict. You will have the opportunity to serve and cooperate with others today, use it. Listen to music or express your feelings through music to get blessings today.

MANTRA FOR TODAY

Kali Durge Namo Nama Om Durge aye nama swaha 108 times

MONEY	LOVE	CAREER	FAMILY	TRAVEL	WEDDING	MOVE	BUSINESS	HEALTH	Lotto #'s	play 3 #s
Good	Excellent	Good	Good	Excellen	Good	Good	Good	Good	42,21,16,11,43,13,3	32

SHOPPING	GAMBLE	SEX	KEYWORD	KEYWORD
Good	Good	is good	LOVE	Romance,Popularity,Visitors,Shopping,Food, Drinks,Co-

STRESS LEVEL	LUCKY COLORS	JEWELERY	MOONS EFFECT	GRAHA EFFECT	DAILY DEITY
Low	Red/Yellow/Pink	Topaz/Diamonds	Conservative	Love Graha	Gauri

DAILY PUJA	DAILY PSALMS
Give Gifts to females andnMother, Serve milk Products, Worship Durga forms	2, 11, 29 ,38, 47, 56, 74, 101, 119

Sunday, February 5, 2023 — This is considered a POSITIVE day for you — Planet: Mercury

ADVICE & DETAILS

You may spend your day at home alone watching TV or may instead opt for luxurious and pleasurable activities that may bring you around fame or famous people. You will be influenced by money, so you will worry about it, make it or spend it.

MANTRA FOR TODAY

Om hareem Kleem Hreem Aem Saraswataye namaha 21 times

MONEY	LOVE	CAREER	FAMILY	TRAVEL	WEDDING	MOVE	BUSINESS	HEALTH	Lotto #'s	play 3 #s
Good	Fair	Good	Good	Excellen	Good	Good	Good	Excellent	61,38,54,3,75,26,9	293

SHOPPING	GAMBLE	SEX	KEYWORD	KEYWORD
Good	Good	is great	SOCIAL	Children,Education,Astrology,Bargains,Social Functions,Childishness,Groups -

STRESS LEVEL	LUCKY COLORS	JEWELERY	MOONS EFFECT	GRAHA EFFECT	DAILY DEITY
Low	Green/Sky Blue/	Diamonds/Silver	Enthusiastic	Social Graha	Vishnu

DAILY PUJA	DAILY PSALMS
Wash the feet of Children, Do Satnarayan Pooja, Read & chant Geeta	3, 12, 30 ,39, 48, 57, 75, 102, 120

Monday, February 6, 2023 — This is considered a NEGATIVE day for you — Planet: Pluto

ADVICE & DETAILS

This will be a positive day if you can control your tongue and do not criticize anyone, particularly your loved ones and especially your partner. The influences are love and marriage. This is the opportunity to create a special surprise meal for your partner and share it with love in a romantic setting with soothing music as background.

MANTRA FOR TODAY

Om Jai Viganeshwaraya.. Lambodaraya Namo Namaha 21 times

MONEY	LOVE	CAREER	FAMILY	TRAVEL	WEDDING	MOVE	BUSINESS	HEALTH	Lotto #'s	play 3 #s
Bad	Fair	Bad	Fair	Bad	Good	Bad	Bad	Bad	32,10,49,6,7,41,61	193

SHOPPING	GAMBLE	SEX	KEYWORD	KEYWORD
Bad	Bad	is tough	CAREER	Career,Hard Work,Co-workers,Low Payment,Job Problems,High Temper,Low

STRESS LEVEL	LUCKY COLORS	JEWELERY	MOONS EFFECT	GRAHA EFFECT	DAILY DEITY
High	Dark Blue/ Purple/	Amethyst/Gold	Emotional	Job Graha	Lingam

DAILY PUJA	DAILY PSALMS
Worship Ganesh, Give gifts to father, and co -workers, Plant gardens, farms	4, 13, 31 ,40, 49, 58, 76, 103, 121

Tuesday, February 7, 2023 — This is considered a POSITIVE day for you — Planet: Venus

ADVICE & DETAILS

Show your affection, cooperate with others and listen to music today; these activities will help you with the paymente of some karmic debts that may become overdue this day.

MANTRA FOR TODAY

Om Graam Greem Graum Sa Gurave namah swaha 21 times

MONEY	LOVE	CAREER	FAMILY	TRAVEL	WEDDING	MOVE	BUSINESS	HEALTH	Lotto #'s	play 3 #s
Bad	Excellent	Fair	Good	Excellen	Good	Excellen	Good	Excellent	24,56,36,54,28,54,3	735

SHOPPING	GAMBLE	SEX	KEYWORD	KEYWORD
Good	Good	is good	CHANGE	Sexuality,Travel,Change,Distant, far,Travel delays,Deception,Excercise,Illicit

STRESS LEVEL	LUCKY COLORS	JEWELERY	MOONS EFFECT	GRAHA EFFECT	DAILY DEITY
Fair	Tan/Green/ Beige	Pearl/Silver/quartz	Courageous	Travel Graha	Nataraja

DAILY PUJA	DAILY PSALMS
Artistic gifts, Pray to Krishna, Do good deeds, do Spiritual trips	5, 14, 32 ,41, 50, 59, 77, 104, 122

Wednesday, February 8, 2023 — This is considered a NEGATIVE day for you — Planet: Mars

ADVICE & DETAILS

You must watch out for misleading statements from others. There will be many changes today. Your sexual energy will be high. You will be thinking a great deal today about very deep and profound subjects.

MANTRA FOR TODAY

Om Mana Swasti Shanti Kuru kuru Swaha Shivoham Shivoham 27 times

MONEY	LOVE	CAREER	FAMILY	TRAVEL	WEDDING	MOVE	BUSINESS	HEALTH	Lotto #'s	play 3 #s
Bad	Bad	Bad	Bad	Bad	Bad	Bad	Fair	Bad	11,7,52,73,47,17,33	612

SHOPPING	GAMBLE	SEX	KEYWORD	KEYWORD
Fair	Bad	is frustrating	POWER	Responsibilty,Disagreement,Family,Back Pain,Family Conflicts,Traffic

STRESS LEVEL	LUCKY COLORS	JEWELERY	MOONS EFFECT	GRAHA EFFECT	DAILY DEITY
High	Purple/Blue/Rose	Emerald/Saphire	Educational	Family Graha	Mahakali

DAILY PUJA	DAILY PSALMS
Meditate, Control temper, Pray to Hanuman, Chant Hanuman Chalisa	6, 15, 33 ,42, 51, 60, 78, 105, 123

Thursday, February 9, 2023 — This is considered a NEUTRAL day for you — Planet: Uranus

ADVICE & DETAILS

You will feel like watching television and would probably prefer the company of children today. You may be acting somewhat immaturely today so be careful of choices and words that may have long term consequences. Today will be a good day for creativity related to writing and publishing.

MANTRA FOR TODAY

Jai Jai Shiva Shambo.(2) ...Mahadeva Shambo (2) 21 times 8

MONEY	LOVE	CAREER	FAMILY	TRAVEL	WEDDING	MOVE	BUSINESS	HEALTH	Lotto #'s	play 3 #s
Good	Good	Fair	Good	Good	Bad	Good	Bad	Fair	27,30,35,24,49,26,3	569

SHOPPING	GAMBLE	SEX	KEYWORD	KEYWORD
Bad	Fair	is quiet	DIVINE	Spirituality,Religious,Astrology,Inner Conflicts,Religious ,Sleepiness,Advice

STRESS LEVEL	LUCKY COLORS	JEWELERY	MOONS EFFECT	GRAHA EFFECT	DAILY DEITY
Fair	Light Blue/Peach	Tiger's eye/Gold/Sil	Affectionate	God'S Graha	Shesnaag

DAILY PUJA	DAILY PSALMS
Chant Shiva Mantras, Take gifts to Ocean - Ganga Puja, Donate to Temple, Priests, etc.	7, 16, 34 ,43, 52, 61, 79, 106, 124

Friday, February 10, 2023 — This is considered a POSITIVE day for you — Planet: Jupiter

ADVICE & DETAILS

You will probably be taking short trips today or you will be moving. You will feel like moving and exercising and you should do it! There will be opportunity for illicit affairs, stay aware of how this affects you and others around you.

MANTRA FOR TODAY

Om Hareem Nama Swaha..Shri Maha Laxmi Aye Namah swaha 12 times

MONEY	LOVE	CAREER	FAMILY	TRAVEL	WEDDING	MOVE	BUSINESS	HEALTH	Lotto #'s	play 3 #s
Excellent	Good	Excellent	Good	Good	Excellent	Good	Excellent	Excellent	71,48,70,45,27,53,1	113

SHOPPING	GAMBLE	SEX	KEYWORD	KEYWORD
Excellent	Excellent	is excellent	MONEY	Business,Major Expense,Money -

STRESS LEVEL	LUCKY COLORS	JEWELERY	MOONS EFFECT	GRAHA EFFECT	DAILY DEITY
Low	Yellow/Silver	Diamonds/Gold/Pea	Secretive	Money Graha	Mahalaxmi

DAILY PUJA	DAILY PSALMS
Decorate Land, Feed the poor, Donate milk /products to all, Feed holy guests,	8, 17, 35 ,44, 53, 62, 80, 107, 125

Saturday, February 11, 2023 — This is considered a NEGATIVE day for you — Planet: Saturn

ADVICE & DETAILS

Try to remember that when you criticize others, you are seeing in others what you think you are missing, be kind and concentrate on the positive characteristics of others not in what you perceive are negatives. The influence of this day will make you introspective and thoughts about your spiritual self will arise. Remember that loves heals all, try to have loving, healing thoughts as much as possible. Rest today if you

MANTRA FOR TODAY

Om Ganga mataye nama swaha Om Varuna Devta aye Pahimam 11 times

MONEY	LOVE	CAREER	FAMILY	TRAVEL	WEDDING	MOVE	BUSINESS	HEALTH	Lotto #'s	play 3 #s
Bad	Bad	Bad	Fair	Bad	Bad	Bad	Bad	Bad	33,23,54,5,34,63,72	694

SHOPPING	GAMBLE	SEX	KEYWORD	KEYWORD
Bad	Bad	is very bad	KARMA	Destruction,Losses,Death,Sickness - cold,Legal matter,Abusive,Karmic debts,God -

STRESS LEVEL	LUCKY COLORS	JEWELERY	MOONS EFFECT	GRAHA EFFECT	DAILY DEITY
High	Gold/Brown//Green	Saphire/Hessonite	Ivestments	Evil Graha	Agnidev

DAILY PUJA	DAILY PSALMS
Remembrance of family members who died, worship of older people. gifts to grand parents	9, 18, 36 ,45, 54, 63, 81, 108, 126

Sunday, February 12, 2023 — This is considered a NEUTRAL day for you — Planet: Sun

ADVICE & DETAILS

The only obstacle to this very positive day is your speech. If you are careful and kind with your words expect money, romance and positive outlook for partnerships in any area.

MANTRA FOR TODAY

Om Namo Bhagawate Mukhtanandaya, 108 times

MONEY	LOVE	CAREER	FAMILY	TRAVEL	WEDDING	MOVE	BUSINESS	HEALTH	Lotto #'s	play 3 #s
Fair	Bad	Good	Bad	Fair	Bad	Fair	Fair	Fair	72,10,57,60,54,11,6	723

SHOPPING	GAMBLE	SEX	KEYWORD	KEYWORD
Fair	Fair	is fair	MIND	Independence,Loneliness,Meditative,Worry,Dominating,Illness - Cold,On Your

STRESS LEVEL	LUCKY COLORS	JEWELERY	MOONS EFFECT	GRAHA EFFECT	DAILY DEITY
High	White/Yellow/	Pearl/Quartz	Arrogance	Status Graha	Saraswaty

DAILY PUJA	DAILY PSALMS
Give Gifts to Priests, Invite holy ones to your home, Feed Swamis and Yogis, Do Shiva Puja.	1, 10, 28 ,37, 46, 55, 73, 100, 118

Monday, February 13, 2023 — This is considered a POSITIVE day for you — Planet: Moon

ADVICE & DETAILS

Every word your lips utter today have great power and they must be used with love and positive intention to avoid conflict. You will have the opportunity to serve and cooperate with others today, use it. Listen to music or express your feelings through music to get blessings today.

MANTRA FOR TODAY

Kali Durge Namo Nama Om Durge aye nama swaha 108 times

MONEY	LOVE	CAREER	FAMILY	TRAVEL	WEDDING	MOVE	BUSINESS	HEALTH	Lotto #'s	play 3 #s
Good	Excellent	Good	Good	Excellen	Good	Good	Good	Good	61,47,64,38,73,62,6	537

SHOPPING	GAMBLE	SEX	KEYWORD	KEYWORD
Good	Good	is good	LOVE	Romance,Popularity,Visitors,Shopping,Food, Drinks,Co-

STRESS LEVEL	LUCKY COLORS	JEWELERY	MOONS EFFECT	GRAHA EFFECT	DAILY DEITY
Low	Red/Yellow/Pink	Topaz/Diamonds	Conservative	Love Graha	Gauri

DAILY PUJA	DAILY PSALMS
Give Gifts to females andnMother, Serve milk Products, Worship Durga forms	2, 11, 29 ,38, 47, 56, 74, 101, 119

Tuesday, February 14, 2023

Tuesday, February 14, 2023	This is considered a POSITIVE day for you				Planet: Mercury

ADVICE & DETAILS — **MANTRA FOR TODAY**

You may spend your day at home alone watching TV or may instead opt for luxurious and pleasurable activities that may bring you around fame or famous people. You will be influenced by money, so you will worry about it, make it or spend it.

Om hareem Kleem Hreem Aem Saraswataye namaha 21 times

MONEY	LOVE	CAREER	FAMILY	TRAVEL	WEDDING	MOVE	BUSINESS	HEALTH	Lotto #'s	play 3 #s
Good	Fair	Good	Good	Excellen	Good	Good	Good	Excellent	35,32,65,11,37,26,3	860

SHOPPING	GAMBLE	SEX	KEYWORD	KEYWORD						
Good	Good	is great	SOCIAL	Children,Education,Astrology,Bargains,Social Functions,Childishness,Groups -						

STRESS LEVEL	LUCKY COLORS	JEWELERY	MOONS EFFECT	GRAHA EFFECT	DAILY DEITY
Low	Green/Sky Blue/	Diamonds/Silver	Enthusiastic	Social Graha	Vishnu

DAILY PUJA	DAILY PSALMS
Wash the feet of Children, Do Satnarayan Pooja, Read & chant Geeta	3, 12, 30 ,39, 48, 57, 75, 102, 120

Wednesday, February 15, 2023

Wednesday, February 15, 2023	This is considered a NEGATIVE day for you				Planet: Pluto

ADVICE & DETAILS — **MANTRA FOR TODAY**

This will be a positive day if you can control your tongue and do not criticize anyone, particularly your loved ones and especially your partner. The influences are love and marriage. This is the opportunity to create a special surprise meal for your partner and share it with love in a romantic setting with soothing music as background.

Om Jai Viganeshwaraya.. Lambodaraya Namo Namaha 21 times

MONEY	LOVE	CAREER	FAMILY	TRAVEL	WEDDING	MOVE	BUSINESS	HEALTH	Lotto #'s	play 3 #s
Bad	Fair	Bad	Fair	Bad	Good	Bad	Bad	Bad	18,51,47,72,16,56,5	254

SHOPPING	GAMBLE	SEX	KEYWORD	KEYWORD						
Bad	Bad	is tough	CAREER	Career,Hard Work,Co-workers,Low Payment,Job Problems,High Temper,Low						

STRESS LEVEL	LUCKY COLORS	JEWELERY	MOONS EFFECT	GRAHA EFFECT	DAILY DEITY
High	Dark Blue/ Purple/	Amethyst/Gold	Emotional	Job Graha	Lingam

DAILY PUJA	DAILY PSALMS
Worship Ganesh, Give gifts to father, and co -workers, Plant gardens, farms	4, 13, 31 ,40, 49, 58, 76, 103, 121

Thursday, February 16, 2023

Thursday, February 16, 2023	This is considered a POSITIVE day for you				Planet: Venus

ADVICE & DETAILS — **MANTRA FOR TODAY**

Show your affection, cooperate with others and listen to music today; these activities will help you with the payment of some karmic debts that may become overdue this day.

Om Graam Greem Graum Sa Gurave namah swaha 21 times

MONEY	LOVE	CAREER	FAMILY	TRAVEL	WEDDING	MOVE	BUSINESS	HEALTH	Lotto #'s	play 3 #s
Bad	Excellent	Fair	Good	Excellen	Good	Excellen	Good	Excellent	45,71,15,18,38,72,6	811

SHOPPING	GAMBLE	SEX	KEYWORD	KEYWORD						
Good	Good	is good	CHANGE	Sexuality,Travel,Change,Distant, far,Travel delays,Deception,Excercise,Illicit						

STRESS LEVEL	LUCKY COLORS	JEWELERY	MOONS EFFECT	GRAHA EFFECT	DAILY DEITY
Fair	Tan/Green/ Beige	Pearl/Silver/quartz	Courageous	Travel Graha	Nataraja

DAILY PUJA	DAILY PSALMS
Artistic gifts, Pray to Krishna, Do good deeds, do Spiritual trips	5, 14, 32 ,41, 50, 59, 77, 104, 122

Friday, February 17, 2023

Friday, February 17, 2023	This is considered a NEGATIVE day for you				Planet: Mars

ADVICE & DETAILS — **MANTRA FOR TODAY**

You must watch out for misleading statements from others. There will be many changes today. Your sexual energy will be high. You will be thinking a great deal today about very deep and profound subjects.

Om Mana Swasti Shanti Kuru kuru Swaha Shivoham Shivoham 27 times

MONEY	LOVE	CAREER	FAMILY	TRAVEL	WEDDING	MOVE	BUSINESS	HEALTH	Lotto #'s	play 3 #s
Bad	Bad	Bad	Bad	Bad	Bad	Bad	Fair	Bad	11,9,45,50,66,17,54	206

SHOPPING	GAMBLE	SEX	KEYWORD	KEYWORD						
Fair	Bad	is frustrating	POWER	Responsibilty,Disagreement,Family,Back Pain,Family Conflicts,Traffic						

STRESS LEVEL	LUCKY COLORS	JEWELERY	MOONS EFFECT	GRAHA EFFECT	DAILY DEITY
High	Purple/Blue/Rose	Emerald/Saphire	Educational	Family Graha	Mahakali

DAILY PUJA	DAILY PSALMS
Meditate, Control temper, Pray to Hanuman, Chant Hanuman Chalisa	6, 15, 33 ,42, 51, 60, 78, 105, 123

Saturday, February 18, 2023 — This is considered a NEUTRAL day for you — Planet: Uranus

ADVICE & DETAILS

You will feel like watching television and would probably prefer the company of children today. You may be acting somewhat immaturely today so be careful of choices and words that may have long term consequences. Today will be a good day for creativity related to writing and publishing.

MANTRA FOR TODAY

Jai Jai Shiva Shambo.(2) ...Mahadeva Shambo (2) 21 times 8

MONEY	LOVE	CAREER	FAMILY	TRAVEL	WEDDING	MOVE	BUSINESS	HEALTH	Lotto #'s	play 3 #s
Good	Good	Fair	Good	Good	Bad	Good	Bad	Fair	5,19,28,63,2,60,31	599

SHOPPING	GAMBLE	SEX	KEYWORD	KEYWORD						
Bad	Fair	is quiet	DIVINE	Spirituality,Religious,Astrology,Inner Conflicts,Religious ,Sleepiness,Advice						

STRESS LEVEL	LUCKY COLORS	JEWELERY	MOONS EFFECT	GRAHA EFFECT	DAILY DEITY
Fair	Light Blue/Peach	Tiger's eye/Gold/Sil	Affectionate	God'S Graha	Shesnaag

DAILY PUJA	DAILY PSALMS
Chant Shiva Mantras, Take gifts to Ocean - Ganga Puja, Donate to Temple, Priests, etc.	7, 16, 34 ,43, 52, 61, 79, 106, 124

Sunday, February 19, 2023 — This is considered a POSITIVE day for you — Planet: Jupiter

ADVICE & DETAILS

You will probably be taking short trips today or you will be moving. You will feel like moving and exercising and you should do it! There will be opportunity for illicit affairs, stay aware of how this affects you and others around you.

MANTRA FOR TODAY

Om Hareem Nama Swaha..Shri Maha Laxmi Aye Namah swaha 12 times

MONEY	LOVE	CAREER	FAMILY	TRAVEL	WEDDING	MOVE	BUSINESS	HEALTH	Lotto #'s	play 3 #s
Excellent	Good	Excellent	Good	Good	Excellent	Good	Excellent	Excellent	51,37,40,64,40,8,39	309

SHOPPING	GAMBLE	SEX	KEYWORD	KEYWORD						
Excellent	Excellent	is excellent	MONEY	Business,Major Expense,Money -						

STRESS LEVEL	LUCKY COLORS	JEWELERY	MOONS EFFECT	GRAHA EFFECT	DAILY DEITY
Low	Yellow/Silver	Diamonds/Gold/Pea	Secretive	Money Graha	Mahalaxmi

DAILY PUJA	DAILY PSALMS
Decorate Land, Feed the poor, Donate milk /products to all, Feed holy guests,	8, 17, 35 ,44, 53, 62, 80, 107, 125

Monday, February 20, 2023 — This is considered a NEGATIVE day for you — Planet: Saturn

ADVICE & DETAILS

Try to remember that when you criticize others, you are seeing in others what you think you are missing, be kind and concentrate on the positive characteristics of others not in what you perceive are negatives. The influence of this day will make you introspective and thoughts about your spiritual self will arise. Remember that loves heals all, try to have loving, healing thoughts as much as possible. Rest today if you

MANTRA FOR TODAY

Om Ganga mataye nama swaha Om Varuna Devta aye Pahimam 11 times

MONEY	LOVE	CAREER	FAMILY	TRAVEL	WEDDING	MOVE	BUSINESS	HEALTH	Lotto #'s	play 3 #s
Bad	Bad	Bad	Fair	Bad	Bad	Bad	Bad	Bad	75,29,46,5,72,63,48	388

SHOPPING	GAMBLE	SEX	KEYWORD	KEYWORD						
Bad	Bad	is very bad	KARMA	Destruction,Losses,Death,Sickness - cold,Legal matter,Abusive,Karmic debts,God -						

STRESS LEVEL	LUCKY COLORS	JEWELERY	MOONS EFFECT	GRAHA EFFECT	DAILY DEITY
High	Gold/Brown//Green	Saphire/Hessonite	Ivestments	Evil Graha	Agnidev

DAILY PUJA	DAILY PSALMS
Remembrance of family members who died, worship of older people. gifts to grand parents	9, 18, 36 ,45, 54, 63, 81, 108, 126

Tuesday, February 21, 2023 — This is considered a NEUTRAL day for you — Planet: Sun

ADVICE & DETAILS

The only obstacle to this very positive day is your speech. If you are careful and kind with your words expect money, romance and positive outlook for partnerships in any area.

MANTRA FOR TODAY

Om Namo Bhagawate Mukhtanandaya, 108 times

MONEY	LOVE	CAREER	FAMILY	TRAVEL	WEDDING	MOVE	BUSINESS	HEALTH	Lotto #'s	play 3 #s
Fair	Bad	Good	Bad	Fair	Bad	Fair	Fair	Fair	26,70,32,45,60,40,3	424

SHOPPING	GAMBLE	SEX	KEYWORD	KEYWORD						
Fair	Fair	is fair	MIND	Independence,Loneliness,Meditative,Worry,Dominating,Illness - Cold,On Your						

STRESS LEVEL	LUCKY COLORS	JEWELERY	MOONS EFFECT	GRAHA EFFECT	DAILY DEITY
High	White/Yellow/	Pearl/Quartz	Arrogance	Status Graha	Saraswaty

DAILY PUJA	DAILY PSALMS
Give Gifts to Priests, Invite holy ones to your home, Feed Swamis and Yogis, Do Shiva Puja.	1, 10, 28 ,37, 46, 55, 73, 100, 118

Wednesday, February 22, 2023 — This is considered a POSITIVE day for you — Planet: Moon

ADVICE & DETAILS

Every word your lips utter today have great power and they must be used with love and positive intention to avoid conflict. You will have the opportunity to serve and cooperate with others today, use it. Listen to music or express your feelings through music to get blessings today.

MANTRA FOR TODAY
Kali Durge Namo Nama Om Durge aye nama swaha 108 times

MONEY	LOVE	CAREER	FAMILY	TRAVEL	WEDDING	MOVE	BUSINESS	HEALTH	Lotto #'s	play 3 #s
Good	Excellent	Good	Good	Excellen	Good	Good	Good	Good	8,73,27,56,56,37,71	266

SHOPPING	GAMBLE	SEX	KEYWORD	KEYWORD						
Good	Good	is good	LOVE	Romance,Popularity,Visitors,Shopping,Food, Drinks,Co-						

STRESS LEVEL	LUCKY COLORS	JEWELERY	MOONS EFFECT	GRAHA EFFECT	DAILY DEITY
Low	Red/Yellow/Pink	Topaz/Diamonds	Conservative	Love Graha	Gauri

DAILY PUJA	DAILY PSALMS
Give Gifts to females andnMother, Serve milk Products, Worship Durga forms	2, 11, 29 ,38, 47, 56, 74, 101, 119

Thursday, February 23, 2023 — This is considered a POSITIVE day for you — Planet: Mercury

ADVICE & DETAILS

You may spend your day at home alone watching TV or may instead opt for luxurious and pleasurable activities that may bring you around fame or famous people. You will be influenced by money, so you will worry about it, make it or spend it.

MANTRA FOR TODAY
Om hareem Kleem Hreem Aem Saraswataye namaha 21 times

MONEY	LOVE	CAREER	FAMILY	TRAVEL	WEDDING	MOVE	BUSINESS	HEALTH	Lotto #'s	play 3 #s
Good	Fair	Good	Good	Excellen	Good	Good	Good	Excellent	69,12,33,36,9,42,61	188

SHOPPING	GAMBLE	SEX	KEYWORD	KEYWORD						
Good	Good	is great	SOCIAL	Children,Education,Astrology,Bargains,Social Functions,Childishness,Groups -						

STRESS LEVEL	LUCKY COLORS	JEWELERY	MOONS EFFECT	GRAHA EFFECT	DAILY DEITY
Low	Green/Sky Blue/	Diamonds/Silver	Enthusiastic	Social Graha	Vishnu

DAILY PUJA	DAILY PSALMS
Wash the feet of Children, Do Satnarayan Pooja, Read & chant Geeta	3, 12, 30 ,39, 48, 57, 75, 102, 120

Friday, February 24, 2023 — This is considered a NEGATIVE day for you — Planet: Pluto

ADVICE & DETAILS

This will be a positive day if you can control your tongue and do not criticize anyone, particularly your loved ones and especially your partner. The influences are love and marriage. This is the opportunity to create a special surprise meal for your partner and share it with love in a romantic setting with soothing music as background.

MANTRA FOR TODAY
Om Jai Viganeshwaraya.. Lambodaraya Namo Namaha 21 times

MONEY	LOVE	CAREER	FAMILY	TRAVEL	WEDDING	MOVE	BUSINESS	HEALTH	Lotto #'s	play 3 #s
Bad	Fair	Bad	Fair	Bad	Good	Bad	Bad	Bad	7,19,69,29,63,61,11	825

SHOPPING	GAMBLE	SEX	KEYWORD	KEYWORD						
Bad	Bad	is tough	CAREER	Career,Hard Work,Co-workers,Low Payment,Job Problems,High Temper,Low						

STRESS LEVEL	LUCKY COLORS	JEWELERY	MOONS EFFECT	GRAHA EFFECT	DAILY DEITY
High	Dark Blue/ Purple/	Amethyst/Gold	Emotional	Job Graha	Lingam

DAILY PUJA	DAILY PSALMS
Worship Ganesh, Give gifts to father, and co -workers, Plant gardens, farms	4, 13, 31 ,40, 49, 58, 76, 103, 121

Saturday, February 25, 2023 — This is considered a POSITIVE day for you — Planet: Venus

ADVICE & DETAILS

Show your affection, cooperate with others and listen to music today; these activities will help you with the paymente of some karmic debts that may become overdue this day.

MANTRA FOR TODAY
Om Graam Greem Graum Sa Gurave namah swaha 21 times

MONEY	LOVE	CAREER	FAMILY	TRAVEL	WEDDING	MOVE	BUSINESS	HEALTH	Lotto #'s	play 3 #s
Bad	Excellent	Fair	Good	Excellen	Good	Excellen	Good	Excellent	66,73,21,24,25,67,7	854

SHOPPING	GAMBLE	SEX	KEYWORD	KEYWORD						
Good	Good	is good	CHANGE	Sexuality,Travel,Change,Distant, far,Travel delays,Deception,Excercise,Illicit						

STRESS LEVEL	LUCKY COLORS	JEWELERY	MOONS EFFECT	GRAHA EFFECT	DAILY DEITY
Fair	Tan/Green/ Beige	Pearl/Silver/quartz	Courageous	Travel Graha	Nataraja

DAILY PUJA	DAILY PSALMS
Artistic gifts, Pray to Krishna, Do good deeds, do Spiritual trips	5, 14, 32 ,41, 50, 59, 77, 104, 122

Sunday, February 26, 2023 — This is considered a NEGATIVE day for you — Planet: Mars

ADVICE & DETAILS

You must watch out for misleading statements from others. There will be many changes today. Your sexual energy will be high. You will be thinking a great deal today about very deep and profound subjects.

MANTRA FOR TODAY

Om Mana Swasti Shanti Kuru kuru Swaha Shivoham Shivoham 27 times

MONEY	LOVE	CAREER	FAMILY	TRAVEL	WEDDING	MOVE	BUSINESS	HEALTH	Lotto #'s	play 3 #s
Bad	Bad	Bad	Bad	Bad	Bad	Bad	Fair	Bad	63,32,37,52,28,55,6	865

SHOPPING	GAMBLE	SEX	KEYWORD	KEYWORD
Fair	Bad	is frustrating	POWER	Responsibilty,Disagreement,Family,Back Pain,Family Conflicts,Traffic

STRESS LEVEL	LUCKY COLORS	JEWELERY	MOONS EFFECT	GRAHA EFFECT	DAILY DEITY
High	Purple/Blue/Rose	Emerald/Saphire	Educational	Family Graha	Mahakali

DAILY PUJA	DAILY PSALMS
Meditate, Control temper, Pray to Hanuman, Chant Hanuman Chalisa	6, 15, 33 ,42, 51, 60, 78, 105, 123

Monday, February 27, 2023 — This is considered a NEUTRAL day for you — Planet: Uranus

ADVICE & DETAILS

You will feel like watching television and would probably prefer the company of children today. You may be acting somewhat immaturely today so be careful of choices and words that may have long term consequences. Today will be a good day for creativity related to writing and publishing.

MANTRA FOR TODAY

Jai Jai Shiva Shambo.(2) ...Mahadeva Shambo (2) 21 times 8

MONEY	LOVE	CAREER	FAMILY	TRAVEL	WEDDING	MOVE	BUSINESS	HEALTH	Lotto #'s	play 3 #s
Good	Good	Fair	Good	Good	Bad	Good	Bad	Fair	25,74,15,14,38,45,1	285

SHOPPING	GAMBLE	SEX	KEYWORD	KEYWORD
Bad	Fair	is quiet	DIVINE	Spirituality,Religious,Astrology,Inner Conflicts,Religious ,Sleepiness,Advice

STRESS LEVEL	LUCKY COLORS	JEWELERY	MOONS EFFECT	GRAHA EFFECT	DAILY DEITY
Fair	Light Blue/Peach	Tiger's eye/Gold/Sil	Affectionate	God'S Graha	Shesnaag

DAILY PUJA	DAILY PSALMS
Chant Shiva Mantras, Take gifts to Ocean - Ganga Puja, Donate to Temple, Priests, etc.	7, 16, 34 ,43, 52, 61, 79, 106, 124

Tuesday, February 28, 2023 — This is considered a POSITIVE day for you — Planet: Jupiter

ADVICE & DETAILS

You will probably be taking short trips today or you will be moving. You will feel like moving and exercising and you should do it! There will be opportunity for illicit affairs, stay aware of how this affects you and others around you.

MANTRA FOR TODAY

Om Hareem Nama Swaha..Shri Maha Laxmi Aye Namah swaha 12 times

MONEY	LOVE	CAREER	FAMILY	TRAVEL	WEDDING	MOVE	BUSINESS	HEALTH	Lotto #'s	play 3 #s
Excellent	Good	Excellent	Good	Good	Excellent	Good	Excellent	Excellent	1,19,47,29,12,3,45	281

SHOPPING	GAMBLE	SEX	KEYWORD	KEYWORD
Excellent	Excellent	is excellent	MONEY	Business,Major Expense,Money -

STRESS LEVEL	LUCKY COLORS	JEWELERY	MOONS EFFECT	GRAHA EFFECT	DAILY DEITY
Low	Yellow/Silver	Diamonds/Gold/Pea	Secretive	Money Graha	Mahalaxmi

DAILY PUJA	DAILY PSALMS
Decorate Land, Feed the poor, Donate milk /products to all, Feed holy guests,	8, 17, 35 ,44, 53, 62, 80, 107, 125

Wednesday, March 1, 2023 — This is considered a POSITIVE day for you — Planet: Jupiter

ADVICE & DETAILS

The power of your expression today is great. Use this power to communicate with others, to write and publish or to entertain others when in groups or parties. There is the influence of someone that is jealous of you, be aware of it and try to be modest.

MANTRA FOR TODAY

Om Hareem Nama Swaha..Shri Maha Laxmi Aye Namah swaha 12 times

MONEY	LOVE	CAREER	FAMILY	TRAVEL	WEDDING	MOVE	BUSINESS	HEALTH	Lotto #'s	play 3 #s
Excellent	Good	Excellent	Good	Good	Excellent	Good	Excellent	Excellent	6,72,62,30,69,52,75	865

SHOPPING	GAMBLE	SEX	KEYWORD	KEYWORD
Excellent	Excellent	is excellent	MONEY	Business,Major Expense,Money -

STRESS LEVEL	LUCKY COLORS	JEWELERY	MOONS EFFECT	GRAHA EFFECT	DAILY DEITY
Low	Yellow/Silver	Diamonds/Gold/Pea	Secretive	Money Graha	Mahalaxmi

DAILY PUJA	DAILY PSALMS
Decorate Land, Feed the poor, Donate milk /products to all, Feed holy guests,	8, 17, 35 ,44, 53, 62, 80, 107, 125

Thursday, March 2, 2023 — This is considered a NEGATIVE day for you — Planet: Saturn

ADVICE & DETAILS

Although this will be a day open for you to socialize with others, you must avoid extremes and parties with alcohol and drugs. Your enemies will take advantage of you today when they see you in your weakest state. Try to rest, you will be sleepy.

MANTRA FOR TODAY

Om Ganga mataye nama swaha Om Varuna Devta aye Pahimam 11 times

MONEY	LOVE	CAREER	FAMILY	TRAVEL	WEDDING	MOVE	BUSINESS	HEALTH	Lotto #'s	play 3 #s
Bad	Bad	Bad	Fair	Bad	Bad	Bad	Bad	Bad	29,48,47,11,8,1,46	934

SHOPPING	GAMBLE	SEX	KEYWORD	KEYWORD
Bad	Bad	is very bad	KARMA	Destruction,Losses,Death,Sickness - cold,Legal matter,Abusive,Karmic debts,God -

STRESS LEVEL	LUCKY COLORS	JEWELERY	MOONS EFFECT	GRAHA EFFECT	DAILY DEITY
High	Gold/Brown//Green	Saphire/Hessonite	Ivestments	Evil Graha	Agnidev

DAILY PUJA	DAILY PSALMS
Remembrance of family members who died, worship of older people. gifts to grand parents	9, 18, 36 ,45, 54, 63, 81, 108, 126

Friday, March 3, 2023 — This is considered a NEUTRAL day for you — Planet: Sun

ADVICE & DETAILS

There may be sickness of children or you may be getting sick. There will be losses and sadness.

MANTRA FOR TODAY

Om Namo Bhagawate Mukhtanandaya, 108 times

MONEY	LOVE	CAREER	FAMILY	TRAVEL	WEDDING	MOVE	BUSINESS	HEALTH	Lotto #'s	play 3 #s
Fair	Bad	Good	Bad	Fair	Bad	Fair	Fair	Fair	45,48,69,45,23,74,8	197

SHOPPING	GAMBLE	SEX	KEYWORD	KEYWORD
Fair	Fair	is fair	MIND	Independence,Loneliness,Meditative,Worry,Dominating,Illness - Cold,On Your

STRESS LEVEL	LUCKY COLORS	JEWELERY	MOONS EFFECT	GRAHA EFFECT	DAILY DEITY
High	White/Yellow/	Pearl/Quartz	Arrogance	Status Graha	Saraswaty

DAILY PUJA	DAILY PSALMS
Give Gifts to Priests, Invite holy ones to your home, Feed Swamis and Yogis, Do Shiva Puja.	1, 10, 28 ,37, 46, 55, 73, 100, 118

Saturday, March 4, 2023 — This is considered a POSITIVE day for you — Planet: Moon

ADVICE & DETAILS

Express your thoughts, opinions or information to partners and/or children. Day is influenced by children and ability to acquire information by reading or other means.

MANTRA FOR TODAY

Kali Durge Namo Nama Om Durge aye nama swaha 108 times

MONEY	LOVE	CAREER	FAMILY	TRAVEL	WEDDING	MOVE	BUSINESS	HEALTH	Lotto #'s	play 3 #s
Good	Excellent	Good	Good	Excellen	Good	Good	Good	Good	69,72,1,29,1,22,34	660

SHOPPING	GAMBLE	SEX	KEYWORD	KEYWORD
Good	Good	is good	LOVE	Romance,Popularity,Visitors,Shopping,Food, Drinks,Co-

STRESS LEVEL	LUCKY COLORS	JEWELERY	MOONS EFFECT	GRAHA EFFECT	DAILY DEITY
Low	Red/Yellow/Pink	Topaz/Diamonds	Conservative	Love Graha	Gauri

DAILY PUJA	DAILY PSALMS
Give Gifts to females andnMother, Serve milk Products, Worship Durga forms	2, 11, 29 ,38, 47, 56, 74, 101, 119

Sunday, March 5, 2023 — This is considered a POSITIVE day for you — Planet: Mercury

ADVICE & DETAILS

Reading will benefit you today. You will have to hone your communication skills and speak clearly and listen carefully, especially when dealing with Real Estate and teachers of any type.

MANTRA FOR TODAY

Om hareem Kleem Hreem Aem Saraswataye namaha 21 times

MONEY	LOVE	CAREER	FAMILY	TRAVEL	WEDDING	MOVE	BUSINESS	HEALTH	Lotto #'s	play 3 #s
Good	Fair	Good	Good	Excellen	Good	Good	Good	Excellent	34,64,55,9,31,3,21	589

SHOPPING	GAMBLE	SEX	KEYWORD	KEYWORD
Good	Good	is great	SOCIAL	Children,Education,Astrology,Bargains,Social Functions,Childishness,Groups -

STRESS LEVEL	LUCKY COLORS	JEWELERY	MOONS EFFECT	GRAHA EFFECT	DAILY DEITY
Low	Green/Sky Blue/	Diamonds/Silver	Enthusiastic	Social Graha	Vishnu

DAILY PUJA	DAILY PSALMS
Wash the feet of Children, Do Satnarayan Pooja, Read & chant Geeta	3, 12, 30 ,39, 48, 57, 75, 102, 120

Monday, March 6, 2023 — This is considered a NEGATIVE day for you — Planet: Pluto

ADVICE & DETAILS

Overcome laziness and low pay today and improve your karma by being industrious, hard working and controlling your high temper.

MANTRA FOR TODAY

Om Jai Viganeshwaraya.. Lambodaraya Namo Namaha 21 times

MONEY	LOVE	CAREER	FAMILY	TRAVEL	WEDDING	MOVE	BUSINESS	HEALTH	Lotto #'s	play 3 #s
Bad	Fair	Bad	Fair	Bad	Good	Bad	Bad	Bad	25,26,8,27,39,11,28	301

SHOPPING	GAMBLE	SEX	KEYWORD	KEYWORD						
Bad	Bad	is tough	CAREER	Career,Hard Work,Co-workers,Low Payment,Job Problems,High Temper,Low						

STRESS LEVEL	LUCKY COLORS	JEWELERY	MOONS EFFECT	GRAHA EFFECT	DAILY DEITY
High	Dark Blue/ Purple/	Amethyst/Gold	Emotional	Job Graha	Lingam

DAILY PUJA	DAILY PSALMS
Worship Ganesh, Give gifts to father, and co-workers, Plant gardens, farms	4, 13, 31 ,40, 49, 58, 76, 103, 121

Tuesday, March 7, 2023 — This is considered a POSITIVE day for you — Planet: Venus

ADVICE & DETAILS

Although this will be a day open for you to socialize with others, you must avoid extremes and parties with alcohol and drugs. Your enemies will take advantage of you today when they see you in your weakest state. Try to rest, you will be sleepy.

MANTRA FOR TODAY

Om Graam Greem Graum Sa Gurave namah swaha 21 times

MONEY	LOVE	CAREER	FAMILY	TRAVEL	WEDDING	MOVE	BUSINESS	HEALTH	Lotto #'s	play 3 #s
Bad	Excellent	Fair	Good	Excellen	Good	Excellen	Good	Excellent	56,68,48,34,75,48,2	316

SHOPPING	GAMBLE	SEX	KEYWORD	KEYWORD						
Good	Good	is good	CHANGE	Sexuality,Travel,Change,Distant, far,Travel delays,Deception,Excercise,Illicit						

STRESS LEVEL	LUCKY COLORS	JEWELERY	MOONS EFFECT	GRAHA EFFECT	DAILY DEITY
Fair	Tan/Green/ Beige	Pearl/Silver/quartz	Courageous	Travel Graha	Nataraja

DAILY PUJA	DAILY PSALMS
Artistic gifts, Pray to Krishna, Do good deeds, do Spiritual trips	5, 14, 32 ,41, 50, 59, 77, 104, 122

Wednesday, March 8, 2023 — This is considered a NEGATIVE day for you — Planet: Mars

ADVICE & DETAILS

Children will be prevalent today. This day is marked with a great deal of creativity ideal for areas related to the left side of the brain such as writing, painting, handcrafts, baking, cooking or needlework.

MANTRA FOR TODAY

Om Mana Swasti Shanti Kuru kuru Swaha Shivoham Shivoham 27 times

MONEY	LOVE	CAREER	FAMILY	TRAVEL	WEDDING	MOVE	BUSINESS	HEALTH	Lotto #'s	play 3 #s
Bad	Bad	Bad	Bad	Bad	Bad	Bad	Fair	Bad	56,36,29,35,31,71,2	672

SHOPPING	GAMBLE	SEX	KEYWORD	KEYWORD						
Fair	Bad	is frustrating	POWER	Responsibilty,Disagreement,Family,Back Pain,Family Conflicts,Traffic						

STRESS LEVEL	LUCKY COLORS	JEWELERY	MOONS EFFECT	GRAHA EFFECT	DAILY DEITY
High	Purple/Blue/Rose	Emerald/Saphire	Educational	Family Graha	Mahakali

DAILY PUJA	DAILY PSALMS
Meditate, Control temper, Pray to Hanuman, Chant Hanuman Chalisa	6, 15, 33 ,42, 51, 60, 78, 105, 123

Thursday, March 9, 2023 — This is considered a NEUTRAL day for you — Planet: Uranus

ADVICE & DETAILS

The thought of watching TV is very appealing today. Spending time with children will benefit your creativity, but you must refrain from allowing immaturity to control your actions today.

MANTRA FOR TODAY

Jai Jai Shiva Shambo.(2) ...Mahadeva Shambo (2) 21 times 8

MONEY	LOVE	CAREER	FAMILY	TRAVEL	WEDDING	MOVE	BUSINESS	HEALTH	Lotto #'s	play 3 #s
Good	Good	Fair	Good	Good	Bad	Good	Bad	Fair	34,70,72,5,48,11,72	626

SHOPPING	GAMBLE	SEX	KEYWORD	KEYWORD						
Bad	Fair	is quiet	DIVINE	Spirituality,Religious,Astrology,Inner Conflicts,Religious ,Sleepiness,Advice						

STRESS LEVEL	LUCKY COLORS	JEWELERY	MOONS EFFECT	GRAHA EFFECT	DAILY DEITY
Fair	Light Blue/Peach	Tiger's eye/Gold/Sil	Affectionate	God'S Graha	Shesnaag

DAILY PUJA	DAILY PSALMS
Chant Shiva Mantras, Take gifts to Ocean - Ganga Puja, Donate to Temple, Priests, etc.	7, 16, 34 ,43, 52, 61, 79, 106, 124

Friday, March 10, 2023 — This is considered a POSITIVE day for you — Planet: Jupiter

ADVICE & DETAILS

The power of your expression today is great. Use this power to communicate with others, to write and publish or to entertain others when in groups or parties. There is the influence of someone that is jealous of you, be aware of it and try to be modest.

MANTRA FOR TODAY

Om Hareem Nama Swaha..Shri Maha Laxmi Aye Namah swaha 12 times

MONEY	LOVE	CAREER	FAMILY	TRAVEL	WEDDING	MOVE	BUSINESS	HEALTH	Lotto #'s	play 3 #s
Excellent	Good	Excellent	Good	Good	Excellent	Good	Excellent	Excellent	67,28,22,66,1,34,18	615

SHOPPING	GAMBLE	SEX	KEYWORD	KEYWORD				
Excellent	Excellent	is excellent	MONEY	Business,Major Expense,Money -				

STRESS LEVEL	LUCKY COLORS	JEWELERY	MOONS EFFECT	GRAHA EFFECT	DAILY DEITY
Low	Yellow/Silver	Diamonds/Gold/Pea	Secretive	Money Graha	Mahalaxmi

DAILY PUJA	DAILY PSALMS
Decorate Land, Feed the poor, Donate milk /products to all, Feed holy guests,	8, 17, 35 ,44, 53, 62, 80, 107, 125

Saturday, March 11, 2023 — This is considered a NEGATIVE day for you — Planet: Saturn

ADVICE & DETAILS

Although this will be a day open for you to socialize with others, you must avoid extremes and parties with alcohol and drugs. Your enemies will take advantage of you today when they see you in your weakest state. Try to rest, you will be sleepy.

MANTRA FOR TODAY

Om Ganga mataye nama swaha Om Varuna Devta aye Pahimam 11 times

MONEY	LOVE	CAREER	FAMILY	TRAVEL	WEDDING	MOVE	BUSINESS	HEALTH	Lotto #'s	play 3 #s
Bad	Bad	Bad	Fair	Bad	Bad	Bad	Bad	Bad	14,42,20,20,1,34,23	554

SHOPPING	GAMBLE	SEX	KEYWORD	KEYWORD				
Bad	Bad	is very bad	KARMA	Destruction,Losses,Death,Sickness - cold,Legal matter,Abusive,Karmic debts,God -				

STRESS LEVEL	LUCKY COLORS	JEWELERY	MOONS EFFECT	GRAHA EFFECT	DAILY DEITY
High	Gold/Brown//Green	Saphire/Hessonite	Ivestments	Evil Graha	Agnidev

DAILY PUJA	DAILY PSALMS
Remembrance of family members who died, worship of older people. gifts to grand parents	9, 18, 36 ,45, 54, 63, 81, 108, 126

Sunday, March 12, 2023 — This is considered a NEUTRAL day for you — Planet: Sun

ADVICE & DETAILS

There may be sickness of children or you may be getting sick. There will be losses and sadness.

MANTRA FOR TODAY

Om Namo Bhagawate Mukhtanandaya, 108 times

MONEY	LOVE	CAREER	FAMILY	TRAVEL	WEDDING	MOVE	BUSINESS	HEALTH	Lotto #'s	play 3 #s
Fair	Bad	Good	Bad	Fair	Bad	Fair	Fair	Fair	73,16,72,48,27,33,4	619

SHOPPING	GAMBLE	SEX	KEYWORD	KEYWORD				
Fair	Fair	is fair	MIND	Independence,Loneliness,Meditative,Worry,Dominating,Illness - Cold,On Your				

STRESS LEVEL	LUCKY COLORS	JEWELERY	MOONS EFFECT	GRAHA EFFECT	DAILY DEITY
High	White/Yellow/	Pearl/Quartz	Arrogance	Status Graha	Saraswaty

DAILY PUJA	DAILY PSALMS
Give Gifts to Priests, Invite holy ones to your home, Feed Swamis and Yogis, Do Shiva Puja.	1, 10, 28 ,37, 46, 55, 73, 100, 118

Monday, March 13, 2023 — This is considered a POSITIVE day for you — Planet: Moon

ADVICE & DETAILS

Express your thoughts, opinions or information to partners and/or children. Day is influenced by children and ability to acquire information by reading or other means.

MANTRA FOR TODAY

Kali Durge Namo Nama Om Durge aye nama swaha 108 times

MONEY	LOVE	CAREER	FAMILY	TRAVEL	WEDDING	MOVE	BUSINESS	HEALTH	Lotto #'s	play 3 #s
Good	Excellent	Good	Good	Excellen	Good	Good	Good	Good	64,71,61,32,4,18,7	612

SHOPPING	GAMBLE	SEX	KEYWORD	KEYWORD				
Good	Good	is good	LOVE	Romance,Popularity,Visitors,Shopping,Food, Drinks,Co-				

STRESS LEVEL	LUCKY COLORS	JEWELERY	MOONS EFFECT	GRAHA EFFECT	DAILY DEITY
Low	Red/Yellow/Pink	Topaz/Diamonds	Conservative	Love Graha	Gauri

DAILY PUJA	DAILY PSALMS
Give Gifts to females andnMother, Serve milk Products, Worship Durga forms	2, 11, 29 ,38, 47, 56, 74, 101, 119

Tuesday, March 14, 2023 — This is considered a POSITIVE day for you — Planet: Mercury

ADVICE & DETAILS

Reading will benefit you today. You will have to hone your communication skills and speak clearly and listen carefully, especially when dealing with Real Estate and teachers of any type.

MANTRA FOR TODAY

Om hareem Kleem Hreem Aem Saraswataye namaha 21 times

MONEY	LOVE	CAREER	FAMILY	TRAVEL	WEDDING	MOVE	BUSINESS	HEALTH	Lotto #'s	play 3 #s
Good	Fair	Good	Good	Excellen	Good	Good	Good	Excellent	36,70,5,49,12,64,68	647

SHOPPING	GAMBLE	SEX	KEYWORD	KEYWORD						
Good	Good	is great	SOCIAL	Children,Education,Astrology,Bargains,Social Functions,Childishness,Groups -						

STRESS LEVEL	LUCKY COLORS	JEWELERY	MOONS EFFECT	GRAHA EFFECT	DAILY DEITY
Low	Green/Sky Blue/	Diamonds/Silver	Enthusiastic	Social Graha	Vishnu

DAILY PUJA	DAILY PSALMS
Wash the feet of Children, Do Satnarayan Pooja, Read & chant Geeta	3, 12, 30 ,39, 48, 57, 75, 102, 120

Wednesday, March 15, 2023 — This is considered a NEGATIVE day for you — Planet: Pluto

ADVICE & DETAILS

Overcome laziness and low pay today and improve your karma by being industrious, hard working and controlling your high temper.

MANTRA FOR TODAY

Om Jai Viganeshwaraya.. Lambodaraya Namo Namaha 21 times

MONEY	LOVE	CAREER	FAMILY	TRAVEL	WEDDING	MOVE	BUSINESS	HEALTH	Lotto #'s	play 3 #s
Bad	Fair	Bad	Fair	Bad	Good	Bad	Bad	Bad	31,36,55,67,49,42,3	189

SHOPPING	GAMBLE	SEX	KEYWORD	KEYWORD						
Bad	Bad	is tough	CAREER	Career,Hard Work,Co-workers,Low Payment,Job Problems,High Temper,Low						

STRESS LEVEL	LUCKY COLORS	JEWELERY	MOONS EFFECT	GRAHA EFFECT	DAILY DEITY
High	Dark Blue/ Purple/	Amethyst/Gold	Emotional	Job Graha	Lingam

DAILY PUJA	DAILY PSALMS
Worship Ganesh, Give gifts to father, and co-workers, Plant gardens, farms	4, 13, 31 ,40, 49, 58, 76, 103, 121

Thursday, March 16, 2023 — This is considered a POSITIVE day for you — Planet: Venus

ADVICE & DETAILS

Although this will be a day open for you to socialize with others, you must avoid extremes and parties with alcohol and drugs. Your enemies will take advantage of you today when they see you in your weakest state. Try to rest, you will be sleepy.

MANTRA FOR TODAY

Om Graam Greem Graum Sa Gurave namah swaha 21 times

MONEY	LOVE	CAREER	FAMILY	TRAVEL	WEDDING	MOVE	BUSINESS	HEALTH	Lotto #'s	play 3 #s
Bad	Excellent	Fair	Good	Excellen	Good	Excellen	Good	Excellent	23,52,18,45,41,39,7	920

SHOPPING	GAMBLE	SEX	KEYWORD	KEYWORD						
Good	Good	is good	CHANGE	Sexuality,Travel,Change,Distant, far,Travel delays,Deception,Excercise,Illicit						

STRESS LEVEL	LUCKY COLORS	JEWELERY	MOONS EFFECT	GRAHA EFFECT	DAILY DEITY
Fair	Tan/Green/ Beige	Pearl/Silver/quartz	Courageous	Travel Graha	Nataraja

DAILY PUJA	DAILY PSALMS
Artistic gifts, Pray to Krishna, Do good deeds, do Spiritual trips	5, 14, 32 ,41, 50, 59, 77, 104, 122

Friday, March 17, 2023 — This is considered a NEGATIVE day for you — Planet: Mars

ADVICE & DETAILS

Children will be prevalent today. This day is marked with a great deal of creativity ideal for areas related to the left side of the brain such as writing, painting, handcrafts, baking, cooking or needlework.

MANTRA FOR TODAY

Om Mana Swasti Shanti Kuru kuru Swaha Shivoham Shivoham 27 times

MONEY	LOVE	CAREER	FAMILY	TRAVEL	WEDDING	MOVE	BUSINESS	HEALTH	Lotto #'s	play 3 #s
Bad	Bad	Bad	Bad	Bad	Bad	Bad	Fair	Bad	12,27,68,42,14,49,5	220

SHOPPING	GAMBLE	SEX	KEYWORD	KEYWORD						
Fair	Bad	is frustrating	POWER	Responsibilty,Disagreement,Family,Back Pain,Family Conflicts,Traffic						

STRESS LEVEL	LUCKY COLORS	JEWELERY	MOONS EFFECT	GRAHA EFFECT	DAILY DEITY
High	Purple/Blue/Rose	Emerald/Saphire	Educational	Family Graha	Mahakali

DAILY PUJA	DAILY PSALMS
Meditate, Control temper, Pray to Hanuman, Chant Hanuman Chalisa	6, 15, 33 ,42, 51, 60, 78, 105, 123

Saturday, March 18, 2023

Saturday, March 18, 2023	This is considered a NEUTRAL day for you	Planet: Uranus
ADVICE & DETAILS		**MANTRA FOR TODAY**
The thought of watching TV is very appealing today. Spending time with children will benefit your creativity, but you must refrain from allowing immaturity to control your actions today.		Jai Jai Shiva Shambo.(2) ...Mahadeva Shambo (2) 21 times 8

MONEY	LOVE	CAREER	FAMILY	TRAVEL	WEDDING	MOVE	BUSINESS	HEALTH	Lotto #'s	play 3 #s
Good	Good	Fair	Good	Good	Bad	Good	Bad	Fair	73,31,14,4,14,47,54	280

SHOPPING	GAMBLE	SEX	KEYWORD	KEYWORD						
Bad	Fair	is quiet	DIVINE	Spirituality,Religious,Astrology,Inner Conflicts,Religious ,Sleepiness,Advice						

STRESS LEVEL	LUCKY COLORS	JEWELERY	MOONS EFFECT	GRAHA EFFECT	DAILY DEITY
Fair	Light Blue/Peach	Tiger's eye/Gold/Silv	Affectionate	God'S Graha	Shesnaag

DAILY PUJA	DAILY PSALMS
Chant Shiva Mantras, Take gifts to Ocean - Ganga Puja, Donate to Temple, Priests, etc.	7, 16, 34 ,43, 52, 61, 79, 106, 124

Sunday, March 19, 2023

Sunday, March 19, 2023	This is considered a POSITIVE day for you	Planet: Jupiter
ADVICE & DETAILS		**MANTRA FOR TODAY**
The power of your expression today is great. Use this power to communicate with others, to write and publish or to entertain others when in groups or parties. There is the influence of someone that is jealous of you, be aware of it and try to be modest.		Om Hareem Nama Swaha..Shri Maha Laxmi Aye Namah swaha 12 times

MONEY	LOVE	CAREER	FAMILY	TRAVEL	WEDDING	MOVE	BUSINESS	HEALTH	Lotto #'s	play 3 #s
Excellent	Good	Excellent	Good	Good	Excellent	Good	Excellent	Excellent	39,53,18,49,57,18,6	741

SHOPPING	GAMBLE	SEX	KEYWORD	KEYWORD						
Excellent	Excellent	is excellent	MONEY	Business,Major Expense,Money -						

STRESS LEVEL	LUCKY COLORS	JEWELERY	MOONS EFFECT	GRAHA EFFECT	DAILY DEITY
Low	Yellow/Silver	Diamonds/Gold/Pea	Secretive	Money Graha	Mahalaxmi

DAILY PUJA	DAILY PSALMS
Decorate Land, Feed the poor, Donate milk /products to all, Feed holy guests,	8, 17, 35 ,44, 53, 62, 80, 107, 125

Monday, March 20, 2023

Monday, March 20, 2023	This is considered a NEGATIVE day for you	Planet: Saturn
ADVICE & DETAILS		**MANTRA FOR TODAY**
Although this will be a day open for you to socialize with others, you must avoid extremes and parties with alcohol and drugs. Your enemies will take advantage of you today when they see you in your weakest state. Try to rest, you will be sleepy.		Om Ganga mataye nama swaha Om Varuna Devta aye Pahimam 11 times

MONEY	LOVE	CAREER	FAMILY	TRAVEL	WEDDING	MOVE	BUSINESS	HEALTH	Lotto #'s	play 3 #s
Bad	Bad	Bad	Fair	Bad	Bad	Bad	Bad	Bad	15,44,30,13,5,50,3	215

SHOPPING	GAMBLE	SEX	KEYWORD	KEYWORD						
Bad	Bad	is very bad	KARMA	Destruction,Losses,Death,Sickness - cold,Legal matter,Abusive,Karmic debts,God -						

STRESS LEVEL	LUCKY COLORS	JEWELERY	MOONS EFFECT	GRAHA EFFECT	DAILY DEITY
High	Gold/Brown//Green	Saphire/Hessonite	Ivestments	Evil Graha	Agnidev

DAILY PUJA	DAILY PSALMS
Remembrance of family members who died, worship of older people. gifts to grand parents	9, 18, 36 ,45, 54, 63, 81, 108, 126

Tuesday, March 21, 2023

Tuesday, March 21, 2023	This is considered a NEUTRAL day for you	Planet: Sun
ADVICE & DETAILS		**MANTRA FOR TODAY**
There may be sickness of children or you may be getting sick. There will be losses and sadness.		Om Namo Bhagawate Mukhtanandaya, 108 times

MONEY	LOVE	CAREER	FAMILY	TRAVEL	WEDDING	MOVE	BUSINESS	HEALTH	Lotto #'s	play 3 #s
Fair	Bad	Good	Bad	Fair	Bad	Fair	Fair	Fair	62,5,4,53,52,60,17	313

SHOPPING	GAMBLE	SEX	KEYWORD	KEYWORD						
Fair	Fair	is fair	MIND	Independence,Loneliness,Meditative,Worry,Dominating,Illness - Cold,On Your						

STRESS LEVEL	LUCKY COLORS	JEWELERY	MOONS EFFECT	GRAHA EFFECT	DAILY DEITY
High	White/Yellow/	Pearl/Quartz	Arrogance	Status Graha	Saraswaty

DAILY PUJA	DAILY PSALMS
Give Gifts to Priests, Invite holy ones to your home, Feed Swamis and Yogis, Do Shiva Puja.	1, 10, 28 ,37, 46, 55, 73, 100, 118

Wednesday, March 22, 2023 — This is considered a POSITIVE day for you — Planet: Moon

ADVICE & DETAILS

Express your thoughts, opinions or information to partners and/or children. Day is influenced by children and ability to acquire information by reading or other means.

MANTRA FOR TODAY

Kali Durge Namo Nama Om Durge aye nama swaha 108 times

MONEY	LOVE	CAREER	FAMILY	TRAVEL	WEDDING	MOVE	BUSINESS	HEALTH	Lotto #'s	play 3 #s
Good	Excellent	Good	Good	Excellen	Good	Good	Good	Good	26,1,4,59,20,18,39	681

SHOPPING	GAMBLE	SEX	KEYWORD	KEYWORD						
Good	Good	is good	LOVE	Romance,Popularity,Visitors,Shopping,Food, Drinks,Co-						

STRESS LEVEL	LUCKY COLORS	JEWELERY	MOONS EFFECT	GRAHA EFFECT	DAILY DEITY
Low	Red/Yellow/Pink	Topaz/Diamonds	Conservative	Love Graha	Gauri

DAILY PUJA	DAILY PSALMS
Give Gifts to females andnMother, Serve milk Products, Worship Durga forms	2, 11, 29 ,38, 47, 56, 74, 101, 119

Thursday, March 23, 2023 — This is considered a POSITIVE day for you — Planet: Mercury

ADVICE & DETAILS

Reading will benefit you today. You will have to hone your communication skills and speak clearly and listen carefully, especially when dealing with Real Estate and teachers of any type.

MANTRA FOR TODAY

Om hareem Kleem Hreem Aem Saraswataye namaha 21 times

MONEY	LOVE	CAREER	FAMILY	TRAVEL	WEDDING	MOVE	BUSINESS	HEALTH	Lotto #'s	play 3 #s
Good	Fair	Good	Good	Excellen	Good	Good	Good	Excellent	68,26,43,61,33,29,2	697

SHOPPING	GAMBLE	SEX	KEYWORD	KEYWORD						
Good	Good	is great	SOCIAL	Children,Education,Astrology,Bargains,Social Functions,Childishness,Groups -						

STRESS LEVEL	LUCKY COLORS	JEWELERY	MOONS EFFECT	GRAHA EFFECT	DAILY DEITY
Low	Green/Sky Blue/	Diamonds/Silver	Enthusiastic	Social Graha	Vishnu

DAILY PUJA	DAILY PSALMS
Wash the feet of Children, Do Satnarayan Pooja, Read & chant Geeta	3, 12, 30 ,39, 48, 57, 75, 102, 120

Friday, March 24, 2023 — This is considered a NEGATIVE day for you — Planet: Pluto

ADVICE & DETAILS

Overcome laziness and low pay today and improve your karma by being industrious, hard working and controlling your high temper.

MANTRA FOR TODAY

Om Jai Viganeshwaraya.. Lambodaraya Namo Namaha 21 times

MONEY	LOVE	CAREER	FAMILY	TRAVEL	WEDDING	MOVE	BUSINESS	HEALTH	Lotto #'s	play 3 #s
Bad	Fair	Bad	Fair	Bad	Good	Bad	Bad	Bad	33,52,29,28,75,15,4	57

SHOPPING	GAMBLE	SEX	KEYWORD	KEYWORD						
Bad	Bad	is tough	CAREER	Career,Hard Work,Co-workers,Low Payment,Job Problems,High Temper,Low						

STRESS LEVEL	LUCKY COLORS	JEWELERY	MOONS EFFECT	GRAHA EFFECT	DAILY DEITY
High	Dark Blue/ Purple/	Amethyst/Gold	Emotional	Job Graha	Lingam

DAILY PUJA	DAILY PSALMS
Worship Ganesh, Give gifts to father, and co -workers, Plant gardens, farms	4, 13, 31 ,40, 49, 58, 76, 103, 121

Saturday, March 25, 2023 — This is considered a POSITIVE day for you — Planet: Venus

ADVICE & DETAILS

Although this will be a day open for you to socialize with others, you must avoid extremes and parties with alcohol and drugs. Your enemies will take advantage of you today when they see you in your weakest state. Try to rest, you will be sleepy.

MANTRA FOR TODAY

Om Graam Greem Graum Sa Gurave namah swaha 21 times

MONEY	LOVE	CAREER	FAMILY	TRAVEL	WEDDING	MOVE	BUSINESS	HEALTH	Lotto #'s	play 3 #s
Bad	Excellent	Fair	Good	Excellen	Good	Excellen	Good	Excellent	20,11,7,55,70,32,4	514

SHOPPING	GAMBLE	SEX	KEYWORD	KEYWORD						
Good	Good	is good	CHANGE	Sexuality,Travel,Change,Distant, far,Travel delays,Deception,Excercise,Illicit						

STRESS LEVEL	LUCKY COLORS	JEWELERY	MOONS EFFECT	GRAHA EFFECT	DAILY DEITY
Fair	Tan/Green/ Beige	Pearl/Silver/quartz	Courageous	Travel Graha	Nataraja

DAILY PUJA	DAILY PSALMS
Artistic gifts, Pray to Krishna, Do good deeds, do Spiritual trips	5, 14, 32 ,41, 50, 59, 77, 104, 122

Sunday, March 26, 2023 — This is considered a NEGATIVE day for you — Planet: Mars

ADVICE & DETAILS

Children will be prevalent today. This day is marked with a great deal of creativity ideal for areas related to the left side of the brain such as writing, painting, handcrafts, baking, cooking or needlework.

MANTRA FOR TODAY

Om Mana Swasti Shanti Kuru kuru Swaha Shivoham Shivoham 27 times

MONEY	LOVE	CAREER	FAMILY	TRAVEL	WEDDING	MOVE	BUSINESS	HEALTH	Lotto #'s	play 3 #s
Bad	Bad	Bad	Bad	Bad	Bad	Bad	Fair	Bad	34,65,22,67,4,38,46	318

SHOPPING	GAMBLE	SEX	KEYWORD	KEYWORD						
Fair	Bad	is frustrating	POWER	Responsibilty,Disagreement,Family,Back Pain,Family Conflicts,Traffic						

STRESS LEVEL		LUCKY COLORS		JEWELERY	MOONS EFFECT	GRAHA EFFECT		DAILY DEITY
High		Purple/Blue/Rose		Emerald/Saphire	Educational	Family Graha		Mahakali

DAILY PUJA	DAILY PSALMS
Meditate, Control temper, Pray to Hanuman, Chant Hanuman Chalisa	6, 15, 33 ,42, 51, 60, 78, 105, 123

Monday, March 27, 2023 — This is considered a NEUTRAL day for you — Planet: Uranus

ADVICE & DETAILS

The thought of watching TV is very appealing today. Spending time with children will benefit your creativity, but you must refrain from allowing immaturity to control your actions today.

MANTRA FOR TODAY

Jai Jai Shiva Shambo.(2) ...Mahadeva Shambo (2) 21 times 8

MONEY	LOVE	CAREER	FAMILY	TRAVEL	WEDDING	MOVE	BUSINESS	HEALTH	Lotto #'s	play 3 #s
Good	Good	Fair	Good	Good	Bad	Good	Bad	Fair	24,33,57,29,12,65,4	205

SHOPPING	GAMBLE	SEX	KEYWORD	KEYWORD						
Bad	Fair	is quiet	DIVINE	Spirituality,Religious,Astrology,Inner Conflicts,Religious ,Sleepiness,Advice						

STRESS LEVEL		LUCKY COLORS		JEWELERY	MOONS EFFECT	GRAHA EFFECT		DAILY DEITY
Fair		Light Blue/Peach		Tiger's eye/Gold/Sil	Affectionate	God'S Graha		Shesnaag

DAILY PUJA	DAILY PSALMS
Chant Shiva Mantras, Take gifts to Ocean - Ganga Puja, Donate to Temple, Priests, etc.	7, 16, 34 ,43, 52, 61, 79, 106, 124

Tuesday, March 28, 2023 — This is considered a POSITIVE day for you — Planet: Jupiter

ADVICE & DETAILS

The power of your expression today is great. Use this power to communicate with others, to write and publish or to entertain others when in groups or parties. There is the influence of someone that is jealous of you, be aware of it and try to be modest.

MANTRA FOR TODAY

Om Hareem Nama Swaha..Shri Maha Laxmi Aye Namah swaha 12 times

MONEY	LOVE	CAREER	FAMILY	TRAVEL	WEDDING	MOVE	BUSINESS	HEALTH	Lotto #'s	play 3 #s
Excellent	Good	Excellent	Good	Good	Excellent	Good	Excellent	Excellent	73,58,45,73,75,3,36	293

SHOPPING	GAMBLE	SEX	KEYWORD	KEYWORD						
Excellent	Excellent	is excellent	MONEY	Business,Major Expense,Money -						

STRESS LEVEL		LUCKY COLORS		JEWELERY	MOONS EFFECT	GRAHA EFFECT		DAILY DEITY
Low		Yellow/Silver		Diamonds/Gold/Pea	Secretive	Money Graha		Mahalaxmi

DAILY PUJA	DAILY PSALMS
Decorate Land, Feed the poor, Donate milk /products to all, Feed holy guests,	8, 17, 35 ,44, 53, 62, 80, 107, 125

Wednesday, March 29, 2023 — This is considered a NEGATIVE day for you — Planet: Saturn

ADVICE & DETAILS

Although this will be a day open for you to socialize with others, you must avoid extremes and parties with alcohol and drugs. Your enemies will take advantage of you today when they see you in your weakest state. Try to rest, you will be sleepy.

MANTRA FOR TODAY

Om Ganga mataye nama swaha Om Varuna Devta aye Pahimam 11 times

MONEY	LOVE	CAREER	FAMILY	TRAVEL	WEDDING	MOVE	BUSINESS	HEALTH	Lotto #'s	play 3 #s
Bad	Bad	Bad	Fair	Bad	Bad	Bad	Bad	Bad	59,24,17,47,16,7,63	503

SHOPPING	GAMBLE	SEX	KEYWORD	KEYWORD						
Bad	Bad	is very bad	KARMA	Destruction,Losses,Death,Sickness - cold,Legal matter,Abusive,Karmic debts,God -						

STRESS LEVEL		LUCKY COLORS		JEWELERY	MOONS EFFECT	GRAHA EFFECT		DAILY DEITY
High		Gold/Brown//Green		Saphire/Hessonite	Ivestments	Evil Graha		Agnidev

DAILY PUJA	DAILY PSALMS
Remembrance of family members who died, worship of older people. gifts to grand parents	9, 18, 36 ,45, 54, 63, 81, 108, 126

Thursday, March 30, 2023 — This is considered a NEUTRAL day for you — Planet: Sun

ADVICE & DETAILS

There may be sickness of children or you may be getting sick. There will be losses and sadness.

MANTRA FOR TODAY

Om Namo Bhagawate Mukhtanandaya, 108 times

MONEY	LOVE	CAREER	FAMILY	TRAVEL	WEDDING	MOVE	BUSINESS	HEALTH	Lotto #'s	play 3 #s
Fair	Bad	Good	Bad	Fair	Bad	Fair	Fair	Fair	25,35,40,40,68,69,2	393

SHOPPING	GAMBLE	SEX	KEYWORD	KEYWORD
Fair	Fair	is fair	MIND	Independence,Loneliness,Meditative,Worry,Dominating,Illness - Cold,On Your

STRESS LEVEL	LUCKY COLORS	JEWELERY	MOONS EFFECT	GRAHA EFFECT	DAILY DEITY
High	White/Yellow/	Pearl/Quartz	Arrogance	Status Graha	Saraswaty

DAILY PUJA	DAILY PSALMS
Give Gifts to Priests, Invite holy ones to your home, Feed Swamis and Yogis, Do Shiva Puja.	1, 10, 28 ,37, 46, 55, 73, 100, 118

Friday, March 31, 2023 — This is considered a POSITIVE day for you — Planet: Moon

ADVICE & DETAILS

Express your thoughts, opinions or information to partners and/or children. Day is influenced by children and ability to acquire information by reading or other means.

MANTRA FOR TODAY

Kali Durge Namo Nama Om Durge aye nama swaha 108 times

MONEY	LOVE	CAREER	FAMILY	TRAVEL	WEDDING	MOVE	BUSINESS	HEALTH	Lotto #'s	play 3 #s
Good	Excellent	Good	Good	Excellen	Good	Good	Good	Good	17,57,63,74,40,44,5	735

SHOPPING	GAMBLE	SEX	KEYWORD	KEYWORD
Good	Good	is good	LOVE	Romance,Popularity,Visitors,Shopping,Food, Drinks,Co-

STRESS LEVEL	LUCKY COLORS	JEWELERY	MOONS EFFECT	GRAHA EFFECT	DAILY DEITY
Low	Red/Yellow/Pink	Topaz/Diamonds	Conservative	Love Graha	Gauri

DAILY PUJA	DAILY PSALMS
Give Gifts to females andnMother, Serve milk Products, Worship Durga forms	2, 11, 29 ,38, 47, 56, 74, 101, 119

Saturday, April 1, 2023 — This is considered a POSITIVE day for you — Planet: Jupiter

ADVICE & DETAILS

Dealings with Real Estate of things related to your professional life may bring beauty and sex into your realm. You will feel fatigued during the day.

MANTRA FOR TODAY

Om Hareem Nama Swaha..Shri Maha Laxmi Aye Namah swaha 12 times

MONEY	LOVE	CAREER	FAMILY	TRAVEL	WEDDING	MOVE	BUSINESS	HEALTH	Lotto #'s	play 3 #s
Excellent	Good	Excellent	Good	Good	Excellent	Good	Excellent	Excellent	47,46,49,57,12,41,4	837

SHOPPING	GAMBLE	SEX	KEYWORD	KEYWORD
Excellent	Excellent	is excellent	MONEY	Business,Major Expense,Money -

STRESS LEVEL	LUCKY COLORS	JEWELERY	MOONS EFFECT	GRAHA EFFECT	DAILY DEITY
Low	Yellow/Silver	Diamonds/Gold/Pea	Secretive	Money Graha	Mahalaxmi

DAILY PUJA	DAILY PSALMS
Decorate Land, Feed the poor, Donate milk /products to all, Feed holy guests,	8, 17, 35 ,44, 53, 62, 80, 107, 125

Sunday, April 2, 2023 — This is considered a NEGATIVE day for you — Planet: Saturn

ADVICE & DETAILS

Be ready to face job difficulties that may come to you today centered in your godliness not your ego. Remember this day is part of your career and the long-term goals you have.

MANTRA FOR TODAY

Om Ganga mataye nama swaha Om Varuna Devta aye Pahimam 11 times

MONEY	LOVE	CAREER	FAMILY	TRAVEL	WEDDING	MOVE	BUSINESS	HEALTH	Lotto #'s	play 3 #s
Bad	Bad	Bad	Fair	Bad	Bad	Bad	Bad	Bad	74,10,51,60,38,67,6	21

SHOPPING	GAMBLE	SEX	KEYWORD	KEYWORD
Bad	Bad	is very bad	KARMA	Destruction,Losses,Death,Sickness - cold,Legal matter,Abusive,Karmic debts, God -

STRESS LEVEL	LUCKY COLORS	JEWELERY	MOONS EFFECT	GRAHA EFFECT	DAILY DEITY
High	Gold/Brown//Green	Saphire/Hessonite	Ivestments	Evil Graha	Agnidev

DAILY PUJA	DAILY PSALMS
Remembrance of family members who died, worship of older people. gifts to grand parents	9, 18, 36 ,45, 54, 63, 81, 108, 126

Monday, April 3, 2023 — This is considered a NEUTRAL day for you — Planet: Sun

ADVICE & DETAILS	MANTRA FOR TODAY
Assiduous dedication to your tasks and responsibilities will be rewarded today. It will be a day when you are busy, but being indolent today will cost you dearly in financial opportunities.	Om Namo Bhagawate Mukhtanandaya, 108 times

MONEY	LOVE	CAREER	FAMILY	TRAVEL	WEDDING	MOVE	BUSINESS	HEALTH	Lotto #'s	play 3 #s
Fair	Bad	Good	Bad	Fair	Bad	Fair	Fair	Fair	30,72,49,53,54,4,30	988

SHOPPING	GAMBLE	SEX	KEYWORD	KEYWORD						
Fair	Fair	is fair	MIND	Independence,Loneliness,Meditative,Worry,Dominating,Illness - Cold,On Your						

STRESS LEVEL	LUCKY COLORS	JEWELERY	MOONS EFFECT	GRAHA EFFECT	DAILY DEITY
High	White/Yellow/	Pearl/Quartz	Arrogance	Status Graha	Saraswaty

DAILY PUJA	DAILY PSALMS
Give Gifts to Priests, Invite holy ones to your home, Feed Swamis and Yogis, Do Shiva Puja.	1, 10, 28 ,37, 46, 55, 73, 100, 118

Tuesday, April 4, 2023 — This is considered a POSITIVE day for you — Planet: Moon

ADVICE & DETAILS	MANTRA FOR TODAY
Your karma for today requires you to be industrious and work very hard. You must put your laziness away. Associates will give you positive input and/or help.	Kali Durge Namo Nama Om Durge aye nama swaha 108 times

MONEY	LOVE	CAREER	FAMILY	TRAVEL	WEDDING	MOVE	BUSINESS	HEALTH	Lotto #'s	play 3 #s
Good	Excellent	Good	Good	Excellen	Good	Good	Good	Good	38,65,70,32,32,17,3	309

SHOPPING	GAMBLE	SEX	KEYWORD	KEYWORD						
Good	Good	is good	LOVE	Romance,Popularity,Visitors,Shopping,Food, Drinks,Co-						

STRESS LEVEL	LUCKY COLORS	JEWELERY	MOONS EFFECT	GRAHA EFFECT	DAILY DEITY
Low	Red/Yellow/Pink	Topaz/Diamonds	Conservative	Love Graha	Gauri

DAILY PUJA	DAILY PSALMS
Give Gifts to females andnMother, Serve milk Products, Worship Durga forms	2, 11, 29 ,38, 47, 56, 74, 101, 119

Wednesday, April 5, 2023 — This is considered a POSITIVE day for you — Planet: Mercury

ADVICE & DETAILS	MANTRA FOR TODAY
Today is a day to work and work even if you feel lazy. You need to be industrious and achieve all tasks that you can today. You will be in association with others while doing these projects, accept the input.	Om hareem Kleem Hreem Aem Saraswataye namaha 21 times

MONEY	LOVE	CAREER	FAMILY	TRAVEL	WEDDING	MOVE	BUSINESS	HEALTH	Lotto #'s	play 3 #s
Good	Fair	Good	Good	Excellen	Good	Good	Good	Excellent	50,44,48,6,15,18,7	275

SHOPPING	GAMBLE	SEX	KEYWORD	KEYWORD						
Good	Good	is great	SOCIAL	Children,Education,Astrology,Bargains,Social Functions,Childishness,Groups -						

STRESS LEVEL	LUCKY COLORS	JEWELERY	MOONS EFFECT	GRAHA EFFECT	DAILY DEITY
Low	Green/Sky Blue/	Diamonds/Silver	Enthusiastic	Social Graha	Vishnu

DAILY PUJA	DAILY PSALMS
Wash the feet of Children, Do Satnarayan Pooja, Read & chant Geeta	3, 12, 30 ,39, 48, 57, 75, 102, 120

Thursday, April 6, 2023 — This is considered a NEGATIVE day for you — Planet: Pluto

ADVICE & DETAILS	MANTRA FOR TODAY
Today you feel lazy, but you will need to work, be industrious and accomplish as much as possible. You will need to control your high temper and accept that today you will feel like they do not pay you enough to do your job.	Om Jai Viganeshwaraya.. Lambodaraya Namo Namaha 21 times

MONEY	LOVE	CAREER	FAMILY	TRAVEL	WEDDING	MOVE	BUSINESS	HEALTH	Lotto #'s	play 3 #s
Bad	Fair	Bad	Fair	Bad	Good	Bad	Bad	Bad	65,34,68,5,25,44,37	171

SHOPPING	GAMBLE	SEX	KEYWORD	KEYWORD						
Bad	Bad	is tough	CAREER	Career,Hard Work,Co-workers,Low Payment,Job Problems,High Temper,Low						

STRESS LEVEL	LUCKY COLORS	JEWELERY	MOONS EFFECT	GRAHA EFFECT	DAILY DEITY
High	Dark Blue/ Purple/	Amethyst/Gold	Emotional	Job Graha	Lingam

DAILY PUJA	DAILY PSALMS
Worship Ganesh, Give gifts to father, and co -workers, Plant gardens, farms	4, 13, 31 ,40, 49, 58, 76, 103, 121

Friday, April 7, 2023 — This is considered a POSITIVE day for you — Planet: Venus

ADVICE & DETAILS

Do not allow the job problems that you may have today to affect your long-term career plans. Remember the foundation of your career is built on a day per day basis at your job. Act and think conscious of your godliness.

MANTRA FOR TODAY

Om Graam Greem Graum Sa Gurave namah swaha 21 times

MONEY	LOVE	CAREER	FAMILY	TRAVEL	WEDDING	MOVE	BUSINESS	HEALTH	Lotto #'s	play 3 #s
Bad	Excellent	Fair	Good	Excellen	Good	Excellen	Good	Excellent	32,12,17,21,61,17,7	744

SHOPPING	GAMBLE	SEX	KEYWORD	KEYWORD						
Good	Good	is good	CHANGE	Sexuality,Travel,Change,Distant, far,Travel delays,Deception,Excercise,Illicit						

STRESS LEVEL	LUCKY COLORS	JEWELERY	MOONS EFFECT	GRAHA EFFECT	DAILY DEITY
Fair	Tan/Green/ Beige	Pearl/Silver/quartz	Courageous	Travel Graha	Nataraja

DAILY PUJA	DAILY PSALMS
Artistic gifts, Pray to Krishna, Do good deeds, do Spiritual trips	5, 14, 32 ,41, 50, 59, 77, 104, 122

Saturday, April 8, 2023 — This is considered a NEGATIVE day for you — Planet: Mars

ADVICE & DETAILS

You are going to feel very lazy today, but you must push through this feeling and devote your day to work with others and work diligently.

MANTRA FOR TODAY

Om Mana Swasti Shanti Kuru kuru Swaha Shivoham Shivoham 27 times

MONEY	LOVE	CAREER	FAMILY	TRAVEL	WEDDING	MOVE	BUSINESS	HEALTH	Lotto #'s	play 3 #s
Bad	Bad	Bad	Bad	Bad	Bad	Bad	Fair	Bad	47,50,59,32,70,7,42	548

SHOPPING	GAMBLE	SEX	KEYWORD	KEYWORD						
Fair	Bad	is frustrating	POWER	Responsibilty,Disagreement,Family,Back Pain,Family Conflicts,Traffic						

STRESS LEVEL	LUCKY COLORS	JEWELERY	MOONS EFFECT	GRAHA EFFECT	DAILY DEITY
High	Purple/Blue/Rose	Emerald/Saphire	Educational	Family Graha	Mahakali

DAILY PUJA	DAILY PSALMS
Meditate, Control temper, Pray to Hanuman, Chant Hanuman Chalisa	6, 15, 33 ,42, 51, 60, 78, 105, 123

Sunday, April 9, 2023 — This is considered a NEUTRAL day for you — Planet: Uranus

ADVICE & DETAILS

Find a reprieve from the weariness of everyday building your professional life by finding a book and reading about something that interests you and makes you happy.

MANTRA FOR TODAY

Jai Jai Shiva Shambo.(2) ...Mahadeva Shambo (2) 21 times 8

MONEY	LOVE	CAREER	FAMILY	TRAVEL	WEDDING	MOVE	BUSINESS	HEALTH	Lotto #'s	play 3 #s
Good	Good	Fair	Good	Good	Bad	Good	Bad	Fair	35,57,37,19,28,32,3	958

SHOPPING	GAMBLE	SEX	KEYWORD	KEYWORD						
Bad	Fair	is quiet	DIVINE	Spirituality,Religious,Astrology,Inner Conflicts,Religious ,Sleepiness,Advice						

STRESS LEVEL	LUCKY COLORS	JEWELERY	MOONS EFFECT	GRAHA EFFECT	DAILY DEITY
Fair	Light Blue/Peach	Tiger's eye/Gold/Sil	Affectionate	God'S Graha	Shesnaag

DAILY PUJA	DAILY PSALMS
Chant Shiva Mantras, Take gifts to Ocean - Ganga Puja, Donate to Temple, Priests, etc.	7, 16, 34 ,43, 52, 61, 79, 106, 124

Monday, April 10, 2023 — This is considered a POSITIVE day for you — Planet: Jupiter

ADVICE & DETAILS

Dealings with Real Estate of things related to your professional life may bring beauty and sex into your realm. You will feel fatigued during the day.

MANTRA FOR TODAY

Om Hareem Nama Swaha..Shri Maha Laxmi Aye Namah swaha 12 times

MONEY	LOVE	CAREER	FAMILY	TRAVEL	WEDDING	MOVE	BUSINESS	HEALTH	Lotto #'s	play 3 #s
Excellent	Good	Excellent	Good	Good	Excellent	Good	Excellent	Excellent	64,24,46,15,67,6,17	866

SHOPPING	GAMBLE	SEX	KEYWORD	KEYWORD						
Excellent	Excellent	is excellent	MONEY	Business,Major Expense,Money -						

STRESS LEVEL	LUCKY COLORS	JEWELERY	MOONS EFFECT	GRAHA EFFECT	DAILY DEITY
Low	Yellow/Silver	Diamonds/Gold/Pea	Secretive	Money Graha	Mahalaxmi

DAILY PUJA	DAILY PSALMS
Decorate Land, Feed the poor, Donate milk /products to all, Feed holy guests,	8, 17, 35 ,44, 53, 62, 80, 107, 125

Tuesday, April 11, 2023 — This is considered a NEGATIVE day for you — Planet: Saturn

ADVICE & DETAILS

Be ready to face job difficulties that may come to you today centered in your godliness not your ego. Remember this day is part of your career and the long-term goals you have.

MANTRA FOR TODAY

Om Ganga mataye nama swaha Om Varuna Devta aye Pahimam 11 times

MONEY	LOVE	CAREER	FAMILY	TRAVEL	WEDDING	MOVE	BUSINESS	HEALTH	Lotto #'s	play 3 #s
Bad	Bad	Bad	Fair	Bad	Bad	Bad	Bad	Bad	58,32,64,46,45,40,5	427

SHOPPING	GAMBLE	SEX	KEYWORD	KEYWORD						
Bad	Bad	is very bad	KARMA	Destruction,Losses,Death,Sickness - cold,Legal matter,Abusive,Karmic debts,God -						

STRESS LEVEL	LUCKY COLORS	JEWELERY	MOONS EFFECT	GRAHA EFFECT	DAILY DEITY
High	Gold/Brown//Green	Saphire/Hessonite	Ivestments	Evil Graha	Agnidev

DAILY PUJA	DAILY PSALMS
Remembrance of family members who died, worship of older people. gifts to grand parents	9, 18, 36 ,45, 54, 63, 81, 108, 126

Wednesday, April 12, 2023 — This is considered a NEUTRAL day for you — Planet: Sun

ADVICE & DETAILS

Assiduous dedication to your tasks and responsibilities will be rewarded today. It will be a day when you are busy, but being indolent today will cost you dearly in financial opportunities.

MANTRA FOR TODAY

Om Namo Bhagawate Mukhtanandaya, 108 times

MONEY	LOVE	CAREER	FAMILY	TRAVEL	WEDDING	MOVE	BUSINESS	HEALTH	Lotto #'s	play 3 #s
Fair	Bad	Good	Bad	Fair	Bad	Fair	Fair	Fair	58,48,23,75,10,18,2	674

SHOPPING	GAMBLE	SEX	KEYWORD	KEYWORD						
Fair	Fair	is fair	MIND	Independence,Loneliness,Meditative,Worry,Dominating,Illness - Cold,On Your						

STRESS LEVEL	LUCKY COLORS	JEWELERY	MOONS EFFECT	GRAHA EFFECT	DAILY DEITY
High	White/Yellow/	Pearl/Quartz	Arrogance	Status Graha	Saraswaty

DAILY PUJA	DAILY PSALMS
Give Gifts to Priests, Invite holy ones to your home, Feed Swamis and Yogis, Do Shiva Puja.	1, 10, 28 ,37, 46, 55, 73, 100, 118

Thursday, April 13, 2023 — This is considered a POSITIVE day for you — Planet: Moon

ADVICE & DETAILS

Your karma for today requires you to be industrious and work very hard. You must put your laziness away. Associates will give you positive input and/or help.

MANTRA FOR TODAY

Kali Durge Namo Nama Om Durge aye nama swaha 108 times

MONEY	LOVE	CAREER	FAMILY	TRAVEL	WEDDING	MOVE	BUSINESS	HEALTH	Lotto #'s	play 3 #s
Good	Excellent	Good	Good	Excellen	Good	Good	Good	Good	25,10,56,15,57,34,3	309

SHOPPING	GAMBLE	SEX	KEYWORD	KEYWORD						
Good	Good	is good	LOVE	Romance,Popularity,Visitors,Shopping,Food, Drinks,Co-						

STRESS LEVEL	LUCKY COLORS	JEWELERY	MOONS EFFECT	GRAHA EFFECT	DAILY DEITY
Low	Red/Yellow/Pink	Topaz/Diamonds	Conservative	Love Graha	Gauri

DAILY PUJA	DAILY PSALMS
Give Gifts to females andnMother, Serve milk Products, Worship Durga forms	2, 11, 29 ,38, 47, 56, 74, 101, 119

Friday, April 14, 2023 — This is considered a POSITIVE day for you — Planet: Mercury

ADVICE & DETAILS

Today is a day to work and work even if you feel lazy. You need to be industrious and achieve all tasks that you can today. You will be in association with others while doing these projects, accept the input.

MANTRA FOR TODAY

Om hareem Kleem Hreem Aem Saraswataye namaha 21 times

MONEY	LOVE	CAREER	FAMILY	TRAVEL	WEDDING	MOVE	BUSINESS	HEALTH	Lotto #'s	play 3 #s
Good	Fair	Good	Good	Excellen	Good	Good	Good	Excellent	32,5,57,55,55,71,68	404

SHOPPING	GAMBLE	SEX	KEYWORD	KEYWORD						
Good	Good	is great	SOCIAL	Children,Education,Astrology,Bargains,Social Functions,Childishness,Groups -						

STRESS LEVEL	LUCKY COLORS	JEWELERY	MOONS EFFECT	GRAHA EFFECT	DAILY DEITY
Low	Green/Sky Blue/	Diamonds/Silver	Enthusiastic	Social Graha	Vishnu

DAILY PUJA	DAILY PSALMS
Wash the feet of Children, Do Satnarayan Pooja, Read & chant Geeta	3, 12, 30 ,39, 48, 57, 75, 102, 120

Saturday, April 15, 2023 — This is considered a NEGATIVE day for you — Planet: Pluto

ADVICE & DETAILS

Today you feel lazy, but you will need to work, be industrious and accomplish as much as possible. You will need to control your high temper and accept that today you will feel like they do not pay you enough to do your job.

MANTRA FOR TODAY
Om Jai Viganeshwaraya.. Lambodaraya Namo Namaha 21 times

MONEY	LOVE	CAREER	FAMILY	TRAVEL	WEDDING	MOVE	BUSINESS	HEALTH	Lotto #'s	play 3 #s
Bad	Fair	Bad	Fair	Bad	Good	Bad	Bad	Bad	68,44,34,19,25,2,38	763

SHOPPING	GAMBLE	SEX	KEYWORD	KEYWORD
Bad	Bad	is tough	CAREER	Career,Hard Work,Co-workers,Low Payment,Job Problems,High Temper,Low

STRESS LEVEL	LUCKY COLORS	JEWELERY	MOONS EFFECT	GRAHA EFFECT	DAILY DEITY
High	Dark Blue/ Purple/	Amethyst/Gold	Emotional	Job Graha	Lingam

DAILY PUJA	DAILY PSALMS
Worship Ganesh, Give gifts to father, and co -workers, Plant gardens, farms	4, 13, 31 ,40, 49, 58, 76, 103, 121

Sunday, April 16, 2023 — This is considered a POSITIVE day for you — Planet: Venus

ADVICE & DETAILS

Do not allow the job problems that you may have today to affect your long-term career plans. Remember the foundation of your career is built on a day per day basis at your job. Act and think conscious of your godliness.

MANTRA FOR TODAY
Om Graam Greem Graum Sa Gurave namah swaha 21 times

MONEY	LOVE	CAREER	FAMILY	TRAVEL	WEDDING	MOVE	BUSINESS	HEALTH	Lotto #'s	play 3 #s
Bad	Excellent	Fair	Good	Excellen	Good	Exceller	Good	Excellent	62,51,28,43,11,68,5	75

SHOPPING	GAMBLE	SEX	KEYWORD	KEYWORD
Good	Good	is good	CHANGE	Sexuality,Travel,Change,Distant, far,Travel delays,Deception,Excercise,Illicit

STRESS LEVEL	LUCKY COLORS	JEWELERY	MOONS EFFECT	GRAHA EFFECT	DAILY DEITY
Fair	Tan/Green/ Beige	Pearl/Silver/quartz	Courageous	Travel Graha	Nataraja

DAILY PUJA	DAILY PSALMS
Artistic gifts, Pray to Krishna, Do good deeds, do Spiritual trips	5, 14, 32 ,41, 50, 59, 77, 104, 122

Monday, April 17, 2023 — This is considered a NEGATIVE day for you — Planet: Mars

ADVICE & DETAILS

You are going to feel very lazy today, but you must push through this feeling and devote your day to work with others and work diligently.

MANTRA FOR TODAY
Om Mana Swasti Shanti Kuru kuru Swaha Shivoham Shivoham 27 times

MONEY	LOVE	CAREER	FAMILY	TRAVEL	WEDDING	MOVE	BUSINESS	HEALTH	Lotto #'s	play 3 #s
Bad	Bad	Bad	Bad	Bad	Bad	Bad	Fair	Bad	57,27,5,35,9,9,75	617

SHOPPING	GAMBLE	SEX	KEYWORD	KEYWORD
Fair	Bad	is frustrating	POWER	Responsibilty,Disagreement,Family,Back Pain,Family Conflicts,Traffic

STRESS LEVEL	LUCKY COLORS	JEWELERY	MOONS EFFECT	GRAHA EFFECT	DAILY DEITY
High	Purple/Blue/Rose	Emerald/Saphire	Educational	Family Graha	Mahakali

DAILY PUJA	DAILY PSALMS
Meditate, Control temper, Pray to Hanuman, Chant Hanuman Chalisa	6, 15, 33 ,42, 51, 60, 78, 105, 123

Tuesday, April 18, 2023 — This is considered a NEUTRAL day for you — Planet: Uranus

ADVICE & DETAILS

Find a reprieve from the weariness of everyday building your professional life by finding a book and reading about something that interests you and makes you happy.

MANTRA FOR TODAY
Jai Jai Shiva Shambo.(2) ...Mahadeva Shambo (2) 21 times 8

MONEY	LOVE	CAREER	FAMILY	TRAVEL	WEDDING	MOVE	BUSINESS	HEALTH	Lotto #'s	play 3 #s
Good	Good	Fair	Good	Good	Bad	Good	Bad	Fair	75,5,71,19,73,59,63	258

SHOPPING	GAMBLE	SEX	KEYWORD	KEYWORD
Bad	Fair	is quiet	DIVINE	Spirituality,Religious,Astrology,Inner Conflicts,Religious ,Sleepiness,Advice

STRESS LEVEL	LUCKY COLORS	JEWELERY	MOONS EFFECT	GRAHA EFFECT	DAILY DEITY
Fair	Light Blue/Peach	Tiger's eye/Gold/Sil	Affectionate	God'S Graha	Shesnaag

DAILY PUJA	DAILY PSALMS
Chant Shiva Mantras, Take gifts to Ocean - Ganga Puja, Donate to Temple, Priests, etc.	7, 16, 34 ,43, 52, 61, 79, 106, 124

Wednesday, April 19, 2023			This is considered a POSITIVE day for you					Planet:	Jupiter	
ADVICE & DETAILS								MANTRA FOR TODAY		
Dealings with Real Estate of things related to your professional life may bring beauty and sex into your realm. You will feel fatigued during the day.								Om Hareem Nama Swaha..Shri Maha Laxmi Aye Namah swaha 12 times		

MONEY	LOVE	CAREER	FAMILY	TRAVEL	WEDDING	MOVE	BUSINESS	HEALTH	Lotto #'s	play 3 #s
Excellent	Good	Excellent	Good	Good	Excellent	Good	Excellent	Excellent	22,37,70,24,1,66,9	97

SHOPPING	GAMBLE	SEX	KEYWORD	KEYWORD						
Excellent	Excellent	is excellent	MONEY	Business,Major Expense,Money -						

STRESS LEVEL		LUCKY COLORS		JEWELERY	MOONS EFFECT	GRAHA EFFECT		DAILY DEITY	
Low		Yellow/Silver		Diamonds/Gold/Pea	Secretive	Money Graha		Mahalaxmi	

DAILY PUJA	DAILY PSALMS
Decorate Land, Feed the poor, Donate milk /products to all, Feed holy guests,	8, 17, 35 ,44, 53, 62, 80, 107, 125

Thursday, April 20, 2023			This is considered a NEGATIVE day for you					Planet:	Saturn	
ADVICE & DETAILS								MANTRA FOR TODAY		
Be ready to face job difficulties that may come to you today centered in your godliness not your ego. Remember this day is part of your career and the long-term goals you have.								Om Ganga mataye nama swaha Om Varuna Devta aye Pahimam 11 times		

MONEY	LOVE	CAREER	FAMILY	TRAVEL	WEDDING	MOVE	BUSINESS	HEALTH	Lotto #'s	play 3 #s
Bad	Bad	Bad	Fair	Bad	Bad	Bad	Bad	Bad	50,64,43,70,40,13,3	403

SHOPPING	GAMBLE	SEX	KEYWORD	KEYWORD						
Bad	Bad	is very bad	KARMA	Destruction,Losses,Death,Sickness - cold,Legal matter,Abusive,Karmic debts,God -						

STRESS LEVEL		LUCKY COLORS		JEWELERY	MOONS EFFECT	GRAHA EFFECT		DAILY DEITY	
High		Gold/Brown//Green		Saphire/Hessonite	Ivestments	Evil Graha		Agnidev	

DAILY PUJA	DAILY PSALMS
Remembrance of family members who died, worship of older people. gifts to grand parents	9, 18, 36 ,45, 54, 63, 81, 108, 126

Friday, April 21, 2023			This is considered a NEUTRAL day for you					Planet:	Sun	
ADVICE & DETAILS								MANTRA FOR TODAY		
Assiduous dedication to your tasks and responsibilities will be rewarded today. It will be a day when you are busy, but being indolent today will cost you dearly in financial opportunities.								Om Namo Bhagawate Mukhtanandaya, 108 times		

MONEY	LOVE	CAREER	FAMILY	TRAVEL	WEDDING	MOVE	BUSINESS	HEALTH	Lotto #'s	play 3 #s
Fair	Bad	Good	Bad	Fair	Bad	Fair	Fair	Fair	69,18,75,73,39,22,3	384

SHOPPING	GAMBLE	SEX	KEYWORD	KEYWORD						
Fair	Fair	is fair	MIND	Independence,Loneliness,Meditative,Worry,Dominating,Illness - Cold,On Your						

STRESS LEVEL		LUCKY COLORS		JEWELERY	MOONS EFFECT	GRAHA EFFECT		DAILY DEITY	
High		White/Yellow/		Pearl/Quartz	Arrogance	Status Graha		Saraswaty	

DAILY PUJA	DAILY PSALMS
Give Gifts to Priests, Invite holy ones to your home, Feed Swamis and Yogis, Do Shiva Puja.	1, 10, 28 ,37, 46, 55, 73, 100, 118

Saturday, April 22, 2023			This is considered a POSITIVE day for you					Planet:	Moon	
ADVICE & DETAILS								MANTRA FOR TODAY		
Your karma for today requires you to be industrious and work very hard. You must put your laziness away. Associates will give you positive input and/or help.								Kali Durge Namo Nama Om Durge aye nama swaha 108 times		

MONEY	LOVE	CAREER	FAMILY	TRAVEL	WEDDING	MOVE	BUSINESS	HEALTH	Lotto #'s	play 3 #s
Good	Excellent	Good	Good	Excellen	Good	Good	Good	Good	75,25,48,6,7,26,63	454

SHOPPING	GAMBLE	SEX	KEYWORD	KEYWORD						
Good	Good	is good	LOVE	Romance,Popularity,Visitors,Shopping,Food, Drinks,Co-						

STRESS LEVEL		LUCKY COLORS		JEWELERY	MOONS EFFECT	GRAHA EFFECT		DAILY DEITY	
Low		Red/Yellow/Pink		Topaz/Diamonds	Conservative	Love Graha		Gauri	

DAILY PUJA	DAILY PSALMS
Give Gifts to females andnMother, Serve milk Products, Worship Durga forms	2, 11, 29 ,38, 47, 56, 74, 101, 119

Sunday, April 23, 2023 — This is considered a POSITIVE day for you — Planet: Mercury

ADVICE & DETAILS

Today is a day to work and work even if you feel lazy. You need to be industrious and achieve all tasks that you can today. You will be in association with others while doing these projects, accept the input.

MANTRA FOR TODAY

Om hareem Kleem Hreem Aem Saraswataye namaha 21 times

MONEY	LOVE	CAREER	FAMILY	TRAVEL	WEDDING	MOVE	BUSINESS	HEALTH	Lotto #'s	play 3 #s
Good	Fair	Good	Good	Excellen	Good	Good	Good	Excellent	3,60,29,36,72,5,5	522

SHOPPING	GAMBLE	SEX	KEYWORD	KEYWORD						
Good	Good	is great	SOCIAL	Children,Education,Astrology,Bargains,Social Functions,Childishness,Groups -						

STRESS LEVEL	LUCKY COLORS	JEWELERY	MOONS EFFECT	GRAHA EFFECT	DAILY DEITY
Low	Green/Sky Blue/	Diamonds/Silver	Enthusiastic	Social Graha	Vishnu

DAILY PUJA	DAILY PSALMS
Wash the feet of Children, Do Satnarayan Pooja, Read & chant Geeta	3, 12, 30 ,39, 48, 57, 75, 102, 120

Monday, April 24, 2023 — This is considered a NEGATIVE day for you — Planet: Pluto

ADVICE & DETAILS

Today you feel lazy, but you will need to work, be industrious and accomplish as much as possible. You will need to control your high temper and accept that today you will feel like they do not pay you enough to do your job.

MANTRA FOR TODAY

Om Jai Viganeshwaraya.. Lambodaraya Namo Namaha 21 times

MONEY	LOVE	CAREER	FAMILY	TRAVEL	WEDDING	MOVE	BUSINESS	HEALTH	Lotto #'s	play 3 #s
Bad	Fair	Bad	Fair	Bad	Good	Bad	Bad	Bad	57,48,34,60,13,32,5	224

SHOPPING	GAMBLE	SEX	KEYWORD	KEYWORD						
Bad	Bad	is tough	CAREER	Career,Hard Work,Co-workers,Low Payment,Job Problems,High Temper,Low						

STRESS LEVEL	LUCKY COLORS	JEWELERY	MOONS EFFECT	GRAHA EFFECT	DAILY DEITY
High	Dark Blue/ Purple/	Amethyst/Gold	Emotional	Job Graha	Lingam

DAILY PUJA	DAILY PSALMS
Worship Ganesh, Give gifts to father, and co -workers, Plant gardens, farms	4, 13, 31 ,40, 49, 58, 76, 103, 121

Tuesday, April 25, 2023 — This is considered a POSITIVE day for you — Planet: Venus

ADVICE & DETAILS

Do not allow the job problems that you may have today to affect your long-term career plans. Remember the foundation of your career is built on a day per day basis at your job. Act and think conscious of your godliness.

MANTRA FOR TODAY

Om Graam Greem Graum Sa Gurave namah swaha 21 times

MONEY	LOVE	CAREER	FAMILY	TRAVEL	WEDDING	MOVE	BUSINESS	HEALTH	Lotto #'s	play 3 #s
Bad	Excellent	Fair	Good	Excellen	Good	Excellen	Good	Excellent	71,34,38,41,64,65,5	259

SHOPPING	GAMBLE	SEX	KEYWORD	KEYWORD						
Good	Good	is good	CHANGE	Sexuality,Travel,Change,Distant, far,Travel delays,Deception,Excercise,Illicit						

STRESS LEVEL	LUCKY COLORS	JEWELERY	MOONS EFFECT	GRAHA EFFECT	DAILY DEITY
Fair	Tan/Green/ Beige	Pearl/Silver/quartz	Courageous	Travel Graha	Nataraja

DAILY PUJA	DAILY PSALMS
Artistic gifts, Pray to Krishna, Do good deeds, do Spiritual trips	5, 14, 32 ,41, 50, 59, 77, 104, 122

Wednesday, April 26, 2023 — This is considered a NEGATIVE day for you — Planet: Mars

ADVICE & DETAILS

You are going to feel very lazy today, but you must push through this feeling and devote your day to work with others and work diligently.

MANTRA FOR TODAY

Om Mana Swasti Shanti Kuru kuru Swaha Shivoham Shivoham 27 times

MONEY	LOVE	CAREER	FAMILY	TRAVEL	WEDDING	MOVE	BUSINESS	HEALTH	Lotto #'s	play 3 #s
Bad	Bad	Bad	Bad	Bad	Bad	Bad	Fair	Bad	64,49,41,59,26,10,3	202

SHOPPING	GAMBLE	SEX	KEYWORD	KEYWORD						
Fair	Bad	is frustrating	POWER	Responsibilty,Disagreement,Family,Back Pain,Family Conflicts,Traffic						

STRESS LEVEL	LUCKY COLORS	JEWELERY	MOONS EFFECT	GRAHA EFFECT	DAILY DEITY
High	Purple/Blue/Rose	Emerald/Saphire	Educational	Family Graha	Mahakali

DAILY PUJA	DAILY PSALMS
Meditate, Control temper, Pray to Hanuman, Chant Hanuman Chalisa	6, 15, 33 ,42, 51, 60, 78, 105, 123

Thursday, April 27, 2023 — This is considered a NEUTRAL day for you — Planet: Uranus

ADVICE & DETAILS

Find a reprieve from the weariness of everyday building your professional life by finding a book and reading about something that interests you and makes you happy.

MANTRA FOR TODAY

Jai Jai Shiva Shambo.(2) ...Mahadeva Shambo (2) 21 times 8

MONEY	LOVE	CAREER	FAMILY	TRAVEL	WEDDING	MOVE	BUSINESS	HEALTH	Lotto #'s	play 3 #s
Good	Good	Fair	Good	Good	Bad	Good	Bad	Fair	57,15,73,9,9,30,24	937

SHOPPING	GAMBLE	SEX	KEYWORD	KEYWORD
Bad	Fair	is quiet	DIVINE	Spirituality,Religious,Astrology,Inner Conflicts,Religious ,Sleepiness,Advice

STRESS LEVEL	LUCKY COLORS	JEWELERY	MOONS EFFECT	GRAHA EFFECT	DAILY DEITY
Fair	Light Blue/Peach	Tiger's eye/Gold/Sil	Affectionate	God'S Graha	Shesnaag

DAILY PUJA	DAILY PSALMS
Chant Shiva Mantras, Take gifts to Ocean - Ganga Puja, Donate to Temple, Priests, etc.	7, 16, 34 ,43, 52, 61, 79, 106, 124

Friday, April 28, 2023 — This is considered a POSITIVE day for you — Planet: Jupiter

ADVICE & DETAILS

Dealings with Real Estate of things related to your professional life may bring beauty and sex into your realm. You will feel fatigued during the day.

MANTRA FOR TODAY

Om Hareem Nama Swaha..Shri Maha Laxmi Aye Namah swaha 12 times

MONEY	LOVE	CAREER	FAMILY	TRAVEL	WEDDING	MOVE	BUSINESS	HEALTH	Lotto #'s	play 3 #s
Excellent	Good	Excellent	Good	Good	Excellent	Good	Excellent	Excellent	22,47,34,31,69,26,1	512

SHOPPING	GAMBLE	SEX	KEYWORD	KEYWORD
Excellent	Excellent	is excellent	MONEY	Business,Major Expense,Money -

STRESS LEVEL	LUCKY COLORS	JEWELERY	MOONS EFFECT	GRAHA EFFECT	DAILY DEITY
Low	Yellow/Silver	Diamonds/Gold/Pea	Secretive	Money Graha	Mahalaxmi

DAILY PUJA	DAILY PSALMS
Decorate Land, Feed the poor, Donate milk /products to all, Feed holy guests,	8, 17, 35 ,44, 53, 62, 80, 107, 125

Saturday, April 29, 2023 — This is considered a NEGATIVE day for you — Planet: Saturn

ADVICE & DETAILS

Be ready to face job difficulties that may come to you today centered in your godliness not your ego. Remember this day is part of your career and the long-term goals you have.

MANTRA FOR TODAY

Om Ganga mataye nama swaha Om Varuna Devta aye Pahimam 11 times

MONEY	LOVE	CAREER	FAMILY	TRAVEL	WEDDING	MOVE	BUSINESS	HEALTH	Lotto #'s	play 3 #s
Bad	Bad	Bad	Fair	Bad	Bad	Bad	Bad	Bad	73,45,73,18,6,45,39	125

SHOPPING	GAMBLE	SEX	KEYWORD	KEYWORD
Bad	Bad	is very bad	KARMA	Destruction,Losses,Death,Sickness - cold,Legal matter,Abusive,Karmic debts,God -

STRESS LEVEL	LUCKY COLORS	JEWELERY	MOONS EFFECT	GRAHA EFFECT	DAILY DEITY
High	Gold/Brown//Green	Saphire/Hessonite	Ivestments	Evil Graha	Agnidev

DAILY PUJA	DAILY PSALMS
Remembrance of family members who died, worship of older people. gifts to grand parents	9, 18, 36 ,45, 54, 63, 81, 108, 126

Sunday, April 30, 2023 — This is considered a NEUTRAL day for you — Planet: Sun

ADVICE & DETAILS

Assiduous dedication to your tasks and responsibilities will be rewarded today. It will be a day when you are busy, but being indolent today will cost you dearly in financial opportunities.

MANTRA FOR TODAY

Om Namo Bhagawate Mukhtanandaya, 108 times

MONEY	LOVE	CAREER	FAMILY	TRAVEL	WEDDING	MOVE	BUSINESS	HEALTH	Lotto #'s	play 3 #s
Fair	Bad	Good	Bad	Fair	Bad	Fair	Fair	Fair	23,20,56,36,22,8,59	587

SHOPPING	GAMBLE	SEX	KEYWORD	KEYWORD
Fair	Fair	is fair	MIND	Independence,Loneliness,Meditative,Worry,Dominating,Illness - Cold,On Your

STRESS LEVEL	LUCKY COLORS	JEWELERY	MOONS EFFECT	GRAHA EFFECT	DAILY DEITY
High	White/Yellow/	Pearl/Quartz	Arrogance	Status Graha	Saraswaty

DAILY PUJA	DAILY PSALMS
Give Gifts to Priests, Invite holy ones to your home, Feed Swamis and Yogis, Do Shiva Puja.	1, 10, 28 ,37, 46, 55, 73, 100, 118

Monday, May 1, 2023 — This is considered a POSITIVE day for you — Planet: Jupiter

ADVICE & DETAILS

There will be moving to and from today. You will experience great pleasure today and will also have to deal with money either receiving it or paying it out. You may be watching TV or meeting someone known related to the entertainment industry.

MANTRA FOR TODAY

Om Hareem Nama Swaha..Shri Maha Laxmi Aye Namah swaha 12 times

MONEY	LOVE	CAREER	FAMILY	TRAVEL	WEDDING	MOVE	BUSINESS	HEALTH	Lotto #'s	play 3 #s
Excellent	Good	Excellent	Good	Good	Excellent	Good	Excellent	Excellent	5,12,24,37,24,13,4	43

SHOPPING	GAMBLE	SEX	KEYWORD	KEYWORD						
Excellent	Excellent	is excellent	MONEY	Business,Major Expense,Money -						

STRESS LEVEL	LUCKY COLORS	JEWELERY	MOONS EFFECT	GRAHA EFFECT	DAILY DEITY
Low	Yellow/Silver	Diamonds/Gold/Pea	Secretive	Money Graha	Mahalaxmi

DAILY PUJA	DAILY PSALMS
Decorate Land, Feed the poor, Donate milk /products to all, Feed holy guests,	8, 17, 35 ,44, 53, 62, 80, 107, 125

Tuesday, May 2, 2023 — This is considered a NEGATIVE day for you — Planet: Saturn

ADVICE & DETAILS

This day is influenced by changes, moves and trips to close by locations. You will change your mind often and this lack of focus may cause you to get into an accident. Try to stay focused on your goals and minimize the multitasking especially when driving from one place to another.

MANTRA FOR TODAY

Om Ganga mataye nama swaha Om Varuna Devta aye Pahimam 11 times

MONEY	LOVE	CAREER	FAMILY	TRAVEL	WEDDING	MOVE	BUSINESS	HEALTH	Lotto #'s	play 3 #s
Bad	Bad	Bad	Fair	Bad	Bad	Bad	Bad	Bad	20,57,26,4,58,20,53	551

SHOPPING	GAMBLE	SEX	KEYWORD	KEYWORD						
Bad	Bad	is very bad	KARMA	Destruction,Losses,Death,Sickness - cold,Legal matter,Abusive,Karmic debts,God -						

STRESS LEVEL	LUCKY COLORS	JEWELERY	MOONS EFFECT	GRAHA EFFECT	DAILY DEITY
High	Gold/Brown//Green	Saphire/Hessonite	Ivestments	Evil Graha	Agnidev

DAILY PUJA	DAILY PSALMS
Remembrance of family members who died, worship of older people. gifts to grand parents	9, 18, 36 ,45, 54, 63, 81, 108, 126

Wednesday, May 3, 2023 — This is considered a NEUTRAL day for you — Planet: Sun

ADVICE & DETAILS

Sex appeal and beauty are important to you today. You must control your ego-based anger and try to understand that every thing in the universe is in perfect order. You will experience travel and changes today

MANTRA FOR TODAY

Om Namo Bhagawate Mukhtanandaya, 108 times

MONEY	LOVE	CAREER	FAMILY	TRAVEL	WEDDING	MOVE	BUSINESS	HEALTH	Lotto #'s	play 3 #s
Fair	Bad	Good	Bad	Fair	Bad	Fair	Fair	Fair	71,65,54,9,12,18,6	291

SHOPPING	GAMBLE	SEX	KEYWORD	KEYWORD						
Fair	Fair	is fair	MIND	Independence,Loneliness,Meditative,Worry,Dominating,Illness - Cold,On Your						

STRESS LEVEL	LUCKY COLORS	JEWELERY	MOONS EFFECT	GRAHA EFFECT	DAILY DEITY
High	White/Yellow/	Pearl/Quartz	Arrogance	Status Graha	Saraswaty

DAILY PUJA	DAILY PSALMS
Give Gifts to Priests, Invite holy ones to your home, Feed Swamis and Yogis, Do Shiva Puja.	1, 10, 28 ,37, 46, 55, 73, 100, 118

Thursday, May 4, 2023 — This is considered a POSITIVE day for you — Planet: Moon

ADVICE & DETAILS

Sexual energy is very high today. It is a good time to enjoy the company of your lover. Do not trust the words of others that may be deceiving, and make sure you are not deceiving others with your words. Accept all changes in your life gracefully.

MANTRA FOR TODAY

Kali Durge Namo Nama Om Durge aye nama swaha 108 times

MONEY	LOVE	CAREER	FAMILY	TRAVEL	WEDDING	MOVE	BUSINESS	HEALTH	Lotto #'s	play 3 #s
Good	Excellent	Good	Good	Excellen	Good	Good	Good	Good	25,12,57,17,5,23,9	523

SHOPPING	GAMBLE	SEX	KEYWORD	KEYWORD						
Good	Good	is good	LOVE	Romance,Popularity,Visitors,Shopping,Food, Drinks,Co-						

STRESS LEVEL	LUCKY COLORS	JEWELERY	MOONS EFFECT	GRAHA EFFECT	DAILY DEITY
Low	Red/Yellow/Pink	Topaz/Diamonds	Conservative	Love Graha	Gauri

DAILY PUJA	DAILY PSALMS
Give Gifts to females andnMother, Serve milk Products, Worship Durga forms	2, 11, 29 ,38, 47, 56, 74, 101, 119

Friday, May 5, 2023 — This is considered a POSITIVE day for you — Planet: Mercury

ADVICE & DETAILS

You will probably experience some type of short trip and/or moving today. Communication is important today so think carefully, speak clearly and listen with intent to transfer messages correctly.

MANTRA FOR TODAY: Om hareem Kleem Hreem Aem Saraswataye namaha 21 times

MONEY	LOVE	CAREER	FAMILY	TRAVEL	WEDDING	MOVE	BUSINESS	HEALTH	Lotto #'s	play 3 #s
Good	Fair	Good	Good	Excellen	Good	Good	Good	Excellent	29,14,59,38,70,6,39	61

SHOPPING	GAMBLE	SEX	KEYWORD	KEYWORD
Good	Good	is great	SOCIAL	Children,Education,Astrology,Bargains,Social Functions,Childishness,Groups -

STRESS LEVEL	LUCKY COLORS	JEWELERY	MOONS EFFECT	GRAHA EFFECT	DAILY DEITY
Low	Green/Sky Blue/	Diamonds/Silver	Enthusiastic	Social Graha	Vishnu

DAILY PUJA: Wash the feet of Children, Do Satnarayan Pooja, Read & chant Geeta

DAILY PSALMS: 3, 12, 30 ,39, 48, 57, 75, 102, 120

Saturday, May 6, 2023 — This is considered a NEGATIVE day for you — Planet: Pluto

ADVICE & DETAILS

You may be deceived today perhaps by a sexual partner or someone else. Use your words carefully today, they are powerful and will have serious consequences. There will be many changes today, make sure you stay truthful regardless.

MANTRA FOR TODAY: Om Jai Viganeshwaraya.. Lambodaraya Namo Namaha 21 times

MONEY	LOVE	CAREER	FAMILY	TRAVEL	WEDDING	MOVE	BUSINESS	HEALTH	Lotto #'s	play 3 #s
Bad	Fair	Bad	Fair	Bad	Good	Bad	Bad	Bad	18,48,10,1,53,30,71	987

SHOPPING	GAMBLE	SEX	KEYWORD	KEYWORD
Bad	Bad	is tough	CAREER	Career,Hard Work,Co-workers,Low Payment,Job Problems,High Temper,Low

STRESS LEVEL	LUCKY COLORS	JEWELERY	MOONS EFFECT	GRAHA EFFECT	DAILY DEITY
High	Dark Blue/ Purple/	Amethyst/Gold	Emotional	Job Graha	Lingam

DAILY PUJA: Worship Ganesh, Give gifts to father, and co -workers, Plant gardens, farms

DAILY PSALMS: 4, 13, 31 ,40, 49, 58, 76, 103, 121

Sunday, May 7, 2023 — This is considered a POSITIVE day for you — Planet: Venus

ADVICE & DETAILS

This day is influenced by changes, moves and trips to close by locations. You will change your mind often and this lack of focus may cause you to get into an accident. Try to stay focused on your goals and minimize the multitasking especially when driving from one place to another.

MANTRA FOR TODAY: Om Graam Greem Graum Sa Gurave namah swaha 21 times

MONEY	LOVE	CAREER	FAMILY	TRAVEL	WEDDING	MOVE	BUSINESS	HEALTH	Lotto #'s	play 3 #s
Bad	Excellent	Fair	Good	Excellen	Good	Excellen	Good	Excellent	49,27,34,47,66,53,5	890

SHOPPING	GAMBLE	SEX	KEYWORD	KEYWORD
Good	Good	is good	CHANGE	Sexuality,Travel,Change,Distant, far,Travel delays,Deception,Excercise,Illicit

STRESS LEVEL	LUCKY COLORS	JEWELERY	MOONS EFFECT	GRAHA EFFECT	DAILY DEITY
Fair	Tan/Green/ Beige	Pearl/Silver/quartz	Courageous	Travel Graha	Nataraja

DAILY PUJA: Artistic gifts, Pray to Krishna, Do good deeds, do Spiritual trips

DAILY PSALMS: 5, 14, 32 ,41, 50, 59, 77, 104, 122

Monday, May 8, 2023 — This is considered a NEGATIVE day for you — Planet: Mars

ADVICE & DETAILS

This day you may feel a bit sad and depressed over health matters and some other type of personal losses. Center your thougts in divine spiritual and religious ideas and try to have an attitude of gratitude to receive blessings.

MANTRA FOR TODAY: Om Mana Swasti Shanti Kuru kuru Swaha Shivoham Shivoham 27 times

MONEY	LOVE	CAREER	FAMILY	TRAVEL	WEDDING	MOVE	BUSINESS	HEALTH	Lotto #'s	play 3 #s
Bad	Bad	Bad	Bad	Bad	Bad	Bad	Fair	Bad	17,35,33,63,61,48,7	248

SHOPPING	GAMBLE	SEX	KEYWORD	KEYWORD
Fair	Bad	is frustrating	POWER	Responsibilty,Disagreement,Family,Back Pain,Family Conflicts,Traffic

STRESS LEVEL	LUCKY COLORS	JEWELERY	MOONS EFFECT	GRAHA EFFECT	DAILY DEITY
High	Purple/Blue/Rose	Emerald/Saphire	Educational	Family Graha	Mahakali

DAILY PUJA: Meditate, Control temper, Pray to Hanuman, Chant Hanuman Chalisa

DAILY PSALMS: 6, 15, 33 ,42, 51, 60, 78, 105, 123

Tuesday, May 9, 2023 — This is considered a NEUTRAL day for you — Planet: Uranus

ADVICE & DETAILS

This is a day of great movement and many short trips. There may be changes in mood, ideas, location, etc. Communication is very important today, make sure other understand what you are trying to say and verify that what you understood is what was said to you.

MANTRA FOR TODAY

Jai Jai Shiva Shambo.(2) ...Mahadeva Shambo (2) 21 times 8

MONEY	LOVE	CAREER	FAMILY	TRAVEL	WEDDING	MOVE	BUSINESS	HEALTH	Lotto #'s	play 3 #s
Good	Good	Fair	Good	Good	Bad	Good	Bad	Fair	27,69,72,44,36,65,4	953

SHOPPING	GAMBLE	SEX	KEYWORD	KEYWORD						
Bad	Fair	is quiet	DIVINE	Spirituality,Religious,Astrology,Inner Conflicts,Religious ,Sleepiness,Advice						

STRESS LEVEL	LUCKY COLORS	JEWELERY	MOONS EFFECT	GRAHA EFFECT	DAILY DEITY
Fair	Light Blue/Peach	Tiger's eye/Gold/Sil	Affectionate	God'S Graha	Shesnaag

DAILY PUJA
Chant Shiva Mantras, Take gifts to Ocean - Ganga Puja, Donate to Temple, Priests, etc.

DAILY PSALMS
7, 16, 34 ,43, 52, 61, 79, 106, 124

Wednesday, May 10, 2023 — This is considered a POSITIVE day for you — Planet: Jupiter

ADVICE & DETAILS

There will be moving to and from today. You will experience great pleasure today and will also have to deal with money either receiving it or paying it out. You may be watching TV or meeting someone known related to the entertainment industry.

MANTRA FOR TODAY

Om Hareem Nama Swaha..Shri Maha Laxmi Aye Namah swaha 12 times

MONEY	LOVE	CAREER	FAMILY	TRAVEL	WEDDING	MOVE	BUSINESS	HEALTH	Lotto #'s	play 3 #s
Excellent	Good	Excellent	Good	Good	Excellent	Good	Excellent	Excellent	45,20,12,1,73,60,51	305

SHOPPING	GAMBLE	SEX	KEYWORD	KEYWORD						
Excellent	Excellent	is excellent	MONEY	Business,Major Expense,Money -						

STRESS LEVEL	LUCKY COLORS	JEWELERY	MOONS EFFECT	GRAHA EFFECT	DAILY DEITY
Low	Yellow/Silver	Diamonds/Gold/Pea	Secretive	Money Graha	Mahalaxmi

DAILY PUJA
Decorate Land, Feed the poor, Donate milk /products to all, Feed holy guests,

DAILY PSALMS
8, 17, 35 ,44, 53, 62, 80, 107, 125

Thursday, May 11, 2023 — This is considered a NEGATIVE day for you — Planet: Saturn

ADVICE & DETAILS

This day is influenced by changes, moves and trips to close by locations. You will change your mind often and this lack of focus may cause you to get into an accident. Try to stay focused on your goals and minimize the multitasking especially when driving from one place to another.

MANTRA FOR TODAY

Om Ganga mataye nama swaha Om Varuna Devta aye Pahimam 11 times

MONEY	LOVE	CAREER	FAMILY	TRAVEL	WEDDING	MOVE	BUSINESS	HEALTH	Lotto #'s	play 3 #s
Bad	Bad	Bad	Fair	Bad	Bad	Bad	Bad	Bad	8,38,31,55,55,3,62	884

SHOPPING	GAMBLE	SEX	KEYWORD	KEYWORD						
Bad	Bad	is very bad	KARMA	Destruction,Losses,Death,Sickness - cold,Legal matter,Abusive,Karmic debts,God -						

STRESS LEVEL	LUCKY COLORS	JEWELERY	MOONS EFFECT	GRAHA EFFECT	DAILY DEITY
High	Gold/Brown//Green	Saphire/Hessonite	Ivestments	Evil Graha	Agnidev

DAILY PUJA
Remembrance of family members who died, worship of older people. gifts to grand parents

DAILY PSALMS
9, 18, 36 ,45, 54, 63, 81, 108, 126

Friday, May 12, 2023 — This is considered a NEUTRAL day for you — Planet: Sun

ADVICE & DETAILS

Sex appeal and beauty are important to you today. You must control your ego-based anger and try to understand that every thing in the universe is in perfect order. You will experience travel and changes today

MANTRA FOR TODAY

Om Namo Bhagawate Mukhtanandaya, 108 times

MONEY	LOVE	CAREER	FAMILY	TRAVEL	WEDDING	MOVE	BUSINESS	HEALTH	Lotto #'s	play 3 #s
Fair	Bad	Good	Bad	Fair	Bad	Fair	Fair	Fair	41,33,72,63,12,41,7	320

SHOPPING	GAMBLE	SEX	KEYWORD	KEYWORD						
Fair	Fair	is fair	MIND	Independence,Loneliness,Meditative,Worry,Dominating,Illness - Cold,On Your						

STRESS LEVEL	LUCKY COLORS	JEWELERY	MOONS EFFECT	GRAHA EFFECT	DAILY DEITY
High	White/Yellow/	Pearl/Quartz	Arrogance	Status Graha	Saraswaty

DAILY PUJA
Give Gifts to Priests, Invite holy ones to your home, Feed Swamis and Yogis, Do Shiva Puja.

DAILY PSALMS
1, 10, 28 ,37, 46, 55, 73, 100, 118

Saturday, May 13, 2023 — This is considered a POSITIVE day for you — Planet: Moon

ADVICE & DETAILS

Sexual energy is very high today. It is a good time to enjoy the company of your lover. Do not trust the words of others that may be deceiving, and make sure you are not deceiving others with your words. Accept all changes in your life gracefully.

MANTRA FOR TODAY

Kali Durge Namo Nama Om Durge aye nama swaha 108 times

MONEY	LOVE	CAREER	FAMILY	TRAVEL	WEDDING	MOVE	BUSINESS	HEALTH	Lotto #'s	play 3 #s
Good	Excellent	Good	Good	Excellen	Good	Good	Good	Good	17,55,59,75,68,60,5	172

SHOPPING	GAMBLE	SEX	KEYWORD	KEYWORD						
Good	Good	is good	LOVE	Romance,Popularity,Visitors,Shopping,Food, Drinks,Co-						

STRESS LEVEL		LUCKY COLORS	JEWELERY	MOONS EFFECT	GRAHA EFFECT	DAILY DEITY
Low		Red/Yellow/Pink	Topaz/Diamonds	Conservative	Love Graha	Gauri

DAILY PUJA	DAILY PSALMS
Give Gifts to females andnMother, Serve milk Products, Worship Durga forms	2, 11, 29 ,38, 47, 56, 74, 101, 119

Sunday, May 14, 2023 — This is considered a POSITIVE day for you — Planet: Mercury

ADVICE & DETAILS

You will probably experience some type of short trip and/or moving today. Communication is important today so think carefully, speak clearly and listen with intent to transfer messages correctly.

MANTRA FOR TODAY

Om hareem Kleem Hreem Aem Saraswataye namaha 21 times

MONEY	LOVE	CAREER	FAMILY	TRAVEL	WEDDING	MOVE	BUSINESS	HEALTH	Lotto #'s	play 3 #s
Good	Fair	Good	Good	Excellen	Good	Good	Good	Excellent	53,52,35,69,69,6,14	707

SHOPPING	GAMBLE	SEX	KEYWORD	KEYWORD						
Good	Good	is great	SOCIAL	Children,Education,Astrology,Bargains,Social Functions,Childishness,Groups -						

STRESS LEVEL		LUCKY COLORS	JEWELERY	MOONS EFFECT	GRAHA EFFECT	DAILY DEITY
Low		Green/Sky Blue/	Diamonds/Silver	Enthusiastic	Social Graha	Vishnu

DAILY PUJA	DAILY PSALMS
Wash the feet of Children, Do Satnarayan Pooja, Read & chant Geeta	3, 12, 30 ,39, 48, 57, 75, 102, 120

Monday, May 15, 2023 — This is considered a NEGATIVE day for you — Planet: Pluto

ADVICE & DETAILS

You may be deceived today perhaps by a sexual partner or someone else. Use your words carefully today, they are powerful and will have serious consequences. There will be many changes today, make sure you stay truthful regardless.

MANTRA FOR TODAY

Om Jai Viganeshwaraya.. Lambodaraya Namo Namaha 21 times

MONEY	LOVE	CAREER	FAMILY	TRAVEL	WEDDING	MOVE	BUSINESS	HEALTH	Lotto #'s	play 3 #s
Bad	Fair	Bad	Fair	Bad	Good	Bad	Bad	Bad	30,41,2,36,74,54,54	179

SHOPPING	GAMBLE	SEX	KEYWORD	KEYWORD						
Bad	Bad	is tough	CAREER	Career,Hard Work,Co-workers,Low Payment,Job Problems,High Temper,Low						

STRESS LEVEL		LUCKY COLORS	JEWELERY	MOONS EFFECT	GRAHA EFFECT	DAILY DEITY
High		Dark Blue/ Purple/	Amethyst/Gold	Emotional	Job Graha	Lingam

DAILY PUJA	DAILY PSALMS
Worship Ganesh, Give gifts to father, and co -workers, Plant gardens, farms	4, 13, 31 ,40, 49, 58, 76, 103, 121

Tuesday, May 16, 2023 — This is considered a POSITIVE day for you — Planet: Venus

ADVICE & DETAILS

This day is influenced by changes, moves and trips to close by locations. You will change your mind often and this lack of focus may cause you to get into an accident. Try to stay focused on your goals and minimize the multitasking especially when driving from one place to another.

MANTRA FOR TODAY

Om Graam Greem Graum Sa Gurave namah swaha 21 times

MONEY	LOVE	CAREER	FAMILY	TRAVEL	WEDDING	MOVE	BUSINESS	HEALTH	Lotto #'s	play 3 #s
Bad	Excellent	Fair	Good	Excellen	Good	Excellen	Good	Excellent	29,4,46,22,45,36,6	942

SHOPPING	GAMBLE	SEX	KEYWORD	KEYWORD						
Good	Good	is good	CHANGE	Sexuality,Travel,Change,Distant, far,Travel delays,Deception,Excercise,Illicit						

STRESS LEVEL		LUCKY COLORS	JEWELERY	MOONS EFFECT	GRAHA EFFECT	DAILY DEITY
Fair		Tan/Green/ Beige	Pearl/Silver/quartz	Courageous	Travel Graha	Nataraja

DAILY PUJA	DAILY PSALMS
Artistic gifts, Pray to Krishna, Do good deeds, do Spiritual trips	5, 14, 32 ,41, 50, 59, 77, 104, 122

Wednesday, May 17, 2023 — This is considered a NEGATIVE day for you — Planet: Mars

ADVICE & DETAILS

This day you may feel a bit sad and depressed over health matters and some other type of personal losses. Center your thougts in divine spiritual and religious ideas and try to have an attitude of gratitude to receive blessings.

MANTRA FOR TODAY

Om Mana Swasti Shanti Kuru kuru Swaha Shivoham Shivoham 27 times

MONEY	LOVE	CAREER	FAMILY	TRAVEL	WEDDING	MOVE	BUSINESS	HEALTH	Lotto #'s	play 3 #s
Bad	Bad	Bad	Bad	Bad	Bad	Bad	Fair	Bad	18,12,6,9,23,62,21	586

SHOPPING	GAMBLE	SEX	KEYWORD	KEYWORD
Fair	Bad	is frustrating	POWER	Responsibilty,Disagreement,Family,Back Pain,Family Conflicts,Traffic

STRESS LEVEL	LUCKY COLORS	JEWELERY	MOONS EFFECT	GRAHA EFFECT	DAILY DEITY
High	Purple/Blue/Rose	Emerald/Saphire	Educational	Family Graha	Mahakali

DAILY PUJA	DAILY PSALMS
Meditate, Control temper, Pray to Hanuman, Chant Hanuman Chalisa	6, 15, 33 ,42, 51, 60, 78, 105, 123

Thursday, May 18, 2023 — This is considered a NEUTRAL day for you — Planet: Uranus

ADVICE & DETAILS

This is a day of great movement and many short trips. There may be changes in mood, ideas, location, etc. Communication is very important today, make sure other understand what you are trying to say and verify that what you understood is what was said to you.

MANTRA FOR TODAY

Jai Jai Shiva Shambo.(2) ...Mahadeva Shambo (2) 21 times 8

MONEY	LOVE	CAREER	FAMILY	TRAVEL	WEDDING	MOVE	BUSINESS	HEALTH	Lotto #'s	play 3 #s
Good	Good	Fair	Good	Good	Bad	Good	Bad	Fair	1,31,16,60,34,12,33	375

SHOPPING	GAMBLE	SEX	KEYWORD	KEYWORD
Bad	Fair	is quiet	DIVINE	Spirituality,Religious,Astrology,Inner Conflicts,Religious ,Sleepiness,Advice

STRESS LEVEL	LUCKY COLORS	JEWELERY	MOONS EFFECT	GRAHA EFFECT	DAILY DEITY
Fair	Light Blue/Peach	Tiger's eye/Gold/Sil	Affectionate	God'S Graha	Shesnaag

DAILY PUJA	DAILY PSALMS
Chant Shiva Mantras, Take gifts to Ocean - Ganga Puja, Donate to Temple, Priests, etc.	7, 16, 34 ,43, 52, 61, 79, 106, 124

Friday, May 19, 2023 — This is considered a POSITIVE day for you — Planet: Jupiter

ADVICE & DETAILS

There will be moving to and from today. You will experience great pleasure today and will also have to deal with money either receiving it or paying it out. You may be watching TV or meeting someone known related to the entertainment industry.

MANTRA FOR TODAY

Om Hareem Nama Swaha..Shri Maha Laxmi Aye Namah swaha 12 times

MONEY	LOVE	CAREER	FAMILY	TRAVEL	WEDDING	MOVE	BUSINESS	HEALTH	Lotto #'s	play 3 #s
Excellent	Good	Excellent	Good	Good	Excellent	Good	Excellent	Excellent	55,60,31,40,25,35,5	197

SHOPPING	GAMBLE	SEX	KEYWORD	KEYWORD
Excellent	Excellent	is excellent	MONEY	Business,Major Expense,Money -

STRESS LEVEL	LUCKY COLORS	JEWELERY	MOONS EFFECT	GRAHA EFFECT	DAILY DEITY
Low	Yellow/Silver	Diamonds/Gold/Pea	Secretive	Money Graha	Mahalaxmi

DAILY PUJA	DAILY PSALMS
Decorate Land, Feed the poor, Donate milk /products to all, Feed holy guests,	8, 17, 35 ,44, 53, 62, 80, 107, 125

Saturday, May 20, 2023 — This is considered a NEGATIVE day for you — Planet: Saturn

ADVICE & DETAILS

This day is influenced by changes, moves and trips to close by locations. You will change your mind often and this lack of focus may cause you to get into an accident. Try to stay focused on your goals and minimize the multitasking especially when driving from one place to another.

MANTRA FOR TODAY

Om Ganga mataye nama swaha Om Varuna Devta aye Pahimam 11 times

MONEY	LOVE	CAREER	FAMILY	TRAVEL	WEDDING	MOVE	BUSINESS	HEALTH	Lotto #'s	play 3 #s
Bad	Bad	Bad	Fair	Bad	Bad	Bad	Bad	Bad	9,51,38,35,24,56,16	767

SHOPPING	GAMBLE	SEX	KEYWORD	KEYWORD
Bad	Bad	is very bad	KARMA	Destruction,Losses,Death,Sickness - cold,Legal matter,Abusive,Karmic debts,God -

STRESS LEVEL	LUCKY COLORS	JEWELERY	MOONS EFFECT	GRAHA EFFECT	DAILY DEITY
High	Gold/Brown//Green	Saphire/Hessonite	Ivestments	Evil Graha	Agnidev

DAILY PUJA	DAILY PSALMS
Remembrance of family members who died, worship of older people. gifts to grand parents	9, 18, 36 ,45, 54, 63, 81, 108, 126

Sunday, May 21, 2023 — This is considered a NEUTRAL day for you — Planet: Sun

ADVICE & DETAILS

Sex appeal and beauty are important to you today. You must control your ego-based anger and try to understand that every thing in the universe is in perfect order. You will experience travel and changes today

MANTRA FOR TODAY

Om Namo Bhagawate Mukhtanandaya, 108 times

MONEY	LOVE	CAREER	FAMILY	TRAVEL	WEDDING	MOVE	BUSINESS	HEALTH	Lotto #'s	play 3 #s
Fair	Bad	Good	Bad	Fair	Bad	Fair	Fair	Fair	28,60,50,4,8,31,9	141

SHOPPING	GAMBLE	SEX	KEYWORD	KEYWORD
Fair	Fair	is fair	MIND	Independence,Loneliness,Meditative,Worry,Dominating,Illness - Cold,On Your

STRESS LEVEL	LUCKY COLORS	JEWELERY	MOONS EFFECT	GRAHA EFFECT	DAILY DEITY
High	White/Yellow/	Pearl/Quartz	Arrogance	Status Graha	Saraswaty

DAILY PUJA	DAILY PSALMS
Give Gifts to Priests, Invite holy ones to your home, Feed Swamis and Yogis, Do Shiva Puja.	1, 10, 28 ,37, 46, 55, 73, 100, 118

Monday, May 22, 2023 — This is considered a POSITIVE day for you — Planet: Moon

ADVICE & DETAILS

Sexual energy is very high today. It is a good time to enjoy the company of your lover. Do not trust the words of others that may be deceiving, and make sure you are not deceiving others with your words. Accept all changes in your life gracefully.

MANTRA FOR TODAY

Kali Durge Namo Nama Om Durge aye nama swaha 108 times

MONEY	LOVE	CAREER	FAMILY	TRAVEL	WEDDING	MOVE	BUSINESS	HEALTH	Lotto #'s	play 3 #s
Good	Excellent	Good	Good	Excellen	Good	Good	Good	Good	7,8,50,26,59,75,30	597

SHOPPING	GAMBLE	SEX	KEYWORD	KEYWORD
Good	Good	is good	LOVE	Romance,Popularity,Visitors,Shopping,Food, Drinks,Co-

STRESS LEVEL	LUCKY COLORS	JEWELERY	MOONS EFFECT	GRAHA EFFECT	DAILY DEITY
Low	Red/Yellow/Pink	Topaz/Diamonds	Conservative	Love Graha	Gauri

DAILY PUJA	DAILY PSALMS
Give Gifts to females andnMother, Serve milk Products, Worship Durga forms	2, 11, 29 ,38, 47, 56, 74, 101, 119

Tuesday, May 23, 2023 — This is considered a POSITIVE day for you — Planet: Mercury

ADVICE & DETAILS

You will probably experience some type of short trip and/or moving today. Communication is important today so think carefully, speak clearly and listen with intent to transfer messages correctly.

MANTRA FOR TODAY

Om hareem Kleem Hreem Aem Saraswataye namaha 21 times

MONEY	LOVE	CAREER	FAMILY	TRAVEL	WEDDING	MOVE	BUSINESS	HEALTH	Lotto #'s	play 3 #s
Good	Fair	Good	Good	Excellen	Good	Good	Good	Excellent	43,11,48,61,73,26,6	390

SHOPPING	GAMBLE	SEX	KEYWORD	KEYWORD
Good	Good	is great	SOCIAL	Children,Education,Astrology,Bargains,Social Functions,Childishness,Groups -

STRESS LEVEL	LUCKY COLORS	JEWELERY	MOONS EFFECT	GRAHA EFFECT	DAILY DEITY
Low	Green/Sky Blue/	Diamonds/Silver	Enthusiastic	Social Graha	Vishnu

DAILY PUJA	DAILY PSALMS
Wash the feet of Children, Do Satnarayan Pooja, Read & chant Geeta	3, 12, 30 ,39, 48, 57, 75, 102, 120

Wednesday, May 24, 2023 — This is considered a NEGATIVE day for you — Planet: Pluto

ADVICE & DETAILS

You may be deceived today perhaps by a sexual partner or someone else. Use your words carefully today, they are powerful and will have serious consequences. There will be many changes today, make sure you stay truthful regardless.

MANTRA FOR TODAY

Om Jai Viganeshwaraya.. Lambodaraya Namo Namaha 21 times

MONEY	LOVE	CAREER	FAMILY	TRAVEL	WEDDING	MOVE	BUSINESS	HEALTH	Lotto #'s	play 3 #s
Bad	Fair	Bad	Fair	Bad	Good	Bad	Bad	Bad	3,4,60,14,69,47,11	879

SHOPPING	GAMBLE	SEX	KEYWORD	KEYWORD
Bad	Bad	is tough	CAREER	Career,Hard Work,Co-workers,Low Payment,Job Problems,High Temper,Low

STRESS LEVEL	LUCKY COLORS	JEWELERY	MOONS EFFECT	GRAHA EFFECT	DAILY DEITY
High	Dark Blue/ Purple/	Amethyst/Gold	Emotional	Job Graha	Lingam

DAILY PUJA	DAILY PSALMS
Worship Ganesh, Give gifts to father, and co -workers, Plant gardens, farms	4, 13, 31 ,40, 49, 58, 76, 103, 121

Thursday, May 25, 2023 — This is considered a POSITIVE day for you — Planet: Venus

ADVICE & DETAILS	MANTRA FOR TODAY
This day is influenced by changes, moves and trips to close by locations. You will change your mind often and this lack of focus may cause you to get into an accident. Try to stay focused on your goals and minimize the multitasking especially when driving from one place to another.	Om Graam Greem Graum Sa Gurave namah swaha 21 times

MONEY	LOVE	CAREER	FAMILY	TRAVEL	WEDDING	MOVE	BUSINESS	HEALTH	Lotto #'s	play 3 #s
Bad	Excellent	Fair	Good	Excellent	Good	Excellent	Good	Excellent	2,15,37,68,42,62,5	26

SHOPPING	GAMBLE	SEX	KEYWORD	KEYWORD						
Good	Good	is good	CHANGE	Sexuality,Travel,Change,Distant, far,Travel delays,Deception,Excercise,Illicit						

STRESS LEVEL	LUCKY COLORS	JEWELERY	MOONS EFFECT	GRAHA EFFECT	DAILY DEITY
Fair	Tan/Green/ Beige	Pearl/Silver/quartz	Courageous	Travel Graha	Nataraja

DAILY PUJA	DAILY PSALMS
Artistic gifts, Pray to Krishna, Do good deeds, do Spiritual trips	5, 14, 32 ,41, 50, 59, 77, 104, 122

Friday, May 26, 2023 — This is considered a NEGATIVE day for you — Planet: Mars

ADVICE & DETAILS	MANTRA FOR TODAY
This day you may feel a bit sad and depressed over health matters and some other type of personal losses. Center your thougts in divine spiritual and religious ideas and try to have an attitude of gratitude to receive blessings.	Om Mana Swasti Shanti Kuru kuru Swaha Shivoham Shivoham 27 times

MONEY	LOVE	CAREER	FAMILY	TRAVEL	WEDDING	MOVE	BUSINESS	HEALTH	Lotto #'s	play 3 #s
Bad	Bad	Bad	Bad	Bad	Bad	Bad	Fair	Bad	45,21,68,30,22,55,5	145

SHOPPING	GAMBLE	SEX	KEYWORD	KEYWORD						
Fair	Bad	is frustrating	POWER	Responsibilty,Disagreement,Family,Back Pain,Family Conflicts,Traffic						

STRESS LEVEL	LUCKY COLORS	JEWELERY	MOONS EFFECT	GRAHA EFFECT	DAILY DEITY
High	Purple/Blue/Rose	Emerald/Saphire	Educational	Family Graha	Mahakali

DAILY PUJA	DAILY PSALMS
Meditate, Control temper, Pray to Hanuman, Chant Hanuman Chalisa	6, 15, 33 ,42, 51, 60, 78, 105, 123

Saturday, May 27, 2023 — This is considered a NEUTRAL day for you — Planet: Uranus

ADVICE & DETAILS	MANTRA FOR TODAY
This is a day of great movement and many short trips. There may be changes in mood, ideas, location, etc. Communication is very important today, make sure other understand what you are trying to say and verify that what you understood is what was said to you.	Jai Jai Shiva Shambo.(2) ...Mahadeva Shambo (2) 21 times 8

MONEY	LOVE	CAREER	FAMILY	TRAVEL	WEDDING	MOVE	BUSINESS	HEALTH	Lotto #'s	play 3 #s
Good	Good	Fair	Good	Good	Bad	Good	Bad	Fair	52,34,63,75,10,3,67	713

SHOPPING	GAMBLE	SEX	KEYWORD	KEYWORD						
Bad	Fair	is quiet	DIVINE	Spirituality,Religious,Astrology,Inner Conflicts,Religious ,Sleepiness,Advice						

STRESS LEVEL	LUCKY COLORS	JEWELERY	MOONS EFFECT	GRAHA EFFECT	DAILY DEITY
Fair	Light Blue/Peach	Tiger's eye/Gold/Sil	Affectionate	God'S Graha	Shesnaag

DAILY PUJA	DAILY PSALMS
Chant Shiva Mantras, Take gifts to Ocean - Ganga Puja, Donate to Temple, Priests, etc.	7, 16, 34 ,43, 52, 61, 79, 106, 124

Sunday, May 28, 2023 — This is considered a POSITIVE day for you — Planet: Jupiter

ADVICE & DETAILS	MANTRA FOR TODAY
There will be moving to and from today. You will experience great pleasure today and will also have to deal with money either receiving it or paying it out. You may be watching TV or meeting someone known related to the entertainment industry.	Om Hareem Nama Swaha..Shri Maha Laxmi Aye Namah swaha 12 times

MONEY	LOVE	CAREER	FAMILY	TRAVEL	WEDDING	MOVE	BUSINESS	HEALTH	Lotto #'s	play 3 #s
Excellent	Good	Excellent	Good	Good	Excellent	Good	Excellent	Excellent	35,17,6,8,55,47,44	212

SHOPPING	GAMBLE	SEX	KEYWORD	KEYWORD						
Excellent	Excellent	is excellent	MONEY	Business,Major Expense,Money -						

STRESS LEVEL	LUCKY COLORS	JEWELERY	MOONS EFFECT	GRAHA EFFECT	DAILY DEITY
Low	Yellow/Silver	Diamonds/Gold/Pea	Secretive	Money Graha	Mahalaxmi

DAILY PUJA	DAILY PSALMS
Decorate Land, Feed the poor, Donate milk /products to all, Feed holy guests,	8, 17, 35 ,44, 53, 62, 80, 107, 125

Monday, May 29, 2023 — This is considered a NEGATIVE day for you — Planet: Saturn

ADVICE & DETAILS	MANTRA FOR TODAY
This day is influenced by changes, moves and trips to close by locations. You will change your mind often and this lack of focus may cause you to get into an accident. Try to stay focused on your goals and minimize the multitasking especially when driving from one place to another.	Om Ganga mataye nama swaha Om Varuna Devta aye Pahimam 11 times

MONEY	LOVE	CAREER	FAMILY	TRAVEL	WEDDING	MOVE	BUSINESS	HEALTH	Lotto #'s	play 3 #s
Bad	Bad	Bad	Fair	Bad	Bad	Bad	Bad	Bad	49,22,45,75,8,74,51	841

SHOPPING	GAMBLE	SEX	KEYWORD	KEYWORD						
Bad	Bad	is very bad	KARMA	Destruction,Losses,Death,Sickness - cold,Legal matter,Abusive,Karmic debts,God -						

STRESS LEVEL		LUCKY COLORS		JEWELERY	MOONS EFFECT	GRAHA EFFECT		DAILY DEITY
High		Gold/Brown//Green		Saphire/Hessonite	Ivestments	Evil Graha		Agnidev

DAILY PUJA	DAILY PSALMS
Remembrance of family members who died, worship of older people. gifts to grand parents	9, 18, 36 ,45, 54, 63, 81, 108, 126

Tuesday, May 30, 2023 — This is considered a NEUTRAL day for you — Planet: Sun

ADVICE & DETAILS	MANTRA FOR TODAY
Sex appeal and beauty are important to you today. You must control your ego-based anger and try to understand that every thing in the universe is in perfect order. You will experience travel and changes today	Om Namo Bhagawate Mukhtanandaya, 108 times

MONEY	LOVE	CAREER	FAMILY	TRAVEL	WEDDING	MOVE	BUSINESS	HEALTH	Lotto #'s	play 3 #s
Fair	Bad	Good	Bad	Fair	Bad	Fair	Fair	Fair	38,20,18,35,45,32,6	226

SHOPPING	GAMBLE	SEX	KEYWORD	KEYWORD						
Fair	Fair	is fair	MIND	Independence,Loneliness,Meditative,Worry,Dominating,Illness - Cold,On Your						

STRESS LEVEL		LUCKY COLORS		JEWELERY	MOONS EFFECT	GRAHA EFFECT		DAILY DEITY
High		White/Yellow/		Pearl/Quartz	Arrogance	Status Graha		Saraswaty

DAILY PUJA	DAILY PSALMS
Give Gifts to Priests, Invite holy ones to your home, Feed Swamis and Yogis, Do Shiva Puja.	1, 10, 28 ,37, 46, 55, 73, 100, 118

Wednesday, May 31, 2023 — This is considered a POSITIVE day for you — Planet: Moon

ADVICE & DETAILS	MANTRA FOR TODAY
Sexual energy is very high today. It is a good time to enjoy the company of your lover. Do not trust the words of others that may be deceiving, and make sure you are not deceiving others with your words. Accept all changes in your life gracefully.	Kali Durge Namo Nama Om Durge aye nama swaha 108 times

MONEY	LOVE	CAREER	FAMILY	TRAVEL	WEDDING	MOVE	BUSINESS	HEALTH	Lotto #'s	play 3 #s
Good	Excellent	Good	Good	Excellen	Good	Good	Good	Good	4,46,10,10,65,20,27	161

SHOPPING	GAMBLE	SEX	KEYWORD	KEYWORD						
Good	Good	is good	LOVE	Romance,Popularity,Visitors,Shopping,Food, Drinks,Co-						

STRESS LEVEL		LUCKY COLORS		JEWELERY	MOONS EFFECT	GRAHA EFFECT		DAILY DEITY
Low		Red/Yellow/Pink		Topaz/Diamonds	Conservative	Love Graha		Gauri

DAILY PUJA	DAILY PSALMS
Give Gifts to females andnMother, Serve milk Products, Worship Durga forms	2, 11, 29 ,38, 47, 56, 74, 101, 119

Thursday, June 1, 2023 — This is considered a POSITIVE day for you — Planet: Jupiter

ADVICE & DETAILS	MANTRA FOR TODAY
Government and police agencies may cross paths with you today; try to follow the law so the encounters are more pleasurable. You will be the target of jealousy today so try to stay humble about your accomplishments or your belongings and remember that the good times also pass what remains is only the purity in your heart. You will have to confront many responsibilities today do it with surrender and	Om Hareem Nama Swaha..Shri Maha Laxmi Aye Namah swaha 12 times

MONEY	LOVE	CAREER	FAMILY	TRAVEL	WEDDING	MOVE	BUSINESS	HEALTH	Lotto #'s	play 3 #s
Excellent	Good	Excellent	Good	Good	Excellent	Good	Excellent	Excellent	24,60,12,67,13,71,6	20

SHOPPING	GAMBLE	SEX	KEYWORD	KEYWORD						
Excellent	Excellent	is excellent	MONEY	Business,Major Expense,Money -						

STRESS LEVEL		LUCKY COLORS		JEWELERY	MOONS EFFECT	GRAHA EFFECT		DAILY DEITY
Low		Yellow/Silver		Diamonds/Gold/Pea	Secretive	Money Graha		Mahalaxmi

DAILY PUJA	DAILY PSALMS
Decorate Land, Feed the poor, Donate milk /products to all, Feed holy guests,	8, 17, 35 ,44, 53, 62, 80, 107, 125

Friday, June 2, 2023 — This is considered a NEGATIVE day for you — Planet: Saturn

ADVICE & DETAILS

You have to deal with a great deal of responsibilities today; regardless of this others will feel jealous and envious of you. There are possible encounters with police and/or government officials.

MANTRA FOR TODAY

Om Ganga mataye nama swaha Om Varuna Devta aye Pahimam 11 times

MONEY	LOVE	CAREER	FAMILY	TRAVEL	WEDDING	MOVE	BUSINESS	HEALTH	Lotto #'s	play 3 #s
Bad	Bad	Bad	Fair	Bad	Bad	Bad	Bad	Bad	59,44,46,32,30,56,8	204

SHOPPING	GAMBLE	SEX	KEYWORD	KEYWORD
Bad	Bad	is very bad	KARMA	Destruction,Losses,Death,Sickness - cold,Legal matter,Abusive,Karmic debts,God -

STRESS LEVEL	LUCKY COLORS	JEWELERY	MOONS EFFECT	GRAHA EFFECT	DAILY DEITY
High	Gold/Brown//Green	Saphire/Hessonite	Ivestments	Evil Graha	Agnidev

DAILY PUJA	DAILY PSALMS
Remembrance of family members who died, worship of older people. gifts to grand parents	9, 18, 36 ,45, 54, 63, 81, 108, 126

Saturday, June 3, 2023 — This is considered a NEUTRAL day for you — Planet: Sun

ADVICE & DETAILS

Your authoritative attitude mixed with arrogance and the need to feel superior may bring you difficulties with government or any of its agencies and may also make you feel lonely. Being humble today will be beneficial.

MANTRA FOR TODAY

Om Namo Bhagawate Mukhtanandaya, 108 times

MONEY	LOVE	CAREER	FAMILY	TRAVEL	WEDDING	MOVE	BUSINESS	HEALTH	Lotto #'s	play 3 #s
Fair	Bad	Good	Bad	Fair	Bad	Fair	Fair	Fair	13,62,2,63,74,12,4	431

SHOPPING	GAMBLE	SEX	KEYWORD	KEYWORD
Fair	Fair	is fair	MIND	Independence,Loneliness,Meditative,Worry,Dominating,Illness - Cold,On Your

STRESS LEVEL	LUCKY COLORS	JEWELERY	MOONS EFFECT	GRAHA EFFECT	DAILY DEITY
High	White/Yellow/	Pearl/Quartz	Arrogance	Status Graha	Saraswaty

DAILY PUJA	DAILY PSALMS
Give Gifts to Priests, Invite holy ones to your home, Feed Swamis and Yogis, Do Shiva Puja.	1, 10, 28 ,37, 46, 55, 73, 100, 118

Sunday, June 4, 2023 — This is considered a POSITIVE day for you — Planet: Moon

ADVICE & DETAILS

Some of the negative influences for this day may be quarrels with loved ones and trouble with government. The positive influences are cooperation, affection and music that can help you counter the negative influences.

MANTRA FOR TODAY

Kali Durge Namo Nama Om Durge aye nama swaha 108 times

MONEY	LOVE	CAREER	FAMILY	TRAVEL	WEDDING	MOVE	BUSINESS	HEALTH	Lotto #'s	play 3 #s
Good	Excellent	Good	Good	Excellen	Good	Good	Good	Good	73,54,39,50,60,13,3	252

SHOPPING	GAMBLE	SEX	KEYWORD	KEYWORD
Good	Good	is good	LOVE	Romance,Popularity,Visitors,Shopping,Food, Drinks,Co-

STRESS LEVEL	LUCKY COLORS	JEWELERY	MOONS EFFECT	GRAHA EFFECT	DAILY DEITY
Low	Red/Yellow/Pink	Topaz/Diamonds	Conservative	Love Graha	Gauri

DAILY PUJA	DAILY PSALMS
Give Gifts to females andnMother, Serve milk Products, Worship Durga forms	2, 11, 29 ,38, 47, 56, 74, 101, 119

Monday, June 5, 2023 — This is considered a POSITIVE day for you — Planet: Mercury

ADVICE & DETAILS

You may feel the exertion from your job and from building the life you have created for you and your family. Take a deep breath, try to take some time for yourself, reading would be beneficial.

MANTRA FOR TODAY

Om hareem Kleem Hreem Aem Saraswataye namaha 21 times

MONEY	LOVE	CAREER	FAMILY	TRAVEL	WEDDING	MOVE	BUSINESS	HEALTH	Lotto #'s	play 3 #s
Good	Fair	Good	Good	Excellen	Good	Good	Good	Excellent	1,11,2,21,50,36,58	169

SHOPPING	GAMBLE	SEX	KEYWORD	KEYWORD
Good	Good	is great	SOCIAL	Children,Education,Astrology,Bargains,Social Functions,Childishness,Groups -

STRESS LEVEL	LUCKY COLORS	JEWELERY	MOONS EFFECT	GRAHA EFFECT	DAILY DEITY
Low	Green/Sky Blue/	Diamonds/Silver	Enthusiastic	Social Graha	Vishnu

DAILY PUJA	DAILY PSALMS
Wash the feet of Children, Do Satnarayan Pooja, Read & chant Geeta	3, 12, 30 ,39, 48, 57, 75, 102, 120

Tuesday, June 6, 2023 — This is considered a NEGATIVE day for you — Planet: Pluto

ADVICE & DETAILS

Your high temper may get the best of you today; try to control it to avoid further karmas. You will have to work today even though you will feel lazy and have the nagging feeling that your pay is very low.

MANTRA FOR TODAY

Om Jai Viganeshwaraya.. Lambodaraya Namo Namaha 21 times

MONEY	LOVE	CAREER	FAMILY	TRAVEL	WEDDING	MOVE	BUSINESS	HEALTH	Lotto #'s	play 3 #s
Bad	Fair	Bad	Fair	Bad	Good	Bad	Bad	Bad	9,11,39,11,61,52,39	841

SHOPPING	GAMBLE	SEX	KEYWORD	KEYWORD
Bad	Bad	is tough	CAREER	Career,Hard Work,Co-workers,Low Payment,Job Problems,High Temper,Low

STRESS LEVEL	LUCKY COLORS	JEWELERY	MOONS EFFECT	GRAHA EFFECT	DAILY DEITY
High	Dark Blue/ Purple/	Amethyst/Gold	Emotional	Job Graha	Lingam

DAILY PUJA	DAILY PSALMS
Worship Ganesh, Give gifts to father, and co-workers, Plant gardens, farms	4, 13, 31 ,40, 49, 58, 76, 103, 121

Wednesday, June 7, 2023 — This is considered a POSITIVE day for you — Planet: Venus

ADVICE & DETAILS

You will feel a great deal of frustration today if your financial matters related to job promotion, profits and money do not work out in the manner that you expect them to. Be patient and try to understand that the universe only send you what you can handle. You have been given what you need the brain and the brawn to work and accomplish your desires.

MANTRA FOR TODAY

Om Graam Greem Graum Sa Gurave namah swaha 21 times

MONEY	LOVE	CAREER	FAMILY	TRAVEL	WEDDING	MOVE	BUSINESS	HEALTH	Lotto #'s	play 3 #s
Bad	Excellent	Fair	Good	Excellen	Good	Excellen	Good	Excellent	37,53,29,71,6,61,30	409

SHOPPING	GAMBLE	SEX	KEYWORD	KEYWORD
Good	Good	is good	CHANGE	Sexuality,Travel,Change,Distant, far,Travel delays,Deception,Excercise,Illicit

STRESS LEVEL	LUCKY COLORS	JEWELERY	MOONS EFFECT	GRAHA EFFECT	DAILY DEITY
Fair	Tan/Green/ Beige	Pearl/Silver/quartz	Courageous	Travel Graha	Nataraja

DAILY PUJA	DAILY PSALMS
Artistic gifts, Pray to Krishna, Do good deeds, do Spiritual trips	5, 14, 32 ,41, 50, 59, 77, 104, 122

Thursday, June 8, 2023 — This is considered a NEGATIVE day for you — Planet: Mars

ADVICE & DETAILS

Although you feel powerful today, you must connect with your inner intelligence and give and receive advice with an open heart and mind. You will have to opportunity to experience high pleasure today and be around or be part of things related to TV or fame.

MANTRA FOR TODAY

Om Mana Swasti Shanti Kuru kuru Swaha Shivoham Shivoham 27 times

MONEY	LOVE	CAREER	FAMILY	TRAVEL	WEDDING	MOVE	BUSINESS	HEALTH	Lotto #'s	play 3 #s
Bad	Bad	Bad	Bad	Bad	Bad	Bad	Fair	Bad	50,10,15,17,23,74,1	530

SHOPPING	GAMBLE	SEX	KEYWORD	KEYWORD
Fair	Bad	is frustrating	POWER	Responsibilty,Disagreement,Family,Back Pain,Family Conflicts,Traffic

STRESS LEVEL	LUCKY COLORS	JEWELERY	MOONS EFFECT	GRAHA EFFECT	DAILY DEITY
High	Purple/Blue/Rose	Emerald/Saphire	Educational	Family Graha	Mahakali

DAILY PUJA	DAILY PSALMS
Meditate, Control temper, Pray to Hanuman, Chant Hanuman Chalisa	6, 15, 33 ,42, 51, 60, 78, 105, 123

Friday, June 9, 2023 — This is considered a NEUTRAL day for you — Planet: Uranus

ADVICE & DETAILS

There will be a feeling of excitement and anticipation, but changes in plans or ideas may leave you feeling frustrated. Use your internal power to overcome the frustration and flow with the changes that at the end will be beneficial.

MANTRA FOR TODAY

Jai Jai Shiva Shambo.(2) ...Mahadeva Shambo (2) 21 times 8

MONEY	LOVE	CAREER	FAMILY	TRAVEL	WEDDING	MOVE	BUSINESS	HEALTH	Lotto #'s	play 3 #s
Good	Good	Fair	Good	Good	Bad	Good	Bad	Fair	18,71,66,33,31,23,5	475

SHOPPING	GAMBLE	SEX	KEYWORD	KEYWORD
Bad	Fair	is quiet	DIVINE	Spirituality,Religious,Astrology,Inner Conflicts,Religious ,Sleepiness,Advice

STRESS LEVEL	LUCKY COLORS	JEWELERY	MOONS EFFECT	GRAHA EFFECT	DAILY DEITY
Fair	Light Blue/Peach	Tiger's eye/Gold/Sil	Affectionate	God'S Graha	Shesnaag

DAILY PUJA	DAILY PSALMS
Chant Shiva Mantras, Take gifts to Ocean - Ganga Puja, Donate to Temple, Priests, etc.	7, 16, 34 ,43, 52, 61, 79, 106, 124

Saturday, June 10, 2023	This is considered a POSITIVE day for you	Planet: Jupiter

ADVICE & DETAILS	MANTRA FOR TODAY
Government and police agencies may cross paths with you today; try to follow the law so the encounters are more pleasurable. You will be the target of jealousy today so try to stay humble about your accomplishments or your belongings and remember that the good times also pass what remains is only the purity in your heart. You will have to confront many responsibilities today do it with surrender and	Om Hareem Nama Swaha..Shri Maha Laxmi Aye Namah swaha 12 times

MONEY	LOVE	CAREER	FAMILY	TRAVEL	WEDDING	MOVE	BUSINESS	HEALTH	Lotto #'s	play 3 #s
Excellent	Good	Excellent	Good	Good	Excellent	Good	Excellent	Excellent	53,19,36,36,35,27,4	911

SHOPPING	GAMBLE	SEX	KEYWORD	KEYWORD
Excellent	Excellent	is excellent	MONEY	Business,Major Expense,Money -

STRESS LEVEL	LUCKY COLORS	JEWELERY	MOONS EFFECT	GRAHA EFFECT	DAILY DEITY
Low	Yellow/Silver	Diamonds/Gold/Pea	Secretive	Money Graha	Mahalaxmi

DAILY PUJA	DAILY PSALMS
Decorate Land, Feed the poor, Donate milk /products to all, Feed holy guests,	8, 17, 35 ,44, 53, 62, 80, 107, 125

Sunday, June 11, 2023	This is considered a NEGATIVE day for you	Planet: Saturn

ADVICE & DETAILS	MANTRA FOR TODAY
You have to deal with a great deal of responsibilities today; regardless of this others will feel jealous and envious of you. There are possible encounters with police and/or government officials.	Om Ganga mataye nama swaha Om Varuna Devta aye Pahimam 11 times

MONEY	LOVE	CAREER	FAMILY	TRAVEL	WEDDING	MOVE	BUSINESS	HEALTH	Lotto #'s	play 3 #s
Bad	Bad	Bad	Fair	Bad	Bad	Bad	Bad	Bad	74,34,52,65,38,4,73	434

SHOPPING	GAMBLE	SEX	KEYWORD	KEYWORD
Bad	Bad	is very bad	KARMA	Destruction,Losses,Death,Sickness - cold,Legal matter,Abusive,Karmic debts,God -

STRESS LEVEL	LUCKY COLORS	JEWELERY	MOONS EFFECT	GRAHA EFFECT	DAILY DEITY
High	Gold/Brown//Green	Saphire/Hessonite	Ivestments	Evil Graha	Agnidev

DAILY PUJA	DAILY PSALMS
Remembrance of family members who died, worship of older people. gifts to grand parents	9, 18, 36 ,45, 54, 63, 81, 108, 126

Monday, June 12, 2023	This is considered a NEUTRAL day for you	Planet: Sun

ADVICE & DETAILS	MANTRA FOR TODAY
Your authoritative attitude mixed with arrogance and the need to feel superior may bring you difficulties with government or any of its agencies and may also make you feel lonely. Being humble today will be beneficial.	Om Namo Bhagawate Mukhtanandaya, 108 times

MONEY	LOVE	CAREER	FAMILY	TRAVEL	WEDDING	MOVE	BUSINESS	HEALTH	Lotto #'s	play 3 #s
Fair	Bad	Good	Bad	Fair	Bad	Fair	Fair	Fair	55,39,20,10,73,27,6	599

SHOPPING	GAMBLE	SEX	KEYWORD	KEYWORD
Fair	Fair	is fair	MIND	Independence,Loneliness,Meditative,Worry,Dominating,Illness - Cold,On Your

STRESS LEVEL	LUCKY COLORS	JEWELERY	MOONS EFFECT	GRAHA EFFECT	DAILY DEITY
High	White/Yellow/	Pearl/Quartz	Arrogance	Status Graha	Saraswaty

DAILY PUJA	DAILY PSALMS
Give Gifts to Priests, Invite holy ones to your home, Feed Swamis and Yogis, Do Shiva Puja.	1, 10, 28 ,37, 46, 55, 73, 100, 118

Tuesday, June 13, 2023	This is considered a POSITIVE day for you	Planet: Moon

ADVICE & DETAILS	MANTRA FOR TODAY
Some of the negative influences for this day may be quarrels with loved ones and trouble with government. The positive influences are cooperation, affection and music that can help you counter the negative influences.	Kali Durge Namo Nama Om Durge aye nama swaha 108 times

MONEY	LOVE	CAREER	FAMILY	TRAVEL	WEDDING	MOVE	BUSINESS	HEALTH	Lotto #'s	play 3 #s
Good	Excellent	Good	Good	Excellen	Good	Good	Good	Good	30,17,70,21,2,74,18	620

SHOPPING	GAMBLE	SEX	KEYWORD	KEYWORD
Good	Good	is good	LOVE	Romance,Popularity,Visitors,Shopping,Food, Drinks,Co-

STRESS LEVEL	LUCKY COLORS	JEWELERY	MOONS EFFECT	GRAHA EFFECT	DAILY DEITY
Low	Red/Yellow/Pink	Topaz/Diamonds	Conservative	Love Graha	Gauri

DAILY PUJA	DAILY PSALMS
Give Gifts to females andnMother, Serve milk Products, Worship Durga forms	2, 11, 29 ,38, 47, 56, 74, 101, 119

Wednesday, June 14, 2023 — This is considered a POSITIVE day for you — Planet: Mercury

ADVICE & DETAILS

You may feel the exertion from your job and from building the life you have created for you and your family. Take a deep breath, try to take some time for yourself, reading would be beneficial.

MANTRA FOR TODAY
Om hareem Kleem Hreem Aem Saraswataye namaha 21 times

MONEY	LOVE	CAREER	FAMILY	TRAVEL	WEDDING	MOVE	BUSINESS	HEALTH	Lotto #'s	play 3 #s
Good	Fair	Good	Good	Excellen	Good	Good	Good	Excellent	21,8,5,50,56,64,20	500

SHOPPING	GAMBLE	SEX	KEYWORD	KEYWORD
Good	Good	is great	SOCIAL	Children,Education,Astrology,Bargains,Social Functions,Childishness,Groups -

STRESS LEVEL	LUCKY COLORS	JEWELERY	MOONS EFFECT	GRAHA EFFECT	DAILY DEITY
Low	Green/Sky Blue/	Diamonds/Silver	Enthusiastic	Social Graha	Vishnu

DAILY PUJA	DAILY PSALMS
Wash the feet of Children, Do Satnarayan Pooja, Read & chant Geeta	3, 12, 30 ,39, 48, 57, 75, 102, 120

Thursday, June 15, 2023 — This is considered a NEGATIVE day for you — Planet: Pluto

ADVICE & DETAILS

Your high temper may get the best of you today; try to control it to avoid further karmas. You will have to work today even though you will feel lazy and have the nagging feeling that your pay is very low.

MANTRA FOR TODAY
Om Jai Viganeshwaraya.. Lambodaraya Namo Namaha 21 times

MONEY	LOVE	CAREER	FAMILY	TRAVEL	WEDDING	MOVE	BUSINESS	HEALTH	Lotto #'s	play 3 #s
Bad	Fair	Bad	Fair	Bad	Good	Bad	Bad	Bad	40,35,17,30,43,16,3	113

SHOPPING	GAMBLE	SEX	KEYWORD	KEYWORD
Bad	Bad	is tough	CAREER	Career,Hard Work,Co-workers,Low Payment,Job Problems,High Temper,Low

STRESS LEVEL	LUCKY COLORS	JEWELERY	MOONS EFFECT	GRAHA EFFECT	DAILY DEITY
High	Dark Blue/ Purple/	Amethyst/Gold	Emotional	Job Graha	Lingam

DAILY PUJA	DAILY PSALMS
Worship Ganesh, Give gifts to father, and co -workers, Plant gardens, farms	4, 13, 31 ,40, 49, 58, 76, 103, 121

Friday, June 16, 2023 — This is considered a POSITIVE day for you — Planet: Venus

ADVICE & DETAILS

You will feel a great deal of frustration today if your financial matters related to job promotion, profits and money do not work out in the manner that you expect them to. Be patient and try to understand that the universe only send you what you can handle. You have been given what you need the brain and the brawn to work and accomplish your desires.

MANTRA FOR TODAY
Om Graam Greem Graum Sa Gurave namah swaha 21 times

MONEY	LOVE	CAREER	FAMILY	TRAVEL	WEDDING	MOVE	BUSINESS	HEALTH	Lotto #'s	play 3 #s
Bad	Excellent	Fair	Good	Excellen	Good	Excellen	Good	Excellent	15,61,72,3,57,72,29	375

SHOPPING	GAMBLE	SEX	KEYWORD	KEYWORD
Good	Good	is good	CHANGE	Sexuality,Travel,Change,Distant, far,Travel delays,Deception,Excercise,Illicit

STRESS LEVEL	LUCKY COLORS	JEWELERY	MOONS EFFECT	GRAHA EFFECT	DAILY DEITY
Fair	Tan/Green/ Beige	Pearl/Silver/quartz	Courageous	Travel Graha	Nataraja

DAILY PUJA	DAILY PSALMS
Artistic gifts, Pray to Krishna, Do good deeds, do Spiritual trips	5, 14, 32 ,41, 50, 59, 77, 104, 122

Saturday, June 17, 2023 — This is considered a NEGATIVE day for you — Planet: Mars

ADVICE & DETAILS

Although you feel powerful today, you must connect with your inner intelligence and give and receive advice with an open heart and mind. You will have to opportunity to experience high pleasure today and be around or be part of things related to TV or fame.

MANTRA FOR TODAY
Om Mana Swasti Shanti Kuru kuru Swaha Shivoham Shivoham 27 times

MONEY	LOVE	CAREER	FAMILY	TRAVEL	WEDDING	MOVE	BUSINESS	HEALTH	Lotto #'s	play 3 #s
Bad	Bad	Bad	Bad	Bad	Bad	Bad	Fair	Bad	43,37,58,31,3,21,31	758

SHOPPING	GAMBLE	SEX	KEYWORD	KEYWORD
Fair	Bad	is frustrating	POWER	Responsibilty,Disagreement,Family,Back Pain,Family Conflicts,Traffic

STRESS LEVEL	LUCKY COLORS	JEWELERY	MOONS EFFECT	GRAHA EFFECT	DAILY DEITY
High	Purple/Blue/Rose	Emerald/Saphire	Educational	Family Graha	Mahakali

DAILY PUJA	DAILY PSALMS
Meditate, Control temper, Pray to Hanuman, Chant Hanuman Chalisa	6, 15, 33 ,42, 51, 60, 78, 105, 123

Sunday, June 18, 2023 — This is considered a NEUTRAL day for you — Planet: Uranus

ADVICE & DETAILS

There will be a feeling of excitement and anticipation, but changes in plans or ideas may leave you feeling frustrated. Use your internal power to overcome the frustration and flow with the changes that at the end will be beneficial.

MANTRA FOR TODAY

Jai Jai Shiva Shambo.(2) ...Mahadeva Shambo (2) 21 times 8

MONEY	LOVE	CAREER	FAMILY	TRAVEL	WEDDING	MOVE	BUSINESS	HEALTH	Lotto #'s	play 3 #s
Good	Good	Fair	Good	Good	Bad	Good	Bad	Fair	2,35,15,24,15,24,12	715

SHOPPING	GAMBLE	SEX	KEYWORD	KEYWORD
Bad	Fair	is quiet	DIVINE	Spirituality,Religious,Astrology,Inner Conflicts,Religious ,Sleepiness,Advice

STRESS LEVEL	LUCKY COLORS	JEWELERY	MOONS EFFECT	GRAHA EFFECT	DAILY DEITY
Fair	Light Blue/Peach	Tiger's eye/Gold/Sil	Affectionate	God'S Graha	Shesnaag

DAILY PUJA	DAILY PSALMS
Chant Shiva Mantras, Take gifts to Ocean - Ganga Puja, Donate to Temple, Priests, etc.	7, 16, 34 ,43, 52, 61, 79, 106, 124

Monday, June 19, 2023 — This is considered a POSITIVE day for you — Planet: Jupiter

ADVICE & DETAILS

Government and police agencies may cross paths with you today; try to follow the law so the encounters are more pleasurable. You will be the target of jealousy today so try to stay humble about your accomplishments or your belongings and remember that the good times also pass what remains is only the purity in your heart. You will have to confront many responsibilities today do it with surrender and

MANTRA FOR TODAY

Om Hareem Nama Swaha..Shri Maha Laxmi Aye Namah swaha 12 times

MONEY	LOVE	CAREER	FAMILY	TRAVEL	WEDDING	MOVE	BUSINESS	HEALTH	Lotto #'s	play 3 #s
Excellent	Good	Excellent	Good	Good	Excellent	Good	Excellent	Excellent	59,1,53,59,18,37,68	775

SHOPPING	GAMBLE	SEX	KEYWORD	KEYWORD
Excellent	Excellent	is excellent	MONEY	Business,Major Expense,Money -

STRESS LEVEL	LUCKY COLORS	JEWELERY	MOONS EFFECT	GRAHA EFFECT	DAILY DEITY
Low	Yellow/Silver	Diamonds/Gold/Pea	Secretive	Money Graha	Mahalaxmi

DAILY PUJA	DAILY PSALMS
Decorate Land, Feed the poor, Donate milk /products to all, Feed holy guests,	8, 17, 35 ,44, 53, 62, 80, 107, 125

Tuesday, June 20, 2023 — This is considered a NEGATIVE day for you — Planet: Saturn

ADVICE & DETAILS

You have to deal with a great deal of responsibilities today; regardless of this others will feel jealous and envious of you. There are possible encounters with police and/or government officials.

MANTRA FOR TODAY

Om Ganga mataye nama swaha Om Varuna Devta aye Pahimam 11 times

MONEY	LOVE	CAREER	FAMILY	TRAVEL	WEDDING	MOVE	BUSINESS	HEALTH	Lotto #'s	play 3 #s
Bad	Bad	Bad	Fair	Bad	Bad	Bad	Bad	Bad	18,3,68,50,16,34,63	703

SHOPPING	GAMBLE	SEX	KEYWORD	KEYWORD
Bad	Bad	is very bad	KARMA	Destruction,Losses,Death,Sickness - cold,Legal matter,Abusive,Karmic debts,God -

STRESS LEVEL	LUCKY COLORS	JEWELERY	MOONS EFFECT	GRAHA EFFECT	DAILY DEITY
High	Gold/Brown//Green	Saphire/Hessonite	Ivestments	Evil Graha	Agnidev

DAILY PUJA	DAILY PSALMS
Remembrance of family members who died, worship of older people. gifts to grand parents	9, 18, 36 ,45, 54, 63, 81, 108, 126

Wednesday, June 21, 2023 — This is considered a NEUTRAL day for you — Planet: Sun

ADVICE & DETAILS

Your authoritative attitude mixed with arrogance and the need to feel superior may bring you difficulties with government or any of its agencies and may also make you feel lonely. Being humble today will be beneficial.

MANTRA FOR TODAY

Om Namo Bhagawate Mukhtanandaya, 108 times

MONEY	LOVE	CAREER	FAMILY	TRAVEL	WEDDING	MOVE	BUSINESS	HEALTH	Lotto #'s	play 3 #s
Fair	Bad	Good	Bad	Fair	Bad	Fair	Fair	Fair	40,63,50,52,71,10,1	927

SHOPPING	GAMBLE	SEX	KEYWORD	KEYWORD
Fair	Fair	is fair	MIND	Independence,Loneliness,Meditative,Worry,Dominating,Illness - Cold,On Your

STRESS LEVEL	LUCKY COLORS	JEWELERY	MOONS EFFECT	GRAHA EFFECT	DAILY DEITY
High	White/Yellow/	Pearl/Quartz	Arrogance	Status Graha	Saraswaty

DAILY PUJA	DAILY PSALMS
Give Gifts to Priests, Invite holy ones to your home, Feed Swamis and Yogis, Do Shiva Puja.	1, 10, 28 ,37, 46, 55, 73, 100, 118

Thursday, June 22, 2023		This is considered a POSITIVE day for you						Planet: Moon		
ADVICE & DETAILS								MANTRA FOR TODAY		
Some of the negative influences for this day may be quarrels with loved ones and trouble with government. The positive influences are cooperation, affection and music that can help you counter the negative influences.								Kali Durge Namo Nama Om Durge aye nama swaha 108 times		

MONEY	LOVE	CAREER	FAMILY	TRAVEL	WEDDING	MOVE	BUSINESS	HEALTH	Lotto #'s	play 3 #s
Good	Excellent	Good	Good	Excellen	Good	Good	Good	Good	16,9,69,37,70,61,5	108

SHOPPING	GAMBLE	SEX	KEYWORD	KEYWORD						
Good	Good	is good	LOVE	Romance,Popularity,Visitors,Shopping,Food, Drinks,Co-						

STRESS LEVEL		LUCKY COLORS		JEWELERY		MOONS EFFECT		GRAHA EFFECT		DAILY DEITY
Low		Red/Yellow/Pink		Topaz/Diamonds		Conservative		Love Graha		Gauri

DAILY PUJA	DAILY PSALMS
Give Gifts to females andnMother, Serve milk Products, Worship Durga forms	2, 11, 29 ,38, 47, 56, 74, 101, 119

Friday, June 23, 2023		This is considered a POSITIVE day for you						Planet: Mercury		
ADVICE & DETAILS								MANTRA FOR TODAY		
You may feel the exertion from your job and from building the life you have created for you and your family. Take a deep breath, try to take some time for yourself, reading would be beneficial.								Om hareem Kleem Hreem Aem Saraswataye namaha 21 times		

MONEY	LOVE	CAREER	FAMILY	TRAVEL	WEDDING	MOVE	BUSINESS	HEALTH	Lotto #'s	play 3 #s
Good	Fair	Good	Good	Excellen	Good	Good	Good	Excellent	70,46,75,23,62,35,1	251

SHOPPING	GAMBLE	SEX	KEYWORD	KEYWORD						
Good	Good	is great	SOCIAL	Children,Education,Astrology,Bargains,Social Functions,Childishness,Groups -						

STRESS LEVEL		LUCKY COLORS		JEWELERY		MOONS EFFECT		GRAHA EFFECT		DAILY DEITY
Low		Green/Sky Blue/		Diamonds/Silver		Enthusiastic		Social Graha		Vishnu

DAILY PUJA	DAILY PSALMS
Wash the feet of Children, Do Satnarayan Pooja, Read & chant Geeta	3, 12, 30 ,39, 48, 57, 75, 102, 120

Saturday, June 24, 2023		This is considered a NEGATIVE day for you						Planet: Pluto		
ADVICE & DETAILS								MANTRA FOR TODAY		
Your high temper may get the best of you today; try to control it to avoid further karmas. You will have to work today even though you will feel lazy and have the nagging feeling that your pay is very low.								Om Jai Viganeshwaraya.. Lambodaraya Namo Namaha 21 times		

MONEY	LOVE	CAREER	FAMILY	TRAVEL	WEDDING	MOVE	BUSINESS	HEALTH	Lotto #'s	play 3 #s
Bad	Fair	Bad	Fair	Bad	Good	Bad	Bad	Bad	58,56,39,49,38,15,2	81

SHOPPING	GAMBLE	SEX	KEYWORD	KEYWORD						
Bad	Bad	is tough	CAREER	Career,Hard Work,Co-workers,Low Payment,Job Problems,High Temper,Low						

STRESS LEVEL		LUCKY COLORS		JEWELERY		MOONS EFFECT		GRAHA EFFECT		DAILY DEITY
High		Dark Blue/ Purple/		Amethyst/Gold		Emotional		Job Graha		Lingam

DAILY PUJA	DAILY PSALMS
Worship Ganesh, Give gifts to father, and co -workers, Plant gardens, farms	4, 13, 31 ,40, 49, 58, 76, 103, 121

Sunday, June 25, 2023		This is considered a POSITIVE day for you						Planet: Venus		
ADVICE & DETAILS								MANTRA FOR TODAY		
You will feel a great deal of frustration today if your financial matters related to job promotion, profits and money do not work out in the manner that you expect them to. Be patient and try to understand that the universe only send you what you can handle. You have been given what you need the brain and the brawn to work and accomplish your desires.								Om Graam Greem Graum Sa Gurave namah swaha 21 times		

MONEY	LOVE	CAREER	FAMILY	TRAVEL	WEDDING	MOVE	BUSINESS	HEALTH	Lotto #'s	play 3 #s
Bad	Excellent	Fair	Good	Excellen	Good	Excellen	Good	Excellent	52,49,53,43,31,14,2	639

SHOPPING	GAMBLE	SEX	KEYWORD	KEYWORD						
Good	Good	is good	CHANGE	Sexuality,Travel,Change,Distant, far,Travel delays,Deception,Excercise,Illicit						

STRESS LEVEL		LUCKY COLORS		JEWELERY		MOONS EFFECT		GRAHA EFFECT		DAILY DEITY
Fair		Tan/Green/ Beige		Pearl/Silver/quartz		Courageous		Travel Graha		Nataraja

DAILY PUJA	DAILY PSALMS
Artistic gifts, Pray to Krishna, Do good deeds, do Spiritual trips	5, 14, 32 ,41, 50, 59, 77, 104, 122

Monday, June 26, 2023 — This is considered a NEGATIVE day for you — Planet: Mars

ADVICE & DETAILS

Although you feel powerful today, you must connect with your inner intelligence and give and receive advice with an open heart and mind. You will have to opportunity to experience high pleasure today and be around or be part of things related to TV or fame.

MANTRA FOR TODAY: Om Mana Swasti Shanti Kuru kuru Swaha Shivoham Shivoham 27 times

MONEY	LOVE	CAREER	FAMILY	TRAVEL	WEDDING	MOVE	BUSINESS	HEALTH	Lotto #'s	play 3 #s
Bad	Bad	Bad	Bad	Bad	Bad	Bad	Fair	Bad	23,39,58,62,58,39,6	594

SHOPPING	GAMBLE	SEX	KEYWORD	KEYWORD
Fair	Bad	is frustrating	POWER	Responsibilty,Disagreement,Family,Back Pain,Family Conflicts,Traffic

STRESS LEVEL	LUCKY COLORS	JEWELERY	MOONS EFFECT	GRAHA EFFECT	DAILY DEITY
High	Purple/Blue/Rose	Emerald/Saphire	Educational	Family Graha	Mahakali

DAILY PUJA	DAILY PSALMS
Meditate, Control temper, Pray to Hanuman, Chant Hanuman Chalisa	6, 15, 33 ,42, 51, 60, 78, 105, 123

Tuesday, June 27, 2023 — This is considered a NEUTRAL day for you — Planet: Uranus

ADVICE & DETAILS

There will be a feeling of excitement and anticipation, but changes in plans or ideas may leave you feeling frustrated. Use your internal power to overcome the frustration and flow with the changes that at the end will be beneficial.

MANTRA FOR TODAY: Jai Jai Shiva Shambo.(2) ...Mahadeva Shambo (2) 21 times 8

MONEY	LOVE	CAREER	FAMILY	TRAVEL	WEDDING	MOVE	BUSINESS	HEALTH	Lotto #'s	play 3 #s
Good	Good	Fair	Good	Good	Bad	Good	Bad	Fair	57,58,43,46,3,40,5	503

SHOPPING	GAMBLE	SEX	KEYWORD	KEYWORD
Bad	Fair	is quiet	DIVINE	Spirituality,Religious,Astrology,Inner Conflicts,Religious ,Sleepiness,Advice

STRESS LEVEL	LUCKY COLORS	JEWELERY	MOONS EFFECT	GRAHA EFFECT	DAILY DEITY
Fair	Light Blue/Peach	Tiger's eye/Gold/Sil	Affectionate	God'S Graha	Shesnaag

DAILY PUJA	DAILY PSALMS
Chant Shiva Mantras, Take gifts to Ocean - Ganga Puja, Donate to Temple, Priests, etc.	7, 16, 34 ,43, 52, 61, 79, 106, 124

Wednesday, June 28, 2023 — This is considered a POSITIVE day for you — Planet: Jupiter

ADVICE & DETAILS

Government and police agencies may cross paths with you today; try to follow the law so the encounters are more pleasurable. You will be the target of jealousy today so try to stay humble about your accomplishments or your belongings and remember that the good times also pass what remains is only the purity in your heart. You will have to confront many responsibilities today do it with surrender and

MANTRA FOR TODAY: Om Hareem Nama Swaha..Shri Maha Laxmi Aye Namah swaha 12 times

MONEY	LOVE	CAREER	FAMILY	TRAVEL	WEDDING	MOVE	BUSINESS	HEALTH	Lotto #'s	play 3 #s
Excellent	Good	Excellent	Good	Good	Excellent	Good	Excellent	Excellent	66,13,8,2,38,43,63	447

SHOPPING	GAMBLE	SEX	KEYWORD	KEYWORD
Excellent	Excellent	is excellent	MONEY	Business,Major Expense,Money -

STRESS LEVEL	LUCKY COLORS	JEWELERY	MOONS EFFECT	GRAHA EFFECT	DAILY DEITY
Low	Yellow/Silver	Diamonds/Gold/Pea	Secretive	Money Graha	Mahalaxmi

DAILY PUJA	DAILY PSALMS
Decorate Land, Feed the poor, Donate milk /products to all, Feed holy guests,	8, 17, 35 ,44, 53, 62, 80, 107, 125

Thursday, June 29, 2023 — This is considered a NEGATIVE day for you — Planet: Saturn

ADVICE & DETAILS

You have to deal with a great deal of responsibilities today; regardless of this others will feel jealous and envious of you. There are possible encounters with police and/or government officials.

MANTRA FOR TODAY: Om Ganga mataye nama swaha Om Varuna Devta aye Pahimam 11 times

MONEY	LOVE	CAREER	FAMILY	TRAVEL	WEDDING	MOVE	BUSINESS	HEALTH	Lotto #'s	play 3 #s
Bad	Bad	Bad	Fair	Bad	Bad	Bad	Bad	Bad	42,64,16,53,50,68,3	707

SHOPPING	GAMBLE	SEX	KEYWORD	KEYWORD
Bad	Bad	is very bad	KARMA	Destruction,Losses,Death,Sickness - cold,Legal matter,Abusive,Karmic debts,God -

STRESS LEVEL	LUCKY COLORS	JEWELERY	MOONS EFFECT	GRAHA EFFECT	DAILY DEITY
High	Gold/Brown//Green	Saphire/Hessonite	Ivestments	Evil Graha	Agnidev

DAILY PUJA	DAILY PSALMS
Remembrance of family members who died, worship of older people. gifts to grand parents	9, 18, 36 ,45, 54, 63, 81, 108, 126

Friday, June 30, 2023				This is considered a NEUTRAL day for you						Planet: Sun	
ADVICE & DETAILS										MANTRA FOR TODAY	

Your authoritative attitude mixed with arrogance and the need to feel superior may bring you difficulties with government or any of its agencies and may also make you feel lonely. Being humble today will be beneficial.

Om Namo Bhagawate Mukhtanandaya, 108 times

MONEY	LOVE	CAREER	FAMILY	TRAVEL	WEDDING	MOVE	BUSINESS	HEALTH	Lotto #'s	play 3 #s
Fair	Bad	Good	Bad	Fair	Bad	Fair	Fair	Fair	11,11,20,66,44,69,6	809

SHOPPING	GAMBLE	SEX	KEYWORD	KEYWORD						
Fair	Fair	is fair	MIND	Independence,Loneliness,Meditative,Worry,Dominating,Illness - Cold,On Your						

STRESS LEVEL		LUCKY COLORS		JEWELERY		MOONS EFFECT		GRAHA EFFECT		DAILY DEITY
High		White/Yellow/		Pearl/Quartz		Arrogance		Status Graha		Saraswaty

DAILY PUJA	DAILY PSALMS
Give Gifts to Priests, Invite holy ones to your home, Feed Swamis and Yogis, Do Shiva Puja.	1, 10, 28 ,37, 46, 55, 73, 100, 118

Saturday, July 1, 2023				This is considered a POSITIVE day for you						Planet: Jupiter	
ADVICE & DETAILS										MANTRA FOR TODAY	

It is important to follow God-like ways in order to receive protection from deceitful people that may want to take advantage of you today. Today you should expect short trips or some movement of some sort either places, people or things.

Om Hareem Nama Swaha..Shri Maha Laxmi Aye Namah swaha 12 times

MONEY	LOVE	CAREER	FAMILY	TRAVEL	WEDDING	MOVE	BUSINESS	HEALTH	Lotto #'s	play 3 #s
Excellent	Good	Excellent	Good	Good	Excellent	Good	Excellent	Excellent	7,61,21,55,74,50,61	384

SHOPPING	GAMBLE	SEX	KEYWORD	KEYWORD						
Excellent	Excellent	is excellent	MONEY	Business,Major Expense,Money -						

STRESS LEVEL		LUCKY COLORS		JEWELERY		MOONS EFFECT		GRAHA EFFECT		DAILY DEITY
Low		Yellow/Silver		Diamonds/Gold/Pea		Secretive		Money Graha		Mahalaxmi

DAILY PUJA	DAILY PSALMS
Decorate Land, Feed the poor, Donate milk /products to all, Feed holy guests,	8, 17, 35 ,44, 53, 62, 80, 107, 125

Sunday, July 2, 2023				This is considered a NEGATIVE day for you						Planet: Saturn	
ADVICE & DETAILS										MANTRA FOR TODAY	

Make sure that the seeds you sow in your life are those of spirituality, devotion, love and understanding so you may reap the same bounty. Prepare yourself for possible accident or sudden changes in your life that give you an opportunity for rebirth .

Om Ganga mataye nama swaha Om Varuna Devta aye Pahimam 11 times

MONEY	LOVE	CAREER	FAMILY	TRAVEL	WEDDING	MOVE	BUSINESS	HEALTH	Lotto #'s	play 3 #s
Bad	Bad	Bad	Fair	Bad	Bad	Bad	Bad	Bad	3,73,74,16,59,40,69	948

SHOPPING	GAMBLE	SEX	KEYWORD	KEYWORD						
Bad	Bad	is very bad	KARMA	Destruction,Losses,Death,Sickness - cold,Legal matter,Abusive,Karmic debts,God -						

STRESS LEVEL		LUCKY COLORS		JEWELERY		MOONS EFFECT		GRAHA EFFECT		DAILY DEITY
High		Gold/Brown//Green		Saphire/Hessonite		Ivestments		Evil Graha		Agnidev

DAILY PUJA	DAILY PSALMS
Remembrance of family members who died, worship of older people. gifts to grand parents	9, 18, 36 ,45, 54, 63, 81, 108, 126

Monday, July 3, 2023				This is considered a NEUTRAL day for you						Planet: Sun	
ADVICE & DETAILS										MANTRA FOR TODAY	

A religious or spiritual demeanor will help you deal today with losses and lack of health. Be grateful for your blessings and offer the difficult lessons to the gods.

Om Namo Bhagawate Mukhtanandaya, 108 times

MONEY	LOVE	CAREER	FAMILY	TRAVEL	WEDDING	MOVE	BUSINESS	HEALTH	Lotto #'s	play 3 #s
Fair	Bad	Good	Bad	Fair	Bad	Fair	Fair	Fair	29,6,18,64,16,51,35	534

SHOPPING	GAMBLE	SEX	KEYWORD	KEYWORD						
Fair	Fair	is fair	MIND	Independence,Loneliness,Meditative,Worry,Dominating,Illness - Cold,On Your						

STRESS LEVEL		LUCKY COLORS		JEWELERY		MOONS EFFECT		GRAHA EFFECT		DAILY DEITY
High		White/Yellow/		Pearl/Quartz		Arrogance		Status Graha		Saraswaty

DAILY PUJA	DAILY PSALMS
Give Gifts to Priests, Invite holy ones to your home, Feed Swamis and Yogis, Do Shiva Puja.	1, 10, 28 ,37, 46, 55, 73, 100, 118

Tuesday, July 4, 2023 — This is considered a POSITIVE day for you — Planet: Moon

ADVICE & DETAILS	MANTRA FOR TODAY
Instead of criticism, offer advice from the heart; not ego. It will be a slow day, but you will feel your connection to God. Do positive actions for good karma.	Kali Durge Namo Nama Om Durge aye nama swaha 108 times

MONEY	LOVE	CAREER	FAMILY	TRAVEL	WEDDING	MOVE	BUSINESS	HEALTH	Lotto #'s	play 3 #s
Good	Excellent	Good	Good	Excellen	Good	Good	Good	Good	9,57,8,51,32,6,21	122

SHOPPING	GAMBLE	SEX	KEYWORD	KEYWORD
Good	Good	is good	LOVE	Romance,Popularity,Visitors,Shopping,Food, Drinks,Co-

STRESS LEVEL	LUCKY COLORS	JEWELERY	MOONS EFFECT	GRAHA EFFECT	DAILY DEITY
Low	Red/Yellow/Pink	Topaz/Diamonds	Conservative	Love Graha	Gauri

DAILY PUJA	DAILY PSALMS
Give Gifts to females andnMother, Serve milk Products, Worship Durga forms	2, 11, 29 ,38, 47, 56, 74, 101, 119

Wednesday, July 5, 2023 — This is considered a POSITIVE day for you — Planet: Mercury

ADVICE & DETAILS	MANTRA FOR TODAY
Today working and communicating with others may further your plans to publish that book you have been thinking about writing. It is a day when expression in any form will be fruitful. You must avoid negative influences of others with such things as alcohol and drugs served in gatherings.	Om hareem Kleem Hreem Aem Saraswataye namaha 21 times

MONEY	LOVE	CAREER	FAMILY	TRAVEL	WEDDING	MOVE	BUSINESS	HEALTH	Lotto #'s	play 3 #s
Good	Fair	Good	Good	Excellen	Good	Good	Good	Excellent	57,54,25,52,64,66,5	786

SHOPPING	GAMBLE	SEX	KEYWORD	KEYWORD
Good	Good	is great	SOCIAL	Children,Education,Astrology,Bargains,Social Functions,Childishness,Groups -

STRESS LEVEL	LUCKY COLORS	JEWELERY	MOONS EFFECT	GRAHA EFFECT	DAILY DEITY
Low	Green/Sky Blue/	Diamonds/Silver	Enthusiastic	Social Graha	Vishnu

DAILY PUJA	DAILY PSALMS
Wash the feet of Children, Do Satnarayan Pooja, Read & chant Geeta	3, 12, 30 ,39, 48, 57, 75, 102, 120

Thursday, July 6, 2023 — This is considered a NEGATIVE day for you — Planet: Pluto

ADVICE & DETAILS	MANTRA FOR TODAY
It is important to follow God-like ways in order to receive protection from deceitful people that may want to take advantage of you today. Today you should expect short trips or some movement of some sort either places, people or things.	Om Jai Viganeshwaraya.. Lambodaraya Namo Namaha 21 times

MONEY	LOVE	CAREER	FAMILY	TRAVEL	WEDDING	MOVE	BUSINESS	HEALTH	Lotto #'s	play 3 #s
Bad	Fair	Bad	Fair	Bad	Good	Bad	Bad	Bad	74,18,14,25,53,63,2	925

SHOPPING	GAMBLE	SEX	KEYWORD	KEYWORD
Bad	Bad	is tough	CAREER	Career,Hard Work,Co-workers,Low Payment,Job Problems,High Temper,Low

STRESS LEVEL	LUCKY COLORS	JEWELERY	MOONS EFFECT	GRAHA EFFECT	DAILY DEITY
High	Dark Blue/ Purple/	Amethyst/Gold	Emotional	Job Graha	Lingam

DAILY PUJA	DAILY PSALMS
Worship Ganesh, Give gifts to father, and co -workers, Plant gardens, farms	4, 13, 31 ,40, 49, 58, 76, 103, 121

Friday, July 7, 2023 — This is considered a POSITIVE day for you — Planet: Venus

ADVICE & DETAILS	MANTRA FOR TODAY
Make sure that the seeds you sow in your life are those of spirituality, devotion, love and understanding so you may reap the same bounty. Prepare yourself for possible accident or sudden changes in your life that give you an opportunity for rebirth .	Om Graam Greem Graum Sa Gurave namah swaha 21 times

MONEY	LOVE	CAREER	FAMILY	TRAVEL	WEDDING	MOVE	BUSINESS	HEALTH	Lotto #'s	play 3 #s
Bad	Excellent	Fair	Good	Excellen	Good	Exceller	Good	Excellent	47,44,60,34,70,15,6	483

SHOPPING	GAMBLE	SEX	KEYWORD	KEYWORD
Good	Good	is good	CHANGE	Sexuality,Travel,Change,Distant, far,Travel delays,Deception,Excercise,Illicit

STRESS LEVEL	LUCKY COLORS	JEWELERY	MOONS EFFECT	GRAHA EFFECT	DAILY DEITY
Fair	Tan/Green/ Beige	Pearl/Silver/quartz	Courageous	Travel Graha	Nataraja

DAILY PUJA	DAILY PSALMS
Artistic gifts, Pray to Krishna, Do good deeds, do Spiritual trips	5, 14, 32 ,41, 50, 59, 77, 104, 122

Saturday, July 8, 2023 — This is considered a NEGATIVE day for you — Planet: Mars

ADVICE & DETAILS

Your manner of expression today may be commanding, make sure you do not go overboard and become bossy or overbearing. Enjoy the company of others in groups or parties. Use this time to work on creative projects like publishing, art or music.

MANTRA FOR TODAY

Om Mana Swasti Shanti Kuru kuru Swaha Shivoham Shivoham 27 times

MONEY	LOVE	CAREER	FAMILY	TRAVEL	WEDDING	MOVE	BUSINESS	HEALTH	Lotto #'s	play 3 #s
Bad	Bad	Bad	Bad	Bad	Bad	Bad	Fair	Bad	68,42,9,8,27,35,31	16

SHOPPING	GAMBLE	SEX	KEYWORD	KEYWORD
Fair	Bad	is frustrating	POWER	Responsibilty,Disagreement,Family,Back Pain,Family Conflicts,Traffic

STRESS LEVEL	LUCKY COLORS	JEWELERY	MOONS EFFECT	GRAHA EFFECT	DAILY DEITY
High	Purple/Blue/Rose	Emerald/Saphire	Educational	Family Graha	Mahakali

DAILY PUJA: Meditate, Control temper, Pray to Hanuman, Chant Hanuman Chalisa

DAILY PSALMS: 6, 15, 33 ,42, 51, 60, 78, 105, 123

Sunday, July 9, 2023 — This is considered a NEUTRAL day for you — Planet: Uranus

ADVICE & DETAILS

Today working and communicating with others may further your plans to publish that book you have been thinking about writing. It is a day when expression in any form will be fruitful. You must avoid negative influences of others with such things as alcohol and drugs served in gatherings.

MANTRA FOR TODAY

Jai Jai Shiva Shambo.(2) ...Mahadeva Shambo (2) 21 times 8

MONEY	LOVE	CAREER	FAMILY	TRAVEL	WEDDING	MOVE	BUSINESS	HEALTH	Lotto #'s	play 3 #s
Good	Good	Fair	Good	Good	Bad	Good	Bad	Fair	65,11,64,7,5,60,72	74

SHOPPING	GAMBLE	SEX	KEYWORD	KEYWORD
Bad	Fair	is quiet	DIVINE	Spirituality,Religious,Astrology,Inner Conflicts,Religious ,Sleepiness,Advice

STRESS LEVEL	LUCKY COLORS	JEWELERY	MOONS EFFECT	GRAHA EFFECT	DAILY DEITY
Fair	Light Blue/Peach	Tiger's eye/Gold/Sil	Affectionate	God'S Graha	Shesnaag

DAILY PUJA: Chant Shiva Mantras, Take gifts to Ocean - Ganga Puja, Donate to Temple, Priests, etc.

DAILY PSALMS: 7, 16, 34 ,43, 52, 61, 79, 106, 124

Monday, July 10, 2023 — This is considered a POSITIVE day for you — Planet: Jupiter

ADVICE & DETAILS

It is important to follow God-like ways in order to receive protection from deceitful people that may want to take advantage of you today. Today you should expect short trips or some movement of some sort either places, people or things.

MANTRA FOR TODAY

Om Hareem Nama Swaha..Shri Maha Laxmi Aye Namah swaha 12 times

MONEY	LOVE	CAREER	FAMILY	TRAVEL	WEDDING	MOVE	BUSINESS	HEALTH	Lotto #'s	play 3 #s
Excellent	Good	Excellent	Good	Good	Excellent	Good	Excellent	Excellent	38,33,21,15,26,39,3	797

SHOPPING	GAMBLE	SEX	KEYWORD	KEYWORD
Excellent	Excellent	is excellent	MONEY	Business,Major Expense,Money -

STRESS LEVEL	LUCKY COLORS	JEWELERY	MOONS EFFECT	GRAHA EFFECT	DAILY DEITY
Low	Yellow/Silver	Diamonds/Gold/Pea	Secretive	Money Graha	Mahalaxmi

DAILY PUJA: Decorate Land, Feed the poor, Donate milk /products to all, Feed holy guests,

DAILY PSALMS: 8, 17, 35 ,44, 53, 62, 80, 107, 125

Tuesday, July 11, 2023 — This is considered a NEGATIVE day for you — Planet: Saturn

ADVICE & DETAILS

Make sure that the seeds you sow in your life are those of spirituality, devotion, love and understanding so you may reap the same bounty. Prepare yourself for possible accident or sudden changes in your life that give you an opportunity for rebirth .

MANTRA FOR TODAY

Om Ganga mataye nama swaha Om Varuna Devta aye Pahimam 11 times

MONEY	LOVE	CAREER	FAMILY	TRAVEL	WEDDING	MOVE	BUSINESS	HEALTH	Lotto #'s	play 3 #s
Bad	Bad	Bad	Fair	Bad	Bad	Bad	Bad	Bad	62,5,46,64,7,14,36	881

SHOPPING	GAMBLE	SEX	KEYWORD	KEYWORD
Bad	Bad	is very bad	KARMA	Destruction,Losses,Death,Sickness - cold,Legal matter,Abusive,Karmic debts,God -

STRESS LEVEL	LUCKY COLORS	JEWELERY	MOONS EFFECT	GRAHA EFFECT	DAILY DEITY
High	Gold/Brown//Green	Saphire/Hessonite	Ivestments	Evil Graha	Agnidev

DAILY PUJA: Remembrance of family members who died, worship of older people. gifts to grand parents

DAILY PSALMS: 9, 18, 36 ,45, 54, 63, 81, 108, 126

Wednesday, July 12, 2023 — This is considered a NEUTRAL day for you — Planet: Sun

ADVICE & DETAILS

A religious or spiritual demeanor will help you deal today with losses and lack of health. Be grateful for your blessings and offer the difficult lessons to the gods.

MANTRA FOR TODAY

Om Namo Bhagawate Mukhtanandaya, 108 times

MONEY	LOVE	CAREER	FAMILY	TRAVEL	WEDDING	MOVE	BUSINESS	HEALTH	Lotto #'s	play 3 #s
Fair	Bad	Good	Bad	Fair	Bad	Fair	Fair	Fair	59,21,3,46,27,57,34	543

SHOPPING	GAMBLE	SEX	KEYWORD	KEYWORD
Fair	Fair	is fair	MIND	Independence,Loneliness,Meditative,Worry,Dominating,Illness - Cold,On Your

STRESS LEVEL	LUCKY COLORS	JEWELERY	MOONS EFFECT	GRAHA EFFECT	DAILY DEITY
High	White/Yellow/	Pearl/Quartz	Arrogance	Status Graha	Saraswaty

DAILY PUJA	DAILY PSALMS
Give Gifts to Priests, Invite holy ones to your home, Feed Swamis and Yogis, Do Shiva Puja.	1, 10, 28 ,37, 46, 55, 73, 100, 118

Thursday, July 13, 2023 — This is considered a POSITIVE day for you — Planet: Moon

ADVICE & DETAILS

Instead of criticism, offer advice from the heart; not ego. It will be a slow day, but you will feel your connection to God. Do positive actions for good karma.

MANTRA FOR TODAY

Kali Durge Namo Nama Om Durge aye nama swaha 108 times

MONEY	LOVE	CAREER	FAMILY	TRAVEL	WEDDING	MOVE	BUSINESS	HEALTH	Lotto #'s	play 3 #s
Good	Excellent	Good	Good	Excellen	Good	Good	Good	Good	69,3,9,11,31,28,22	894

SHOPPING	GAMBLE	SEX	KEYWORD	KEYWORD
Good	Good	is good	LOVE	Romance,Popularity,Visitors,Shopping,Food, Drinks,Co-

STRESS LEVEL	LUCKY COLORS	JEWELERY	MOONS EFFECT	GRAHA EFFECT	DAILY DEITY
Low	Red/Yellow/Pink	Topaz/Diamonds	Conservative	Love Graha	Gauri

DAILY PUJA	DAILY PSALMS
Give Gifts to females andnMother, Serve milk Products, Worship Durga forms	2, 11, 29 ,38, 47, 56, 74, 101, 119

Friday, July 14, 2023 — This is considered a POSITIVE day for you — Planet: Mercury

ADVICE & DETAILS

Today working and communicating with others may further your plans to publish that book you have been thinking about writing. It is a day when expression in any form will be fruitful. You must avoid negative influences of others with such things as alcohol and drugs served in gatherings.

MANTRA FOR TODAY

Om hareem Kleem Hreem Aem Saraswataye namaha 21 times

MONEY	LOVE	CAREER	FAMILY	TRAVEL	WEDDING	MOVE	BUSINESS	HEALTH	Lotto #'s	play 3 #s
Good	Fair	Good	Good	Excellen	Good	Good	Good	Excellent	47,64,66,14,33,7,55	212

SHOPPING	GAMBLE	SEX	KEYWORD	KEYWORD
Good	Good	is great	SOCIAL	Children,Education,Astrology,Bargains,Social Functions,Childishness,Groups -

STRESS LEVEL	LUCKY COLORS	JEWELERY	MOONS EFFECT	GRAHA EFFECT	DAILY DEITY
Low	Green/Sky Blue/	Diamonds/Silver	Enthusiastic	Social Graha	Vishnu

DAILY PUJA	DAILY PSALMS
Wash the feet of Children, Do Satnarayan Pooja, Read & chant Geeta	3, 12, 30 ,39, 48, 57, 75, 102, 120

Saturday, July 15, 2023 — This is considered a NEGATIVE day for you — Planet: Pluto

ADVICE & DETAILS

It is important to follow God-like ways in order to receive protection from deceitful people that may want to take advantage of you today. Today you should expect short trips or some movement of some sort either places, people or things.

MANTRA FOR TODAY

Om Jai Viganeshwaraya.. Lambodaraya Namo Namaha 21 times

MONEY	LOVE	CAREER	FAMILY	TRAVEL	WEDDING	MOVE	BUSINESS	HEALTH	Lotto #'s	play 3 #s
Bad	Fair	Bad	Fair	Bad	Good	Bad	Bad	Bad	9,20,34,71,6,54,56	348

SHOPPING	GAMBLE	SEX	KEYWORD	KEYWORD
Bad	Bad	is tough	CAREER	Career,Hard Work,Co-workers,Low Payment,Job Problems,High Temper,Low

STRESS LEVEL	LUCKY COLORS	JEWELERY	MOONS EFFECT	GRAHA EFFECT	DAILY DEITY
High	Dark Blue/ Purple/	Amethyst/Gold	Emotional	Job Graha	Lingam

DAILY PUJA	DAILY PSALMS
Worship Ganesh, Give gifts to father, and co -workers, Plant gardens, farms	4, 13, 31 ,40, 49, 58, 76, 103, 121

Sunday, July 16, 2023 — This is considered a POSITIVE day for you — Planet: Venus

ADVICE & DETAILS

Make sure that the seeds you sow in your life are those of spirituality, devotion, love and understanding so you may reap the same bounty. Prepare yourself for possible accident or sudden changes in your life that give you an opportunity for rebirth .

MANTRA FOR TODAY

Om Graam Greem Graum Sa Gurave namah swaha 21 times

MONEY	LOVE	CAREER	FAMILY	TRAVEL	WEDDING	MOVE	BUSINESS	HEALTH	Lotto #'s	play 3 #s
Bad	Excellent	Fair	Good	Excellen	Good	Excellen	Good	Excellent	41,59,3,44,26,31,62	49

SHOPPING	GAMBLE	SEX	KEYWORD	KEYWORD
Good	Good	is good	CHANGE	Sexuality,Travel,Change,Distant, far,Travel delays,Deception,Excercise,Illicit

STRESS LEVEL	LUCKY COLORS	JEWELERY	MOONS EFFECT	GRAHA EFFECT	DAILY DEITY
Fair	Tan/Green/ Beige	Pearl/Silver/quartz	Courageous	Travel Graha	Nataraja

DAILY PUJA	DAILY PSALMS
Artistic gifts, Pray to Krishna, Do good deeds, do Spiritual trips	5, 14, 32 ,41, 50, 59, 77, 104, 122

Monday, July 17, 2023 — This is considered a NEGATIVE day for you — Planet: Mars

ADVICE & DETAILS

Your manner of expression today may be commanding, make sure you do not go overboard and become bossy or overbearing. Enjoy the company of others in groups or parties. Use this time to work on creative projects like publishing, art or music.

MANTRA FOR TODAY

Om Mana Swasti Shanti Kuru kuru Swaha Shivoham Shivoham 27 times

MONEY	LOVE	CAREER	FAMILY	TRAVEL	WEDDING	MOVE	BUSINESS	HEALTH	Lotto #'s	play 3 #s
Bad	Bad	Bad	Bad	Bad	Bad	Bad	Fair	Bad	51,42,30,15,19,30,4	129

SHOPPING	GAMBLE	SEX	KEYWORD	KEYWORD
Fair	Bad	is frustrating	POWER	Responsibilty,Disagreement,Family,Back Pain,Family Conflicts,Traffic

STRESS LEVEL	LUCKY COLORS	JEWELERY	MOONS EFFECT	GRAHA EFFECT	DAILY DEITY
High	Purple/Blue/Rose	Emerald/Saphire	Educational	Family Graha	Mahakali

DAILY PUJA	DAILY PSALMS
Meditate, Control temper, Pray to Hanuman, Chant Hanuman Chalisa	6, 15, 33 ,42, 51, 60, 78, 105, 123

Tuesday, July 18, 2023 — This is considered a NEUTRAL day for you — Planet: Uranus

ADVICE & DETAILS

Today working and communicating with others may further your plans to publish that book you have been thinking about writing. It is a day when expression in any form will be fruitful. You must avoid negative influences of others with such things as alcohol and drugs served in gatherings.

MANTRA FOR TODAY

Jai Jai Shiva Shambo.(2) ...Mahadeva Shambo (2) 21 times 8

MONEY	LOVE	CAREER	FAMILY	TRAVEL	WEDDING	MOVE	BUSINESS	HEALTH	Lotto #'s	play 3 #s
Good	Good	Fair	Good	Good	Bad	Good	Bad	Fair	10,18,19,69,23,40,4	841

SHOPPING	GAMBLE	SEX	KEYWORD	KEYWORD
Bad	Fair	is quiet	DIVINE	Spirituality,Religious,Astrology,Inner Conflicts,Religious ,Sleepiness,Advice

STRESS LEVEL	LUCKY COLORS	JEWELERY	MOONS EFFECT	GRAHA EFFECT	DAILY DEITY
Fair	Light Blue/Peach	Tiger's eye/Gold/Sil	Affectionate	God'S Graha	Shesnaag

DAILY PUJA	DAILY PSALMS
Chant Shiva Mantras, Take gifts to Ocean - Ganga Puja, Donate to Temple, Priests, etc.	7, 16, 34 ,43, 52, 61, 79, 106, 124

Wednesday, July 19, 2023 — This is considered a POSITIVE day for you — Planet: Jupiter

ADVICE & DETAILS

It is important to follow God-like ways in order to receive protection from deceitful people that may want to take advantage of you today. Today you should expect short trips or some movement of some sort either places, people or things.

MANTRA FOR TODAY

Om Hareem Nama Swaha..Shri Maha Laxmi Aye Namah swaha 12 times

MONEY	LOVE	CAREER	FAMILY	TRAVEL	WEDDING	MOVE	BUSINESS	HEALTH	Lotto #'s	play 3 #s
Excellent	Good	Excellent	Good	Good	Excellent	Good	Excellent	Excellent	72,39,11,28,72,49,5	873

SHOPPING	GAMBLE	SEX	KEYWORD	KEYWORD
Excellent	Excellent	is excellent	MONEY	Business,Major Expense,Money -

STRESS LEVEL	LUCKY COLORS	JEWELERY	MOONS EFFECT	GRAHA EFFECT	DAILY DEITY
Low	Yellow/Silver	Diamonds/Gold/Pea	Secretive	Money Graha	Mahalaxmi

DAILY PUJA	DAILY PSALMS
Decorate Land, Feed the poor, Donate milk /products to all, Feed holy guests,	8, 17, 35 ,44, 53, 62, 80, 107, 125

Thursday, July 20, 2023 — This is considered a NEGATIVE day for you — Planet: Saturn

ADVICE & DETAILS	MANTRA FOR TODAY
Make sure that the seeds you sow in your life are those of spirituality, devotion, love and understanding so you may reap the same bounty. Prepare yourself for possible accident or sudden changes in your life that give you an opportunity for rebirth .	Om Ganga mataye nama swaha Om Varuna Devta aye Pahimam 11 times

MONEY	LOVE	CAREER	FAMILY	TRAVEL	WEDDING	MOVE	BUSINESS	HEALTH	Lotto #'s	play 3 #s
Bad	Bad	Bad	Fair	Bad	Bad	Bad	Bad	Bad	68,2,9,13,10,5,10	256

SHOPPING	GAMBLE	SEX	KEYWORD	KEYWORD						
Bad	Bad	is very bad	KARMA	Destruction,Losses,Death,Sickness - cold,Legal matter,Abusive,Karmic debts,God -						

STRESS LEVEL	LUCKY COLORS	JEWELERY	MOONS EFFECT	GRAHA EFFECT	DAILY DEITY
High	Gold/Brown//Green	Saphire/Hessonite	Ivestments	Evil Graha	Agnidev

DAILY PUJA	DAILY PSALMS
Remembrance of family members who died, worship of older people. gifts to grand parents	9, 18, 36 ,45, 54, 63, 81, 108, 126

Friday, July 21, 2023 — This is considered a NEUTRAL day for you — Planet: Sun

ADVICE & DETAILS	MANTRA FOR TODAY
A religious or spiritual demeanor will help you deal today with losses and lack of health. Be grateful for your blessings and offer the difficult lessons to the gods.	Om Namo Bhagawate Mukhtanandaya, 108 times

MONEY	LOVE	CAREER	FAMILY	TRAVEL	WEDDING	MOVE	BUSINESS	HEALTH	Lotto #'s	play 3 #s
Fair	Bad	Good	Bad	Fair	Bad	Fair	Fair	Fair	18,72,70,75,4,34,23	759

SHOPPING	GAMBLE	SEX	KEYWORD	KEYWORD						
Fair	Fair	is fair	MIND	Independence,Loneliness,Meditative,Worry,Dominating,Illness - Cold,On Your						

STRESS LEVEL	LUCKY COLORS	JEWELERY	MOONS EFFECT	GRAHA EFFECT	DAILY DEITY
High	White/Yellow/	Pearl/Quartz	Arrogance	Status Graha	Saraswaty

DAILY PUJA	DAILY PSALMS
Give Gifts to Priests, Invite holy ones to your home, Feed Swamis and Yogis, Do Shiva Puja.	1, 10, 28 ,37, 46, 55, 73, 100, 118

Saturday, July 22, 2023 — This is considered a POSITIVE day for you — Planet: Moon

ADVICE & DETAILS	MANTRA FOR TODAY
Instead of criticism, offer advice from the heart; not ego. It will be a slow day, but you will feel your connection to God. Do positive actions for good karma.	Kali Durge Namo Nama Om Durge aye nama swaha 108 times

MONEY	LOVE	CAREER	FAMILY	TRAVEL	WEDDING	MOVE	BUSINESS	HEALTH	Lotto #'s	play 3 #s
Good	Excellent	Good	Good	Excellen	Good	Good	Good	Good	54,9,38,26,15,2,12	146

SHOPPING	GAMBLE	SEX	KEYWORD	KEYWORD						
Good	Good	is good	LOVE	Romance,Popularity,Visitors,Shopping,Food, Drinks,Co-						

STRESS LEVEL	LUCKY COLORS	JEWELERY	MOONS EFFECT	GRAHA EFFECT	DAILY DEITY
Low	Red/Yellow/Pink	Topaz/Diamonds	Conservative	Love Graha	Gauri

DAILY PUJA	DAILY PSALMS
Give Gifts to females andnMother, Serve milk Products, Worship Durga forms	2, 11, 29 ,38, 47, 56, 74, 101, 119

Sunday, July 23, 2023 — This is considered a POSITIVE day for you — Planet: Mercury

ADVICE & DETAILS	MANTRA FOR TODAY
Today working and communicating with others may further your plans to publish that book you have been thinking about writing. It is a day when expression in any form will be fruitful. You must avoid negative influences of others with such things as alcohol and drugs served in gatherings.	Om hareem Kleem Hreem Aem Saraswataye namaha 21 times

MONEY	LOVE	CAREER	FAMILY	TRAVEL	WEDDING	MOVE	BUSINESS	HEALTH	Lotto #'s	play 3 #s
Good	Fair	Good	Good	Excellen	Good	Good	Good	Excellent	2,70,74,66,8,27,71	600

SHOPPING	GAMBLE	SEX	KEYWORD	KEYWORD						
Good	Good	is great	SOCIAL	Children,Education,Astrology,Bargains,Social Functions,Childishness,Groups -						

STRESS LEVEL	LUCKY COLORS	JEWELERY	MOONS EFFECT	GRAHA EFFECT	DAILY DEITY
Low	Green/Sky Blue/	Diamonds/Silver	Enthusiastic	Social Graha	Vishnu

DAILY PUJA	DAILY PSALMS
Wash the feet of Children, Do Satnarayan Pooja, Read & chant Geeta	3, 12, 30 ,39, 48, 57, 75, 102, 120

Monday, July 24, 2023 — This is considered a NEGATIVE day for you — Planet: Pluto

ADVICE & DETAILS

It is important to follow God-like ways in order to receive protection from deceitful people that may want to take advantage of you today. Today you should expect short trips or some movement of some sort either places, people or things.

MANTRA FOR TODAY

Om Jai Viganeshwaraya.. Lambodaraya Namo Namaha 21 times

MONEY	LOVE	CAREER	FAMILY	TRAVEL	WEDDING	MOVE	BUSINESS	HEALTH	Lotto #'s	play 3 #s
Bad	Fair	Bad	Fair	Bad	Good	Bad	Bad	Bad	63,20,11,64,18,45,7	271

SHOPPING	GAMBLE	SEX	KEYWORD	KEYWORD
Bad	Bad	is tough	CAREER	Career,Hard Work,Co-workers,Low Payment,Job Problems,High Temper,Low

STRESS LEVEL	LUCKY COLORS	JEWELERY	MOONS EFFECT	GRAHA EFFECT	DAILY DEITY
High	Dark Blue/ Purple/	Amethyst/Gold	Emotional	Job Graha	Lingam

DAILY PUJA	DAILY PSALMS
Worship Ganesh, Give gifts to father, and co -workers, Plant gardens, farms	4, 13, 31 ,40, 49, 58, 76, 103, 121

Tuesday, July 25, 2023 — This is considered a POSITIVE day for you — Planet: Venus

ADVICE & DETAILS

Make sure that the seeds you sow in your life are those of spirituality, devotion, love and understanding so you may reap the same bounty. Prepare yourself for possible accident or sudden changes in your life that give you an opportunity for rebirth .

MANTRA FOR TODAY

Om Graam Greem Graum Sa Gurave namah swaha 21 times

MONEY	LOVE	CAREER	FAMILY	TRAVEL	WEDDING	MOVE	BUSINESS	HEALTH	Lotto #'s	play 3 #s
Bad	Excellent	Fair	Good	Excellen	Good	Excellen	Good	Excellent	57,34,34,30,75,20,4	915

SHOPPING	GAMBLE	SEX	KEYWORD	KEYWORD
Good	Good	is good	CHANGE	Sexuality,Travel,Change,Distant, far,Travel delays,Deception,Excercise,Illicit

STRESS LEVEL	LUCKY COLORS	JEWELERY	MOONS EFFECT	GRAHA EFFECT	DAILY DEITY
Fair	Tan/Green/ Beige	Pearl/Silver/quartz	Courageous	Travel Graha	Nataraja

DAILY PUJA	DAILY PSALMS
Artistic gifts, Pray to Krishna, Do good deeds, do Spiritual trips	5, 14, 32 ,41, 50, 59, 77, 104, 122

Wednesday, July 26, 2023 — This is considered a NEGATIVE day for you — Planet: Mars

ADVICE & DETAILS

Your manner of expression today may be commanding, make sure you do not go overboard and become bossy or overbearing. Enjoy the company of others in groups or parties. Use this time to work on creative projects like publishing, art or music.

MANTRA FOR TODAY

Om Mana Swasti Shanti Kuru kuru Swaha Shivoham Shivoham 27 times

MONEY	LOVE	CAREER	FAMILY	TRAVEL	WEDDING	MOVE	BUSINESS	HEALTH	Lotto #'s	play 3 #s
Bad	Bad	Bad	Bad	Bad	Bad	Bad	Fair	Bad	6,59,5,48,47,16,8	269

SHOPPING	GAMBLE	SEX	KEYWORD	KEYWORD
Fair	Bad	is frustrating	POWER	Responsibilty,Disagreement,Family,Back Pain,Family Conflicts,Traffic

STRESS LEVEL	LUCKY COLORS	JEWELERY	MOONS EFFECT	GRAHA EFFECT	DAILY DEITY
High	Purple/Blue/Rose	Emerald/Saphire	Educational	Family Graha	Mahakali

DAILY PUJA	DAILY PSALMS
Meditate, Control temper, Pray to Hanuman, Chant Hanuman Chalisa	6, 15, 33 ,42, 51, 60, 78, 105, 123

Thursday, July 27, 2023 — This is considered a NEUTRAL day for you — Planet: Uranus

ADVICE & DETAILS

Today working and communicating with others may further your plans to publish that book you have been thinking about writing. It is a day when expression in any form will be fruitful. You must avoid negative influences of others with such things as alcohol and drugs served in gatherings.

MANTRA FOR TODAY

Jai Jai Shiva Shambo.(2) ...Mahadeva Shambo (2) 21 times 8

MONEY	LOVE	CAREER	FAMILY	TRAVEL	WEDDING	MOVE	BUSINESS	HEALTH	Lotto #'s	play 3 #s
Good	Good	Fair	Good	Good	Bad	Good	Bad	Fair	18,15,24,65,3,33,67	961

SHOPPING	GAMBLE	SEX	KEYWORD	KEYWORD
Bad	Fair	is quiet	DIVINE	Spirituality,Religious,Astrology,Inner Conflicts,Religious ,Sleepiness,Advice

STRESS LEVEL	LUCKY COLORS	JEWELERY	MOONS EFFECT	GRAHA EFFECT	DAILY DEITY
Fair	Light Blue/Peach	Tiger's eye/Gold/Sil	Affectionate	God'S Graha	Shesnaag

DAILY PUJA	DAILY PSALMS
Chant Shiva Mantras, Take gifts to Ocean - Ganga Puja, Donate to Temple, Priests, etc.	7, 16, 34 ,43, 52, 61, 79, 106, 124

Friday, July 28, 2023 — This is considered a POSITIVE day for you — Planet: Jupiter

ADVICE & DETAILS

It is important to follow God-like ways in order to receive protection from deceitful people that may want to take advantage of you today. Today you should expect short trips or some movement of some sort either places, people or things.

MANTRA FOR TODAY

Om Hareem Nama Swaha..Shri Maha Laxmi Aye Namah swaha 12 times

MONEY	LOVE	CAREER	FAMILY	TRAVEL	WEDDING	MOVE	BUSINESS	HEALTH	Lotto #'s	play 3 #s
Excellent	Good	Excellent	Good	Good	Excellent	Good	Excellent	Excellent	7,33,30,21,19,28,57	949

SHOPPING	GAMBLE	SEX	KEYWORD	KEYWORD
Excellent	Excellent	is excellent	MONEY	Business,Major Expense,Money -

STRESS LEVEL	LUCKY COLORS	JEWELERY	MOONS EFFECT	GRAHA EFFECT	DAILY DEITY
Low	Yellow/Silver	Diamonds/Gold/Pea	Secretive	Money Graha	Mahalaxmi

DAILY PUJA	DAILY PSALMS
Decorate Land, Feed the poor, Donate milk /products to all, Feed holy guests,	8, 17, 35 ,44, 53, 62, 80, 107, 125

Saturday, July 29, 2023 — This is considered a NEGATIVE day for you — Planet: Saturn

ADVICE & DETAILS

Make sure that the seeds you sow in your life are those of spirituality, devotion, love and understanding so you may reap the same bounty. Prepare yourself for possible accident or sudden changes in your life that give you an opportunity for rebirth .

MANTRA FOR TODAY

Om Ganga mataye nama swaha Om Varuna Devta aye Pahimam 11 times

MONEY	LOVE	CAREER	FAMILY	TRAVEL	WEDDING	MOVE	BUSINESS	HEALTH	Lotto #'s	play 3 #s
Bad	Bad	Bad	Fair	Bad	Bad	Bad	Bad	Bad	32,25,30,44,45,69,3	504

SHOPPING	GAMBLE	SEX	KEYWORD	KEYWORD
Bad	Bad	is very bad	KARMA	Destruction,Losses,Death,Sickness - cold,Legal matter,Abusive,Karmic debts,God -

STRESS LEVEL	LUCKY COLORS	JEWELERY	MOONS EFFECT	GRAHA EFFECT	DAILY DEITY
High	Gold/Brown//Green	Saphire/Hessonite	Ivestments	Evil Graha	Agnidev

DAILY PUJA	DAILY PSALMS
Remembrance of family members who died, worship of older people. gifts to grand parents	9, 18, 36 ,45, 54, 63, 81, 108, 126

Sunday, July 30, 2023 — This is considered a NEUTRAL day for you — Planet: Sun

ADVICE & DETAILS

A religious or spiritual demeanor will help you deal today with losses and lack of health. Be grateful for your blessings and offer the difficult lessons to the gods.

MANTRA FOR TODAY

Om Namo Bhagawate Mukhtanandaya, 108 times

MONEY	LOVE	CAREER	FAMILY	TRAVEL	WEDDING	MOVE	BUSINESS	HEALTH	Lotto #'s	play 3 #s
Fair	Bad	Good	Bad	Fair	Bad	Fair	Fair	Fair	24,69,9,50,59,7,61	405

SHOPPING	GAMBLE	SEX	KEYWORD	KEYWORD
Fair	Fair	is fair	MIND	Independence,Loneliness,Meditative,Worry,Dominating,Illness - Cold,On Your

STRESS LEVEL	LUCKY COLORS	JEWELERY	MOONS EFFECT	GRAHA EFFECT	DAILY DEITY
High	White/Yellow/	Pearl/Quartz	Arrogance	Status Graha	Saraswaty

DAILY PUJA	DAILY PSALMS
Give Gifts to Priests, Invite holy ones to your home, Feed Swamis and Yogis, Do Shiva Puja.	1, 10, 28 ,37, 46, 55, 73, 100, 118

Monday, July 31, 2023 — This is considered a POSITIVE day for you — Planet: Moon

ADVICE & DETAILS

Instead of criticism, offer advice from the heart; not ego. It will be a slow day, but you will feel your connection to God. Do positive actions for good karma.

MANTRA FOR TODAY

Kali Durge Namo Nama Om Durge aye nama swaha 108 times

MONEY	LOVE	CAREER	FAMILY	TRAVEL	WEDDING	MOVE	BUSINESS	HEALTH	Lotto #'s	play 3 #s
Good	Excellent	Good	Good	Excellen	Good	Good	Good	Good	10,54,19,43,59,57,9	701

SHOPPING	GAMBLE	SEX	KEYWORD	KEYWORD
Good	Good	is good	LOVE	Romance,Popularity,Visitors,Shopping,Food, Drinks,Co-

STRESS LEVEL	LUCKY COLORS	JEWELERY	MOONS EFFECT	GRAHA EFFECT	DAILY DEITY
Low	Red/Yellow/Pink	Topaz/Diamonds	Conservative	Love Graha	Gauri

DAILY PUJA	DAILY PSALMS
Give Gifts to females andnMother, Serve milk Products, Worship Durga forms	2, 11, 29 ,38, 47, 56, 74, 101, 119

Tuesday, August 1, 2023 — This is considered a POSITIVE day for you — Planet: Jupiter

ADVICE & DETAILS

Money is coming and/or going out today, but it will be pleasurable. You may be changing locations and enjoying the company of someone known or famous from TV or the entertainment industry.

MANTRA FOR TODAY

Om Hareem Nama Swaha..Shri Maha Laxmi Aye Namah swaha 12 times

MONEY	LOVE	CAREER	FAMILY	TRAVEL	WEDDING	MOVE	BUSINESS	HEALTH	Lotto #'s	play 3 #s
Excellent	Good	Excellent	Good	Good	Excellent	Good	Excellent	Excellent	53,30,33,47,37,21,3	888

SHOPPING	GAMBLE	SEX	KEYWORD	KEYWORD
Excellent	Excellent	is excellent	MONEY	Business,Major Expense,Money -

STRESS LEVEL	LUCKY COLORS	JEWELERY	MOONS EFFECT	GRAHA EFFECT	DAILY DEITY
Low	Yellow/Silver	Diamonds/Gold/Pea	Secretive	Money Graha	Mahalaxmi

DAILY PUJA	DAILY PSALMS
Decorate Land, Feed the poor, Donate milk /products to all, Feed holy guests,	8, 17, 35 ,44, 53, 62, 80, 107, 125

Wednesday, August 2, 2023 — This is considered a NEGATIVE day for you — Planet: Saturn

ADVICE & DETAILS

Today could be a very positive day influenced by promotion, profits and money; but there may be also a degree of frustation if your expectations are not fulfilled the way you feel they should. Concentrate in the positive and learn from what you perceive as negative.

MANTRA FOR TODAY

Om Ganga mataye nama swaha Om Varuna Devta aye Pahimam 11 times

MONEY	LOVE	CAREER	FAMILY	TRAVEL	WEDDING	MOVE	BUSINESS	HEALTH	Lotto #'s	play 3 #s
Bad	Bad	Bad	Fair	Bad	Bad	Bad	Bad	Bad	12,52,25,5,4,66,17	228

SHOPPING	GAMBLE	SEX	KEYWORD	KEYWORD
Bad	Bad	is very bad	KARMA	Destruction,Losses,Death,Sickness - cold,Legal matter,Abusive,Karmic debts,God -

STRESS LEVEL	LUCKY COLORS	JEWELERY	MOONS EFFECT	GRAHA EFFECT	DAILY DEITY
High	Gold/Brown//Green	Saphire/Hessonite	Ivestments	Evil Graha	Agnidev

DAILY PUJA	DAILY PSALMS
Remembrance of family members who died, worship of older people. gifts to grand parents	9, 18, 36 ,45, 54, 63, 81, 108, 126

Thursday, August 3, 2023 — This is considered a NEUTRAL day for you — Planet: Sun

ADVICE & DETAILS

You will be enjoying profits and money from your endeavors today, but on the other hand you will have sizable expenses that will give you great pleasure.

MANTRA FOR TODAY

Om Namo Bhagawate Mukhtanandaya, 108 times

MONEY	LOVE	CAREER	FAMILY	TRAVEL	WEDDING	MOVE	BUSINESS	HEALTH	Lotto #'s	play 3 #s
Fair	Bad	Good	Bad	Fair	Bad	Fair	Fair	Fair	26,15,32,47,27,56,4	53

SHOPPING	GAMBLE	SEX	KEYWORD	KEYWORD
Fair	Fair	is fair	MIND	Independence,Loneliness,Meditative,Worry,Dominating,Illness - Cold,On Your

STRESS LEVEL	LUCKY COLORS	JEWELERY	MOONS EFFECT	GRAHA EFFECT	DAILY DEITY
High	White/Yellow/	Pearl/Quartz	Arrogance	Status Graha	Saraswaty

DAILY PUJA	DAILY PSALMS
Give Gifts to Priests, Invite holy ones to your home, Feed Swamis and Yogis, Do Shiva Puja.	1, 10, 28 ,37, 46, 55, 73, 100, 118

Friday, August 4, 2023 — This is considered a POSITIVE day for you — Planet: Moon

ADVICE & DETAILS

This is a very positive day as long as you are willing to serve and cooperate with others. Make sure that every word your lips utter is with purpose, loving and kind. It is a propitious day for marriage and romance.

MANTRA FOR TODAY

Kali Durge Namo Nama Om Durge aye nama swaha 108 times

MONEY	LOVE	CAREER	FAMILY	TRAVEL	WEDDING	MOVE	BUSINESS	HEALTH	Lotto #'s	play 3 #s
Good	Excellent	Good	Good	Excellen	Good	Good	Good	Good	7,40,7,68,12,17,10	656

SHOPPING	GAMBLE	SEX	KEYWORD	KEYWORD
Good	Good	is good	LOVE	Romance,Popularity,Visitors,Shopping,Food, Drinks,Co-

STRESS LEVEL	LUCKY COLORS	JEWELERY	MOONS EFFECT	GRAHA EFFECT	DAILY DEITY
Low	Red/Yellow/Pink	Topaz/Diamonds	Conservative	Love Graha	Gauri

DAILY PUJA	DAILY PSALMS
Give Gifts to females andnMother, Serve milk Products, Worship Durga forms	2, 11, 29 ,38, 47, 56, 74, 101, 119

Saturday, August 5, 2023 — This is considered a POSITIVE day for you — Planet: Mercury

ADVICE & DETAILS

Finances are in your mind today. It is a great day to make money, get profits and get a promotion at your job. You may also have to deal with children or younger adults and their financial needs.

MANTRA FOR TODAY

Om hareem Kleem Hreem Aem Saraswataye namaha 21 times

MONEY	LOVE	CAREER	FAMILY	TRAVEL	WEDDING	MOVE	BUSINESS	HEALTH	Lotto #'s	play 3 #s
Good	Fair	Good	Good	Excellen	Good	Good	Good	Excellent	69,38,8,71,7,4,9	768

SHOPPING	GAMBLE	SEX	KEYWORD	KEYWORD
Good	Good	is great	SOCIAL	Children,Education,Astrology,Bargains,Social Functions,Childishness,Groups -

STRESS LEVEL	LUCKY COLORS	JEWELERY	MOONS EFFECT	GRAHA EFFECT	DAILY DEITY
Low	Green/Sky Blue/	Diamonds/Silver	Enthusiastic	Social Graha	Vishnu

DAILY PUJA	DAILY PSALMS
Wash the feet of Children, Do Satnarayan Pooja, Read & chant Geeta	3, 12, 30 ,39, 48, 57, 75, 102, 120

Sunday, August 6, 2023 — This is considered a NEGATIVE day for you — Planet: Pluto

ADVICE & DETAILS

Money is coming and/or going out today, but it will be pleasurable. You may be changing locations and enjoying the company of someone known or famous from TV or the entertainment industry.

MANTRA FOR TODAY

Om Jai Viganeshwaraya.. Lambodaraya Namo Namaha 21 times

MONEY	LOVE	CAREER	FAMILY	TRAVEL	WEDDING	MOVE	BUSINESS	HEALTH	Lotto #'s	play 3 #s
Bad	Fair	Bad	Fair	Bad	Good	Bad	Bad	Bad	41,46,2,72,6,39,58	733

SHOPPING	GAMBLE	SEX	KEYWORD	KEYWORD
Bad	Bad	is tough	CAREER	Career,Hard Work,Co-workers,Low Payment,Job Problems,High Temper,Low

STRESS LEVEL	LUCKY COLORS	JEWELERY	MOONS EFFECT	GRAHA EFFECT	DAILY DEITY
High	Dark Blue/ Purple/	Amethyst/Gold	Emotional	Job Graha	Lingam

DAILY PUJA	DAILY PSALMS
Worship Ganesh, Give gifts to father, and co -workers, Plant gardens, farms	4, 13, 31 ,40, 49, 58, 76, 103, 121

Monday, August 7, 2023 — This is considered a POSITIVE day for you — Planet: Venus

ADVICE & DETAILS

This is a positive day to invest. To improve your results in this arena make sure you show gratitude to the universe by praying and meditating.

MANTRA FOR TODAY

Om Graam Greem Graum Sa Gurave namah swaha 21 times

MONEY	LOVE	CAREER	FAMILY	TRAVEL	WEDDING	MOVE	BUSINESS	HEALTH	Lotto #'s	play 3 #s
Bad	Excellent	Fair	Good	Excellen	Good	Excellen	Good	Excellent	39,3,3,34,58,46,2	1

SHOPPING	GAMBLE	SEX	KEYWORD	KEYWORD
Good	Good	is good	CHANGE	Sexuality,Travel,Change,Distant, far,Travel delays,Deception,Excercise,Illicit

STRESS LEVEL	LUCKY COLORS	JEWELERY	MOONS EFFECT	GRAHA EFFECT	DAILY DEITY
Fair	Tan/Green/ Beige	Pearl/Silver/quartz	Courageous	Travel Graha	Nataraja

DAILY PUJA	DAILY PSALMS
Artistic gifts, Pray to Krishna, Do good deeds, do Spiritual trips	5, 14, 32 ,41, 50, 59, 77, 104, 122

Tuesday, August 8, 2023 — This is considered a NEGATIVE day for you — Planet: Mars

ADVICE & DETAILS

It will be difficult, but possible to overcome your sadness today. Your mind will tend to veer towards thoughts of losses, doubts, denial and death; if you cannot control it you will be creating this in your life. Pray, meditate and place your trust in the Higher Power.

MANTRA FOR TODAY

Om Mana Swasti Shanti Kuru kuru Swaha Shivoham Shivoham 27 times

MONEY	LOVE	CAREER	FAMILY	TRAVEL	WEDDING	MOVE	BUSINESS	HEALTH	Lotto #'s	play 3 #s
Bad	Bad	Bad	Bad	Bad	Bad	Bad	Fair	Bad	51,59,29,38,52,60,1	435

SHOPPING	GAMBLE	SEX	KEYWORD	KEYWORD
Fair	Bad	is frustrating	POWER	Responsibilty,Disagreement,Family,Back Pain,Family Conflicts,Traffic

STRESS LEVEL	LUCKY COLORS	JEWELERY	MOONS EFFECT	GRAHA EFFECT	DAILY DEITY
High	Purple/Blue/Rose	Emerald/Saphire	Educational	Family Graha	Mahakali

DAILY PUJA	DAILY PSALMS
Meditate, Control temper, Pray to Hanuman, Chant Hanuman Chalisa	6, 15, 33 ,42, 51, 60, 78, 105, 123

Wednesday, August 9, 2023 — This is considered a NEUTRAL day for you — Planet: Uranus

ADVICE & DETAILS

Finances are in your mind today. It is a great day to make money, get profits and get a promotion at your job. You may also have to deal with children or younger adults and their financial needs.

MANTRA FOR TODAY

Jai Jai Shiva Shambo.(2) ...Mahadeva Shambo (2) 21 times 8

MONEY	LOVE	CAREER	FAMILY	TRAVEL	WEDDING	MOVE	BUSINESS	HEALTH	Lotto #'s	play 3 #s
Good	Good	Fair	Good	Good	Bad	Good	Bad	Fair	8,61,3,53,17,17,50	585

SHOPPING	GAMBLE	SEX	KEYWORD	KEYWORD
Bad	Fair	is quiet	DIVINE	Spirituality,Religious,Astrology,Inner Conflicts,Religious ,Sleepiness,Advice

STRESS LEVEL	LUCKY COLORS	JEWELERY	MOONS EFFECT	GRAHA EFFECT	DAILY DEITY
Fair	Light Blue/Peach	Tiger's eye/Gold/Sil	Affectionate	God'S Graha	Shesnaag

DAILY PUJA	DAILY PSALMS
Chant Shiva Mantras, Take gifts to Ocean - Ganga Puja, Donate to Temple, Priests, etc.	7, 16, 34 ,43, 52, 61, 79, 106, 124

Thursday, August 10, 2023 — This is considered a POSITIVE day for you — Planet: Jupiter

ADVICE & DETAILS

Money is coming and/or going out today, but it will be pleasurable. You may be changing locations and enjoying the company of someone known or famous from TV or the entertainment industry.

MANTRA FOR TODAY

Om Hareem Nama Swaha..Shri Maha Laxmi Aye Namah swaha 12 times

MONEY	LOVE	CAREER	FAMILY	TRAVEL	WEDDING	MOVE	BUSINESS	HEALTH	Lotto #'s	play 3 #s
Excellent	Good	Excellent	Good	Good	Excellent	Good	Excellent	Excellent	70,49,56,38,7,55,36	561

SHOPPING	GAMBLE	SEX	KEYWORD	KEYWORD
Excellent	Excellent	is excellent	MONEY	Business,Major Expense,Money -

STRESS LEVEL	LUCKY COLORS	JEWELERY	MOONS EFFECT	GRAHA EFFECT	DAILY DEITY
Low	Yellow/Silver	Diamonds/Gold/Pea	Secretive	Money Graha	Mahalaxmi

DAILY PUJA	DAILY PSALMS
Decorate Land, Feed the poor, Donate milk /products to all, Feed holy guests,	8, 17, 35 ,44, 53, 62, 80, 107, 125

Friday, August 11, 2023 — This is considered a NEGATIVE day for you — Planet: Saturn

ADVICE & DETAILS

Today could be a very positive day influenced by promotion, profits and money; but there may be also a degree of frustation if your expectations are not fulfilled the way you feel they should. Concentrate in the positive and learn from what you perceive as negative.

MANTRA FOR TODAY

Om Ganga mataye nama swaha Om Varuna Devta aye Pahimam 11 times

MONEY	LOVE	CAREER	FAMILY	TRAVEL	WEDDING	MOVE	BUSINESS	HEALTH	Lotto #'s	play 3 #s
Bad	Bad	Bad	Fair	Bad	Bad	Bad	Bad	Bad	50,48,47,41,53,62,5	197

SHOPPING	GAMBLE	SEX	KEYWORD	KEYWORD
Bad	Bad	is very bad	KARMA	Destruction,Losses,Death,Sickness - cold,Legal matter,Abusive,Karmic debts,God -

STRESS LEVEL	LUCKY COLORS	JEWELERY	MOONS EFFECT	GRAHA EFFECT	DAILY DEITY
High	Gold/Brown//Green	Saphire/Hessonite	Ivestments	Evil Graha	Agnidev

DAILY PUJA	DAILY PSALMS
Remembrance of family members who died, worship of older people. gifts to grand parents	9, 18, 36 ,45, 54, 63, 81, 108, 126

Saturday, August 12, 2023 — This is considered a NEUTRAL day for you — Planet: Sun

ADVICE & DETAILS

You will be enjoying profits and money from your endeavors today, but on the other hand you will have sizable expenses that will give you great pleasure.

MANTRA FOR TODAY

Om Namo Bhagawate Mukhtanandaya, 108 times

MONEY	LOVE	CAREER	FAMILY	TRAVEL	WEDDING	MOVE	BUSINESS	HEALTH	Lotto #'s	play 3 #s
Fair	Bad	Good	Bad	Fair	Bad	Fair	Fair	Fair	65,52,43,13,75,19,7	760

SHOPPING	GAMBLE	SEX	KEYWORD	KEYWORD
Fair	Fair	is fair	MIND	Independence,Loneliness,Meditative,Worry,Dominating,Illness - Cold,On Your

STRESS LEVEL	LUCKY COLORS	JEWELERY	MOONS EFFECT	GRAHA EFFECT	DAILY DEITY
High	White/Yellow/	Pearl/Quartz	Arrogance	Status Graha	Saraswaty

DAILY PUJA	DAILY PSALMS
Give Gifts to Priests, Invite holy ones to your home, Feed Swamis and Yogis, Do Shiva Puja.	1, 10, 28 ,37, 46, 55, 73, 100, 118

Sunday, August 13, 2023 — This is considered a POSITIVE day for you — Planet: Moon

ADVICE & DETAILS

This is a very positive day as long as you are willing to serve and cooperate with others. Make sure that every word your lips utter is with purpose, loving and kind. It is a propitious day for marriage and romance.

MANTRA FOR TODAY: Kali Durge Namo Nama Om Durge aye nama swaha 108 times

MONEY	LOVE	CAREER	FAMILY	TRAVEL	WEDDING	MOVE	BUSINESS	HEALTH	Lotto #'s	play 3 #s
Good	Excellent	Good	Good	Excellen	Good	Good	Good	Good	68,16,10,40,35,32,2	253

SHOPPING	GAMBLE	SEX	KEYWORD	KEYWORD
Good	Good	is good	LOVE	Romance,Popularity,Visitors,Shopping,Food, Drinks,Co-

STRESS LEVEL	LUCKY COLORS	JEWELERY	MOONS EFFECT	GRAHA EFFECT	DAILY DEITY
Low	Red/Yellow/Pink	Topaz/Diamonds	Conservative	Love Graha	Gauri

DAILY PUJA: Give Gifts to females andnMother, Serve milk Products, Worship Durga forms

DAILY PSALMS: 2, 11, 29 ,38, 47, 56, 74, 101, 119

Monday, August 14, 2023 — This is considered a POSITIVE day for you — Planet: Mercury

ADVICE & DETAILS

Finances are in your mind today. It is a great day to make money, get profits and get a promotion at your job. You may also have to deal with children or younger adults and their financial needs.

MANTRA FOR TODAY: Om hareem Kleem Hreem Aem Saraswataye namaha 21 times

MONEY	LOVE	CAREER	FAMILY	TRAVEL	WEDDING	MOVE	BUSINESS	HEALTH	Lotto #'s	play 3 #s
Good	Fair	Good	Good	Excellen	Good	Good	Good	Excellent	23,50,70,24,27,23,4	178

SHOPPING	GAMBLE	SEX	KEYWORD	KEYWORD
Good	Good	is great	SOCIAL	Children,Education,Astrology,Bargains,Social Functions,Childishness,Groups -

STRESS LEVEL	LUCKY COLORS	JEWELERY	MOONS EFFECT	GRAHA EFFECT	DAILY DEITY
Low	Green/Sky Blue/	Diamonds/Silver	Enthusiastic	Social Graha	Vishnu

DAILY PUJA: Wash the feet of Children, Do Satnarayan Pooja, Read & chant Geeta

DAILY PSALMS: 3, 12, 30 ,39, 48, 57, 75, 102, 120

Tuesday, August 15, 2023 — This is considered a NEGATIVE day for you — Planet: Pluto

ADVICE & DETAILS

Money is coming and/or going out today, but it will be pleasurable. You may be changing locations and enjoying the company of someone known or famous from TV or the entertainment industry.

MANTRA FOR TODAY: Om Jai Viganeshwaraya.. Lambodaraya Namo Namaha 21 times

MONEY	LOVE	CAREER	FAMILY	TRAVEL	WEDDING	MOVE	BUSINESS	HEALTH	Lotto #'s	play 3 #s
Bad	Fair	Bad	Fair	Bad	Good	Bad	Bad	Bad	9,4,62,72,27,17,39	394

SHOPPING	GAMBLE	SEX	KEYWORD	KEYWORD
Bad	Bad	is tough	CAREER	Career,Hard Work,Co-workers,Low Payment,Job Problems,High Temper,Low

STRESS LEVEL	LUCKY COLORS	JEWELERY	MOONS EFFECT	GRAHA EFFECT	DAILY DEITY
High	Dark Blue/ Purple/	Amethyst/Gold	Emotional	Job Graha	Lingam

DAILY PUJA: Worship Ganesh, Give gifts to father, and co -workers, Plant gardens, farms

DAILY PSALMS: 4, 13, 31 ,40, 49, 58, 76, 103, 121

Wednesday, August 16, 2023 — This is considered a POSITIVE day for you — Planet: Venus

ADVICE & DETAILS

This is a positive day to invest. To improve your results in this arena make sure you show gratitude to the universe by praying and meditating.

MANTRA FOR TODAY: Om Graam Greem Graum Sa Gurave namah swaha 21 times

MONEY	LOVE	CAREER	FAMILY	TRAVEL	WEDDING	MOVE	BUSINESS	HEALTH	Lotto #'s	play 3 #s
Bad	Excellent	Fair	Good	Excellen	Good	Excellen	Good	Excellent	64,39,51,22,53,26,1	598

SHOPPING	GAMBLE	SEX	KEYWORD	KEYWORD
Good	Good	is good	CHANGE	Sexuality,Travel,Change,Distant, far,Travel delays,Deception,Excercise,Illicit

STRESS LEVEL	LUCKY COLORS	JEWELERY	MOONS EFFECT	GRAHA EFFECT	DAILY DEITY
Fair	Tan/Green/ Beige	Pearl/Silver/quartz	Courageous	Travel Graha	Nataraja

DAILY PUJA: Artistic gifts, Pray to Krishna, Do good deeds, do Spiritual trips

DAILY PSALMS: 5, 14, 32 ,41, 50, 59, 77, 104, 122

Thursday, August 17, 2023 — This is considered a NEGATIVE day for you — Planet: Mars

ADVICE & DETAILS

It will be difficult, but possible to overcome your sadness today. Your mind will tend to veer towards thoughts of losses, doubts, denial and death; if you cannot control it you will be creating this in your life. Pray, meditate and place your trust in the Higher Power.

MANTRA FOR TODAY

Om Mana Swasti Shanti Kuru kuru Swaha Shivoham Shivoham 27 times

MONEY	LOVE	CAREER	FAMILY	TRAVEL	WEDDING	MOVE	BUSINESS	HEALTH	Lotto #'s	play 3 #s
Bad	Bad	Bad	Bad	Bad	Bad	Bad	Fair	Bad	43,23,2,73,51,27,65	384

SHOPPING	GAMBLE	SEX	KEYWORD	KEYWORD
Fair	Bad	is frustrating	POWER	Responsibilty,Disagreement,Family,Back Pain,Family Conflicts,Traffic

STRESS LEVEL	LUCKY COLORS	JEWELERY	MOONS EFFECT	GRAHA EFFECT	DAILY DEITY
High	Purple/Blue/Rose	Emerald/Saphire	Educational	Family Graha	Mahakali

DAILY PUJA	DAILY PSALMS
Meditate, Control temper, Pray to Hanuman, Chant Hanuman Chalisa	6, 15, 33 ,42, 51, 60, 78, 105, 123

Friday, August 18, 2023 — This is considered a NEUTRAL day for you — Planet: Uranus

ADVICE & DETAILS

Finances are in your mind today. It is a great day to make money, get profits and get a promotion at your job. You may also have to deal with children or younger adults and their financial needs.

MANTRA FOR TODAY

Jai Jai Shiva Shambo.(2) ...Mahadeva Shambo (2) 21 times 8

MONEY	LOVE	CAREER	FAMILY	TRAVEL	WEDDING	MOVE	BUSINESS	HEALTH	Lotto #'s	play 3 #s
Good	Good	Fair	Good	Good	Bad	Good	Bad	Fair	6,66,64,17,11,48,10	219

SHOPPING	GAMBLE	SEX	KEYWORD	KEYWORD
Bad	Fair	is quiet	DIVINE	Spirituality,Religious,Astrology,Inner Conflicts,Religious ,Sleepiness,Advice

STRESS LEVEL	LUCKY COLORS	JEWELERY	MOONS EFFECT	GRAHA EFFECT	DAILY DEITY
Fair	Light Blue/Peach	Tiger's eye/Gold/Sil	Affectionate	God'S Graha	Shesnaag

DAILY PUJA	DAILY PSALMS
Chant Shiva Mantras, Take gifts to Ocean - Ganga Puja, Donate to Temple, Priests, etc.	7, 16, 34 ,43, 52, 61, 79, 106, 124

Saturday, August 19, 2023 — This is considered a POSITIVE day for you — Planet: Jupiter

ADVICE & DETAILS

Money is coming and/or going out today, but it will be pleasurable. You may be changing locations and enjoying the company of someone known or famous from TV or the entertainment industry.

MANTRA FOR TODAY

Om Hareem Nama Swaha..Shri Maha Laxmi Aye Namah swaha 12 times

MONEY	LOVE	CAREER	FAMILY	TRAVEL	WEDDING	MOVE	BUSINESS	HEALTH	Lotto #'s	play 3 #s
Excellent	Good	Excellent	Good	Good	Excellent	Good	Excellent	Excellent	3,60,71,14,58,22,36	843

SHOPPING	GAMBLE	SEX	KEYWORD	KEYWORD
Excellent	Excellent	is excellent	MONEY	Business,Major Expense,Money -

STRESS LEVEL	LUCKY COLORS	JEWELERY	MOONS EFFECT	GRAHA EFFECT	DAILY DEITY
Low	Yellow/Silver	Diamonds/Gold/Pea	Secretive	Money Graha	Mahalaxmi

DAILY PUJA	DAILY PSALMS
Decorate Land, Feed the poor, Donate milk /products to all, Feed holy guests,	8, 17, 35 ,44, 53, 62, 80, 107, 125

Sunday, August 20, 2023 — This is considered a NEGATIVE day for you — Planet: Saturn

ADVICE & DETAILS

Today could be a very positive day influenced by promotion, profits and money; but there may be also a degree of frustation if your expectations are not fulfilled the way you feel they should. Concentrate in the positive and learn from what you perceive as negative.

MANTRA FOR TODAY

Om Ganga mataye nama swaha Om Varuna Devta aye Pahimam 11 times

MONEY	LOVE	CAREER	FAMILY	TRAVEL	WEDDING	MOVE	BUSINESS	HEALTH	Lotto #'s	play 3 #s
Bad	Bad	Bad	Fair	Bad	Bad	Bad	Bad	Bad	44,8,10,19,22,35,73	122

SHOPPING	GAMBLE	SEX	KEYWORD	KEYWORD
Bad	Bad	is very bad	KARMA	Destruction,Losses,Death,Sickness - cold,Legal matter,Abusive,Karmic debts,God -

STRESS LEVEL	LUCKY COLORS	JEWELERY	MOONS EFFECT	GRAHA EFFECT	DAILY DEITY
High	Gold/Brown//Green	Saphire/Hessonite	Ivestments	Evil Graha	Agnidev

DAILY PUJA	DAILY PSALMS
Remembrance of family members who died, worship of older people. gifts to grand parents	9, 18, 36 ,45, 54, 63, 81, 108, 126

Monday, August 21, 2023			This is considered a NEUTRAL day for you						Planet: Sun	
ADVICE & DETAILS									MANTRA FOR TODAY	

You will be enjoying profits and money from your endeavors today, but on the other hand you will have sizable expenses that will give you great pleasure.

Om Namo Bhagawate Mukhtanandaya, 108 times

MONEY	LOVE	CAREER	FAMILY	TRAVEL	WEDDING	MOVE	BUSINESS	HEALTH	Lotto #'s	play 3 #s
Fair	Bad	Good	Bad	Fair	Bad	Fair	Fair	Fair	18,60,66,70,64,74,5	592

SHOPPING	GAMBLE	SEX	KEYWORD	KEYWORD						
Fair	Fair	is fair	MIND	Independence,Loneliness,Meditative,Worry,Dominating,Illness - Cold,On Your						

STRESS LEVEL		LUCKY COLORS		JEWELERY		MOONS EFFECT	GRAHA EFFECT		DAILY DEITY	
High		White/Yellow/		Pearl/Quartz		Arrogance	Status Graha		Saraswaty	

DAILY PUJA	DAILY PSALMS
Give Gifts to Priests, Invite holy ones to your home, Feed Swamis and Yogis, Do Shiva Puja.	1, 10, 28 ,37, 46, 55, 73, 100, 118

Tuesday, August 22, 2023			This is considered a POSITIVE day for you						Planet: Moon	
ADVICE & DETAILS									MANTRA FOR TODAY	

This is a very positive day as long as you are willing to serve and cooperate with others. Make sure that every word your lips utter is with purpose, loving and kind. It is a propitious day for marriage and romance.

Kali Durge Namo Nama Om Durge aye nama swaha 108 times

MONEY	LOVE	CAREER	FAMILY	TRAVEL	WEDDING	MOVE	BUSINESS	HEALTH	Lotto #'s	play 3 #s
Good	Excellent	Good	Good	Excellent	Good	Good	Good	Good	10,19,13,60,18,53,5	420

SHOPPING	GAMBLE	SEX	KEYWORD	KEYWORD						
Good	Good	is good	LOVE	Romance,Popularity,Visitors,Shopping,Food, Drinks,Co-						

STRESS LEVEL		LUCKY COLORS		JEWELERY		MOONS EFFECT	GRAHA EFFECT		DAILY DEITY	
Low		Red/Yellow/Pink		Topaz/Diamonds		Conservative	Love Graha		Gauri	

DAILY PUJA	DAILY PSALMS
Give Gifts to females andnMother, Serve milk Products, Worship Durga forms	2, 11, 29 ,38, 47, 56, 74, 101, 119

Wednesday, August 23, 2023			This is considered a POSITIVE day for you						Planet: Mercury	
ADVICE & DETAILS									MANTRA FOR TODAY	

Finances are in your mind today. It is a great day to make money, get profits and get a promotion at your job. You may also have to deal with children or younger adults and their financial needs.

Om hareem Kleem Hreem Aem Saraswataye namaha 21 times

MONEY	LOVE	CAREER	FAMILY	TRAVEL	WEDDING	MOVE	BUSINESS	HEALTH	Lotto #'s	play 3 #s
Good	Fair	Good	Good	Excellent	Good	Good	Good	Excellent	1,41,66,60,1,8,49	774

SHOPPING	GAMBLE	SEX	KEYWORD	KEYWORD						
Good	Good	is great	SOCIAL	Children,Education,Astrology,Bargains,Social Functions,Childishness,Groups -						

STRESS LEVEL		LUCKY COLORS		JEWELERY		MOONS EFFECT	GRAHA EFFECT		DAILY DEITY	
Low		Green/Sky Blue/		Diamonds/Silver		Enthusiastic	Social Graha		Vishnu	

DAILY PUJA	DAILY PSALMS
Wash the feet of Children, Do Satnarayan Pooja, Read & chant Geeta	3, 12, 30 ,39, 48, 57, 75, 102, 120

Thursday, August 24, 2023			This is considered a NEGATIVE day for you						Planet: Pluto	
ADVICE & DETAILS									MANTRA FOR TODAY	

Money is coming and/or going out today, but it will be pleasurable. You may be changing locations and enjoying the company of someone known or famous from TV or the entertainment industry.

Om Jai Viganeshwaraya.. Lambodaraya Namo Namaha 21 times

MONEY	LOVE	CAREER	FAMILY	TRAVEL	WEDDING	MOVE	BUSINESS	HEALTH	Lotto #'s	play 3 #s
Bad	Fair	Bad	Fair	Bad	Good	Bad	Bad	Bad	69,15,19,25,61,30,5	285

SHOPPING	GAMBLE	SEX	KEYWORD	KEYWORD						
Bad	Bad	is tough	CAREER	Career,Hard Work,Co-workers,Low Payment,Job Problems,High Temper,Low						

STRESS LEVEL		LUCKY COLORS		JEWELERY		MOONS EFFECT	GRAHA EFFECT		DAILY DEITY	
High		Dark Blue/ Purple/		Amethyst/Gold		Emotional	Job Graha		Lingam	

DAILY PUJA	DAILY PSALMS
Worship Ganesh, Give gifts to father, and co -workers, Plant gardens, farms	4, 13, 31 ,40, 49, 58, 76, 103, 121

Friday, August 25, 2023 — This is considered a POSITIVE day for you — Planet: Venus

ADVICE & DETAILS

This is a positive day to invest. To improve your results in this arena make sure you show gratitude to the universe by praying and meditating.

MANTRA FOR TODAY: Om Graam Greem Graum Sa Gurave namah swaha 21 times

MONEY	LOVE	CAREER	FAMILY	TRAVEL	WEDDING	MOVE	BUSINESS	HEALTH	Lotto #'s	play 3 #s
Bad	Excellent	Fair	Good	Excellen	Good	Excellen	Good	Excellent	67,55,39,71,67,49,4	734

SHOPPING	GAMBLE	SEX	KEYWORD	KEYWORD
Good	Good	is good	CHANGE	Sexuality,Travel,Change,Distant, far,Travel delays,Deception,Excercise,Illicit

STRESS LEVEL	LUCKY COLORS	JEWELERY	MOONS EFFECT	GRAHA EFFECT	DAILY DEITY
Fair	Tan/Green/ Beige	Pearl/Silver/quartz	Courageous	Travel Graha	Nataraja

DAILY PUJA: Artistic gifts, Pray to Krishna, Do good deeds, do Spiritual trips

DAILY PSALMS: 5, 14, 32 ,41, 50, 59, 77, 104, 122

Saturday, August 26, 2023 — This is considered a NEGATIVE day for you — Planet: Mars

ADVICE & DETAILS

It will be difficult, but possible to overcome your sadness today. Your mind will tend to veer towards thoughts of losses, doubts, denial and death; if you cannot control it you will be creating this in your life. Pray, meditate and place your trust in the Higher Power.

MANTRA FOR TODAY: Om Mana Swasti Shanti Kuru kuru Swaha Shivoham Shivoham 27 times

MONEY	LOVE	CAREER	FAMILY	TRAVEL	WEDDING	MOVE	BUSINESS	HEALTH	Lotto #'s	play 3 #s
Bad	Bad	Bad	Bad	Bad	Bad	Bad	Fair	Bad	31,57,73,57,68,41,7	667

SHOPPING	GAMBLE	SEX	KEYWORD	KEYWORD
Fair	Bad	is frustrating	POWER	Responsibilty,Disagreement,Family,Back Pain,Family Conflicts,Traffic

STRESS LEVEL	LUCKY COLORS	JEWELERY	MOONS EFFECT	GRAHA EFFECT	DAILY DEITY
High	Purple/Blue/Rose	Emerald/Saphire	Educational	Family Graha	Mahakali

DAILY PUJA: Meditate, Control temper, Pray to Hanuman, Chant Hanuman Chalisa

DAILY PSALMS: 6, 15, 33 ,42, 51, 60, 78, 105, 123

Sunday, August 27, 2023 — This is considered a NEUTRAL day for you — Planet: Uranus

ADVICE & DETAILS

Finances are in your mind today. It is a great day to make money, get profits and get a promotion at your job. You may also have to deal with children or younger adults and their financial needs.

MANTRA FOR TODAY: Jai Jai Shiva Shambo.(2) ...Mahadeva Shambo (2) 21 times 8

MONEY	LOVE	CAREER	FAMILY	TRAVEL	WEDDING	MOVE	BUSINESS	HEALTH	Lotto #'s	play 3 #s
Good	Good	Fair	Good	Good	Bad	Good	Bad	Fair	45,66,52,56,41,9,12	766

SHOPPING	GAMBLE	SEX	KEYWORD	KEYWORD
Bad	Fair	is quiet	DIVINE	Spirituality,Religious,Astrology,Inner Conflicts,Religious ,Sleepiness,Advice

STRESS LEVEL	LUCKY COLORS	JEWELERY	MOONS EFFECT	GRAHA EFFECT	DAILY DEITY
Fair	Light Blue/Peach	Tiger's eye/Gold/Sil	Affectionate	God'S Graha	Shesnaag

DAILY PUJA: Chant Shiva Mantras, Take gifts to Ocean - Ganga Puja, Donate to Temple, Priests, etc.

DAILY PSALMS: 7, 16, 34 ,43, 52, 61, 79, 106, 124

Monday, August 28, 2023 — This is considered a POSITIVE day for you — Planet: Jupiter

ADVICE & DETAILS

Money is coming and/or going out today, but it will be pleasurable. You may be changing locations and enjoying the company of someone known or famous from TV or the entertainment industry.

MANTRA FOR TODAY: Om Hareem Nama Swaha..Shri Maha Laxmi Aye Namah swaha 12 times

MONEY	LOVE	CAREER	FAMILY	TRAVEL	WEDDING	MOVE	BUSINESS	HEALTH	Lotto #'s	play 3 #s
Excellent	Good	Excellent	Good	Good	Excellent	Good	Excellent	Excellent	71,12,53,14,43,74,1	340

SHOPPING	GAMBLE	SEX	KEYWORD	KEYWORD
Excellent	Excellent	is excellent	MONEY	Business,Major Expense,Money -

STRESS LEVEL	LUCKY COLORS	JEWELERY	MOONS EFFECT	GRAHA EFFECT	DAILY DEITY
Low	Yellow/Silver	Diamonds/Gold/Pea	Secretive	Money Graha	Mahalaxmi

DAILY PUJA: Decorate Land, Feed the poor, Donate milk /products to all, Feed holy guests,

DAILY PSALMS: 8, 17, 35 ,44, 53, 62, 80, 107, 125

Tuesday, August 29, 2023 — This is considered a NEGATIVE day for you — Planet: Saturn

ADVICE & DETAILS
Today could be a very positive day influenced by promotion, profits and money; but there may be also a degree of frustation if your expectations are not fulfilled the way you feel they should. Concentrate in the positive and learn from what you perceive as negative.

MANTRA FOR TODAY
Om Ganga mataye nama swaha Om Varuna Devta aye Pahimam 11 times

MONEY	LOVE	CAREER	FAMILY	TRAVEL	WEDDING	MOVE	BUSINESS	HEALTH	Lotto #'s	play 3 #s
Bad	Bad	Bad	Fair	Bad	Bad	Bad	Bad	Bad	49,13,72,44,9,14,26	116

SHOPPING	GAMBLE	SEX	KEYWORD	KEYWORD						
Bad	Bad	is very bad	KARMA	Destruction,Losses,Death,Sickness - cold,Legal matter,Abusive,Karmic debts,God -						

STRESS LEVEL	LUCKY COLORS	JEWELERY	MOONS EFFECT	GRAHA EFFECT	DAILY DEITY
High	Gold/Brown//Green	Saphire/Hessonite	Ivestments	Evil Graha	Agnidev

DAILY PUJA	DAILY PSALMS
Remembrance of family members who died, worship of older people. gifts to grand parents	9, 18, 36 ,45, 54, 63, 81, 108, 126

Wednesday, August 30, 2023 — This is considered a NEUTRAL day for you — Planet: Sun

ADVICE & DETAILS
You will be enjoying profits and money from your endeavors today, but on the other hand you will have sizable expenses that will give you great pleasure.

MANTRA FOR TODAY
Om Namo Bhagawate Mukhtanandaya, 108 times

MONEY	LOVE	CAREER	FAMILY	TRAVEL	WEDDING	MOVE	BUSINESS	HEALTH	Lotto #'s	play 3 #s
Fair	Bad	Good	Bad	Fair	Bad	Fair	Fair	Fair	20,30,19,18,62,31,4	700

SHOPPING	GAMBLE	SEX	KEYWORD	KEYWORD						
Fair	Fair	is fair	MIND	Independence,Loneliness,Meditative,Worry,Dominating,Illness - Cold,On Your						

STRESS LEVEL	LUCKY COLORS	JEWELERY	MOONS EFFECT	GRAHA EFFECT	DAILY DEITY
High	White/Yellow/	Pearl/Quartz	Arrogance	Status Graha	Saraswaty

DAILY PUJA	DAILY PSALMS
Give Gifts to Priests, Invite holy ones to your home, Feed Swamis and Yogis, Do Shiva Puja.	1, 10, 28 ,37, 46, 55, 73, 100, 118

Thursday, August 31, 2023 — This is considered a POSITIVE day for you — Planet: Moon

ADVICE & DETAILS
This is a very positive day as long as you are willing to serve and cooperate with others. Make sure that every word your lips utter is with purpose, loving and kind. It is a propitious day for marriage and romance.

MANTRA FOR TODAY
Kali Durge Namo Nama Om Durge aye nama swaha 108 times

MONEY	LOVE	CAREER	FAMILY	TRAVEL	WEDDING	MOVE	BUSINESS	HEALTH	Lotto #'s	play 3 #s
Good	Excellent	Good	Good	Excellen	Good	Good	Good	Good	34,16,10,60,50,22,7	51

SHOPPING	GAMBLE	SEX	KEYWORD	KEYWORD						
Good	Good	is good	LOVE	Romance,Popularity,Visitors,Shopping,Food, Drinks,Co-						

STRESS LEVEL	LUCKY COLORS	JEWELERY	MOONS EFFECT	GRAHA EFFECT	DAILY DEITY
Low	Red/Yellow/Pink	Topaz/Diamonds	Conservative	Love Graha	Gauri

DAILY PUJA	DAILY PSALMS
Give Gifts to females andnMother, Serve milk Products, Worship Durga forms	2, 11, 29 ,38, 47, 56, 74, 101, 119

Friday, September 1, 2023 — This is considered a POSITIVE day for you — Planet: Jupiter

ADVICE & DETAILS
Watch out for accidents or tickets, today is a day of moving or trips that if you are not careful could have negative consequences.

MANTRA FOR TODAY
Om Hareem Nama Swaha..Shri Maha Laxmi Aye Namah swaha 12 times

MONEY	LOVE	CAREER	FAMILY	TRAVEL	WEDDING	MOVE	BUSINESS	HEALTH	Lotto #'s	play 3 #s
Excellent	Good	Excellent	Good	Good	Excellent	Good	Excellent	Excellent	43,2,52,68,61,35,18	972

SHOPPING	GAMBLE	SEX	KEYWORD	KEYWORD						
Excellent	Excellent	is excellent	MONEY	Business,Major Expense,Money -						

STRESS LEVEL	LUCKY COLORS	JEWELERY	MOONS EFFECT	GRAHA EFFECT	DAILY DEITY
Low	Yellow/Silver	Diamonds/Gold/Pea	Secretive	Money Graha	Mahalaxmi

DAILY PUJA	DAILY PSALMS
Decorate Land, Feed the poor, Donate milk /products to all, Feed holy guests,	8, 17, 35 ,44, 53, 62, 80, 107, 125

Saturday, September 2, 2023 — This is considered a NEGATIVE day for you — Planet: Saturn

ADVICE & DETAILS	MANTRA FOR TODAY
The law of "action and reaction" or karma will be present in your life today. Stay God-centered while maintaining your full attention to avoid troubles with government, accidents and/or death.	Om Ganga mataye nama swaha Om Varuna Devta aye Pahimam 11 times

MONEY	LOVE	CAREER	FAMILY	TRAVEL	WEDDING	MOVE	BUSINESS	HEALTH	Lotto #'s	play 3 #s
Bad	Bad	Bad	Fair	Bad	Bad	Bad	Bad	Bad	15,57,17,32,74,9,36	699

SHOPPING	GAMBLE	SEX	KEYWORD	KEYWORD
Bad	Bad	is very bad	KARMA	Destruction,Losses,Death,Sickness - cold,Legal matter,Abusive,Karmic debts,God -

STRESS LEVEL	LUCKY COLORS	JEWELERY	MOONS EFFECT	GRAHA EFFECT	DAILY DEITY
High	Gold/Brown//Green	Saphire/Hessonite	Ivestments	Evil Graha	Agnidev

DAILY PUJA	DAILY PSALMS
Remembrance of family members who died, worship of older people. gifts to grand parents	9, 18, 36 ,45, 54, 63, 81, 108, 126

Sunday, September 3, 2023 — This is considered a NEUTRAL day for you — Planet: Sun

ADVICE & DETAILS	MANTRA FOR TODAY
This is not a day to begin any new project. Concentrate on finishing anything you have started before. There is the possibility of death or end of someone, a project, a situation, an idea or thought; it may be positive or negative. Watch out for accidents, they may have serious consequences. Stay in a prayerful attitude.	Om Namo Bhagawate Mukhtanandaya, 108 times

MONEY	LOVE	CAREER	FAMILY	TRAVEL	WEDDING	MOVE	BUSINESS	HEALTH	Lotto #'s	play 3 #s
Fair	Bad	Good	Bad	Fair	Bad	Fair	Fair	Fair	14,71,54,29,15,44,4	73

SHOPPING	GAMBLE	SEX	KEYWORD	KEYWORD
Fair	Fair	is fair	MIND	Independence,Loneliness,Meditative,Worry,Dominating,Illness - Cold,On Your

STRESS LEVEL	LUCKY COLORS	JEWELERY	MOONS EFFECT	GRAHA EFFECT	DAILY DEITY
High	White/Yellow/	Pearl/Quartz	Arrogance	Status Graha	Saraswaty

DAILY PUJA	DAILY PSALMS
Give Gifts to Priests, Invite holy ones to your home, Feed Swamis and Yogis, Do Shiva Puja.	1, 10, 28 ,37, 46, 55, 73, 100, 118

Monday, September 4, 2023 — This is considered a POSITIVE day for you — Planet: Moon

ADVICE & DETAILS	MANTRA FOR TODAY
It is a great day to begin partnerships, associations or friendships with people that are or may become your teachers or have something to offer you.	Kali Durge Namo Nama Om Durge aye nama swaha 108 times

MONEY	LOVE	CAREER	FAMILY	TRAVEL	WEDDING	MOVE	BUSINESS	HEALTH	Lotto #'s	play 3 #s
Good	Excellent	Good	Good	Excellen	Good	Good	Good	Good	41,57,5,17,5,33,14	555

SHOPPING	GAMBLE	SEX	KEYWORD	KEYWORD
Good	Good	is good	LOVE	Romance,Popularity,Visitors,Shopping,Food, Drinks,Co-

STRESS LEVEL	LUCKY COLORS	JEWELERY	MOONS EFFECT	GRAHA EFFECT	DAILY DEITY
Low	Red/Yellow/Pink	Topaz/Diamonds	Conservative	Love Graha	Gauri

DAILY PUJA	DAILY PSALMS
Give Gifts to females andnMother, Serve milk Products, Worship Durga forms	2, 11, 29 ,38, 47, 56, 74, 101, 119

Tuesday, September 5, 2023 — This is considered a POSITIVE day for you — Planet: Mercury

ADVICE & DETAILS	MANTRA FOR TODAY
Doubts and denial will plague your mind today. You may have encounters today with people in government agencies; people that are famous or are somewhat related to television. Anything that you perceive as negative that happens today is probably a payment of a karmic debt.	Om hareem Kleem Hreem Aem Saraswataye namaha 21 times

MONEY	LOVE	CAREER	FAMILY	TRAVEL	WEDDING	MOVE	BUSINESS	HEALTH	Lotto #'s	play 3 #s
Good	Fair	Good	Good	Excellen	Good	Good	Good	Excellent	5,44,1,65,31,5,51	474

SHOPPING	GAMBLE	SEX	KEYWORD	KEYWORD
Good	Good	is great	SOCIAL	Children,Education,Astrology,Bargains,Social Functions,Childishness,Groups -

STRESS LEVEL	LUCKY COLORS	JEWELERY	MOONS EFFECT	GRAHA EFFECT	DAILY DEITY
Low	Green/Sky Blue/	Diamonds/Silver	Enthusiastic	Social Graha	Vishnu

DAILY PUJA	DAILY PSALMS
Wash the feet of Children, Do Satnarayan Pooja, Read & chant Geeta	3, 12, 30 ,39, 48, 57, 75, 102, 120

Wednesday, September 6, 2023 — This is considered a NEGATIVE day for you — Planet: Pluto

ADVICE & DETAILS

Your doubts may bring losses in the financial or personal arenas, you are advised not to deny facts that are in front of you and that are valuable information; you need to face them. Your day may be influenced by interaction with government agencies.

MANTRA FOR TODAY

Om Jai Viganeshwaraya.. Lambodaraya Namo Namaha 21 times

MONEY	LOVE	CAREER	FAMILY	TRAVEL	WEDDING	MOVE	BUSINESS	HEALTH	Lotto #'s	play 3 #s
Bad	Fair	Bad	Fair	Bad	Good	Bad	Bad	Bad	65,39,46,44,73,32,5	721

SHOPPING	GAMBLE	SEX	KEYWORD	KEYWORD
Bad	Bad	is tough	CAREER	Career,Hard Work,Co-workers,Low Payment,Job Problems,High Temper,Low

STRESS LEVEL	LUCKY COLORS	JEWELERY	MOONS EFFECT	GRAHA EFFECT	DAILY DEITY
High	Dark Blue/ Purple/	Amethyst/Gold	Emotional	Job Graha	Lingam

DAILY PUJA	DAILY PSALMS
Worship Ganesh, Give gifts to father, and co -workers, Plant gardens, farms	4, 13, 31 ,40, 49, 58, 76, 103, 121

Thursday, September 7, 2023 — This is considered a POSITIVE day for you — Planet: Venus

ADVICE & DETAILS

This is a day when you may have a big expense, make sure it is the right decision; otherwise you may find out that you wasted your money. Do not make any rushed decisions and do not purchase on impulse. You may be promoted in some manner as long as you are not lazy or inactive.

MANTRA FOR TODAY

Om Graam Greem Graum Sa Gurave namah swaha 21 times

MONEY	LOVE	CAREER	FAMILY	TRAVEL	WEDDING	MOVE	BUSINESS	HEALTH	Lotto #'s	play 3 #s
Bad	Excellent	Fair	Good	Excellen	Good	Exceller	Good	Excellent	66,61,49,49,69,56,7	29

SHOPPING	GAMBLE	SEX	KEYWORD	KEYWORD
Good	Good	is good	CHANGE	Sexuality,Travel,Change,Distant, far,Travel delays,Deception,Excercise,Illicit

STRESS LEVEL	LUCKY COLORS	JEWELERY	MOONS EFFECT	GRAHA EFFECT	DAILY DEITY
Fair	Tan/Green/ Beige	Pearl/Silver/quartz	Courageous	Travel Graha	Nataraja

DAILY PUJA	DAILY PSALMS
Artistic gifts, Pray to Krishna, Do good deeds, do Spiritual trips	5, 14, 32 ,41, 50, 59, 77, 104, 122

Friday, September 8, 2023 — This is considered a NEGATIVE day for you — Planet: Mars

ADVICE & DETAILS

Karmic debts may make you infamous today. You have influences from the law, doubts and denial and a karmic account that is overdue.

MANTRA FOR TODAY

Om Mana Swasti Shanti Kuru kuru Swaha Shivoham Shivoham 27 times

MONEY	LOVE	CAREER	FAMILY	TRAVEL	WEDDING	MOVE	BUSINESS	HEALTH	Lotto #'s	play 3 #s
Bad	Bad	Bad	Bad	Bad	Bad	Bad	Fair	Bad	12,25,53,49,42,48,6	176

SHOPPING	GAMBLE	SEX	KEYWORD	KEYWORD
Fair	Bad	is frustrating	POWER	Responsibilty,Disagreement,Family,Back Pain,Family Conflicts,Traffic

STRESS LEVEL	LUCKY COLORS	JEWELERY	MOONS EFFECT	GRAHA EFFECT	DAILY DEITY
High	Purple/Blue/Rose	Emerald/Saphire	Educational	Family Graha	Mahakali

DAILY PUJA	DAILY PSALMS
Meditate, Control temper, Pray to Hanuman, Chant Hanuman Chalisa	6, 15, 33 ,42, 51, 60, 78, 105, 123

Saturday, September 9, 2023 — This is considered a NEUTRAL day for you — Planet: Uranus

ADVICE & DETAILS

Doubts and denial will plague your mind today. You may have encounters today with people in government agencies; people that are famous or are somewhat related to television. Anything that you perceive as negative that happens today is probably a payment of a karmic debt.

MANTRA FOR TODAY

Jai Jai Shiva Shambo.(2) ...Mahadeva Shambo (2) 21 times 8

MONEY	LOVE	CAREER	FAMILY	TRAVEL	WEDDING	MOVE	BUSINESS	HEALTH	Lotto #'s	play 3 #s
Good	Good	Fair	Good	Good	Bad	Good	Bad	Fair	28,56,26,32,44,23,6	941

SHOPPING	GAMBLE	SEX	KEYWORD	KEYWORD
Bad	Fair	is quiet	DIVINE	Spirituality,Religious,Astrology,Inner Conflicts,Religious ,Sleepiness,Advice

STRESS LEVEL	LUCKY COLORS	JEWELERY	MOONS EFFECT	GRAHA EFFECT	DAILY DEITY
Fair	Light Blue/Peach	Tiger's eye/Gold/Sil	Affectionate	God'S Graha	Shesnaag

DAILY PUJA	DAILY PSALMS
Chant Shiva Mantras, Take gifts to Ocean - Ganga Puja, Donate to Temple, Priests, etc.	7, 16, 34 ,43, 52, 61, 79, 106, 124

Sunday, September 10, 2023 — This is considered a POSITIVE day for you — Planet: Jupiter

ADVICE & DETAILS

Watch out for accidents or tickets, today is a day of moving or trips that if you are not careful could have negative consequences.

MANTRA FOR TODAY

Om Hareem Nama Swaha..Shri Maha Laxmi Aye Namah swaha 12 times

MONEY	LOVE	CAREER	FAMILY	TRAVEL	WEDDING	MOVE	BUSINESS	HEALTH	Lotto #'s	play 3 #s
Excellent	Good	Excellent	Good	Good	Excellent	Good	Excellent	Excellent	18,5,42,59,10,38,45	412

SHOPPING	GAMBLE	SEX	KEYWORD	KEYWORD						
Excellent	Excellent	is excellent	MONEY	Business,Major Expense,Money -						

STRESS LEVEL		LUCKY COLORS	JEWELERY	MOONS EFFECT	GRAHA EFFECT	DAILY DEITY
Low		Yellow/Silver	Diamonds/Gold/Pea	Secretive	Money Graha	Mahalaxmi

DAILY PUJA	DAILY PSALMS
Decorate Land, Feed the poor, Donate milk /products to all, Feed holy guests,	8, 17, 35 ,44, 53, 62, 80, 107, 125

Monday, September 11, 2023 — This is considered a NEGATIVE day for you — Planet: Saturn

ADVICE & DETAILS

The law of "action and reaction" or karma will be present in your life today. Stay God-centered while maintaining your full attention to avoid troubles with government, accidents and/or death.

MANTRA FOR TODAY

Om Ganga mataye nama swaha Om Varuna Devta aye Pahimam 11 times

MONEY	LOVE	CAREER	FAMILY	TRAVEL	WEDDING	MOVE	BUSINESS	HEALTH	Lotto #'s	play 3 #s
Bad	Bad	Bad	Fair	Bad	Bad	Bad	Bad	Bad	41,48,38,57,39,71,1	540

SHOPPING	GAMBLE	SEX	KEYWORD	KEYWORD						
Bad	Bad	is very bad	KARMA	Destruction,Losses,Death,Sickness - cold,Legal matter,Abusive,Karmic debts,God -						

STRESS LEVEL		LUCKY COLORS	JEWELERY	MOONS EFFECT	GRAHA EFFECT	DAILY DEITY
High		Gold/Brown//Green	Saphire/Hessonite	Ivestments	Evil Graha	Agnidev

DAILY PUJA	DAILY PSALMS
Remembrance of family members who died, worship of older people. gifts to grand parents	9, 18, 36 ,45, 54, 63, 81, 108, 126

Tuesday, September 12, 2023 — This is considered a NEUTRAL day for you — Planet: Sun

ADVICE & DETAILS

This is not a day to begin any new project. Concentrate on finishing anything you have started before. There is the possibility of death or end of someone, a project, a situation, an idea or thought; it may be positive or negative. Watch out for accidents, they may have serious consequences. Stay in a prayerful attitude.

MANTRA FOR TODAY

Om Namo Bhagawate Mukhtanandaya, 108 times

MONEY	LOVE	CAREER	FAMILY	TRAVEL	WEDDING	MOVE	BUSINESS	HEALTH	Lotto #'s	play 3 #s
Fair	Bad	Good	Bad	Fair	Bad	Fair	Fair	Fair	3,13,15,73,39,10,27	352

SHOPPING	GAMBLE	SEX	KEYWORD	KEYWORD						
Fair	Fair	is fair	MIND	Independence,Loneliness,Meditative,Worry,Dominating,Illness - Cold,On Your						

STRESS LEVEL		LUCKY COLORS	JEWELERY	MOONS EFFECT	GRAHA EFFECT	DAILY DEITY
High		White/Yellow/	Pearl/Quartz	Arrogance	Status Graha	Saraswaty

DAILY PUJA	DAILY PSALMS
Give Gifts to Priests, Invite holy ones to your home, Feed Swamis and Yogis, Do Shiva Puja.	1, 10, 28 ,37, 46, 55, 73, 100, 118

Wednesday, September 13, 2023 — This is considered a POSITIVE day for you — Planet: Moon

ADVICE & DETAILS

It is a great day to begin partnerships, associations or friendships with people that are or may become your teachers or have something to offer you.

MANTRA FOR TODAY

Kali Durge Namo Nama Om Durge aye nama swaha 108 times

MONEY	LOVE	CAREER	FAMILY	TRAVEL	WEDDING	MOVE	BUSINESS	HEALTH	Lotto #'s	play 3 #s
Good	Excellent	Good	Good	Excellen	Good	Good	Good	Good	15,13,42,27,66,44,7	565

SHOPPING	GAMBLE	SEX	KEYWORD	KEYWORD						
Good	Good	is good	LOVE	Romance,Popularity,Visitors,Shopping,Food, Drinks,Co-						

STRESS LEVEL		LUCKY COLORS	JEWELERY	MOONS EFFECT	GRAHA EFFECT	DAILY DEITY
Low		Red/Yellow/Pink	Topaz/Diamonds	Conservative	Love Graha	Gauri

DAILY PUJA	DAILY PSALMS
Give Gifts to females andnMother, Serve milk Products, Worship Durga forms	2, 11, 29 ,38, 47, 56, 74, 101, 119

Thursday, September 14, 2023 — This is considered a POSITIVE day for you — Planet: Mercury

ADVICE & DETAILS

Doubts and denial will plague your mind today. You may have encounters today with people in government agencies; people that are famous or are somewhat related to television. Anything that you perceive as negative that happens today is probably a payment of a karmic debt.

MANTRA FOR TODAY

Om hareem Kleem Hreem Aem Saraswataye namaha 21 times

MONEY	LOVE	CAREER	FAMILY	TRAVEL	WEDDING	MOVE	BUSINESS	HEALTH	Lotto #'s	play 3 #s
Good	Fair	Good	Good	Excellen	Good	Good	Good	Excellent	61,5,48,7,65,64,31	987

SHOPPING	GAMBLE	SEX	KEYWORD	KEYWORD
Good	Good	is great	SOCIAL	Children,Education,Astrology,Bargains,Social Functions,Childishness,Groups -

STRESS LEVEL	LUCKY COLORS	JEWELERY	MOONS EFFECT	GRAHA EFFECT	DAILY DEITY
Low	Green/Sky Blue/	Diamonds/Silver	Enthusiastic	Social Graha	Vishnu

DAILY PUJA	DAILY PSALMS
Wash the feet of Children, Do Satnarayan Pooja, Read & chant Geeta	3, 12, 30 ,39, 48, 57, 75, 102, 120

Friday, September 15, 2023 — This is considered a NEGATIVE day for you — Planet: Pluto

ADVICE & DETAILS

Your doubts may bring losses in the financial or personal arenas, you are advised not to deny facts that are in front of you and that are valuable information; you need to face them. Your day may be influenced by interaction with government agencies.

MANTRA FOR TODAY

Om Jai Viganeshwaraya.. Lambodaraya Namo Namaha 21 times

MONEY	LOVE	CAREER	FAMILY	TRAVEL	WEDDING	MOVE	BUSINESS	HEALTH	Lotto #'s	play 3 #s
Bad	Fair	Bad	Fair	Bad	Good	Bad	Bad	Bad	51,52,28,10,51,59,2	746

SHOPPING	GAMBLE	SEX	KEYWORD	KEYWORD
Bad	Bad	is tough	CAREER	Career,Hard Work,Co-workers,Low Payment,Job Problems,High Temper,Low

STRESS LEVEL	LUCKY COLORS	JEWELERY	MOONS EFFECT	GRAHA EFFECT	DAILY DEITY
High	Dark Blue/ Purple/	Amethyst/Gold	Emotional	Job Graha	Lingam

DAILY PUJA	DAILY PSALMS
Worship Ganesh, Give gifts to father, and co -workers, Plant gardens, farms	4, 13, 31 ,40, 49, 58, 76, 103, 121

Saturday, September 16, 2023 — This is considered a POSITIVE day for you — Planet: Venus

ADVICE & DETAILS

This is a day when you may have a big expense, make sure it is the right decision; otherwise you may find out that you wasted your money. Do not make any rushed decisions and do not purchase on impulse. You may be promoted in some manner as long as you are not lazy or inactive.

MANTRA FOR TODAY

Om Graam Greem Graum Sa Gurave namah swaha 21 times

MONEY	LOVE	CAREER	FAMILY	TRAVEL	WEDDING	MOVE	BUSINESS	HEALTH	Lotto #'s	play 3 #s
Bad	Excellent	Fair	Good	Excellen	Good	Excellen	Good	Excellent	34,6,31,17,40,43,44	351

SHOPPING	GAMBLE	SEX	KEYWORD	KEYWORD
Good	Good	is good	CHANGE	Sexuality,Travel,Change,Distant, far,Travel delays,Deception,Excercise,Illicit

STRESS LEVEL	LUCKY COLORS	JEWELERY	MOONS EFFECT	GRAHA EFFECT	DAILY DEITY
Fair	Tan/Green/ Beige	Pearl/Silver/quartz	Courageous	Travel Graha	Nataraja

DAILY PUJA	DAILY PSALMS
Artistic gifts, Pray to Krishna, Do good deeds, do Spiritual trips	5, 14, 32 ,41, 50, 59, 77, 104, 122

Sunday, September 17, 2023 — This is considered a NEGATIVE day for you — Planet: Mars

ADVICE & DETAILS

Karmic debts may make you infamous today. You have influences from the law, doubts and denial and a karmic account that is overdue.

MANTRA FOR TODAY

Om Mana Swasti Shanti Kuru kuru Swaha Shivoham Shivoham 27 times

MONEY	LOVE	CAREER	FAMILY	TRAVEL	WEDDING	MOVE	BUSINESS	HEALTH	Lotto #'s	play 3 #s
Bad	Bad	Bad	Bad	Bad	Bad	Bad	Fair	Bad	59,10,25,8,29,3,22	175

SHOPPING	GAMBLE	SEX	KEYWORD	KEYWORD
Fair	Bad	is frustrating	POWER	Responsibilty,Disagreement,Family,Back Pain,Family Conflicts,Traffic

STRESS LEVEL	LUCKY COLORS	JEWELERY	MOONS EFFECT	GRAHA EFFECT	DAILY DEITY
High	Purple/Blue/Rose	Emerald/Saphire	Educational	Family Graha	Mahakali

DAILY PUJA	DAILY PSALMS
Meditate, Control temper, Pray to Hanuman, Chant Hanuman Chalisa	6, 15, 33 ,42, 51, 60, 78, 105, 123

Monday, September 18, 2023 — This is considered a NEUTRAL day for you — Planet: Uranus

ADVICE & DETAILS

Doubts and denial will plague your mind today. You may have encounters today with people in government agencies; people that are famous or are somewhat related to television. Anything that you perceive as negative that happens today is probably a payment of a karmic debt.

MANTRA FOR TODAY

Jai Jai Shiva Shambo.(2) ...Mahadeva Shambo (2) 21 times 8

MONEY	LOVE	CAREER	FAMILY	TRAVEL	WEDDING	MOVE	BUSINESS	HEALTH	Lotto #'s	play 3 #s
Good	Good	Fair	Good	Good	Bad	Good	Bad	Fair	20,34,68,46,21,41,1	618

SHOPPING	GAMBLE	SEX	KEYWORD	KEYWORD						
Bad	Fair	is quiet	DIVINE	Spirituality,Religious,Astrology,Inner Conflicts,Religious ,Sleepiness,Advice						

STRESS LEVEL	LUCKY COLORS	JEWELERY	MOONS EFFECT	GRAHA EFFECT	DAILY DEITY
Fair	Light Blue/Peach	Tiger's eye/Gold/Sil	Affectionate	God'S Graha	Shesnaag

DAILY PUJA	DAILY PSALMS
Chant Shiva Mantras, Take gifts to Ocean - Ganga Puja, Donate to Temple, Priests, etc.	7, 16, 34 ,43, 52, 61, 79, 106, 124

Tuesday, September 19, 2023 — This is considered a POSITIVE day for you — Planet: Jupiter

ADVICE & DETAILS

Watch out for accidents or tickets, today is a day of moving or trips that if you are not careful could have negative consequences.

MANTRA FOR TODAY

Om Hareem Nama Swaha..Shri Maha Laxmi Aye Namah swaha 12 times

MONEY	LOVE	CAREER	FAMILY	TRAVEL	WEDDING	MOVE	BUSINESS	HEALTH	Lotto #'s	play 3 #s
Excellent	Good	Excellent	Good	Good	Excellent	Good	Excellent	Excellent	14,48,54,44,44,22,3	140

SHOPPING	GAMBLE	SEX	KEYWORD	KEYWORD						
Excellent	Excellent	is excellent	MONEY	Business,Major Expense,Money -						

STRESS LEVEL	LUCKY COLORS	JEWELERY	MOONS EFFECT	GRAHA EFFECT	DAILY DEITY
Low	Yellow/Silver	Diamonds/Gold/Pea	Secretive	Money Graha	Mahalaxmi

DAILY PUJA	DAILY PSALMS
Decorate Land, Feed the poor, Donate milk /products to all, Feed holy guests,	8, 17, 35 ,44, 53, 62, 80, 107, 125

Wednesday, September 20, 2023 — This is considered a NEGATIVE day for you — Planet: Saturn

ADVICE & DETAILS

The law of "action and reaction" or karma will be present in your life today. Stay God-centered while maintaining your full attention to avoid troubles with government, accidents and/or death.

MANTRA FOR TODAY

Om Ganga mataye nama swaha Om Varuna Devta aye Pahimam 11 times

MONEY	LOVE	CAREER	FAMILY	TRAVEL	WEDDING	MOVE	BUSINESS	HEALTH	Lotto #'s	play 3 #s
Bad	Bad	Bad	Fair	Bad	Bad	Bad	Bad	Bad	22,47,40,4,71,56,42	741

SHOPPING	GAMBLE	SEX	KEYWORD	KEYWORD						
Bad	Bad	is very bad	KARMA	Destruction,Losses,Death,Sickness - cold,Legal matter,Abusive,Karmic debts,God -						

STRESS LEVEL	LUCKY COLORS	JEWELERY	MOONS EFFECT	GRAHA EFFECT	DAILY DEITY
High	Gold/Brown//Green	Saphire/Hessonite	Ivestments	Evil Graha	Agnidev

DAILY PUJA	DAILY PSALMS
Remembrance of family members who died, worship of older people. gifts to grand parents	9, 18, 36 ,45, 54, 63, 81, 108, 126

Thursday, September 21, 2023 — This is considered a NEUTRAL day for you — Planet: Sun

ADVICE & DETAILS

This is not a day to begin any new project. Concentrate on finishing anything you have started before. There is the possibility of death or end of someone, a project, a situation, an idea or thought; it may be positive or negative. Watch out for accidents, they may have serious consequences. Stay in a prayerful attitude.

MANTRA FOR TODAY

Om Namo Bhagawate Mukhtanandaya, 108 times

MONEY	LOVE	CAREER	FAMILY	TRAVEL	WEDDING	MOVE	BUSINESS	HEALTH	Lotto #'s	play 3 #s
Fair	Bad	Good	Bad	Fair	Bad	Fair	Fair	Fair	16,16,60,59,71,71,7	783

SHOPPING	GAMBLE	SEX	KEYWORD	KEYWORD						
Fair	Fair	is fair	MIND	Independence,Loneliness,Meditative,Worry,Dominating,Illness - Cold,On Your						

STRESS LEVEL	LUCKY COLORS	JEWELERY	MOONS EFFECT	GRAHA EFFECT	DAILY DEITY
High	White/Yellow/	Pearl/Quartz	Arrogance	Status Graha	Saraswaty

DAILY PUJA	DAILY PSALMS
Give Gifts to Priests, Invite holy ones to your home, Feed Swamis and Yogis, Do Shiva Puja.	1, 10, 28 ,37, 46, 55, 73, 100, 118

Friday, September 22, 2023			This is considered a POSITIVE day for you					Planet: Moon		

ADVICE & DETAILS | MANTRA FOR TODAY

It is a great day to begin partnerships, associations or friendships with people that are or may become your teachers or have something to offer you.

MANTRA FOR TODAY: Kali Durge Namo Nama Om Durge aye nama swaha 108 times

MONEY	LOVE	CAREER	FAMILY	TRAVEL	WEDDING	MOVE	BUSINESS	HEALTH	Lotto #'s	play 3 #s
Good	Excellent	Good	Good	Excellen	Good	Good	Good	Good	31,57,34,13,67,53,2	249

SHOPPING	GAMBLE	SEX	KEYWORD	KEYWORD						
Good	Good	is good	LOVE	Romance,Popularity,Visitors,Shopping,Food, Drinks,Co-						

STRESS LEVEL	LUCKY COLORS	JEWELERY	MOONS EFFECT	GRAHA EFFECT	DAILY DEITY
Low	Red/Yellow/Pink	Topaz/Diamonds	Conservative	Love Graha	Gauri

DAILY PUJA	DAILY PSALMS
Give Gifts to females andnMother, Serve milk Products, Worship Durga forms	2, 11, 29 ,38, 47, 56, 74, 101, 119

Saturday, September 23, 2023			This is considered a POSITIVE day for you					Planet: Mercury		

ADVICE & DETAILS | MANTRA FOR TODAY

Doubts and denial will plague your mind today. You may have encounters today with people in government agencies; people that are famous or are somewhat related to television. Anything that you perceive as negative that happens today is probably a payment of a karmic debt.

MANTRA FOR TODAY: Om hareem Kleem Hreem Aem Saraswataye namaha 21 times

MONEY	LOVE	CAREER	FAMILY	TRAVEL	WEDDING	MOVE	BUSINESS	HEALTH	Lotto #'s	play 3 #s
Good	Fair	Good	Good	Excellen	Good	Good	Good	Excellent	51,46,28,44,37,70,6	467

SHOPPING	GAMBLE	SEX	KEYWORD	KEYWORD						
Good	Good	is great	SOCIAL	Children,Education,Astrology,Bargains,Social Functions,Childishness,Groups -						

STRESS LEVEL	LUCKY COLORS	JEWELERY	MOONS EFFECT	GRAHA EFFECT	DAILY DEITY
Low	Green/Sky Blue/	Diamonds/Silver	Enthusiastic	Social Graha	Vishnu

DAILY PUJA	DAILY PSALMS
Wash the feet of Children, Do Satnarayan Pooja, Read & chant Geeta	3, 12, 30 ,39, 48, 57, 75, 102, 120

Sunday, September 24, 2023			This is considered a NEGATIVE day for you					Planet: Pluto		

ADVICE & DETAILS | MANTRA FOR TODAY

Your doubts may bring losses in the financial or personal arenas, you are advised not to deny facts that are in front of you and that are valuable information; you need to face them. Your day may be influenced by interaction with government agencies.

MANTRA FOR TODAY: Om Jai Viganeshwaraya.. Lambodaraya Namo Namaha 21 times

MONEY	LOVE	CAREER	FAMILY	TRAVEL	WEDDING	MOVE	BUSINESS	HEALTH	Lotto #'s	play 3 #s
Bad	Fair	Bad	Fair	Bad	Good	Bad	Bad	Bad	8,48,9,42,42,34,25	704

SHOPPING	GAMBLE	SEX	KEYWORD	KEYWORD						
Bad	Bad	is tough	CAREER	Career,Hard Work,Co-workers,Low Payment,Job Problems,High Temper,Low						

STRESS LEVEL	LUCKY COLORS	JEWELERY	MOONS EFFECT	GRAHA EFFECT	DAILY DEITY
High	Dark Blue/ Purple/	Amethyst/Gold	Emotional	Job Graha	Lingam

DAILY PUJA	DAILY PSALMS
Worship Ganesh, Give gifts to father, and co -workers, Plant gardens, farms	4, 13, 31 ,40, 49, 58, 76, 103, 121

Monday, September 25, 2023			This is considered a POSITIVE day for you					Planet: Venus		

ADVICE & DETAILS | MANTRA FOR TODAY

This is a day when you may have a big expense, make sure it is the right decision; otherwise you may find out that you wasted your money. Do not make any rushed decisions and do not purchase on impulse. You may be promoted in some manner as long as you are not lazy or inactive.

MANTRA FOR TODAY: Om Graam Greem Graum Sa Gurave namah swaha 21 times

MONEY	LOVE	CAREER	FAMILY	TRAVEL	WEDDING	MOVE	BUSINESS	HEALTH	Lotto #'s	play 3 #s
Bad	Excellent	Fair	Good	Excellen	Good	Exceller	Good	Excellent	50,39,52,5,32,20,1	397

SHOPPING	GAMBLE	SEX	KEYWORD	KEYWORD						
Good	Good	is good	CHANGE	Sexuality,Travel,Change,Distant, far,Travel delays,Deception,Excercise,Illicit						

STRESS LEVEL	LUCKY COLORS	JEWELERY	MOONS EFFECT	GRAHA EFFECT	DAILY DEITY
Fair	Tan/Green/ Beige	Pearl/Silver/quartz	Courageous	Travel Graha	Nataraja

DAILY PUJA	DAILY PSALMS
Artistic gifts, Pray to Krishna, Do good deeds, do Spiritual trips	5, 14, 32 ,41, 50, 59, 77, 104, 122

Tuesday, September 26, 2023 — This is considered a NEGATIVE day for you — Planet: Mars

ADVICE & DETAILS

Karmic debts may make you infamous today. You have influences from the law, doubts and denial and a karmic account that is overdue.

MANTRA FOR TODAY

Om Mana Swasti Shanti Kuru kuru Swaha Shivoham Shivoham 27 times

MONEY	LOVE	CAREER	FAMILY	TRAVEL	WEDDING	MOVE	BUSINESS	HEALTH	Lotto #'s	play 3 #s
Bad	Bad	Bad	Bad	Bad	Bad	Bad	Fair	Bad	14,21,60,19,66,46,7	232

SHOPPING	GAMBLE	SEX	KEYWORD	KEYWORD
Fair	Bad	is frustrating	POWER	Responsibilty,Disagreement,Family,Back Pain,Family Conflicts,Traffic

STRESS LEVEL	LUCKY COLORS	JEWELERY	MOONS EFFECT	GRAHA EFFECT	DAILY DEITY
High	Purple/Blue/Rose	Emerald/Saphire	Educational	Family Graha	Mahakali

DAILY PUJA	DAILY PSALMS
Meditate, Control temper, Pray to Hanuman, Chant Hanuman Chalisa	6, 15, 33 ,42, 51, 60, 78, 105, 123

Wednesday, September 27, 2023 — This is considered a NEUTRAL day for you — Planet: Uranus

ADVICE & DETAILS

Doubts and denial will plague your mind today. You may have encounters today with people in government agencies; people that are famous or are somewhat related to television. Anything that you perceive as negative that happens today is probably a payment of a karmic debt.

MANTRA FOR TODAY

Jai Jai Shiva Shambo.(2) ...Mahadeva Shambo (2) 21 times 8

MONEY	LOVE	CAREER	FAMILY	TRAVEL	WEDDING	MOVE	BUSINESS	HEALTH	Lotto #'s	play 3 #s
Good	Good	Fair	Good	Good	Bad	Good	Bad	Fair	11,75,52,14,13,10,7	296

SHOPPING	GAMBLE	SEX	KEYWORD	KEYWORD
Bad	Fair	is quiet	DIVINE	Spirituality,Religious,Astrology,Inner Conflicts,Religious ,Sleepiness,Advice

STRESS LEVEL	LUCKY COLORS	JEWELERY	MOONS EFFECT	GRAHA EFFECT	DAILY DEITY
Fair	Light Blue/Peach	Tiger's eye/Gold/Sil	Affectionate	God'S Graha	Shesnaag

DAILY PUJA	DAILY PSALMS
Chant Shiva Mantras, Take gifts to Ocean - Ganga Puja, Donate to Temple, Priests, etc.	7, 16, 34 ,43, 52, 61, 79, 106, 124

Thursday, September 28, 2023 — This is considered a POSITIVE day for you — Planet: Jupiter

ADVICE & DETAILS

Watch out for accidents or tickets, today is a day of moving or trips that if you are not careful could have negative consequences.

MANTRA FOR TODAY

Om Hareem Nama Swaha..Shri Maha Laxmi Aye Namah swaha 12 times

MONEY	LOVE	CAREER	FAMILY	TRAVEL	WEDDING	MOVE	BUSINESS	HEALTH	Lotto #'s	play 3 #s
Excellent	Good	Excellent	Good	Good	Excellent	Good	Excellent	Excellent	59,44,15,50,60,25,4	715

SHOPPING	GAMBLE	SEX	KEYWORD	KEYWORD
Excellent	Excellent	is excellent	MONEY	Business,Major Expense,Money -

STRESS LEVEL	LUCKY COLORS	JEWELERY	MOONS EFFECT	GRAHA EFFECT	DAILY DEITY
Low	Yellow/Silver	Diamonds/Gold/Pea	Secretive	Money Graha	Mahalaxmi

DAILY PUJA	DAILY PSALMS
Decorate Land, Feed the poor, Donate milk /products to all, Feed holy guests,	8, 17, 35 ,44, 53, 62, 80, 107, 125

Friday, September 29, 2023 — This is considered a NEGATIVE day for you — Planet: Saturn

ADVICE & DETAILS

The law of "action and reaction" or karma will be present in your life today. Stay God-centered while maintaining your full attention to avoid troubles with government, accidents and/or death.

MANTRA FOR TODAY

Om Ganga mataye nama swaha Om Varuna Devta aye Pahimam 11 times

MONEY	LOVE	CAREER	FAMILY	TRAVEL	WEDDING	MOVE	BUSINESS	HEALTH	Lotto #'s	play 3 #s
Bad	Bad	Bad	Fair	Bad	Bad	Bad	Bad	Bad	71,30,39,49,75,2,33	193

SHOPPING	GAMBLE	SEX	KEYWORD	KEYWORD
Bad	Bad	is very bad	KARMA	Destruction,Losses,Death,Sickness - cold,Legal matter,Abusive,Karmic debts,God -

STRESS LEVEL	LUCKY COLORS	JEWELERY	MOONS EFFECT	GRAHA EFFECT	DAILY DEITY
High	Gold/Brown//Green	Saphire/Hessonite	Ivestments	Evil Graha	Agnidev

DAILY PUJA	DAILY PSALMS
Remembrance of family members who died, worship of older people. gifts to grand parents	9, 18, 36 ,45, 54, 63, 81, 108, 126

Saturday, September 30, 2023				This is considered a NEUTRAL day for you					Planet: Sun	

ADVICE & DETAILS — **MANTRA FOR TODAY**

This is not a day to begin any new project. Concentrate on finishing anything you have started before. There is the possibility of death or end of someone, a project, a situation, an idea or thought; it may be positive or negative. Watch out for accidents, they may have serious consequences. Stay in a prayerful attitude.

Om Namo Bhagawate Mukhtanandaya, 108 times

MONEY	LOVE	CAREER	FAMILY	TRAVEL	WEDDING	MOVE	BUSINESS	HEALTH	Lotto #'s	play 3 #s
Fair	Bad	Good	Bad	Fair	Bad	Fair	Fair	Fair	41,40,46,55,31,27,4	844

SHOPPING	GAMBLE	SEX	KEYWORD	KEYWORD						
Fair	Fair	is fair	MIND	Independence,Loneliness,Meditative,Worry,Dominating,Illness - Cold,On Your						

STRESS LEVEL	LUCKY COLORS	JEWELERY	MOONS EFFECT	GRAHA EFFECT	DAILY DEITY
High	White/Yellow/	Pearl/Quartz	Arrogance	Status Graha	Saraswaty

DAILY PUJA	DAILY PSALMS
Give Gifts to Priests, Invite holy ones to your home, Feed Swamis and Yogis, Do Shiva Puja.	1, 10, 28 ,37, 46, 55, 73, 100, 118

Sunday, October 1, 2023				This is considered a POSITIVE day for you					Planet: Jupiter	

ADVICE & DETAILS — **MANTRA FOR TODAY**

If you can, take short trips and enjoy high pleasure. There will be lots of moving today.

Om Hareem Nama Swaha..Shri Maha Laxmi Aye Namah swaha 12 times

MONEY	LOVE	CAREER	FAMILY	TRAVEL	WEDDING	MOVE	BUSINESS	HEALTH	Lotto #'s	play 3 #s
Excellent	Good	Excellent	Good	Good	Excellent	Good	Excellent	Excellent	49,52,34,71,28,35,7	300

SHOPPING	GAMBLE	SEX	KEYWORD	KEYWORD						
Excellent	Excellent	is excellent	MONEY	Business,Major Expense,Money -						

STRESS LEVEL	LUCKY COLORS	JEWELERY	MOONS EFFECT	GRAHA EFFECT	DAILY DEITY
Low	Yellow/Silver	Diamonds/Gold/Pe	Secretive	Money Graha	Mahalaxmi

DAILY PUJA	DAILY PSALMS
Decorate Land, Feed the poor, Donate milk /products to all, Feed holy guests,	8, 17, 35 ,44, 53, 62, 80, 107, 125

Monday, October 2, 2023				This is considered a NEGATIVE day for you					Planet: Saturn	

ADVICE & DETAILS — **MANTRA FOR TODAY**

Connect with the God within today so you can avoid the loneliness that can result from being boastful and criticizing others. Look at yourself first instead of trying to fix others.

Om Ganga mataye nama swaha Om Varuna Devta aye Pahimam 11 times

MONEY	LOVE	CAREER	FAMILY	TRAVEL	WEDDING	MOVE	BUSINESS	HEALTH	Lotto #'s	play 3 #s
Bad	Bad	Bad	Fair	Bad	Bad	Bad	Bad	Bad	31,69,66,28,42,35,1	204

SHOPPING	GAMBLE	SEX	KEYWORD	KEYWORD						
Bad	Bad	is very bad	KARMA	Destruction,Losses,Death,Sickness - cold,Legal matter,Abusive,Karmic debts,God -						

STRESS LEVEL	LUCKY COLORS	JEWELERY	MOONS EFFECT	GRAHA EFFECT	DAILY DEITY
High	Gold/Brown//Green	Saphire/Hessonite	Ivestments	Evil Graha	Agnidev

DAILY PUJA	DAILY PSALMS
Remembrance of family members who died, worship of older people. gifts to grand parents	9, 18, 36 ,45, 54, 63, 81, 108, 126

Tuesday, October 3, 2023				This is considered a NEUTRAL day for you					Planet: Sun	

ADVICE & DETAILS — **MANTRA FOR TODAY**

Today, you may be home alone, you may feel a bit confined, but at the same time you will have a sense of independence and the realization of your capabilities. This day may be influenced by dealings with the government, courts or legal institutions.

Om Namo Bhagawate Mukhtanandaya, 108 times

MONEY	LOVE	CAREER	FAMILY	TRAVEL	WEDDING	MOVE	BUSINESS	HEALTH	Lotto #'s	play 3 #s
Fair	Bad	Good	Bad	Fair	Bad	Fair	Fair	Fair	24,25,74,48,12,16,5	136

SHOPPING	GAMBLE	SEX	KEYWORD	KEYWORD						
Fair	Fair	is fair	MIND	Independence,Loneliness,Meditative,Worry,Dominating,Illness - Cold,On Your						

STRESS LEVEL	LUCKY COLORS	JEWELERY	MOONS EFFECT	GRAHA EFFECT	DAILY DEITY
High	White/Yellow/	Pearl/Quartz	Arrogance	Status Graha	Saraswaty

DAILY PUJA	DAILY PSALMS
Give Gifts to Priests, Invite holy ones to your home, Feed Swamis and Yogis, Do Shiva Puja.	1, 10, 28 ,37, 46, 55, 73, 100, 118

Wednesday, October 4, 2023 — This is considered a POSITIVE day for you — Planet: Moon

ADVICE & DETAILS

There will be opportunity for romantic dates or encounters. You will make money today and get profits. There is a good chance of promotion.

MANTRA FOR TODAY

Kali Durge Namo Nama Om Durge aye nama swaha 108 times

MONEY	LOVE	CAREER	FAMILY	TRAVEL	WEDDING	MOVE	BUSINESS	HEALTH	Lotto #'s	play 3 #s
Good	Excellent	Good	Good	Excellen	Good	Good	Good	Good	18,13,42,75,13,41,5	422

SHOPPING	GAMBLE	SEX	KEYWORD	KEYWORD
Good	Good	is good	LOVE	Romance,Popularity,Visitors,Shopping,Food, Drinks,Co-

STRESS LEVEL	LUCKY COLORS	JEWELERY	MOONS EFFECT	GRAHA EFFECT	DAILY DEITY
Low	Red/Yellow/Pink	Topaz/Diamonds	Conservative	Love Graha	Gauri

DAILY PUJA	DAILY PSALMS
Give Gifts to females andnMother, Serve milk Products, Worship Durga forms	2, 11, 29 ,38, 47, 56, 74, 101, 119

Thursday, October 5, 2023 — This is considered a POSITIVE day for you — Planet: Mercury

ADVICE & DETAILS

This is slow and lazy day, but for your karma you are advised to work and to be industrious. Your accomplishments today will be important for your personal growth.

MANTRA FOR TODAY

Om hareem Kleem Hreem Aem Saraswataye namaha 21 times

MONEY	LOVE	CAREER	FAMILY	TRAVEL	WEDDING	MOVE	BUSINESS	HEALTH	Lotto #'s	play 3 #s
Good	Fair	Good	Good	Excellen	Good	Good	Good	Excellent	63,34,26,44,29,53,7	549

SHOPPING	GAMBLE	SEX	KEYWORD	KEYWORD
Good	Good	is great	SOCIAL	Children,Education,Astrology,Bargains,Social Functions,Childishness,Groups -

STRESS LEVEL	LUCKY COLORS	JEWELERY	MOONS EFFECT	GRAHA EFFECT	DAILY DEITY
Low	Green/Sky Blue/	Diamonds/Silver	Enthusiastic	Social Graha	Vishnu

DAILY PUJA	DAILY PSALMS
Wash the feet of Children, Do Satnarayan Pooja, Read & chant Geeta	3, 12, 30 ,39, 48, 57, 75, 102, 120

Friday, October 6, 2023 — This is considered a NEGATIVE day for you — Planet: Pluto

ADVICE & DETAILS

If you can, take short trips and enjoy high pleasure. There will be lots of moving today.

MANTRA FOR TODAY

Om Jai Viganeshwaraya.. Lambodaraya Namo Namaha 21 times

MONEY	LOVE	CAREER	FAMILY	TRAVEL	WEDDING	MOVE	BUSINESS	HEALTH	Lotto #'s	play 3 #s
Bad	Fair	Bad	Fair	Bad	Good	Bad	Bad	Bad	29,25,59,75,27,68,5	857

SHOPPING	GAMBLE	SEX	KEYWORD	KEYWORD
Bad	Bad	is tough	CAREER	Career,Hard Work,Co-workers,Low Payment,Job Problems,High Temper,Low

STRESS LEVEL	LUCKY COLORS	JEWELERY	MOONS EFFECT	GRAHA EFFECT	DAILY DEITY
High	Dark Blue/ Purple/	Amethyst/Gold	Emotional	Job Graha	Lingam

DAILY PUJA	DAILY PSALMS
Worship Ganesh, Give gifts to father, and co -workers, Plant gardens, farms	4, 13, 31 ,40, 49, 58, 76, 103, 121

Saturday, October 7, 2023 — This is considered a POSITIVE day for you — Planet: Venus

ADVICE & DETAILS

Today is a positive day to spend with others. You will be surrounded by partners, friends, associates and teachers. The exchange is beneficial, even if it is not what you expect.

MANTRA FOR TODAY

Om Graam Greem Graum Sa Gurave namah swaha 21 times

MONEY	LOVE	CAREER	FAMILY	TRAVEL	WEDDING	MOVE	BUSINESS	HEALTH	Lotto #'s	play 3 #s
Bad	Excellent	Fair	Good	Excellen	Good	Excellen	Good	Excellent	7,46,73,61,2,25,68	474

SHOPPING	GAMBLE	SEX	KEYWORD	KEYWORD
Good	Good	is good	CHANGE	Sexuality,Travel,Change,Distant, far,Travel delays,Deception,Excercise,Illicit

STRESS LEVEL	LUCKY COLORS	JEWELERY	MOONS EFFECT	GRAHA EFFECT	DAILY DEITY
Fair	Tan/Green/ Beige	Pearl/Silver/quartz	Courageous	Travel Graha	Nataraja

DAILY PUJA	DAILY PSALMS
Artistic gifts, Pray to Krishna, Do good deeds, do Spiritual trips	5, 14, 32 ,41, 50, 59, 77, 104, 122

Sunday, October 8, 2023 — This is considered a NEGATIVE day for you — Planet: Mars

ADVICE & DETAILS

You will feel in command of everything today, be careful not to be too bossy and to be careful with your expression. It is a good day for creative endeavors such as publishing or writing. You will have an opportunity to work or be in groups or to be invited to parties.

MANTRA FOR TODAY

Om Mana Swasti Shanti Kuru kuru Swaha Shivoham Shivoham 27 times

MONEY	LOVE	CAREER	FAMILY	TRAVEL	WEDDING	MOVE	BUSINESS	HEALTH	Lotto #'s	play 3 #s
Bad	Bad	Bad	Bad	Bad	Bad	Bad	Fair	Bad	36,3,37,1,41,5,26	913

SHOPPING	GAMBLE	SEX	KEYWORD	KEYWORD
Fair	Bad	is frustrating	POWER	Responsibilty,Disagreement,Family,Back Pain,Family Conflicts,Traffic

STRESS LEVEL	LUCKY COLORS	JEWELERY	MOONS EFFECT	GRAHA EFFECT	DAILY DEITY
High	Purple/Blue/Rose	Emerald/Saphire	Educational	Family Graha	Mahakali

DAILY PUJA	DAILY PSALMS
Meditate, Control temper, Pray to Hanuman, Chant Hanuman Chalisa	6, 15, 33 ,42, 51, 60, 78, 105, 123

Monday, October 9, 2023 — This is considered a NEUTRAL day for you — Planet: Uranus

ADVICE & DETAILS

This is a day for expressing yourself in oral, visual or written form. Talk to others possibly in a group or at a gathering, paint or write a poem, book or article. This is also a day that if you are negative the use of alcohol or drugs will create danger for you, try to avoid it.

MANTRA FOR TODAY

Jai Jai Shiva Shambo.(2) ...Mahadeva Shambo (2) 21 times 8

MONEY	LOVE	CAREER	FAMILY	TRAVEL	WEDDING	MOVE	BUSINESS	HEALTH	Lotto #'s	play 3 #s
Good	Good	Fair	Good	Good	Bad	Good	Bad	Fair	12,73,33,65,30,56,2	368

SHOPPING	GAMBLE	SEX	KEYWORD	KEYWORD
Bad	Fair	is quiet	DIVINE	Spirituality,Religious,Astrology,Inner Conflicts,Religious ,Sleepiness,Advice

STRESS LEVEL	LUCKY COLORS	JEWELERY	MOONS EFFECT	GRAHA EFFECT	DAILY DEITY
Fair	Light Blue/Peach	Tiger's eye/Gold/Sil	Affectionate	God'S Graha	Shesnaag

DAILY PUJA	DAILY PSALMS
Chant Shiva Mantras, Take gifts to Ocean - Ganga Puja, Donate to Temple, Priests, etc.	7, 16, 34 ,43, 52, 61, 79, 106, 124

Tuesday, October 10, 2023 — This is considered a POSITIVE day for you — Planet: Jupiter

ADVICE & DETAILS

If you can, take short trips and enjoy high pleasure. There will be lots of moving today.

MANTRA FOR TODAY

Om Hareem Nama Swaha..Shri Maha Laxmi Aye Namah swaha 12 times

MONEY	LOVE	CAREER	FAMILY	TRAVEL	WEDDING	MOVE	BUSINESS	HEALTH	Lotto #'s	play 3 #s
Excellent	Good	Excellent	Good	Good	Excellent	Good	Excellent	Excellent	48,53,40,17,75,17,5	550

SHOPPING	GAMBLE	SEX	KEYWORD	KEYWORD
Excellent	Excellent	is excellent	MONEY	Business,Major Expense,Money -

STRESS LEVEL	LUCKY COLORS	JEWELERY	MOONS EFFECT	GRAHA EFFECT	DAILY DEITY
Low	Yellow/Silver	Diamonds/Gold/Pea	Secretive	Money Graha	Mahalaxmi

DAILY PUJA	DAILY PSALMS
Decorate Land, Feed the poor, Donate milk /products to all, Feed holy guests,	8, 17, 35 ,44, 53, 62, 80, 107, 125

Wednesday, October 11, 2023 — This is considered a NEGATIVE day for you — Planet: Saturn

ADVICE & DETAILS

Connect with the God within today so you can avoid the loneliness that can result from being boastful and criticizing others. Look at yourself first instead of trying to fix others.

MANTRA FOR TODAY

Om Ganga mataye nama swaha Om Varuna Devta aye Pahimam 11 times

MONEY	LOVE	CAREER	FAMILY	TRAVEL	WEDDING	MOVE	BUSINESS	HEALTH	Lotto #'s	play 3 #s
Bad	Bad	Bad	Fair	Bad	Bad	Bad	Bad	Bad	51,62,3,6,15,12,7	179

SHOPPING	GAMBLE	SEX	KEYWORD	KEYWORD
Bad	Bad	is very bad	KARMA	Destruction,Losses,Death,Sickness - cold,Legal matter,Abusive,Karmic debts,God -

STRESS LEVEL	LUCKY COLORS	JEWELERY	MOONS EFFECT	GRAHA EFFECT	DAILY DEITY
High	Gold/Brown//Green	Saphire/Hessonite	Ivestments	Evil Graha	Agnidev

DAILY PUJA	DAILY PSALMS
Remembrance of family members who died, worship of older people. gifts to grand parents	9, 18, 36 ,45, 54, 63, 81, 108, 126

Thursday, October 12, 2023		This is considered a NEUTRAL day for you							Planet: Sun	
ADVICE & DETAILS									MANTRA FOR TODAY	

Today, you may be home alone, you may feel a bit confined, but at the same time you will have a sense of independence and the realization of your capabilities. This day may be influenced by dealings with the government, courts or legal institutions.

Om Namo Bhagawate Mukhtanandaya, 108 times

MONEY	LOVE	CAREER	FAMILY	TRAVEL	WEDDING	MOVE	BUSINESS	HEALTH	Lotto #'s	play 3 #s
Fair	Bad	Good	Bad	Fair	Bad	Fair	Fair	Fair	68,74,70,57,44,60,6	55
SHOPPING	GAMBLE	SEX	KEYWORD	KEYWORD						
Fair	Fair	is fair	MIND	Independence,Loneliness,Meditative,Worry,Dominating,Illness - Cold,On Your						
STRESS LEVEL		LUCKY COLORS		JEWELERY		MOONS EFFECT		GRAHA EFFECT		DAILY DEITY
High		White/Yellow/		Pearl/Quartz		Arrogance		Status Graha		Saraswaty
DAILY PUJA								DAILY PSALMS		
Give Gifts to Priests, Invite holy ones to your home, Feed Swamis and Yogis, Do Shiva Puja.								1, 10, 28 ,37, 46, 55, 73, 100, 118		

Friday, October 13, 2023		This is considered a POSITIVE day for you							Planet: Moon	
ADVICE & DETAILS									MANTRA FOR TODAY	

There will be opportunity for romantic dates or encounters. You will make money today and get profits. There is a good chance of promotion.

Kali Durge Namo Nama Om Durge aye nama swaha 108 times

MONEY	LOVE	CAREER	FAMILY	TRAVEL	WEDDING	MOVE	BUSINESS	HEALTH	Lotto #'s	play 3 #s
Good	Excellent	Good	Good	Excellen	Good	Good	Good	Good	40,15,37,52,30,44,6	763
SHOPPING	GAMBLE	SEX	KEYWORD	KEYWORD						
Good	Good	is good	LOVE	Romance,Popularity,Visitors,Shopping,Food, Drinks,Co-						
STRESS LEVEL		LUCKY COLORS		JEWELERY		MOONS EFFECT		GRAHA EFFECT		DAILY DEITY
Low		Red/Yellow/Pink		Topaz/Diamonds		Conservative		Love Graha		Gauri
DAILY PUJA								DAILY PSALMS		
Give Gifts to females andnMother, Serve milk Products, Worship Durga forms								2, 11, 29 ,38, 47, 56, 74, 101, 119		

Saturday, October 14, 2023		This is considered a POSITIVE day for you							Planet: Mercury	
ADVICE & DETAILS									MANTRA FOR TODAY	

This is slow and lazy day, but for your karma you are advised to work and to be industrious. Your accomplishments today will be important for your personal growth.

Om hareem Kleem Hreem Aem Saraswataye namaha 21 times

MONEY	LOVE	CAREER	FAMILY	TRAVEL	WEDDING	MOVE	BUSINESS	HEALTH	Lotto #'s	play 3 #s
Good	Fair	Good	Good	Excellen	Good	Good	Good	Excellent	19,32,75,12,55,44,4	998
SHOPPING	GAMBLE	SEX	KEYWORD	KEYWORD						
Good	Good	is great	SOCIAL	Children,Education,Astrology,Bargains,Social Functions,Childishness,Groups -						
STRESS LEVEL		LUCKY COLORS		JEWELERY		MOONS EFFECT		GRAHA EFFECT		DAILY DEITY
Low		Green/Sky Blue/		Diamonds/Silver		Enthusiastic		Social Graha		Vishnu
DAILY PUJA								DAILY PSALMS		
Wash the feet of Children, Do Satnarayan Pooja, Read & chant Geeta								3, 12, 30 ,39, 48, 57, 75, 102, 120		

Sunday, October 15, 2023		This is considered a NEGATIVE day for you							Planet: Pluto	
ADVICE & DETAILS									MANTRA FOR TODAY	

If you can, take short trips and enjoy high pleasure. There will be lots of moving today.

Om Jai Viganeshwaraya.. Lambodaraya Namo Namaha 21 times

MONEY	LOVE	CAREER	FAMILY	TRAVEL	WEDDING	MOVE	BUSINESS	HEALTH	Lotto #'s	play 3 #s
Bad	Fair	Bad	Fair	Bad	Good	Bad	Bad	Bad	56,22,57,5,68,52,55	548
SHOPPING	GAMBLE	SEX	KEYWORD	KEYWORD						
Bad	Bad	is tough	CAREER	Career,Hard Work,Co-workers,Low Payment,Job Problems,High Temper,Low						
STRESS LEVEL		LUCKY COLORS		JEWELERY		MOONS EFFECT		GRAHA EFFECT		DAILY DEITY
High		Dark Blue/ Purple/		Amethyst/Gold		Emotional		Job Graha		Lingam
DAILY PUJA								DAILY PSALMS		
Worship Ganesh, Give gifts to father, and co -workers, Plant gardens, farms								4, 13, 31 ,40, 49, 58, 76, 103, 121		

Monday, October 16, 2023 — This is considered a POSITIVE day for you — Planet: Venus

ADVICE & DETAILS

Today is a positive day to spend with others. You will be surrounded by partners, friends, associates and teachers. The exchange is beneficial, even if it is not what you expect.

MANTRA FOR TODAY

Om Graam Greem Graum Sa Gurave namah swaha 21 times

MONEY	LOVE	CAREER	FAMILY	TRAVEL	WEDDING	MOVE	BUSINESS	HEALTH	Lotto #'s	play 3 #s
Bad	Excellent	Fair	Good	Excellen	Good	Excellen	Good	Excellent	1,50,37,56,6,17,47	524

SHOPPING	GAMBLE	SEX	KEYWORD	KEYWORD						
Good	Good	is good	CHANGE	Sexuality,Travel,Change,Distant, far,Travel delays,Deception,Excercise,Illicit						

STRESS LEVEL		LUCKY COLORS	JEWELERY	MOONS EFFECT	GRAHA EFFECT	DAILY DEITY
Fair		Tan/Green/ Beige	Pearl/Silver/quartz	Courageous	Travel Graha	Nataraja

DAILY PUJA	DAILY PSALMS
Artistic gifts, Pray to Krishna, Do good deeds, do Spiritual trips	5, 14, 32 ,41, 50, 59, 77, 104, 122

Tuesday, October 17, 2023 — This is considered a NEGATIVE day for you — Planet: Mars

ADVICE & DETAILS

You will feel in command of everything today, be careful not to be too bossy and to be careful with your expression. It is a good day for creative endeavors such as publishing or writing. You will have an opportunity to work or be in groups or to be invited to parties.

MANTRA FOR TODAY

Om Mana Swasti Shanti Kuru kuru Swaha Shivoham Shivoham 27 times

MONEY	LOVE	CAREER	FAMILY	TRAVEL	WEDDING	MOVE	BUSINESS	HEALTH	Lotto #'s	play 3 #s
Bad	Bad	Bad	Bad	Bad	Bad	Bad	Fair	Bad	28,16,36,55,38,2,73	959

SHOPPING	GAMBLE	SEX	KEYWORD	KEYWORD						
Fair	Bad	is frustrating	POWER	Responsibilty,Disagreement,Family,Back Pain,Family Conflicts,Traffic						

STRESS LEVEL		LUCKY COLORS	JEWELERY	MOONS EFFECT	GRAHA EFFECT	DAILY DEITY
High		Purple/Blue/Rose	Emerald/Saphire	Educational	Family Graha	Mahakali

DAILY PUJA	DAILY PSALMS
Meditate, Control temper, Pray to Hanuman, Chant Hanuman Chalisa	6, 15, 33 ,42, 51, 60, 78, 105, 123

Wednesday, October 18, 2023 — This is considered a NEUTRAL day for you — Planet: Uranus

ADVICE & DETAILS

This is a day for expressing yourself in oral, visual or written form. Talk to others possibly in a group or at a gathering, paint or write a poem, book or article. This is also a day that if you are negative the use of alcohol or drugs will create danger for you, try to avoid it.

MANTRA FOR TODAY

Jai Jai Shiva Shambo.(2) ...Mahadeva Shambo (2) 21 times 8

MONEY	LOVE	CAREER	FAMILY	TRAVEL	WEDDING	MOVE	BUSINESS	HEALTH	Lotto #'s	play 3 #s
Good	Good	Fair	Good	Good	Bad	Good	Bad	Fair	4,45,22,5,75,6,62	563

SHOPPING	GAMBLE	SEX	KEYWORD	KEYWORD						
Bad	Fair	is quiet	DIVINE	Spirituality,Religious,Astrology,Inner Conflicts,Religious ,Sleepiness,Advice						

STRESS LEVEL		LUCKY COLORS	JEWELERY	MOONS EFFECT	GRAHA EFFECT	DAILY DEITY
Fair		Light Blue/Peach	Tiger's eye/Gold/Sil	Affectionate	God'S Graha	Shesnaag

DAILY PUJA	DAILY PSALMS
Chant Shiva Mantras, Take gifts to Ocean - Ganga Puja, Donate to Temple, Priests, etc.	7, 16, 34 ,43, 52, 61, 79, 106, 124

Thursday, October 19, 2023 — This is considered a POSITIVE day for you — Planet: Jupiter

ADVICE & DETAILS

If you can, take short trips and enjoy high pleasure. There will be lots of moving today.

MANTRA FOR TODAY

Om Hareem Nama Swaha..Shri Maha Laxmi Aye Namah swaha 12 times

MONEY	LOVE	CAREER	FAMILY	TRAVEL	WEDDING	MOVE	BUSINESS	HEALTH	Lotto #'s	play 3 #s
Excellent	Good	Excellent	Good	Good	Excellent	Good	Excellent	Excellent	24,64,11,47,58,8,70	104

SHOPPING	GAMBLE	SEX	KEYWORD	KEYWORD						
Excellent	Excellent	is excellent	MONEY	Business,Major Expense,Money -						

STRESS LEVEL		LUCKY COLORS	JEWELERY	MOONS EFFECT	GRAHA EFFECT	DAILY DEITY
Low		Yellow/Silver	Diamonds/Gold/Pea	Secretive	Money Graha	Mahalaxmi

DAILY PUJA	DAILY PSALMS
Decorate Land, Feed the poor, Donate milk /products to all, Feed holy guests,	8, 17, 35 ,44, 53, 62, 80, 107, 125

Friday, October 20, 2023 — This is considered a NEGATIVE day for you — Planet: Saturn

ADVICE & DETAILS
Connect with the God within today so you can avoid the loneliness that can result from being boastful and criticizing others. Look at yourself first instead of trying to fix others.

MANTRA FOR TODAY
Om Ganga mataye nama swaha Om Varuna Devta aye Pahimam 11 times

MONEY	LOVE	CAREER	FAMILY	TRAVEL	WEDDING	MOVE	BUSINESS	HEALTH	Lotto #'s	play 3 #s
Bad	Bad	Bad	Fair	Bad	Bad	Bad	Bad	Bad	7,63,60,36,20,72,32	441

SHOPPING	GAMBLE	SEX	KEYWORD	KEYWORD
Bad	Bad	is very bad	KARMA	Destruction,Losses,Death,Sickness - cold,Legal matter,Abusive,Karmic debts,God -

STRESS LEVEL	LUCKY COLORS	JEWELERY	MOONS EFFECT	GRAHA EFFECT	DAILY DEITY
High	Gold/Brown//Green	Saphire/Hessonite	Ivestments	Evil Graha	Agnidev

DAILY PUJA	DAILY PSALMS
Remembrance of family members who died, worship of older people. gifts to grand parents	9, 18, 36 ,45, 54, 63, 81, 108, 126

Saturday, October 21, 2023 — This is considered a NEUTRAL day for you — Planet: Sun

ADVICE & DETAILS
Today, you may be home alone, you may feel a bit confined, but at the same time you will have a sense of independence and the realization of your capabilities. This day may be influenced by dealings with the government, courts or legal institutions.

MANTRA FOR TODAY
Om Namo Bhagawate Mukhtanandaya, 108 times

MONEY	LOVE	CAREER	FAMILY	TRAVEL	WEDDING	MOVE	BUSINESS	HEALTH	Lotto #'s	play 3 #s
Fair	Bad	Good	Bad	Fair	Bad	Fair	Fair	Fair	8,74,23,27,73,70,50	737

SHOPPING	GAMBLE	SEX	KEYWORD	KEYWORD
Fair	Fair	is fair	MIND	Independence,Loneliness,Meditative,Worry,Dominating,Illness - Cold,On Your

STRESS LEVEL	LUCKY COLORS	JEWELERY	MOONS EFFECT	GRAHA EFFECT	DAILY DEITY
High	White/Yellow/	Pearl/Quartz	Arrogance	Status Graha	Saraswaty

DAILY PUJA	DAILY PSALMS
Give Gifts to Priests, Invite holy ones to your home, Feed Swamis and Yogis, Do Shiva Puja.	1, 10, 28 ,37, 46, 55, 73, 100, 118

Sunday, October 22, 2023 — This is considered a POSITIVE day for you — Planet: Moon

ADVICE & DETAILS
There will be opportunity for romantic dates or encounters. You will make money today and get profits. There is a good chance of promotion.

MANTRA FOR TODAY
Kali Durge Namo Nama Om Durge aye nama swaha 108 times

MONEY	LOVE	CAREER	FAMILY	TRAVEL	WEDDING	MOVE	BUSINESS	HEALTH	Lotto #'s	play 3 #s
Good	Excellent	Good	Good	Excellen	Good	Good	Good	Good	14,45,42,52,28,23,1	548

SHOPPING	GAMBLE	SEX	KEYWORD	KEYWORD
Good	Good	is good	LOVE	Romance,Popularity,Visitors,Shopping,Food, Drinks,Co-

STRESS LEVEL	LUCKY COLORS	JEWELERY	MOONS EFFECT	GRAHA EFFECT	DAILY DEITY
Low	Red/Yellow/Pink	Topaz/Diamonds	Conservative	Love Graha	Gauri

DAILY PUJA	DAILY PSALMS
Give Gifts to females andnMother, Serve milk Products, Worship Durga forms	2, 11, 29 ,38, 47, 56, 74, 101, 119

Monday, October 23, 2023 — This is considered a POSITIVE day for you — Planet: Mercury

ADVICE & DETAILS
This is slow and lazy day, but for your karma you are advised to work and to be industrious. Your accomplishments today will be important for your personal growth.

MANTRA FOR TODAY
Om hareem Kleem Hreem Aem Saraswataye namaha 21 times

MONEY	LOVE	CAREER	FAMILY	TRAVEL	WEDDING	MOVE	BUSINESS	HEALTH	Lotto #'s	play 3 #s
Good	Fair	Good	Good	Excellen	Good	Good	Good	Excellent	40,26,63,19,2,25,22	571

SHOPPING	GAMBLE	SEX	KEYWORD	KEYWORD
Good	Good	is great	SOCIAL	Children,Education,Astrology,Bargains,Social Functions,Childishness,Groups -

STRESS LEVEL	LUCKY COLORS	JEWELERY	MOONS EFFECT	GRAHA EFFECT	DAILY DEITY
Low	Green/Sky Blue/	Diamonds/Silver	Enthusiastic	Social Graha	Vishnu

DAILY PUJA	DAILY PSALMS
Wash the feet of Children, Do Satnarayan Pooja, Read & chant Geeta	3, 12, 30 ,39, 48, 57, 75, 102, 120

Tuesday, October 24, 2023 — This is considered a NEGATIVE day for you — Planet: Pluto

ADVICE & DETAILS

If you can, take short trips and enjoy high pleasure. There will be lots of moving today.

MANTRA FOR TODAY

Om Jai Viganeshwaraya.. Lambodaraya Namo Namaha 21 times

MONEY	LOVE	CAREER	FAMILY	TRAVEL	WEDDING	MOVE	BUSINESS	HEALTH	Lotto #'s	play 3 #s
Bad	Fair	Bad	Fair	Bad	Good	Bad	Bad	Bad	20,64,17,19,59,70,6	474

SHOPPING	GAMBLE	SEX	KEYWORD	KEYWORD
Bad	Bad	is tough	CAREER	Career,Hard Work,Co-workers,Low Payment,Job Problems,High Temper,Low

STRESS LEVEL	LUCKY COLORS	JEWELERY	MOONS EFFECT	GRAHA EFFECT	DAILY DEITY
High	Dark Blue/ Purple/	Amethyst/Gold	Emotional	Job Graha	Lingam

DAILY PUJA	DAILY PSALMS
Worship Ganesh, Give gifts to father, and co -workers, Plant gardens, farms	4, 13, 31 ,40, 49, 58, 76, 103, 121

Wednesday, October 25, 2023 — This is considered a POSITIVE day for you — Planet: Venus

ADVICE & DETAILS

Today is a positive day to spend with others. You will be surrounded by partners, friends, associates and teachers. The exchange is beneficial, even if it is not what you expect.

MANTRA FOR TODAY

Om Graam Greem Graum Sa Gurave namah swaha 21 times

MONEY	LOVE	CAREER	FAMILY	TRAVEL	WEDDING	MOVE	BUSINESS	HEALTH	Lotto #'s	play 3 #s
Bad	Excellent	Fair	Good	Excellen	Good	Excellen	Good	Excellent	54,33,17,40,7,41,13	742

SHOPPING	GAMBLE	SEX	KEYWORD	KEYWORD
Good	Good	is good	CHANGE	Sexuality,Travel,Change,Distant, far,Travel delays,Deception,Excercise,Illicit

STRESS LEVEL	LUCKY COLORS	JEWELERY	MOONS EFFECT	GRAHA EFFECT	DAILY DEITY
Fair	Tan/Green/ Beige	Pearl/Silver/quartz	Courageous	Travel Graha	Nataraja

DAILY PUJA	DAILY PSALMS
Artistic gifts, Pray to Krishna, Do good deeds, do Spiritual trips	5, 14, 32 ,41, 50, 59, 77, 104, 122

Thursday, October 26, 2023 — This is considered a NEGATIVE day for you — Planet: Mars

ADVICE & DETAILS

You will feel in command of everything today, be careful not to be too bossy and to be careful with your expression. It is a good day for creative endeavors such as publishing or writing. You will have an opportunity to work or be in groups or to be invited to parties.

MANTRA FOR TODAY

Om Mana Swasti Shanti Kuru kuru Swaha Shivoham Shivoham 27 times

MONEY	LOVE	CAREER	FAMILY	TRAVEL	WEDDING	MOVE	BUSINESS	HEALTH	Lotto #'s	play 3 #s
Bad	Bad	Bad	Bad	Bad	Bad	Bad	Fair	Bad	11,50,4,45,73,27,20	290

SHOPPING	GAMBLE	SEX	KEYWORD	KEYWORD
Fair	Bad	is frustrating	POWER	Responsibilty,Disagreement,Family,Back Pain,Family Conflicts,Traffic

STRESS LEVEL	LUCKY COLORS	JEWELERY	MOONS EFFECT	GRAHA EFFECT	DAILY DEITY
High	Purple/Blue/Rose	Emerald/Saphire	Educational	Family Graha	Mahakali

DAILY PUJA	DAILY PSALMS
Meditate, Control temper, Pray to Hanuman, Chant Hanuman Chalisa	6, 15, 33 ,42, 51, 60, 78, 105, 123

Friday, October 27, 2023 — This is considered a NEUTRAL day for you — Planet: Uranus

ADVICE & DETAILS

This is a day for expressing yourself in oral, visual or written form. Talk to others possibly in a group or at a gathering, paint or write a poem, book or article. This is also a day that if you are negative the use of alcohol or drugs will create danger for you, try to avoid it.

MANTRA FOR TODAY

Jai Jai Shiva Shambo.(2) ...Mahadeva Shambo (2) 21 times 8

MONEY	LOVE	CAREER	FAMILY	TRAVEL	WEDDING	MOVE	BUSINESS	HEALTH	Lotto #'s	play 3 #s
Good	Good	Fair	Good	Good	Bad	Good	Bad	Fair	23,43,73,48,70,7,53	523

SHOPPING	GAMBLE	SEX	KEYWORD	KEYWORD
Bad	Fair	is quiet	DIVINE	Spirituality,Religious,Astrology,Inner Conflicts,Religious ,Sleepiness,Advice

STRESS LEVEL	LUCKY COLORS	JEWELERY	MOONS EFFECT	GRAHA EFFECT	DAILY DEITY
Fair	Light Blue/Peach	Tiger's eye/Gold/Sil	Affectionate	God'S Graha	Shesnaag

DAILY PUJA	DAILY PSALMS
Chant Shiva Mantras, Take gifts to Ocean - Ganga Puja, Donate to Temple, Priests, etc.	7, 16, 34 ,43, 52, 61, 79, 106, 124

Saturday, October 28, 2023 — This is considered a POSITIVE day for you — Planet: Jupiter

ADVICE & DETAILS

If you can, take short trips and enjoy high pleasure. There will be lots of moving today.

MANTRA FOR TODAY

Om Hareem Nama Swaha..Shri Maha Laxmi Aye Namah swaha 12 times

MONEY	LOVE	CAREER	FAMILY	TRAVEL	WEDDING	MOVE	BUSINESS	HEALTH	Lotto #'s	play 3 #s
Excellent	Good	Excellent	Good	Good	Excellent	Good	Excellent	Excellent	17,49,17,37,37,66,2	228

SHOPPING	GAMBLE	SEX	KEYWORD	KEYWORD						
Excellent	Excellent	is excellent	MONEY	Business,Major Expense,Money -						

STRESS LEVEL	LUCKY COLORS	JEWELERY	MOONS EFFECT	GRAHA EFFECT	DAILY DEITY
Low	Yellow/Silver	Diamonds/Gold/Pea	Secretive	Money Graha	Mahalaxmi

DAILY PUJA	DAILY PSALMS
Decorate Land, Feed the poor, Donate milk /products to all, Feed holy guests,	8, 17, 35 ,44, 53, 62, 80, 107, 125

Sunday, October 29, 2023 — This is considered a NEGATIVE day for you — Planet: Saturn

ADVICE & DETAILS

Connect with the God within today so you can avoid the loneliness that can result from being boastful and criticizing others. Look at yourself first instead of trying to fix others.

MANTRA FOR TODAY

Om Ganga mataye nama swaha Om Varuna Devta aye Pahimam 11 times

MONEY	LOVE	CAREER	FAMILY	TRAVEL	WEDDING	MOVE	BUSINESS	HEALTH	Lotto #'s	play 3 #s
Bad	Bad	Bad	Fair	Bad	Bad	Bad	Bad	Bad	55,43,53,48,58,14,2	643

SHOPPING	GAMBLE	SEX	KEYWORD	KEYWORD						
Bad	Bad	is very bad	KARMA	Destruction,Losses,Death,Sickness - cold,Legal matter,Abusive,Karmic debts,God -						

STRESS LEVEL	LUCKY COLORS	JEWELERY	MOONS EFFECT	GRAHA EFFECT	DAILY DEITY
High	Gold/Brown//Green	Saphire/Hessonite	Ivestments	Evil Graha	Agnidev

DAILY PUJA	DAILY PSALMS
Remembrance of family members who died, worship of older people. gifts to grand parents	9, 18, 36 ,45, 54, 63, 81, 108, 126

Monday, October 30, 2023 — This is considered a NEUTRAL day for you — Planet: Sun

ADVICE & DETAILS

Today, you may be home alone, you may feel a bit confined, but at the same time you will have a sense of independence and the realization of your capabilities. This day may be influenced by dealings with the government, courts or legal institutions.

MANTRA FOR TODAY

Om Namo Bhagawate Mukhtanandaya, 108 times

MONEY	LOVE	CAREER	FAMILY	TRAVEL	WEDDING	MOVE	BUSINESS	HEALTH	Lotto #'s	play 3 #s
Fair	Bad	Good	Bad	Fair	Bad	Fair	Fair	Fair	64,1,70,52,4,5,41	855

SHOPPING	GAMBLE	SEX	KEYWORD	KEYWORD						
Fair	Fair	is fair	MIND	Independence,Loneliness,Meditative,Worry,Dominating,Illness - Cold,On Your						

STRESS LEVEL	LUCKY COLORS	JEWELERY	MOONS EFFECT	GRAHA EFFECT	DAILY DEITY
High	White/Yellow/	Pearl/Quartz	Arrogance	Status Graha	Saraswaty

DAILY PUJA	DAILY PSALMS
Give Gifts to Priests, Invite holy ones to your home, Feed Swamis and Yogis, Do Shiva Puja.	1, 10, 28 ,37, 46, 55, 73, 100, 118

Tuesday, October 31, 2023 — This is considered a POSITIVE day for you — Planet: Moon

ADVICE & DETAILS

There will be opportunity for romantic dates or encounters. You will make money today and get profits. There is a good chance of promotion.

MANTRA FOR TODAY

Kali Durge Namo Nama Om Durge aye nama swaha 108 times

MONEY	LOVE	CAREER	FAMILY	TRAVEL	WEDDING	MOVE	BUSINESS	HEALTH	Lotto #'s	play 3 #s
Good	Excellent	Good	Good	Excellen	Good	Good	Good	Good	68,1,20,63,57,26,27	411

SHOPPING	GAMBLE	SEX	KEYWORD	KEYWORD						
Good	Good	is good	LOVE	Romance,Popularity,Visitors,Shopping,Food, Drinks,Co-						

STRESS LEVEL	LUCKY COLORS	JEWELERY	MOONS EFFECT	GRAHA EFFECT	DAILY DEITY
Low	Red/Yellow/Pink	Topaz/Diamonds	Conservative	Love Graha	Gauri

DAILY PUJA	DAILY PSALMS
Give Gifts to females andnMother, Serve milk Products, Worship Durga forms	2, 11, 29 ,38, 47, 56, 74, 101, 119

Wednesday, November 1, 2023 — This is considered a POSITIVE day for you — Planet: Jupiter

ADVICE & DETAILS

You will probably be taking short trips today or you will be moving. You will feel like moving and exercising and you should do it! There will be opportunity for illicit affairs, stay aware of how this affects you and others around you.

MANTRA FOR TODAY

Om Hareem Nama Swaha..Shri Maha Laxmi Aye Namah swaha 12 times

MONEY	LOVE	CAREER	FAMILY	TRAVEL	WEDDING	MOVE	BUSINESS	HEALTH	Lotto #'s	play 3 #s
Excellent	Good	Excellent	Good	Good	Excellent	Good	Excellent	Excellent	28,20,9,21,62,15,29	588

SHOPPING	GAMBLE	SEX	KEYWORD	KEYWORD						
Excellent	Excellent	is excellent	MONEY	Business,Major Expense,Money -						

STRESS LEVEL	LUCKY COLORS	JEWELERY	MOONS EFFECT	GRAHA EFFECT	DAILY DEITY
Low	Yellow/Silver	Diamonds/Gold/Pea	Secretive	Money Graha	Mahalaxmi

DAILY PUJA	DAILY PSALMS
Decorate Land, Feed the poor, Donate milk /products to all, Feed holy guests,	8, 17, 35 ,44, 53, 62, 80, 107, 125

Thursday, November 2, 2023 — This is considered a NEGATIVE day for you — Planet: Saturn

ADVICE & DETAILS

Try to remember that when you criticize others, you are seeing in others what you think you are missing, be kind and concentrate on the positive characteristics of others not in what you perceive are negatives. The influence of this day will make you introspective and thoughts about your spiritual self will arise. Remember that loves heals all, try to have loving, healing thoughts as much as possible. Rest today if you

MANTRA FOR TODAY

Om Ganga mataye nama swaha Om Varuna Devta aye Pahimam 11 times

MONEY	LOVE	CAREER	FAMILY	TRAVEL	WEDDING	MOVE	BUSINESS	HEALTH	Lotto #'s	play 3 #s
Bad	Bad	Bad	Fair	Bad	Bad	Bad	Bad	Bad	37,27,61,2,12,26,35	746

SHOPPING	GAMBLE	SEX	KEYWORD	KEYWORD						
Bad	Bad	is very bad	KARMA	Destruction,Losses,Death,Sickness - cold,Legal matter,Abusive,Karmic debts,God -						

STRESS LEVEL	LUCKY COLORS	JEWELERY	MOONS EFFECT	GRAHA EFFECT	DAILY DEITY
High	Gold/Brown//Green	Saphire/Hessonite	Ivestments	Evil Graha	Agnidev

DAILY PUJA	DAILY PSALMS
Remembrance of family members who died, worship of older people. gifts to grand parents	9, 18, 36 ,45, 54, 63, 81, 108, 126

Friday, November 3, 2023 — This is considered a NEUTRAL day for you — Planet: Sun

ADVICE & DETAILS

The only obstacle to this very positive day is your speech. If you are careful and kind with your words expect money, romance and positive outlook for partnerships in any area.

MANTRA FOR TODAY

Om Namo Bhagawate Mukhtanandaya, 108 times

MONEY	LOVE	CAREER	FAMILY	TRAVEL	WEDDING	MOVE	BUSINESS	HEALTH	Lotto #'s	play 3 #s
Fair	Bad	Good	Bad	Fair	Bad	Fair	Fair	Fair	9,35,62,42,32,74,51	410

SHOPPING	GAMBLE	SEX	KEYWORD	KEYWORD						
Fair	Fair	is fair	MIND	Independence,Loneliness,Meditative,Worry,Dominating,Illness - Cold,On Your						

STRESS LEVEL	LUCKY COLORS	JEWELERY	MOONS EFFECT	GRAHA EFFECT	DAILY DEITY
High	White/Yellow/	Pearl/Quartz	Arrogance	Status Graha	Saraswaty

DAILY PUJA	DAILY PSALMS
Give Gifts to Priests, Invite holy ones to your home, Feed Swamis and Yogis, Do Shiva Puja.	1, 10, 28 ,37, 46, 55, 73, 100, 118

Saturday, November 4, 2023 — This is considered a POSITIVE day for you — Planet: Moon

ADVICE & DETAILS

Every word your lips utter today have great power and they must be used with love and positive intention to avoid conflict. You will have the opportunity to serve and cooperate with others today, use it. Listen to music or express your feelings through music to get blessings today.

MANTRA FOR TODAY

Kali Durge Namo Nama Om Durge aye nama swaha 108 times

MONEY	LOVE	CAREER	FAMILY	TRAVEL	WEDDING	MOVE	BUSINESS	HEALTH	Lotto #'s	play 3 #s
Good	Excellent	Good	Good	Excellen	Good	Good	Good	Good	2,24,23,65,24,13,59	190

SHOPPING	GAMBLE	SEX	KEYWORD	KEYWORD						
Good	Good	is good	LOVE	Romance,Popularity,Visitors,Shopping,Food, Drinks,Co-						

STRESS LEVEL	LUCKY COLORS	JEWELERY	MOONS EFFECT	GRAHA EFFECT	DAILY DEITY
Low	Red/Yellow/Pink	Topaz/Diamonds	Conservative	Love Graha	Gauri

DAILY PUJA	DAILY PSALMS
Give Gifts to females andnMother, Serve milk Products, Worship Durga forms	2, 11, 29 ,38, 47, 56, 74, 101, 119

Sunday, November 5, 2023 — This is considered a POSITIVE day for you — Planet: Mercury

ADVICE & DETAILS

You may spend your day at home alone watching TV or may instead opt for luxurious and pleasurable activities that may bring you around fame or famous people. You will be influenced by money, so you will worry about it, make it or spend it.

MANTRA FOR TODAY

Om hareem Kleem Hreem Aem Saraswataye namaha 21 times

MONEY	LOVE	CAREER	FAMILY	TRAVEL	WEDDING	MOVE	BUSINESS	HEALTH	Lotto #'s	play 3 #s
Good	Fair	Good	Good	Excellen	Good	Good	Good	Excellent	55,30,36,5,56,22,37	515

SHOPPING	GAMBLE	SEX	KEYWORD	KEYWORD						
Good	Good	is great	SOCIAL	Children,Education,Astrology,Bargains,Social Functions,Childishness,Groups -						

STRESS LEVEL		LUCKY COLORS	JEWELERY	MOONS EFFECT	GRAHA EFFECT	DAILY DEITY
Low		Green/Sky Blue/	Diamonds/Silver	Enthusiastic	Social Graha	Vishnu

DAILY PUJA	DAILY PSALMS
Wash the feet of Children, Do Satnarayan Pooja, Read & chant Geeta	3, 12, 30 ,39, 48, 57, 75, 102, 120

Monday, November 6, 2023 — This is considered a NEGATIVE day for you — Planet: Pluto

ADVICE & DETAILS

This will be a positive day if you can control your tongue and do not criticize anyone, particularly your loved ones and especially your partner. The influences are love and marriage. This is the opportunity to create a special surprise meal for your partner and share it with love in a romantic setting with soothing music as background.

MANTRA FOR TODAY

Om Jai Viganeshwaraya.. Lambodaraya Namo Namaha 21 times

MONEY	LOVE	CAREER	FAMILY	TRAVEL	WEDDING	MOVE	BUSINESS	HEALTH	Lotto #'s	play 3 #s
Bad	Fair	Bad	Fair	Bad	Good	Bad	Bad	Bad	33,5,6,75,20,38,13	334

SHOPPING	GAMBLE	SEX	KEYWORD	KEYWORD						
Bad	Bad	is tough	CAREER	Career,Hard Work,Co-workers,Low Payment,Job Problems,High Temper,Low						

STRESS LEVEL		LUCKY COLORS	JEWELERY	MOONS EFFECT	GRAHA EFFECT	DAILY DEITY
High		Dark Blue/ Purple/	Amethyst/Gold	Emotional	Job Graha	Lingam

DAILY PUJA	DAILY PSALMS
Worship Ganesh, Give gifts to father, and co -workers, Plant gardens, farms	4, 13, 31 ,40, 49, 58, 76, 103, 121

Tuesday, November 7, 2023 — This is considered a POSITIVE day for you — Planet: Venus

ADVICE & DETAILS

Show your affection, cooperate with others and listen to music today; these activities will help you with the paymente of some karmic debts that may become overdue this day.

MANTRA FOR TODAY

Om Graam Greem Graum Sa Gurave namah swaha 21 times

MONEY	LOVE	CAREER	FAMILY	TRAVEL	WEDDING	MOVE	BUSINESS	HEALTH	Lotto #'s	play 3 #s
Bad	Excellent	Fair	Good	Excellen	Good	Excellen	Good	Excellent	22,63,30,29,37,17,6	907

SHOPPING	GAMBLE	SEX	KEYWORD	KEYWORD						
Good	Good	is good	CHANGE	Sexuality,Travel,Change,Distant, far,Travel delays,Deception,Excercise,Illicit						

STRESS LEVEL		LUCKY COLORS	JEWELERY	MOONS EFFECT	GRAHA EFFECT	DAILY DEITY
Fair		Tan/Green/ Beige	Pearl/Silver/quartz	Courageous	Travel Graha	Nataraja

DAILY PUJA	DAILY PSALMS
Artistic gifts, Pray to Krishna, Do good deeds, do Spiritual trips	5, 14, 32 ,41, 50, 59, 77, 104, 122

Wednesday, November 8, 2023 — This is considered a NEGATIVE day for you — Planet: Mars

ADVICE & DETAILS

You must watch out for misleading statements from others. There will be many changes today. Your sexual energy will be high. You will be thinking a great deal today about very deep and profound subjects.

MANTRA FOR TODAY

Om Mana Swasti Shanti Kuru kuru Swaha Shivoham Shivoham 27 times

MONEY	LOVE	CAREER	FAMILY	TRAVEL	WEDDING	MOVE	BUSINESS	HEALTH	Lotto #'s	play 3 #s
Bad	Bad	Bad	Bad	Bad	Bad	Bad	Fair	Bad	67,43,27,52,43,5,61	815

SHOPPING	GAMBLE	SEX	KEYWORD	KEYWORD						
Fair	Bad	is frustrating	POWER	Responsibilty,Disagreement,Family,Back Pain,Family Conflicts,Traffic						

STRESS LEVEL		LUCKY COLORS	JEWELERY	MOONS EFFECT	GRAHA EFFECT	DAILY DEITY
High		Purple/Blue/Rose	Emerald/Saphire	Educational	Family Graha	Mahakali

DAILY PUJA	DAILY PSALMS
Meditate, Control temper, Pray to Hanuman, Chant Hanuman Chalisa	6, 15, 33 ,42, 51, 60, 78, 105, 123

Thursday, November 9, 2023 — This is considered a NEUTRAL day for you — Planet: Uranus

ADVICE & DETAILS

You will feel like watching television and would probably prefer the company of children today. You may be acting somewhat immaturely today so be careful of choices and words that may have long term consequences. Today will be a good day for creativity related to writing and publishing.

MANTRA FOR TODAY

Jai Jai Shiva Shambo.(2) ...Mahadeva Shambo (2) 21 times 8

MONEY	LOVE	CAREER	FAMILY	TRAVEL	WEDDING	MOVE	BUSINESS	HEALTH	Lotto #'s	play 3 #s
Good	Good	Fair	Good	Good	Bad	Good	Bad	Fair	57,9,17,75,37,28,35	649

SHOPPING	GAMBLE	SEX	KEYWORD	KEYWORD
Bad	Fair	is quiet	DIVINE	Spirituality,Religious,Astrology,Inner Conflicts,Religious ,Sleepiness,Advice

STRESS LEVEL	LUCKY COLORS	JEWELERY	MOONS EFFECT	GRAHA EFFECT	DAILY DEITY
Fair	Light Blue/Peach	Tiger's eye/Gold/Sil	Affectionate	God'S Graha	Shesnaag

DAILY PUJA	DAILY PSALMS
Chant Shiva Mantras, Take gifts to Ocean - Ganga Puja, Donate to Temple, Priests, etc.	7, 16, 34 ,43, 52, 61, 79, 106, 124

Friday, November 10, 2023 — This is considered a POSITIVE day for you — Planet: Jupiter

ADVICE & DETAILS

You will probably be taking short trips today or you will be moving. You will feel like moving and exercising and you should do it! There will be opportunity for illicit affairs, stay aware of how this affects you and others around you.

MANTRA FOR TODAY

Om Hareem Nama Swaha..Shri Maha Laxmi Aye Namah swaha 12 times

MONEY	LOVE	CAREER	FAMILY	TRAVEL	WEDDING	MOVE	BUSINESS	HEALTH	Lotto #'s	play 3 #s
Excellent	Good	Excellent	Good	Good	Excellent	Good	Excellent	Excellent	65,39,41,64,36,42,3	249

SHOPPING	GAMBLE	SEX	KEYWORD	KEYWORD
Excellent	Excellent	is excellent	MONEY	Business,Major Expense,Money -

STRESS LEVEL	LUCKY COLORS	JEWELERY	MOONS EFFECT	GRAHA EFFECT	DAILY DEITY
Low	Yellow/Silver	Diamonds/Gold/Pea	Secretive	Money Graha	Mahalaxmi

DAILY PUJA	DAILY PSALMS
Decorate Land, Feed the poor, Donate milk /products to all, Feed holy guests,	8, 17, 35 ,44, 53, 62, 80, 107, 125

Saturday, November 11, 2023 — This is considered a NEGATIVE day for you — Planet: Saturn

ADVICE & DETAILS

Try to remember that when you criticize others, you are seeing in others what you think you are missing, be kind and concentrate on the positive characteristics of others not in what you perceive are negatives. The influence of this day will make you introspective and thoughts about your spiritual self will arise. Remember that loves heals all, try to have loving, healing thoughts as much as possible. Rest today if you

MANTRA FOR TODAY

Om Ganga mataye nama swaha Om Varuna Devta aye Pahimam 11 times

MONEY	LOVE	CAREER	FAMILY	TRAVEL	WEDDING	MOVE	BUSINESS	HEALTH	Lotto #'s	play 3 #s
Bad	Bad	Bad	Fair	Bad	Bad	Bad	Bad	Bad	3,28,27,9,12,67,57	223

SHOPPING	GAMBLE	SEX	KEYWORD	KEYWORD
Bad	Bad	is very bad	KARMA	Destruction,Losses,Death,Sickness - cold,Legal matter,Abusive,Karmic debts,God -

STRESS LEVEL	LUCKY COLORS	JEWELERY	MOONS EFFECT	GRAHA EFFECT	DAILY DEITY
High	Gold/Brown//Green	Saphire/Hessonite	Ivestments	Evil Graha	Agnidev

DAILY PUJA	DAILY PSALMS
Remembrance of family members who died, worship of older people. gifts to grand parents	9, 18, 36 ,45, 54, 63, 81, 108, 126

Sunday, November 12, 2023 — This is considered a NEUTRAL day for you — Planet: Sun

ADVICE & DETAILS

The only obstacle to this very positive day is your speech. If you are careful and kind with your words expect money, romance and positive outlook for partnerships in any area.

MANTRA FOR TODAY

Om Namo Bhagawate Mukhtanandaya, 108 times

MONEY	LOVE	CAREER	FAMILY	TRAVEL	WEDDING	MOVE	BUSINESS	HEALTH	Lotto #'s	play 3 #s
Fair	Bad	Good	Bad	Fair	Bad	Fair	Fair	Fair	11,37,30,32,25,18,2	241

SHOPPING	GAMBLE	SEX	KEYWORD	KEYWORD
Fair	Fair	is fair	MIND	Independence,Loneliness,Meditative,Worry,Dominating,Illness - Cold,On Your

STRESS LEVEL	LUCKY COLORS	JEWELERY	MOONS EFFECT	GRAHA EFFECT	DAILY DEITY
High	White/Yellow/	Pearl/Quartz	Arrogance	Status Graha	Saraswaty

DAILY PUJA	DAILY PSALMS
Give Gifts to Priests, Invite holy ones to your home, Feed Swamis and Yogis, Do Shiva Puja.	1, 10, 28 ,37, 46, 55, 73, 100, 118

Monday, November 13, 2023 — This is considered a POSITIVE day for you — Planet: Moon

ADVICE & DETAILS

Every word your lips utter today have great power and they must be used with love and positive intention to avoid conflict. You will have the opportunity to serve and cooperate with others today, use it. Listen to music or express your feelings through music to get blessings today.

MANTRA FOR TODAY

Kali Durge Namo Nama Om Durge aye nama swaha 108 times

MONEY	LOVE	CAREER	FAMILY	TRAVEL	WEDDING	MOVE	BUSINESS	HEALTH	Lotto #'s	play 3 #s
Good	Excellent	Good	Good	Excellen	Good	Good	Good	Good	9,57,9,16,58,18,61	190

SHOPPING	GAMBLE	SEX	KEYWORD	KEYWORD
Good	Good	is good	LOVE	Romance,Popularity,Visitors,Shopping,Food, Drinks,Co-

STRESS LEVEL	LUCKY COLORS	JEWELERY	MOONS EFFECT	GRAHA EFFECT	DAILY DEITY
Low	Red/Yellow/Pink	Topaz/Diamonds	Conservative	Love Graha	Gauri

DAILY PUJA	DAILY PSALMS
Give Gifts to females andnMother, Serve milk Products, Worship Durga forms	2, 11, 29 ,38, 47, 56, 74, 101, 119

Tuesday, November 14, 2023 — This is considered a POSITIVE day for you — Planet: Mercury

ADVICE & DETAILS

You may spend your day at home alone watching TV or may instead opt for luxurious and pleasurable activities that may bring you around fame or famous people. You will be influenced by money, so you will worry about it, make it or spend it.

MANTRA FOR TODAY

Om hareem Kleem Hreem Aem Saraswataye namaha 21 times

MONEY	LOVE	CAREER	FAMILY	TRAVEL	WEDDING	MOVE	BUSINESS	HEALTH	Lotto #'s	play 3 #s
Good	Fair	Good	Good	Excellen	Good	Good	Good	Excellent	23,74,58,62,9,19,51	363

SHOPPING	GAMBLE	SEX	KEYWORD	KEYWORD
Good	Good	is great	SOCIAL	Children,Education,Astrology,Bargains,Social Functions,Childishness,Groups -

STRESS LEVEL	LUCKY COLORS	JEWELERY	MOONS EFFECT	GRAHA EFFECT	DAILY DEITY
Low	Green/Sky Blue/	Diamonds/Silver	Enthusiastic	Social Graha	Vishnu

DAILY PUJA	DAILY PSALMS
Wash the feet of Children, Do Satnarayan Pooja, Read & chant Geeta	3, 12, 30 ,39, 48, 57, 75, 102, 120

Wednesday, November 15, 2023 — This is considered a NEGATIVE day for you — Planet: Pluto

ADVICE & DETAILS

This will be a positive day if you can control your tongue and do not criticize anyone, particularly your loved ones and especially your partner. The influences are love and marriage. This is the opportunity to create a special surprise meal for your partner and share it with love in a romantic setting with soothing music as background.

MANTRA FOR TODAY

Om Jai Viganeshwaraya.. Lambodaraya Namo Namaha 21 times

MONEY	LOVE	CAREER	FAMILY	TRAVEL	WEDDING	MOVE	BUSINESS	HEALTH	Lotto #'s	play 3 #s
Bad	Fair	Bad	Fair	Bad	Good	Bad	Bad	Bad	39,31,4,58,74,8,18	822

SHOPPING	GAMBLE	SEX	KEYWORD	KEYWORD
Bad	Bad	is tough	CAREER	Career,Hard Work,Co-workers,Low Payment,Job Problems,High Temper,Low

STRESS LEVEL	LUCKY COLORS	JEWELERY	MOONS EFFECT	GRAHA EFFECT	DAILY DEITY
High	Dark Blue/ Purple/	Amethyst/Gold	Emotional	Job Graha	Lingam

DAILY PUJA	DAILY PSALMS
Worship Ganesh, Give gifts to father, and co -workers, Plant gardens, farms	4, 13, 31 ,40, 49, 58, 76, 103, 121

Thursday, November 16, 2023 — This is considered a POSITIVE day for you — Planet: Venus

ADVICE & DETAILS

Show your affection, cooperate with others and listen to music today; these activities will help you with the paymente of some karmic debts that may become overdue this day.

MANTRA FOR TODAY

Om Graam Greem Graum Sa Gurave namah swaha 21 times

MONEY	LOVE	CAREER	FAMILY	TRAVEL	WEDDING	MOVE	BUSINESS	HEALTH	Lotto #'s	play 3 #s
Bad	Excellent	Fair	Good	Excellen	Good	Excellen	Good	Excellent	23,16,62,42,65,47,8	958

SHOPPING	GAMBLE	SEX	KEYWORD	KEYWORD
Good	Good	is good	CHANGE	Sexuality,Travel,Change,Distant, far,Travel delays,Deception,Excercise,Illicit

STRESS LEVEL	LUCKY COLORS	JEWELERY	MOONS EFFECT	GRAHA EFFECT	DAILY DEITY
Fair	Tan/Green/ Beige	Pearl/Silver/quartz	Courageous	Travel Graha	Nataraja

DAILY PUJA	DAILY PSALMS
Artistic gifts, Pray to Krishna, Do good deeds, do Spiritual trips	5, 14, 32 ,41, 50, 59, 77, 104, 122

Friday, November 17, 2023 — This is considered a NEGATIVE day for you — Planet: Mars

ADVICE & DETAILS

You must watch out for misleading statements from others. There will be many changes today. Your sexual energy will be high. You will be thinking a great deal today about very deep and profound subjects.

MANTRA FOR TODAY

Om Mana Swasti Shanti Kuru kuru Swaha Shivoham Shivoham 27 times

MONEY	LOVE	CAREER	FAMILY	TRAVEL	WEDDING	MOVE	BUSINESS	HEALTH	Lotto #'s	play 3 #s
Bad	Bad	Bad	Bad	Bad	Bad	Bad	Fair	Bad	4,51,7,47,58,68,48	395

SHOPPING	GAMBLE	SEX	KEYWORD	KEYWORD
Fair	Bad	is frustrating	POWER	Responsibilty,Disagreement,Family,Back Pain,Family Conflicts,Traffic

STRESS LEVEL	LUCKY COLORS	JEWELERY	MOONS EFFECT	GRAHA EFFECT	DAILY DEITY
High	Purple/Blue/Rose	Emerald/Saphire	Educational	Family Graha	Mahakali

DAILY PUJA	DAILY PSALMS
Meditate, Control temper, Pray to Hanuman, Chant Hanuman Chalisa	6, 15, 33 ,42, 51, 60, 78, 105, 123

Saturday, November 18, 2023 — This is considered a NEUTRAL day for you — Planet: Uranus

ADVICE & DETAILS

You will feel like watching television and would probably prefer the company of children today. You may be acting somewhat immaturely today so be careful of choices and words that may have long term consequences. Today will be a good day for creativity related to writing and publishing.

MANTRA FOR TODAY

Jai Jai Shiva Shambo.(2) ...Mahadeva Shambo (2) 21 times 8

MONEY	LOVE	CAREER	FAMILY	TRAVEL	WEDDING	MOVE	BUSINESS	HEALTH	Lotto #'s	play 3 #s
Good	Good	Fair	Good	Good	Bad	Good	Bad	Fair	70,40,73,15,43,45,6	9

SHOPPING	GAMBLE	SEX	KEYWORD	KEYWORD
Bad	Fair	is quiet	DIVINE	Spirituality,Religious,Astrology,Inner Conflicts,Religious ,Sleepiness,Advice

STRESS LEVEL	LUCKY COLORS	JEWELERY	MOONS EFFECT	GRAHA EFFECT	DAILY DEITY
Fair	Light Blue/Peach	Tiger's eye/Gold/Sil	Affectionate	God'S Graha	Shesnaag

DAILY PUJA	DAILY PSALMS
Chant Shiva Mantras, Take gifts to Ocean - Ganga Puja, Donate to Temple, Priests, etc.	7, 16, 34 ,43, 52, 61, 79, 106, 124

Sunday, November 19, 2023 — This is considered a POSITIVE day for you — Planet: Jupiter

ADVICE & DETAILS

You will probably be taking short trips today or you will be moving. You will feel like moving and exercising and you should do it! There will be opportunity for illicit affairs, stay aware of how this affects you and others around you.

MANTRA FOR TODAY

Om Hareem Nama Swaha..Shri Maha Laxmi Aye Namah swaha 12 times

MONEY	LOVE	CAREER	FAMILY	TRAVEL	WEDDING	MOVE	BUSINESS	HEALTH	Lotto #'s	play 3 #s
Excellent	Good	Excellent	Good	Good	Excellent	Good	Excellent	Excellent	2,6,15,26,61,35,23	137

SHOPPING	GAMBLE	SEX	KEYWORD	KEYWORD
Excellent	Excellent	is excellent	MONEY	Business,Major Expense,Money -

STRESS LEVEL	LUCKY COLORS	JEWELERY	MOONS EFFECT	GRAHA EFFECT	DAILY DEITY
Low	Yellow/Silver	Diamonds/Gold/Pea	Secretive	Money Graha	Mahalaxmi

DAILY PUJA	DAILY PSALMS
Decorate Land, Feed the poor, Donate milk /products to all, Feed holy guests,	8, 17, 35 ,44, 53, 62, 80, 107, 125

Monday, November 20, 2023 — This is considered a NEGATIVE day for you — Planet: Saturn

ADVICE & DETAILS

Try to remember that when you criticize others, you are seeing in others what you think you are missing, be kind and concentrate on the positive characteristics of others not in what you perceive are negatives. The influence of this day will make you introspective and thoughts about your spiritual self will arise. Remember that loves heals all, try to have loving, healing thoughts as much as possible. Rest today if you

MANTRA FOR TODAY

Om Ganga mataye nama swaha Om Varuna Devta aye Pahimam 11 times

MONEY	LOVE	CAREER	FAMILY	TRAVEL	WEDDING	MOVE	BUSINESS	HEALTH	Lotto #'s	play 3 #s
Bad	Bad	Bad	Fair	Bad	Bad	Bad	Bad	Bad	57,19,15,16,3,46,2	308

SHOPPING	GAMBLE	SEX	KEYWORD	KEYWORD
Bad	Bad	is very bad	KARMA	Destruction,Losses,Death,Sickness - cold,Legal matter,Abusive,Karmic debts,God -

STRESS LEVEL	LUCKY COLORS	JEWELERY	MOONS EFFECT	GRAHA EFFECT	DAILY DEITY
High	Gold/Brown//Green	Saphire/Hessonite	Ivestments	Evil Graha	Agnidev

DAILY PUJA	DAILY PSALMS
Remembrance of family members who died, worship of older people. gifts to grand parents	9, 18, 36 ,45, 54, 63, 81, 108, 126

Tuesday, November 21, 2023 — This is considered a NEUTRAL day for you — Planet: Sun

ADVICE & DETAILS

The only obstacle to this very positive day is your speech. If you are careful and kind with your words expect money, romance and positive outlook for partnerships in any area.

MANTRA FOR TODAY: Om Namo Bhagawate Mukhtanandaya, 108 times

MONEY	LOVE	CAREER	FAMILY	TRAVEL	WEDDING	MOVE	BUSINESS	HEALTH	Lotto #'s	play 3 #s
Fair	Bad	Good	Bad	Fair	Bad	Fair	Fair	Fair	2,9,26,10,41,9,72	628

SHOPPING	GAMBLE	SEX	KEYWORD	KEYWORD
Fair	Fair	is fair	MIND	Independence,Loneliness,Meditative,Worry,Dominating,Illness - Cold,On Your

STRESS LEVEL	LUCKY COLORS	JEWELERY	MOONS EFFECT	GRAHA EFFECT	DAILY DEITY
High	White/Yellow/	Pearl/Quartz	Arrogance	Status Graha	Saraswaty

DAILY PUJA	DAILY PSALMS
Give Gifts to Priests, Invite holy ones to your home, Feed Swamis and Yogis, Do Shiva Puja.	1, 10, 28 ,37, 46, 55, 73, 100, 118

Wednesday, November 22, 2023 — This is considered a POSITIVE day for you — Planet: Moon

ADVICE & DETAILS

Every word your lips utter today have great power and they must be used with love and positive intention to avoid conflict. You will have the opportunity to serve and cooperate with others today, use it. Listen to music or express your feelings through music to get blessings today.

MANTRA FOR TODAY: Kali Durge Namo Nama Om Durge aye nama swaha 108 times

MONEY	LOVE	CAREER	FAMILY	TRAVEL	WEDDING	MOVE	BUSINESS	HEALTH	Lotto #'s	play 3 #s
Good	Excellent	Good	Good	Excellen	Good	Good	Good	Good	11,23,13,55,34,18,2	624

SHOPPING	GAMBLE	SEX	KEYWORD	KEYWORD
Good	Good	is good	LOVE	Romance,Popularity,Visitors,Shopping,Food, Drinks,Co-

STRESS LEVEL	LUCKY COLORS	JEWELERY	MOONS EFFECT	GRAHA EFFECT	DAILY DEITY
Low	Red/Yellow/Pink	Topaz/Diamonds	Conservative	Love Graha	Gauri

DAILY PUJA	DAILY PSALMS
Give Gifts to females andnMother, Serve milk Products, Worship Durga forms	2, 11, 29 ,38, 47, 56, 74, 101, 119

Thursday, November 23, 2023 — This is considered a POSITIVE day for you — Planet: Mercury

ADVICE & DETAILS

You may spend your day at home alone watching TV or may instead opt for luxurious and pleasurable activities that may bring you around fame or famous people. You will be influenced by money, so you will worry about it, make it or spend it.

MANTRA FOR TODAY: Om hareem Kleem Hreem Aem Saraswataye namaha 21 times

MONEY	LOVE	CAREER	FAMILY	TRAVEL	WEDDING	MOVE	BUSINESS	HEALTH	Lotto #'s	play 3 #s
Good	Fair	Good	Good	Excellen	Good	Good	Good	Excellent	4,2,27,70,6,58,38	157

SHOPPING	GAMBLE	SEX	KEYWORD	KEYWORD
Good	Good	is great	SOCIAL	Children,Education,Astrology,Bargains,Social Functions,Childishness,Groups -

STRESS LEVEL	LUCKY COLORS	JEWELERY	MOONS EFFECT	GRAHA EFFECT	DAILY DEITY
Low	Green/Sky Blue/	Diamonds/Silver	Enthusiastic	Social Graha	Vishnu

DAILY PUJA	DAILY PSALMS
Wash the feet of Children, Do Satnarayan Pooja, Read & chant Geeta	3, 12, 30 ,39, 48, 57, 75, 102, 120

Friday, November 24, 2023 — This is considered a NEGATIVE day for you — Planet: Pluto

ADVICE & DETAILS

This will be a positive day if you can control your tongue and do not criticize anyone, particularly your loved ones and especially your partner. The influences are love and marriage. This is the opportunity to create a special surprise meal for your partner and share it with love in a romantic setting with soothing music as background.

MANTRA FOR TODAY: Om Jai Viganeshwaraya.. Lambodaraya Namo Namaha 21 times

MONEY	LOVE	CAREER	FAMILY	TRAVEL	WEDDING	MOVE	BUSINESS	HEALTH	Lotto #'s	play 3 #s
Bad	Fair	Bad	Fair	Bad	Good	Bad	Bad	Bad	40,57,71,11,47,61,2	223

SHOPPING	GAMBLE	SEX	KEYWORD	KEYWORD
Bad	Bad	is tough	CAREER	Career,Hard Work,Co-workers,Low Payment,Job Problems,High Temper,Low

STRESS LEVEL	LUCKY COLORS	JEWELERY	MOONS EFFECT	GRAHA EFFECT	DAILY DEITY
High	Dark Blue/ Purple/	Amethyst/Gold	Emotional	Job Graha	Lingam

DAILY PUJA	DAILY PSALMS
Worship Ganesh, Give gifts to father, and co -workers, Plant gardens, farms	4, 13, 31 ,40, 49, 58, 76, 103, 121

Saturday, November 25, 2023 — This is considered a POSITIVE day for you — Planet: Venus

ADVICE & DETAILS
Show your affection, cooperate with others and listen to music today; these activities will help you with the payment of some karmic debts that may become overdue this day.

MANTRA FOR TODAY
Om Graam Greem Graum Sa Gurave namah swaha 21 times

MONEY	LOVE	CAREER	FAMILY	TRAVEL	WEDDING	MOVE	BUSINESS	HEALTH	Lotto #'s	play 3 #s
Bad	Excellent	Fair	Good	Excellen	Good	Excellen	Good	Excellent	9,4,12,40,32,36,24	703

SHOPPING	GAMBLE	SEX	KEYWORD	KEYWORD						
Good	Good	is good	CHANGE	Sexuality,Travel,Change,Distant, far,Travel delays,Deception,Excercise,Illicit						

STRESS LEVEL	LUCKY COLORS	JEWELERY	MOONS EFFECT	GRAHA EFFECT	DAILY DEITY
Fair	Tan/Green/ Beige	Pearl/Silver/quartz	Courageous	Travel Graha	Nataraja

DAILY PUJA: Artistic gifts, Pray to Krishna, Do good deeds, do Spiritual trips

DAILY PSALMS: 5, 14, 32 ,41, 50, 59, 77, 104, 122

Sunday, November 26, 2023 — This is considered a NEGATIVE day for you — Planet: Mars

ADVICE & DETAILS
You must watch out for misleading statements from others. There will be many changes today. Your sexual energy will be high. You will be thinking a great deal today about very deep and profound subjects.

MANTRA FOR TODAY
Om Mana Swasti Shanti Kuru kuru Swaha Shivoham Shivoham 27 times

MONEY	LOVE	CAREER	FAMILY	TRAVEL	WEDDING	MOVE	BUSINESS	HEALTH	Lotto #'s	play 3 #s
Bad	Bad	Bad	Bad	Bad	Bad	Bad	Fair	Bad	29,17,45,30,59,6,42	967

SHOPPING	GAMBLE	SEX	KEYWORD	KEYWORD						
Fair	Bad	is frustrating	POWER	Responsibilty,Disagreement,Family,Back Pain,Family Conflicts,Traffic						

STRESS LEVEL	LUCKY COLORS	JEWELERY	MOONS EFFECT	GRAHA EFFECT	DAILY DEITY
High	Purple/Blue/Rose	Emerald/Saphire	Educational	Family Graha	Mahakali

DAILY PUJA: Meditate, Control temper, Pray to Hanuman, Chant Hanuman Chalisa

DAILY PSALMS: 6, 15, 33 ,42, 51, 60, 78, 105, 123

Monday, November 27, 2023 — This is considered a NEUTRAL day for you — Planet: Uranus

ADVICE & DETAILS
You will feel like watching television and would probably prefer the company of children today. You may be acting somewhat immaturely today so be careful of choices and words that may have long term consequences. Today will be a good day for creativity related to writing and publishing.

MANTRA FOR TODAY
Jai Jai Shiva Shambo.(2) ...Mahadeva Shambo (2) 21 times 8

MONEY	LOVE	CAREER	FAMILY	TRAVEL	WEDDING	MOVE	BUSINESS	HEALTH	Lotto #'s	play 3 #s
Good	Good	Fair	Good	Good	Bad	Good	Bad	Fair	5,9,64,2,27,67,3	626

SHOPPING	GAMBLE	SEX	KEYWORD	KEYWORD						
Bad	Fair	is quiet	DIVINE	Spirituality,Religious,Astrology,Inner Conflicts,Religious ,Sleepiness,Advice						

STRESS LEVEL	LUCKY COLORS	JEWELERY	MOONS EFFECT	GRAHA EFFECT	DAILY DEITY
Fair	Light Blue/Peach	Tiger's eye/Gold/Sil	Affectionate	God'S Graha	Shesnaag

DAILY PUJA: Chant Shiva Mantras, Take gifts to Ocean - Ganga Puja, Donate to Temple, Priests, etc.

DAILY PSALMS: 7, 16, 34 ,43, 52, 61, 79, 106, 124

Tuesday, November 28, 2023 — This is considered a POSITIVE day for you — Planet: Jupiter

ADVICE & DETAILS
You will probably be taking short trips today or you will be moving. You will feel like moving and exercising and you should do it! There will be opportunity for illicit affairs, stay aware of how this affects you and others around you.

MANTRA FOR TODAY
Om Hareem Nama Swaha..Shri Maha Laxmi Aye Namah swaha 12 times

MONEY	LOVE	CAREER	FAMILY	TRAVEL	WEDDING	MOVE	BUSINESS	HEALTH	Lotto #'s	play 3 #s
Excellent	Good	Excellent	Good	Good	Excellent	Good	Excellent	Excellent	12,54,65,48,57,45,1	489

SHOPPING	GAMBLE	SEX	KEYWORD	KEYWORD						
Excellent	Excellent	is excellent	MONEY	Business,Major Expense,Money -						

STRESS LEVEL	LUCKY COLORS	JEWELERY	MOONS EFFECT	GRAHA EFFECT	DAILY DEITY
Low	Yellow/Silver	Diamonds/Gold/Pea	Secretive	Money Graha	Mahalaxmi

DAILY PUJA: Decorate Land, Feed the poor, Donate milk /products to all, Feed holy guests,

DAILY PSALMS: 8, 17, 35 ,44, 53, 62, 80, 107, 125

Wednesday, November 29, 2023 — This is considered a NEGATIVE day for you — Planet: Saturn

ADVICE & DETAILS

Try to remember that when you criticize others, you are seeing in others what you think you are missing, be kind and concentrate on the positive characteristics of others not in what you perceive are negatives. The influence of this day will make you introspective and thoughts about your spiritual self will arise. Remember that loves heals all, try to have loving, healing thoughts as much as possible. Rest today if you

MANTRA FOR TODAY: Om Ganga mataye nama swaha Om Varuna Devta aye Pahimam 11 times

MONEY	LOVE	CAREER	FAMILY	TRAVEL	WEDDING	MOVE	BUSINESS	HEALTH	Lotto #'s	play 3 #s
Bad	Bad	Bad	Fair	Bad	Bad	Bad	Bad	Bad	11,9,30,51,2,14,59	665

SHOPPING	GAMBLE	SEX	KEYWORD	KEYWORD
Bad	Bad	is very bad	KARMA	Destruction,Losses,Death,Sickness - cold,Legal matter,Abusive,Karmic debts,God -

STRESS LEVEL	LUCKY COLORS	JEWELERY	MOONS EFFECT	GRAHA EFFECT	DAILY DEITY
High	Gold/Brown//Green	Saphire/Hessonite	Ivestments	Evil Graha	Agnidev

DAILY PUJA	DAILY PSALMS
Remembrance of family members who died, worship of older people. gifts to grand parents	9, 18, 36 ,45, 54, 63, 81, 108, 126

Thursday, November 30, 2023 — This is considered a NEUTRAL day for you — Planet: Sun

ADVICE & DETAILS

The only obstacle to this very positive day is your speech. If you are careful and kind with your words expect money, romance and positive outlook for partnerships in any area.

MANTRA FOR TODAY: Om Namo Bhagawate Mukhtanandaya, 108 times

MONEY	LOVE	CAREER	FAMILY	TRAVEL	WEDDING	MOVE	BUSINESS	HEALTH	Lotto #'s	play 3 #s
Fair	Bad	Good	Bad	Fair	Bad	Fair	Fair	Fair	33,74,27,58,61,65,7	513

SHOPPING	GAMBLE	SEX	KEYWORD	KEYWORD
Fair	Fair	is fair	MIND	Independence,Loneliness,Meditative,Worry,Dominating,Illness - Cold,On Your

STRESS LEVEL	LUCKY COLORS	JEWELERY	MOONS EFFECT	GRAHA EFFECT	DAILY DEITY
High	White/Yellow/	Pearl/Quartz	Arrogance	Status Graha	Saraswaty

DAILY PUJA	DAILY PSALMS
Give Gifts to Priests, Invite holy ones to your home, Feed Swamis and Yogis, Do Shiva Puja.	1, 10, 28 ,37, 46, 55, 73, 100, 118

Friday, December 1, 2023 — This is considered a POSITIVE day for you — Planet: Jupiter

ADVICE & DETAILS

The power of your expression today is great. Use this power to communicate with others, to write and publish or to entertain others when in groups or parties. There is the influence of someone that is jealous of you, be aware of it and try to be modest.

MANTRA FOR TODAY: Om Hareem Nama Swaha..Shri Maha Laxmi Aye Namah swaha 12 times

MONEY	LOVE	CAREER	FAMILY	TRAVEL	WEDDING	MOVE	BUSINESS	HEALTH	Lotto #'s	play 3 #s
Excellent	Good	Excellent	Good	Good	Excellent	Good	Excellent	Excellent	9,67,49,14,15,31,7	849

SHOPPING	GAMBLE	SEX	KEYWORD	KEYWORD
Excellent	Excellent	is excellent	MONEY	Business,Major Expense,Money -

STRESS LEVEL	LUCKY COLORS	JEWELERY	MOONS EFFECT	GRAHA EFFECT	DAILY DEITY
Low	Yellow/Silver	Diamonds/Gold/Pea	Secretive	Money Graha	Mahalaxmi

DAILY PUJA	DAILY PSALMS
Decorate Land, Feed the poor, Donate milk /products to all, Feed holy guests,	8, 17, 35 ,44, 53, 62, 80, 107, 125

Saturday, December 2, 2023 — This is considered a NEGATIVE day for you — Planet: Saturn

ADVICE & DETAILS

Although this will be a day open for you to socialize with others, you must avoid extremes and parties with alcohol and drugs. Your enemies will take advantage of you today when they see you in your weakest state. Try to rest, you will be sleepy.

MANTRA FOR TODAY: Om Ganga mataye nama swaha Om Varuna Devta aye Pahimam 11 times

MONEY	LOVE	CAREER	FAMILY	TRAVEL	WEDDING	MOVE	BUSINESS	HEALTH	Lotto #'s	play 3 #s
Bad	Bad	Bad	Fair	Bad	Bad	Bad	Bad	Bad	47,55,74,16,59,59,6	722

SHOPPING	GAMBLE	SEX	KEYWORD	KEYWORD
Bad	Bad	is very bad	KARMA	Destruction,Losses,Death,Sickness - cold,Legal matter,Abusive,Karmic debts,God -

STRESS LEVEL	LUCKY COLORS	JEWELERY	MOONS EFFECT	GRAHA EFFECT	DAILY DEITY
High	Gold/Brown//Green	Saphire/Hessonite	Ivestments	Evil Graha	Agnidev

DAILY PUJA	DAILY PSALMS
Remembrance of family members who died, worship of older people. gifts to grand parents	9, 18, 36 ,45, 54, 63, 81, 108, 126

Sunday, December 3, 2023 — This is considered a NEUTRAL day for you — Planet: Sun

ADVICE & DETAILS

There may be sickness of children or you may be getting sick. There will be losses and sadness.

MANTRA FOR TODAY

Om Namo Bhagawate Mukhtanandaya, 108 times

MONEY	LOVE	CAREER	FAMILY	TRAVEL	WEDDING	MOVE	BUSINESS	HEALTH	Lotto #'s	play 3 #s
Fair	Bad	Good	Bad	Fair	Bad	Fair	Fair	Fair	54,22,35,64,15,36,1	933

SHOPPING	GAMBLE	SEX	KEYWORD	KEYWORD						
Fair	Fair	is fair	MIND	Independence,Loneliness,Meditative,Worry,Dominating,Illness - Cold,On Your						

STRESS LEVEL	LUCKY COLORS	JEWELERY	MOONS EFFECT	GRAHA EFFECT	DAILY DEITY
High	White/Yellow/	Pearl/Quartz	Arrogance	Status Graha	Saraswaty

DAILY PUJA	DAILY PSALMS
Give Gifts to Priests, Invite holy ones to your home, Feed Swamis and Yogis, Do Shiva Puja.	1, 10, 28 ,37, 46, 55, 73, 100, 118

Monday, December 4, 2023 — This is considered a POSITIVE day for you — Planet: Moon

ADVICE & DETAILS

Express your thoughts, opinions or information to partners and/or children. Day is influenced by children and ability to acquire information by reading or other means.

MANTRA FOR TODAY

Kali Durge Namo Nama Om Durge aye nama swaha 108 times

MONEY	LOVE	CAREER	FAMILY	TRAVEL	WEDDING	MOVE	BUSINESS	HEALTH	Lotto #'s	play 3 #s
Good	Excellent	Good	Good	Excellen	Good	Good	Good	Good	59,46,24,38,53,22,1	761

SHOPPING	GAMBLE	SEX	KEYWORD	KEYWORD						
Good	Good	is good	LOVE	Romance,Popularity,Visitors,Shopping,Food, Drinks,Co-						

STRESS LEVEL	LUCKY COLORS	JEWELERY	MOONS EFFECT	GRAHA EFFECT	DAILY DEITY
Low	Red/Yellow/Pink	Topaz/Diamonds	Conservative	Love Graha	Gauri

DAILY PUJA	DAILY PSALMS
Give Gifts to females andnMother, Serve milk Products, Worship Durga forms	2, 11, 29 ,38, 47, 56, 74, 101, 119

Tuesday, December 5, 2023 — This is considered a POSITIVE day for you — Planet: Mercury

ADVICE & DETAILS

Reading will benefit you today. You will have to hone your communication skills and speak clearly and listen carefully, especially when dealing with Real Estate and teachers of any type.

MANTRA FOR TODAY

Om hareem Kleem Hreem Aem Saraswataye namaha 21 times

MONEY	LOVE	CAREER	FAMILY	TRAVEL	WEDDING	MOVE	BUSINESS	HEALTH	Lotto #'s	play 3 #s
Good	Fair	Good	Good	Excellen	Good	Good	Good	Excellent	64,45,43,15,39,11,3	244

SHOPPING	GAMBLE	SEX	KEYWORD	KEYWORD						
Good	Good	is great	SOCIAL	Children,Education,Astrology,Bargains,Social Functions,Childishness,Groups -						

STRESS LEVEL	LUCKY COLORS	JEWELERY	MOONS EFFECT	GRAHA EFFECT	DAILY DEITY
Low	Green/Sky Blue/	Diamonds/Silver	Enthusiastic	Social Graha	Vishnu

DAILY PUJA	DAILY PSALMS
Wash the feet of Children, Do Satnarayan Pooja, Read & chant Geeta	3, 12, 30 ,39, 48, 57, 75, 102, 120

Wednesday, December 6, 2023 — This is considered a NEGATIVE day for you — Planet: Pluto

ADVICE & DETAILS

Overcome laziness and low pay today and improve your karma by being industrious, hard working and controlling your high temper.

MANTRA FOR TODAY

Om Jai Viganeshwaraya.. Lambodaraya Namo Namaha 21 times

MONEY	LOVE	CAREER	FAMILY	TRAVEL	WEDDING	MOVE	BUSINESS	HEALTH	Lotto #'s	play 3 #s
Bad	Fair	Bad	Fair	Bad	Good	Bad	Bad	Bad	27,5,49,70,74,73,18	957

SHOPPING	GAMBLE	SEX	KEYWORD	KEYWORD						
Bad	Bad	is tough	CAREER	Career,Hard Work,Co-workers,Low Payment,Job Problems,High Temper,Low						

STRESS LEVEL	LUCKY COLORS	JEWELERY	MOONS EFFECT	GRAHA EFFECT	DAILY DEITY
High	Dark Blue/ Purple/	Amethyst/Gold	Emotional	Job Graha	Lingam

DAILY PUJA	DAILY PSALMS
Worship Ganesh, Give gifts to father, and co -workers, Plant gardens, farms	4, 13, 31 ,40, 49, 58, 76, 103, 121

Thursday, December 7, 2023 — This is considered a POSITIVE day for you — Planet: Venus

ADVICE & DETAILS

Although this will be a day open for you to socialize with others, you must avoid extremes and parties with alcohol and drugs. Your enemies will take advantage of you today when they see you in your weakest state. Try to rest, you will be sleepy.

MANTRA FOR TODAY: Om Graam Greem Graum Sa Gurave namah swaha 21 times

MONEY	LOVE	CAREER	FAMILY	TRAVEL	WEDDING	MOVE	BUSINESS	HEALTH	Lotto #'s	play 3 #s
Bad	Excellent	Fair	Good	Excellen	Good	Exceller	Good	Excellent	46,7,25,63,50,21,65	946

SHOPPING	GAMBLE	SEX	KEYWORD	KEYWORD
Good	Good	is good	CHANGE	Sexuality,Travel,Change,Distant, far,Travel delays,Deception,Excercise,Illicit

STRESS LEVEL	LUCKY COLORS	JEWELERY	MOONS EFFECT	GRAHA EFFECT	DAILY DEITY
Fair	Tan/Green/ Beige	Pearl/Silver/quartz	Courageous	Travel Graha	Nataraja

DAILY PUJA	DAILY PSALMS
Artistic gifts, Pray to Krishna, Do good deeds, do Spiritual trips	5, 14, 32 ,41, 50, 59, 77, 104, 122

Friday, December 8, 2023 — This is considered a NEGATIVE day for you — Planet: Mars

ADVICE & DETAILS

Children will be prevalent today. This day is marked with a great deal of creativity ideal for areas related to the left side of the brain such as writing, painting, handcrafts, baking, cooking or needlework.

MANTRA FOR TODAY: Om Mana Swasti Shanti Kuru kuru Swaha Shivoham Shivoham 27 times

MONEY	LOVE	CAREER	FAMILY	TRAVEL	WEDDING	MOVE	BUSINESS	HEALTH	Lotto #'s	play 3 #s
Bad	Bad	Bad	Bad	Bad	Bad	Bad	Fair	Bad	47,2,41,23,63,19,13	278

SHOPPING	GAMBLE	SEX	KEYWORD	KEYWORD
Fair	Bad	is frustrating	POWER	Responsibilty,Disagreement,Family,Back Pain,Family Conflicts,Traffic

STRESS LEVEL	LUCKY COLORS	JEWELERY	MOONS EFFECT	GRAHA EFFECT	DAILY DEITY
High	Purple/Blue/Rose	Emerald/Saphire	Educational	Family Graha	Mahakali

DAILY PUJA	DAILY PSALMS
Meditate, Control temper, Pray to Hanuman, Chant Hanuman Chalisa	6, 15, 33 ,42, 51, 60, 78, 105, 123

Saturday, December 9, 2023 — This is considered a NEUTRAL day for you — Planet: Uranus

ADVICE & DETAILS

The thought of watching TV is very appealing today. Spending time with children will benefit your creativity, but you must refrain from allowing immaturity to control your actions today.

MANTRA FOR TODAY: Jai Jai Shiva Shambo.(2) ...Mahadeva Shambo (2) 21 times 8

MONEY	LOVE	CAREER	FAMILY	TRAVEL	WEDDING	MOVE	BUSINESS	HEALTH	Lotto #'s	play 3 #s
Good	Good	Fair	Good	Good	Bad	Good	Bad	Fair	26,39,73,4,66,31,30	551

SHOPPING	GAMBLE	SEX	KEYWORD	KEYWORD
Bad	Fair	is quiet	DIVINE	Spirituality,Religious,Astrology,Inner Conflicts,Religious ,Sleepiness,Advice

STRESS LEVEL	LUCKY COLORS	JEWELERY	MOONS EFFECT	GRAHA EFFECT	DAILY DEITY
Fair	Light Blue/Peach	Tiger's eye/Gold/Sil	Affectionate	God'S Graha	Shesnaag

DAILY PUJA	DAILY PSALMS
Chant Shiva Mantras, Take gifts to Ocean - Ganga Puja, Donate to Temple, Priests, etc.	7, 16, 34 ,43, 52, 61, 79, 106, 124

Sunday, December 10, 2023 — This is considered a POSITIVE day for you — Planet: Jupiter

ADVICE & DETAILS

The power of your expression today is great. Use this power to communicate with others, to write and publish or to entertain others when in groups or parties. There is the influence of someone that is jealous of you, be aware of it and try to be modest.

MANTRA FOR TODAY: Om Hareem Nama Swaha..Shri Maha Laxmi Aye Namah swaha 12 times

MONEY	LOVE	CAREER	FAMILY	TRAVEL	WEDDING	MOVE	BUSINESS	HEALTH	Lotto #'s	play 3 #s
Excellent	Good	Excellent	Good	Good	Excellent	Good	Excellent	Excellent	32,31,43,53,33,1,59	562

SHOPPING	GAMBLE	SEX	KEYWORD	KEYWORD
Excellent	Excellent	is excellent	MONEY	Business,Major Expense,Money -

STRESS LEVEL	LUCKY COLORS	JEWELERY	MOONS EFFECT	GRAHA EFFECT	DAILY DEITY
Low	Yellow/Silver	Diamonds/Gold/Pea	Secretive	Money Graha	Mahalaxmi

DAILY PUJA	DAILY PSALMS
Decorate Land, Feed the poor, Donate milk /products to all, Feed holy guests,	8, 17, 35 ,44, 53, 62, 80, 107, 125

Monday, December 11, 2023 — This is considered a NEGATIVE day for you — Planet: Saturn

ADVICE & DETAILS

Although this will be a day open for you to socialize with others, you must avoid extremes and parties with alcohol and drugs. Your enemies will take advantage of you today when they see you in your weakest state. Try to rest, you will be sleepy.

MANTRA FOR TODAY

Om Ganga mataye nama swaha Om Varuna Devta aye Pahimam 11 times

MONEY	LOVE	CAREER	FAMILY	TRAVEL	WEDDING	MOVE	BUSINESS	HEALTH	Lotto #'s	play 3 #s
Bad	Bad	Bad	Fair	Bad	Bad	Bad	Bad	Bad	51,24,57,41,23,38,7	695

SHOPPING	GAMBLE	SEX	KEYWORD	KEYWORD						
Bad	Bad	is very bad	KARMA	Destruction,Losses,Death,Sickness - cold,Legal matter,Abusive,Karmic debts,God -						

STRESS LEVEL	LUCKY COLORS	JEWELERY	MOONS EFFECT	GRAHA EFFECT	DAILY DEITY
High	Gold/Brown//Green	Saphire/Hessonite	Ivestments	Evil Graha	Agnidev

DAILY PUJA	DAILY PSALMS
Remembrance of family members who died, worship of older people. gifts to grand parents	9, 18, 36 ,45, 54, 63, 81, 108, 126

Tuesday, December 12, 2023 — This is considered a NEUTRAL day for you — Planet: Sun

ADVICE & DETAILS

There may be sickness of children or you may be getting sick. There will be losses and sadness.

MANTRA FOR TODAY

Om Namo Bhagawate Mukhtanandaya, 108 times

MONEY	LOVE	CAREER	FAMILY	TRAVEL	WEDDING	MOVE	BUSINESS	HEALTH	Lotto #'s	play 3 #s
Fair	Bad	Good	Bad	Fair	Bad	Fair	Fair	Fair	15,14,71,69,67,54,5	66

SHOPPING	GAMBLE	SEX	KEYWORD	KEYWORD						
Fair	Fair	is fair	MIND	Independence,Loneliness,Meditative,Worry,Dominating,Illness - Cold,On Your						

STRESS LEVEL	LUCKY COLORS	JEWELERY	MOONS EFFECT	GRAHA EFFECT	DAILY DEITY
High	White/Yellow/	Pearl/Quartz	Arrogance	Status Graha	Saraswaty

DAILY PUJA	DAILY PSALMS
Give Gifts to Priests, Invite holy ones to your home, Feed Swamis and Yogis, Do Shiva Puja.	1, 10, 28 ,37, 46, 55, 73, 100, 118

Wednesday, December 13, 2023 — This is considered a POSITIVE day for you — Planet: Moon

ADVICE & DETAILS

Express your thoughts, opinions or information to partners and/or children. Day is influenced by children and ability to acquire information by reading or other means.

MANTRA FOR TODAY

Kali Durge Namo Nama Om Durge aye nama swaha 108 times

MONEY	LOVE	CAREER	FAMILY	TRAVEL	WEDDING	MOVE	BUSINESS	HEALTH	Lotto #'s	play 3 #s
Good	Excellent	Good	Good	Excellen	Good	Good	Good	Good	12,1,56,50,60,11,5	285

SHOPPING	GAMBLE	SEX	KEYWORD	KEYWORD						
Good	Good	is good	LOVE	Romance,Popularity,Visitors,Shopping,Food, Drinks,Co-						

STRESS LEVEL	LUCKY COLORS	JEWELERY	MOONS EFFECT	GRAHA EFFECT	DAILY DEITY
Low	Red/Yellow/Pink	Topaz/Diamonds	Conservative	Love Graha	Gauri

DAILY PUJA	DAILY PSALMS
Give Gifts to females andnMother, Serve milk Products, Worship Durga forms	2, 11, 29 ,38, 47, 56, 74, 101, 119

Thursday, December 14, 2023 — This is considered a POSITIVE day for you — Planet: Mercury

ADVICE & DETAILS

Reading will benefit you today. You will have to hone your communication skills and speak clearly and listen carefully, especially when dealing with Real Estate and teachers of any type.

MANTRA FOR TODAY

Om hareem Kleem Hreem Aem Saraswataye namaha 21 times

MONEY	LOVE	CAREER	FAMILY	TRAVEL	WEDDING	MOVE	BUSINESS	HEALTH	Lotto #'s	play 3 #s
Good	Fair	Good	Good	Excellen	Good	Good	Good	Excellent	8,24,54,35,5,32,59	828

SHOPPING	GAMBLE	SEX	KEYWORD	KEYWORD						
Good	Good	is great	SOCIAL	Children,Education,Astrology,Bargains,Social Functions,Childishness,Groups -						

STRESS LEVEL	LUCKY COLORS	JEWELERY	MOONS EFFECT	GRAHA EFFECT	DAILY DEITY
Low	Green/Sky Blue/	Diamonds/Silver	Enthusiastic	Social Graha	Vishnu

DAILY PUJA	DAILY PSALMS
Wash the feet of Children, Do Satnarayan Pooja, Read & chant Geeta	3, 12, 30 ,39, 48, 57, 75, 102, 120

Friday, December 15, 2023 — This is considered a NEGATIVE day for you — Planet: Pluto

ADVICE & DETAILS
Overcome laziness and low pay today and improve your karma by being industrious, hard working and controlling your high temper.

MANTRA FOR TODAY
Om Jai Viganeshwaraya.. Lambodaraya Namo Namaha 21 times

MONEY	LOVE	CAREER	FAMILY	TRAVEL	WEDDING	MOVE	BUSINESS	HEALTH	Lotto #'s	play 3 #s
Bad	Fair	Bad	Fair	Bad	Good	Bad	Bad	Bad	33,72,40,32,12,49,5	291

SHOPPING	GAMBLE	SEX	KEYWORD	KEYWORD
Bad	Bad	is tough	CAREER	Career,Hard Work,Co-workers,Low Payment,Job Problems,High Temper,Low

STRESS LEVEL	LUCKY COLORS	JEWELERY	MOONS EFFECT	GRAHA EFFECT	DAILY DEITY
High	Dark Blue/ Purple/	Amethyst/Gold	Emotional	Job Graha	Lingam

DAILY PUJA	DAILY PSALMS
Worship Ganesh, Give gifts to father, and co-workers, Plant gardens, farms	4, 13, 31 ,40, 49, 58, 76, 103, 121

Saturday, December 16, 2023 — This is considered a POSITIVE day for you — Planet: Venus

ADVICE & DETAILS
Although this will be a day open for you to socialize with others, you must avoid extremes and parties with alcohol and drugs. Your enemies will take advantage of you today when they see you in your weakest state. Try to rest, you will be sleepy.

MANTRA FOR TODAY
Om Graam Greem Graum Sa Gurave namah swaha 21 times

MONEY	LOVE	CAREER	FAMILY	TRAVEL	WEDDING	MOVE	BUSINESS	HEALTH	Lotto #'s	play 3 #s
Bad	Excellent	Fair	Good	Excellen	Good	Excellen	Good	Excellent	39,16,29,18,47,16,3	972

SHOPPING	GAMBLE	SEX	KEYWORD	KEYWORD
Good	Good	is good	CHANGE	Sexuality,Travel,Change,Distant, far,Travel delays,Deception,Excercise,Illicit

STRESS LEVEL	LUCKY COLORS	JEWELERY	MOONS EFFECT	GRAHA EFFECT	DAILY DEITY
Fair	Tan/Green/ Beige	Pearl/Silver/quartz	Courageous	Travel Graha	Nataraja

DAILY PUJA	DAILY PSALMS
Artistic gifts, Pray to Krishna, Do good deeds, do Spiritual trips	5, 14, 32 ,41, 50, 59, 77, 104, 122

Sunday, December 17, 2023 — This is considered a NEGATIVE day for you — Planet: Mars

ADVICE & DETAILS
Children will be prevalent today. This day is marked with a great deal of creativity ideal for areas related to the left side of the brain such as writing, painting, handcrafts, baking, cooking or needlework.

MANTRA FOR TODAY
Om Mana Swasti Shanti Kuru kuru Swaha Shivoham Shivoham 27 times

MONEY	LOVE	CAREER	FAMILY	TRAVEL	WEDDING	MOVE	BUSINESS	HEALTH	Lotto #'s	play 3 #s
Bad	Bad	Bad	Bad	Bad	Bad	Bad	Fair	Bad	14,21,5,39,52,32,16	169

SHOPPING	GAMBLE	SEX	KEYWORD	KEYWORD
Fair	Bad	is frustrating	POWER	Responsibilty,Disagreement,Family,Back Pain,Family Conflicts,Traffic

STRESS LEVEL	LUCKY COLORS	JEWELERY	MOONS EFFECT	GRAHA EFFECT	DAILY DEITY
High	Purple/Blue/Rose	Emerald/Saphire	Educational	Family Graha	Mahakali

DAILY PUJA	DAILY PSALMS
Meditate, Control temper, Pray to Hanuman, Chant Hanuman Chalisa	6, 15, 33 ,42, 51, 60, 78, 105, 123

Monday, December 18, 2023 — This is considered a NEUTRAL day for you — Planet: Uranus

ADVICE & DETAILS
The thought of watching TV is very appealing today. Spending time with children will benefit your creativity, but you must refrain from allowing immaturity to control your actions today.

MANTRA FOR TODAY
Jai Jai Shiva Shambo.(2) ...Mahadeva Shambo (2) 21 times 8

MONEY	LOVE	CAREER	FAMILY	TRAVEL	WEDDING	MOVE	BUSINESS	HEALTH	Lotto #'s	play 3 #s
Good	Good	Fair	Good	Good	Bad	Good	Bad	Fair	65,26,53,10,51,40,6	304

SHOPPING	GAMBLE	SEX	KEYWORD	KEYWORD
Bad	Fair	is quiet	DIVINE	Spirituality,Religious,Astrology,Inner Conflicts,Religious ,Sleepiness,Advice

STRESS LEVEL	LUCKY COLORS	JEWELERY	MOONS EFFECT	GRAHA EFFECT	DAILY DEITY
Fair	Light Blue/Peach	Tiger's eye/Gold/Sil	Affectionate	God'S Graha	Shesnaag

DAILY PUJA	DAILY PSALMS
Chant Shiva Mantras, Take gifts to Ocean - Ganga Puja, Donate to Temple, Priests, etc.	7, 16, 34 ,43, 52, 61, 79, 106, 124

Tuesday, December 19, 2023 — This is considered a POSITIVE day for you — Planet: Jupiter

ADVICE & DETAILS

The power of your expression today is great. Use this power to communicate with others, to write and publish or to entertain others when in groups or parties. There is the influence of someone that is jealous of you, be aware of it and try to be modest.

MANTRA FOR TODAY: Om Hareem Nama Swaha..Shri Maha Laxmi Aye Namah swaha 12 times

MONEY	LOVE	CAREER	FAMILY	TRAVEL	WEDDING	MOVE	BUSINESS	HEALTH	Lotto #'s	play 3 #s
Excellent	Good	Excellent	Good	Good	Excellent	Good	Excellent	Excellent	26,27,66,62,31,11,7	313

SHOPPING	GAMBLE	SEX	KEYWORD	KEYWORD
Excellent	Excellent	is excellent	MONEY	Business,Major Expense,Money -

STRESS LEVEL	LUCKY COLORS	JEWELERY	MOONS EFFECT	GRAHA EFFECT	DAILY DEITY
Low	Yellow/Silver	Diamonds/Gold/Pea	Secretive	Money Graha	Mahalaxmi

DAILY PUJA	DAILY PSALMS
Decorate Land, Feed the poor, Donate milk /products to all, Feed holy guests,	8, 17, 35 ,44, 53, 62, 80, 107, 125

Wednesday, December 20, 2023 — This is considered a NEGATIVE day for you — Planet: Saturn

ADVICE & DETAILS

Although this will be a day open for you to socialize with others, you must avoid extremes and parties with alcohol and drugs. Your enemies will take advantage of you today when they see you in your weakest state. Try to rest, you will be sleepy.

MANTRA FOR TODAY: Om Ganga mataye nama swaha Om Varuna Devta aye Pahimam 11 times

MONEY	LOVE	CAREER	FAMILY	TRAVEL	WEDDING	MOVE	BUSINESS	HEALTH	Lotto #'s	play 3 #s
Bad	Bad	Bad	Fair	Bad	Bad	Bad	Bad	Bad	16,51,71,3,31,27,46	277

SHOPPING	GAMBLE	SEX	KEYWORD	KEYWORD
Bad	Bad	is very bad	KARMA	Destruction,Losses,Death,Sickness - cold,Legal matter,Abusive,Karmic debts,God -

STRESS LEVEL	LUCKY COLORS	JEWELERY	MOONS EFFECT	GRAHA EFFECT	DAILY DEITY
High	Gold/Brown//Green	Saphire/Hessonite	Ivestments	Evil Graha	Agnidev

DAILY PUJA	DAILY PSALMS
Remembrance of family members who died, worship of older people. gifts to grand parents	9, 18, 36 ,45, 54, 63, 81, 108, 126

Thursday, December 21, 2023 — This is considered a NEUTRAL day for you — Planet: Sun

ADVICE & DETAILS

There may be sickness of children or you may be getting sick. There will be losses and sadness.

MANTRA FOR TODAY: Om Namo Bhagawate Mukhtanandaya, 108 times

MONEY	LOVE	CAREER	FAMILY	TRAVEL	WEDDING	MOVE	BUSINESS	HEALTH	Lotto #'s	play 3 #s
Fair	Bad	Good	Bad	Fair	Bad	Fair	Fair	Fair	74,28,61,5,26,13,16	906

SHOPPING	GAMBLE	SEX	KEYWORD	KEYWORD
Fair	Fair	is fair	MIND	Independence,Loneliness,Meditative,Worry,Dominating,Illness - Cold,On Your

STRESS LEVEL	LUCKY COLORS	JEWELERY	MOONS EFFECT	GRAHA EFFECT	DAILY DEITY
High	White/Yellow/	Pearl/Quartz	Arrogance	Status Graha	Saraswaty

DAILY PUJA	DAILY PSALMS
Give Gifts to Priests, Invite holy ones to your home, Feed Swamis and Yogis, Do Shiva Puja.	1, 10, 28 ,37, 46, 55, 73, 100, 118

Friday, December 22, 2023 — This is considered a POSITIVE day for you — Planet: Moon

ADVICE & DETAILS

Express your thoughts, opinions or information to partners and/or children. Day is influenced by children and ability to acquire information by reading or other means.

MANTRA FOR TODAY: Kali Durge Namo Nama Om Durge aye nama swaha 108 times

MONEY	LOVE	CAREER	FAMILY	TRAVEL	WEDDING	MOVE	BUSINESS	HEALTH	Lotto #'s	play 3 #s
Good	Excellent	Good	Good	Excellen	Good	Good	Good	Good	71,35,69,9,32,26,15	741

SHOPPING	GAMBLE	SEX	KEYWORD	KEYWORD
Good	Good	is good	LOVE	Romance,Popularity,Visitors,Shopping,Food, Drinks,Co-

STRESS LEVEL	LUCKY COLORS	JEWELERY	MOONS EFFECT	GRAHA EFFECT	DAILY DEITY
Low	Red/Yellow/Pink	Topaz/Diamonds	Conservative	Love Graha	Gauri

DAILY PUJA	DAILY PSALMS
Give Gifts to females andnMother, Serve milk Products, Worship Durga forms	2, 11, 29 ,38, 47, 56, 74, 101, 119

Saturday, December 23, 2023 — This is considered a POSITIVE day for you — Planet: Mercury

ADVICE & DETAILS

Reading will benefit you today. You will have to hone your communication skills and speak clearly and listen carefully, especially when dealing with Real Estate and teachers of any type.

MANTRA FOR TODAY

Om hareem Kleem Hreem Aem Saraswataye namaha 21 times

MONEY	LOVE	CAREER	FAMILY	TRAVEL	WEDDING	MOVE	BUSINESS	HEALTH	Lotto #'s	play 3 #s
Good	Fair	Good	Good	Excellen	Good	Good	Good	Excellent	33,38,11,48,8,13,44	215

SHOPPING	GAMBLE	SEX	KEYWORD	KEYWORD						
Good	Good	is great	SOCIAL	Children,Education,Astrology,Bargains,Social Functions,Childishness,Groups -						

STRESS LEVEL	LUCKY COLORS	JEWELERY	MOONS EFFECT	GRAHA EFFECT	DAILY DEITY
Low	Green/Sky Blue/	Diamonds/Silver	Enthusiastic	Social Graha	Vishnu

DAILY PUJA	DAILY PSALMS
Wash the feet of Children, Do Satnarayan Pooja, Read & chant Geeta	3, 12, 30 ,39, 48, 57, 75, 102, 120

Sunday, December 24, 2023 — This is considered a NEGATIVE day for you — Planet: Pluto

ADVICE & DETAILS

Overcome laziness and low pay today and improve your karma by being industrious, hard working and controlling your high temper.

MANTRA FOR TODAY

Om Jai Viganeshwaraya.. Lambodaraya Namo Namaha 21 times

MONEY	LOVE	CAREER	FAMILY	TRAVEL	WEDDING	MOVE	BUSINESS	HEALTH	Lotto #'s	play 3 #s
Bad	Fair	Bad	Fair	Bad	Good	Bad	Bad	Bad	24,65,29,31,8,5,74	44

SHOPPING	GAMBLE	SEX	KEYWORD	KEYWORD						
Bad	Bad	is tough	CAREER	Career,Hard Work,Co-workers,Low Payment,Job Problems,High Temper,Low						

STRESS LEVEL	LUCKY COLORS	JEWELERY	MOONS EFFECT	GRAHA EFFECT	DAILY DEITY
High	Dark Blue/ Purple/	Amethyst/Gold	Emotional	Job Graha	Lingam

DAILY PUJA	DAILY PSALMS
Worship Ganesh, Give gifts to father, and co -workers, Plant gardens, farms	4, 13, 31 ,40, 49, 58, 76, 103, 121

Monday, December 25, 2023 — This is considered a POSITIVE day for you — Planet: Venus

ADVICE & DETAILS

Although this will be a day open for you to socialize with others, you must avoid extremes and parties with alcohol and drugs. Your enemies will take advantage of you today when they see you in your weakest state. Try to rest, you will be sleepy.

MANTRA FOR TODAY

Om Graam Greem Graum Sa Gurave namah swaha 21 times

MONEY	LOVE	CAREER	FAMILY	TRAVEL	WEDDING	MOVE	BUSINESS	HEALTH	Lotto #'s	play 3 #s
Bad	Excellent	Fair	Good	Excellen	Good	Excellen	Good	Excellent	17,33,17,33,58,62,6	992

SHOPPING	GAMBLE	SEX	KEYWORD	KEYWORD						
Good	Good	is good	CHANGE	Sexuality,Travel,Change,Distant, far,Travel delays,Deception,Excercise,Illicit						

STRESS LEVEL	LUCKY COLORS	JEWELERY	MOONS EFFECT	GRAHA EFFECT	DAILY DEITY
Fair	Tan/Green/ Beige	Pearl/Silver/quartz	Courageous	Travel Graha	Nataraja

DAILY PUJA	DAILY PSALMS
Artistic gifts, Pray to Krishna, Do good deeds, do Spiritual trips	5, 14, 32 ,41, 50, 59, 77, 104, 122

Tuesday, December 26, 2023 — This is considered a NEGATIVE day for you — Planet: Mars

ADVICE & DETAILS

Children will be prevalent today. This day is marked with a great deal of creativity ideal for areas related to the left side of the brain such as writing, painting, handcrafts, baking, cooking or needlework.

MANTRA FOR TODAY

Om Mana Swasti Shanti Kuru kuru Swaha Shivoham Shivoham 27 times

MONEY	LOVE	CAREER	FAMILY	TRAVEL	WEDDING	MOVE	BUSINESS	HEALTH	Lotto #'s	play 3 #s
Bad	Bad	Bad	Bad	Bad	Bad	Bad	Fair	Bad	48,66,72,63,4,64,74	660

SHOPPING	GAMBLE	SEX	KEYWORD	KEYWORD						
Fair	Bad	is frustrating	POWER	Responsibilty,Disagreement,Family,Back Pain,Family Conflicts,Traffic						

STRESS LEVEL	LUCKY COLORS	JEWELERY	MOONS EFFECT	GRAHA EFFECT	DAILY DEITY
High	Purple/Blue/Rose	Emerald/Saphire	Educational	Family Graha	Mahakali

DAILY PUJA	DAILY PSALMS
Meditate, Control temper, Pray to Hanuman, Chant Hanuman Chalisa	6, 15, 33 ,42, 51, 60, 78, 105, 123

Wednesday, December 27, 2023 — This is considered a NEUTRAL day for you — Planet: Uranus

ADVICE & DETAILS

The thought of watching TV is very appealing today. Spending time with children will benefit your creativity, but you must refrain from allowing immaturity to control your actions today.

MANTRA FOR TODAY

Jai Jai Shiva Shambo.(2) ...Mahadeva Shambo (2) 21 times 8

MONEY	LOVE	CAREER	FAMILY	TRAVEL	WEDDING	MOVE	BUSINESS	HEALTH	Lotto #'s	play 3 #s
Good	Good	Fair	Good	Good	Bad	Good	Bad	Fair	49,57,46,53,30,19,1	224

SHOPPING	GAMBLE	SEX	KEYWORD	KEYWORD
Bad	Fair	is quiet	DIVINE	Spirituality,Religious,Astrology,Inner Conflicts,Religious ,Sleepiness,Advice

STRESS LEVEL	LUCKY COLORS	JEWELERY	MOONS EFFECT	GRAHA EFFECT	DAILY DEITY
Fair	Light Blue/Peach	Tiger's eye/Gold/Sil	Affectionate	God'S Graha	Shesnaag

DAILY PUJA	DAILY PSALMS
Chant Shiva Mantras, Take gifts to Ocean - Ganga Puja, Donate to Temple, Priests, etc.	7, 16, 34 ,43, 52, 61, 79, 106, 124

Thursday, December 28, 2023 — This is considered a POSITIVE day for you — Planet: Jupiter

ADVICE & DETAILS

The power of your expression today is great. Use this power to communicate with others, to write and publish or to entertain others when in groups or parties. There is the influence of someone that is jealous of you, be aware of it and try to be modest.

MANTRA FOR TODAY

Om Hareem Nama Swaha..Shri Maha Laxmi Aye Namah swaha 12 times

MONEY	LOVE	CAREER	FAMILY	TRAVEL	WEDDING	MOVE	BUSINESS	HEALTH	Lotto #'s	play 3 #s
Excellent	Good	Excellent	Good	Good	Excellent	Good	Excellent	Excellent	64,36,62,2,56,6,48	560

SHOPPING	GAMBLE	SEX	KEYWORD	KEYWORD
Excellent	Excellent	is excellent	MONEY	Business,Major Expense,Money -

STRESS LEVEL	LUCKY COLORS	JEWELERY	MOONS EFFECT	GRAHA EFFECT	DAILY DEITY
Low	Yellow/Silver	Diamonds/Gold/Pea	Secretive	Money Graha	Mahalaxmi

DAILY PUJA	DAILY PSALMS
Decorate Land, Feed the poor, Donate milk /products to all, Feed holy guests,	8, 17, 35 ,44, 53, 62, 80, 107, 125

Friday, December 29, 2023 — This is considered a NEGATIVE day for you — Planet: Saturn

ADVICE & DETAILS

Although this will be a day open for you to socialize with others, you must avoid extremes and parties with alcohol and drugs. Your enemies will take advantage of you today when they see you in your weakest state. Try to rest, you will be sleepy.

MANTRA FOR TODAY

Om Ganga mataye nama swaha Om Varuna Devta aye Pahimam 11 times

MONEY	LOVE	CAREER	FAMILY	TRAVEL	WEDDING	MOVE	BUSINESS	HEALTH	Lotto #'s	play 3 #s
Bad	Bad	Bad	Fair	Bad	Bad	Bad	Bad	Bad	36,68,73,33,50,40,3	111

SHOPPING	GAMBLE	SEX	KEYWORD	KEYWORD
Bad	Bad	is very bad	KARMA	Destruction,Losses,Death,Sickness - cold,Legal matter,Abusive,Karmic debts,God -

STRESS LEVEL	LUCKY COLORS	JEWELERY	MOONS EFFECT	GRAHA EFFECT	DAILY DEITY
High	Gold/Brown//Green	Saphire/Hessonite	Ivestments	Evil Graha	Agnidev

DAILY PUJA	DAILY PSALMS
Remembrance of family members who died, worship of older people. gifts to grand parents	9, 18, 36 ,45, 54, 63, 81, 108, 126

Saturday, December 30, 2023 — This is considered a NEUTRAL day for you — Planet: Sun

ADVICE & DETAILS

There may be sickness of children or you may be getting sick. There will be losses and sadness.

MANTRA FOR TODAY

Om Namo Bhagawate Mukhtanandaya, 108 times

MONEY	LOVE	CAREER	FAMILY	TRAVEL	WEDDING	MOVE	BUSINESS	HEALTH	Lotto #'s	play 3 #s
Fair	Bad	Good	Bad	Fair	Bad	Fair	Fair	Fair	24,10,22,29,56,58,5	232

SHOPPING	GAMBLE	SEX	KEYWORD	KEYWORD
Fair	Fair	is fair	MIND	Independence,Loneliness,Meditative,Worry,Dominating,Illness - Cold,On Your

STRESS LEVEL	LUCKY COLORS	JEWELERY	MOONS EFFECT	GRAHA EFFECT	DAILY DEITY
High	White/Yellow/	Pearl/Quartz	Arrogance	Status Graha	Saraswaty

DAILY PUJA	DAILY PSALMS
Give Gifts to Priests, Invite holy ones to your home, Feed Swamis and Yogis, Do Shiva Puja.	1, 10, 28 ,37, 46, 55, 73, 100, 118

Sunday, December 31, 2023 — This is considered a POSITIVE day for you — Planet: Moon

ADVICE & DETAILS

Express your thoughts, opinions or information to partners and/or children. Day is influenced by children and ability to acquire information by reading or other means.

MANTRA FOR TODAY

Kali Durge Namo Nama Om Durge aye nama swaha 108 times

MONEY	LOVE	CAREER	FAMILY	TRAVEL	WEDDING	MOVE	BUSINESS	HEALTH	Lotto #'s	play 3 #s
Good	Excellent	Good	Good	Excellen	Good	Good	Good	Good	51,22,24,23,67,27,5	451

SHOPPING	GAMBLE	SEX	KEYWORD	KEYWORD						
Good	Good	is good	LOVE	Romance,Popularity,Visitors,Shopping,Food, Drinks,Co-						

STRESS LEVEL		LUCKY COLORS	JEWELERY	MOONS EFFECT	GRAHA EFFECT	DAILY DEITY
Low		Red/Yellow/Pink	Topaz/Diamonds	Conservative	Love Graha	Gauri

DAILY PUJA	DAILY PSALMS
Give Gifts to females andnMother, Serve milk Products, Worship Durga forms	2, 11, 29 ,38, 47, 56, 74, 101, 119

Monday, January 1, 2024 — This is considered a POSITIVE day for you — Planet: Jupiter

ADVICE & DETAILS

If you can, take short trips and enjoy high pleasure. There will be lots of moving today.

MANTRA FOR TODAY

Om Hareem Nama Swaha..Shri Maha Laxmi Aye Namah swaha 12 times

MONEY	LOVE	CAREER	FAMILY	TRAVEL	WEDDING	MOVE	BUSINESS	HEALTH	Lotto #'s	play 3 #s
Excellent	Good	Excellent	Good	Good	Excellent	Good	Excellent	Excellent	7,67,48,36,61,56,28	645

SHOPPING	GAMBLE	SEX	KEYWORD	KEYWORD						
Excellent	Excellent	is excellent	MONEY	Business,Major Expense,Money -						

STRESS LEVEL		LUCKY COLORS	JEWELERY	MOONS EFFECT	GRAHA EFFECT	DAILY DEITY
Low		Yellow/Silver	Diamonds/Gold/Pea	Secretive	Money Graha	Mahalaxmi

DAILY PUJA	DAILY PSALMS
Decorate Land, Feed the poor, Donate milk /products to all, Feed holy guests,	8, 17, 35 ,44, 53, 62, 80, 107, 125

Tuesday, January 2, 2024 — This is considered a NEGATIVE day for you — Planet: Saturn

ADVICE & DETAILS

Connect with the God within today so you can avoid the loneliness that can result from being boastful and criticizing others. Look at yourself first instead of trying to fix others.

MANTRA FOR TODAY

Om Ganga mataye nama swaha Om Varuna Devta aye Pahimam 11 times

MONEY	LOVE	CAREER	FAMILY	TRAVEL	WEDDING	MOVE	BUSINESS	HEALTH	Lotto #'s	play 3 #s
Bad	Bad	Bad	Fair	Bad	Bad	Bad	Bad	Bad	36,36,37,63,40,42,3	372

SHOPPING	GAMBLE	SEX	KEYWORD	KEYWORD						
Bad	Bad	is very bad	KARMA	Destruction,Losses,Death,Sickness - cold,Legal matter,Abusive,Karmic debts,God -						

STRESS LEVEL		LUCKY COLORS	JEWELERY	MOONS EFFECT	GRAHA EFFECT	DAILY DEITY
High		Gold/Brown//Green	Saphire/Hessonite	Ivestments	Evil Graha	Agnidev

DAILY PUJA	DAILY PSALMS
Remembrance of family members who died, worship of older people. gifts to grand parents	9, 18, 36 ,45, 54, 63, 81, 108, 126

Wednesday, January 3, 2024 — This is considered a NEUTRAL day for you — Planet: Sun

ADVICE & DETAILS

Today, you may be home alone, you may feel a bit confined, but at the same time you will have a sense of independence and the realization of your capabilities. This day may be influenced by dealings with the government, courts or legal institutions.

MANTRA FOR TODAY

Om Namo Bhagawate Mukhtanandaya, 108 times

MONEY	LOVE	CAREER	FAMILY	TRAVEL	WEDDING	MOVE	BUSINESS	HEALTH	Lotto #'s	play 3 #s
Fair	Bad	Good	Bad	Fair	Bad	Fair	Fair	Fair	21,32,51,7,46,19,24	721

SHOPPING	GAMBLE	SEX	KEYWORD	KEYWORD						
Fair	Fair	is fair	MIND	Independence,Loneliness,Meditative,Worry,Dominating,Illness - Cold,On Your						

STRESS LEVEL		LUCKY COLORS	JEWELERY	MOONS EFFECT	GRAHA EFFECT	DAILY DEITY
High		White/Yellow/	Pearl/Quartz	Arrogance	Status Graha	Saraswaty

DAILY PUJA	DAILY PSALMS
Give Gifts to Priests, Invite holy ones to your home, Feed Swamis and Yogis, Do Shiva Puja.	1, 10, 28 ,37, 46, 55, 73, 100, 118

APPENDIX I

The Purpose and Benefits of The LifeCode

1   To provide ALL PEOPLE with accurate predictions of his or her life so that steps can be taken to avoid negative experiences.

2   To help ALL PEOPLE determine when it's a good time to:

a)	Get married	e)	Invest
b)	Move into a new home	f)	Travel
c)	Undergo medical operations	g)	and more....
d)	Buy a vehicle		

3   To provide ALL PEOPLE person with monthly, yearly, and daily forecast of his or her life based on their LifeCode

4   To assist ALL PEOPLE, to take control or change his destiny and avoid negative experiences in his life through the help of Vedic Science, used in this book.

5   To assist ALL PEOPLE by bringing back the use of ancient formulas that were used by the great Rishis and Sages for creating a successful lifestyle so that we can properly use it for the elimination of bad marriages, unhealthy babies, financial disasters, and so on. To bring back the old science of the ALL PEOPLE, a science greater than the science of today, thereby creating a better world for our future generation.

6   If you wish to perform yearly forecast predictions on your own life then you need to know these very details as shown above based on your actual date of birth. Since this book only covers the present year to get your birth information you may need to get a "100 YEAR LIFECODE BOOK" that we publish and personalize according to you.

7   In this book you can find out who your ISHTA DEVTA or Karmic Ruler is and the same for anyone in your family. Using this you will be able to predict most of the experiences that you will have in this year or the coming year. You will also be able to predict your monthly and your daily experiences, determine if your marriage is compatible

and whether your home is a good location for you....and many more.

8 Suggestions for timing certain events in your life such as when to move, when to travel, when to borrow money, when to file a court case, and so on, can be found on the DAILY HOROSCOPE section called "CONTROL THE POSITIVE AND NEGATIVE DAYS IN YOUR LIFE" in the latter half of this book. It is well known that the time or day that you start something will determine its success or failure.

PLEASE NOTE:
ANY QUESTIONS ABOUT THIS BOOK OR ABOUT LEARNING THE SCIENCE CAN BE ANSWERED BY CALLING THE CHAKRA SQUARE HEALING CENTER AT (305) 253-5410 OR EMAILING SWAMICHARRAN@GMAIL.COM

Appendix II
LIFE CODE BOOKS AVALABLE

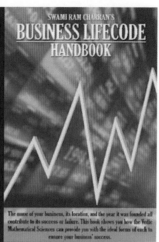

Books & Products Available from Chakra Square Healing Center

To Order Any Products Listed Contact the Center at (305) 253 – 5410 or via Email Swamicharran@gmail.com

SHIPPING/HANDLING IS NOT INCLUDED IN THE FOLLOWING PRICES

- **THE LIFE CODE SERIES**
  1. Life Code – The Vedic Code of Your Life $24.99
  2. The Equation of Your Life $39.99
  3. The Square of Life Vol. 1 $39.99
  4. The Square of Life Vol. 2 $39.99
  5. LifeCode Handbook $19.99
  6. Codigo de la Vida (Spanish LifeCode) $29.99
  7. Whole Life Handbook for Life Code Book #1 $54.99
  8. Whole Life Handbook for Life Code Book #2 $54.99
  9. Whole Life Handbook for Life Code Book #3 $54.99
  10. Whole Life Handbook for Life Code Book #4 $54.99
  11. Whole Life Handbook for Life Code Book #5 $54.99
  12. Whole Life Handbook for Life Code Book #6 $54.99
  13. Whole Life Handbook for Life Code Book #7 $54.99
  14. Whole Life Handbook for Life Code Book #8 $54.99
  15. Whole Life Handbook for Life Code Book #9 $54.99
  16. Vedic Yearly Guide Life Code #1 Book for 2023 BRAHMA $44.99
  17. Vedic Yearly Guide Life Code #2 Book for 2023 DURGA $44.99
  18. Vedic Yearly Guide Life Code #3 Book for 2023 VISHNU $44.99
  19. Vedic Yearly Guide Life Code #4 Book for 2023 RUDRA $44.99
  20. Vedic Yearly Guide Life Code #5 Book for 2023 NARAYAN $44.99
  21. Vedic Yearly Guide Life Code #6 Book for 2023 HANUMAN/KALI $44.99
  22. Vedic Yearly Guide Life Code #7 Book for 2023 SHIVA $44.99
  23. Vedic Yearly Guide Life Code #8 Book for 2023 LAXMI $44.99
  24. Vedic Yearly Guide Life Code #9 Book for 2023 INDRA $44.99

- **THE VEDIC SCIENCE SERIES**
  25. The Science Of The Hindu Gods (Black & White Version) $29.99
  26. The Science Of The Hindu Gods (Color Version) $44.99
  27. The Kalbhairo Vs. Lord Shiva $29.99
  28. Hanuman Jyotish (Ram's Book of Fate) $49.99
  29. Book of Yantras $29.99

30. Challenging God- Is Sacrifice Part Of God Or Devil? $29.99
31. Challenging Temptation: The Good Vs. The Evil $29.99
32. The Vedic Health Life Code $24.99
33. The Vedic Sexual Life Code $34.99
34. Sexual Death $39.99
35. The Power Of A Woman $39.99
36. The Location Life Code $19.99
37. The Vedic Name Life Code $29.99.
38. The Vedic Code Of Wealth And Prosperity Book $39.99.
39. The Heendu Learning Center Handbook $9.99
40. The Vedic Mathematics $39.99
    o This Book Will Revolutionize The Way The World Looks At Mathematics. Swami Ram Charran Uncovers The Mysteries Behind Numbers Through Times. AVAILABLE SOON!

- THE VEDIC ASTROLOGY SERIES
    41. 100 Year Patra Volume 1 $99.99
    42. 100 Year Patra Volume 1A $99.99
    43. 100 Year Patra Volume 2 $99.99
    44. 100 Year Patra Volume 3 $74.99
    45. 100 Year Patra Volume 4 $99.99
    46. 100 Year Patra Volume 5 $99.99
    47. Vedic Patra 2022 Color Edition $54.99
    48. Charan Mala –Vedic Birth Name Code $39.99
    49. Nakshatra Mala- Vedic Birth Star Code $39.99
    50. Rasimala- Vedic Birth Sign Code Book $39.99

- THE VEDIC RITUAL SCIENCE SERIES
    Every time a person is born, the whole universe re-arranges itself. When the karma of the parents follow the child in the form of negative spiritual genetics, and a spiritual operation to change the karma is required to re-change the universe, then a universal correction ritual called a "PUJA" is needed where the person goes backward in time and re-corrects his or her karma....whether in finance, health, marriage, family structure or children then a specific puja ritual is geared for its correction.

    51. Antyesi Puja Handbook $39.99 (Funeral Puja)
    52. Durga Puja Handbook $39.99 (Love Puja)
    53. Ganesh Puja Handbook $39.99 (Career & Remove Obstacle Puja)
    54. Ganga Puja Handbook $39.99
    55. Garbhadan Sanskar Puja $39.99 (Childbirth)
    56. Guru Initiation Puja $39.99
    57. Hanuman Puja Handbook $39.99
    58. Havan Puja Handbook $39.99 (Agni Fire Ritual)
    59. Laxmi Puja Handbook $39.99 (Wealth & Prosperity Puja)

60. Moola Puja Handbook $39.99 (Children Born Unlucky)
61. Nav-Graha Puja $39.99 (Nine Planets)
62. Panchanka Puja Handbook $39.99 (Untimely Deaths)
63. Pitri Puja Handbook $39.99 (Ancestors)
64. Shiva Puja Handbook $39.99
65. Lord Satnarayan Puja $39.99
66. Lord Surya Narayan Puja $39.99
67. Vijay Bhava Puja Handbook $39.99
68. Vivaah Puja Handbook $39.99

- <u>SWAMI RAM'S AYURVEDIC HERBAL CURES</u>

  Includes all herbal capsules and medicine, hair cream etc

  69. **Ayurvedic Oil for Men** $29.99.
      - Used for: Aligning your spine, Removes Back Pain, Headaches, Stomach Problems, Enhances your Energy and Love Life, Removes Skin Problems*
  70. **Pregnancy Oil** $19.99
      - Used FOR PROTECTING THE BABY from miscarriage, menstrual problems, self-abortions, and to remove stretch marks around the belly*
  71. **Herbal Bath $19.99**
      - A spiritual bath that will drive all evil spirits away from your body & soul. A pure Ayurvedic mixture of herbal plant elements that has been specially prepared with mantras and prayers chanted by holy and divine priests of a Hindu temple(ashram), specially prepared to make people avoid blockages to progress in all aspects of their life*
  72. **Hair Cream $14.99**
      - Natural Blend of Herbal Medicines proven to stop hair loss and promote healthy hair growth*
  73. **Florida Water $4.99**
  74. **Ashwagandha Powder Vegetarian Capsules** 100CT $19.99.
      - Promotes Circulatory Health. Controls Sugar and Glucose Levels, Reduces High Blood Pressures, Aids Diabetics*
  75. **Cinnamon Powder Vegetarian Capsules** 100Ct $14.99.
      - Aids with digestion and removes stomach pain*
  76. **Diabetic Powder Vegetarian Capsules** 100CT $19.99.
      - Aids in bittering of blood, lowers glucose levels, and helps pancreatic islet cells to naturally produce more insulin.*
  77. **Ginger Vegetarian Capsules** 100CT $14.99.
      - Good for creating body heat, Cures Cold Fever, and helps Blood Circulation*
  78. **HIV/AIDS Vegetarian Capsule** 100CT $19.99
      - Reduces symptoms and helps in healing immune system in those affected by the disease*
  79. **Kundalini Vegetarian Capsules** 50 CT $19.99 100 CT 39.99

- o Good for enhancing Sexual Energy
80. **Neem Powder Vegetarian Capsules** 100CT 19.99.
  - o Promotes Circulatory Health. Aids in bittering of blood, lowers glucose levels, and clears acne and blemishes*
81. **Triphala Powder Vegetarian Capsules** 100 CT $14.99
  - o Blood Cleanser*
82. **Turmeric Vegetarian Capsules** 100CT $6.99
  - o Aids in bittering of blood, lowers glucose levels, clears acne and blemishes. Recommended for those with arthritis*

*Here's the legal disclaimer that WE HAVE to place on our catalog by law. The Statements on this catalog have not been evaluated by the FDA. Natural supplements or herbal remedies are not to be used to diagnose, treat, cure or prevent any disease. Any information provided on these herbal remedies is not a substitute for the advice of a licensed medical practitioner, naturopath, physician, alternative medicine doctor, licensed chiropractor, registered pharmacist or holistic medical physician. Individuals are advised not to self-medicate in the presence of significant illness. Ingredients in natural supplements or herbal remedies are not drugs and may not be foods.

- <u>SWAMI RAM'S AUDIO SERIES</u> – CD's

83. Kali Durge CD $5.99
84. Remove Obstacles CD $5.99
85. Wealth CD $5.99
86. Remove Illness CD $5.99
87. Knowledge CD $5.99
88. Love and Marriage CD $5.99
89. Pregnancy CD $5.99
90. Love and Romance CD $5.99
91. Remove Ghosts CD $5.99
92. Kundalini Yoga CD $5.99
93. Shiva Lingam CD (Lover) $5.99
94. Nav-Graha CD $5.99
95. Jaya Guru OM CD $5.99
96. Govinda Jai Jai CD $5.99
97. Om Nama Shivaya CD $5.99
98. How to Meditate CD $5.99
99. Morning Prayer CD $5.99
100. Fire Ritual CD $5.99
101. Daily Prayer CD $5.99
102. Court Cases CD $5.99
103. Winning Debates CD $5.99
104. Immigration CD $5.99
105. Remove Anger CD $5.99
106. Happy Marriage Life CD $5.99
107. Return Someone CD $5.99
108. Improve Career CD $5.99
109. Business CD $5.99
110. Rid of Curses CD $5.99
111. Interview with Swami 1 CD $5.99
112. Interview with Swami 1 CD $5.99
113. Interview with Swami 1 CD $5.99
114. Interview with Swami 1 CD $5.99
115. Interview with Swami 1 CD $5.99
116. Interview with Swami 1 CD $5.99
117. Gauri Mantra CD $5.99

- ## INSTRUCTIONAL BOOKLETS AND PAMPHLETS

  ### MANTRA BOOK $39.99

  1. Mantra to Remove Negative Energy from your life
  2. Mantra to Remove Obstacles and Enemies
  3. Mantra to Remove Illness and Health Problems
  4. Mantra for Wealth and Prosperity & Harmony
  5. Mantra to Improve Knowledge and Education
  6. Mantra to improve your Love & Marriage Life
  7. Mantra to Promote Pregnancy and Child birth
  8. Mantra to Attract Love and Romance in your life
  9. Mantra to Remove Ghosts and Spiritual Entities
  10. Mantra to Energize the Kundalini and Chakras
  11. Mantra to Obtain a Handsome & Great Lover (Lingam)
  12. Mantra to be in Harmony with the Universe (OM Nama)
  13. Mantra to learn how to meditate and relax
  14. Morning Prayers with Swami Ram Charran
  15. Mantras to use for Fire Rituals and Agni Hotra
  16. Mantras for the Daily Prayers and Peaceful Life
  17. Mantras for Winning Court Cases and Hearings
  18. Mantras for Winning Competitions and Debates
  19. Mantras for Immigration and Naturalization Cases
  20. Mantras to remove anger and High Temper
  21. Mantras to Create Peace and Good Relationships
  22. Mantras for Returning Someone Back into Your Life
  23. Mantra for Improving Career and Getting Promotions
  24. Mantra to Promote Business and Sales
  25. Mantra to Take Away Curses, Bad Eyes and Depression

- ## RITUAL INSTRUCTIONS - $3.00

  1. Puja Ritual to Change Life Karmas & Solve Problems
  2. Ritual for Success in Love and Marriage (Lingam Puja)
  3. House Blessing and Protection Ritual
  4. Business Location Blessing Ritual
  5. Car Blessing Ritual

- ## RITUAL PACKAGES & KITS

  1. House Cleaning Package 1 Day $14.99
  2. House Cleaning 3 Day Kit $44.99
  3. Car Blessing Package $29.99
  4. Business Blessing and Cleansing Package $50

5. Shiva Puja Package $99.99
6. Laxmi Puja Package $99.99
7. Hanuman Puja Package $99.99
8. Ganesh Puja Package $99.99
9. Complete Health Rejuvenation Package $150
10. Love, Marriage and Shiva Lingam Package $50
11. Court and Government Problems Package $20
12. Job and Career Promotion Package $20
13. Havan Puja and Fire Ritual Package $50
14. Pregnancy Promotion and Childbirth Kit $50
15. Wealth Promotion and Investment Kit $500

- PERSONALIZED SERVICES

Swami Ram Charran will create personalized Vedic astrological and life code charts. He also provides financial, performance and profit charges for companies.

1. Vedic ASTROLOGICAL Charts for specific birthdates…$300.00
2. Life code charts for 10year and more…$300.00
3. Vedic financial charts for specific companies and commodities $200.00 Each company
4. Vedic cycle charts for company performance and profits $100.00

- FRESH LEAVES AVAILABLE FOR PUJAS AND PRAYERS

SHIPPED FROM MIAMI FL VIA UPS OVERNIGHT. Prices vary by season and availability, call center for details or email swamicharran@gmail.com

1. Bael Patra Leaves 30 ct $34.99
2. Peepal Leaves 30 ct $29.99
3. Neem leaves (30 STEMS) 30 ct $29.99
4. Mango Leaves 30 ct $29.99
5. Paan Leaves 30 ct $29.99
6. Tulsi Leaves (by stem of approx. 30-50 leaves) 10 ct $29.99
7. Kush Grass 25 ct $29.99
8. Bahamia Grass 1 bunch $19.99
9. Kowa Leaves 30 ct $29.99
10. Madar Flowers (Purple/White) 25 ct $29.99

Swami Ram™ Presents
The Meditation Mantra Kit.

Mantras are words of power spoken in Sanskrit; An ancient Hindu language based on the scientific laws of sound & vibration. Meditating & Chanting These Sounds Creates A vibration Through The Universe - Bringing Love, Health, Wealth, Prosperity, Knowledge, Positivity & The Ever Presence Of The Supreme God To Reign In Your Life.

Swami Ram™ Presents
The Home Energy Cleansing Kit

A scientifically proven method of driving away negative energies from your home or business. By burning specially mixed aromas and elements in the home or business for at least one hour for one day. This packet will guarantee the user at least six months of peaceful existence in his or her home and larger profits at his or her business.

Cleanse Your Surroundings...

Begin the process to living a richer... healthier... Clearer life...

Want to learn how to rid your life and home of bad energy and start leading a healthier more prosperous life? Swami Ram has the answers! He's developed easy to use kits to get you on the right track on your path to a happy and fulfilled life. See what Swami Ram has in store for you in a portable kit form! Healing has arrived.

Cleanse Your Inner Self...

Begin the process to living a richer... healthier... Clearer life...

Want to learn how to rid your life and home of bad energy and start leading a healthier more prosperous life? Swami Ram has the answers! He's developed easy to use kits to get you on the right track on your path to a happy and fulfilled life. See what Swami Ram has in store for you in a portable kit form! Healing has arrived.

Swami Ram™ Presents
Health Maintenance Essentials Kit

Control and maintain a healthier life, naturally; avoid wasting time and money on treatments and medicines that are full of chemicals & may produce worse side effects. These natural ingredients have shown to help improve overall health and help control different illnesses & conditions.

Swami Ram™ Presents
The Hair Rejuvenation Kit.

This crème mixture contains a special blend of 10 essential nutrient oils proven to aid hair growth & thickness. These special blends of oils are formulated to prevent further hair loss as well as help to rejuvenate thinning hair and strengthen hair at the follicle.

Cleanse Your Surroundings...

Begin the process to living a richer... healthier... Clearer life...

Want to learn how to rid your life and home of bad energy and start leading a healthier more prosperous life? Swami Ram has the answers! He's developed easy to use kits to get you on the right track on your path to a happy and fulfilled life. See what Swami Ram has in .store for you in a portable kit form! Healing has arrived.

Cleanse Your Inner Self...

Begin the process to living a richer... healthier... Clearer life...

Want to learn how to rid your life and home of bad energy and start leading a healthier more prosperous life? Swami Ram has the answers! He's developed easy to use kits to get you on the right track on your path to a happy and fulfilled life. See what Swami Ram has in store for you in a portable kit form! Healing has arrived.

Swami Ram™
Presents
Diabetes Control Essentials Kit

Regain control of your life with the Diabetes essentials that work. These organic remedies will help you to naturally produce more insulin and regulate glucose levels. Additionally experience the other benefits to a better wellbeing.

Swami Ram™
Presents
The Rejuvenating Energy Bath Kit

Revitalize. Refresh. Renew. Swami Ram launches a newly redesigned take home product. Developed to help individuals begin to lead a better life. Restore good energy flow to your body. This life changing bath promotes tranquility, well-being, balances chakra energy and helps reduce stress. Cleanse and allow yourself to feel renewed.

Begin the process to living a richer... healthier... Clearer life...

Cleanse Your Surroundings...

Want to learn how to rid your life and home of bad energy and start leading a healthier more prosperous life? Swami Ram has the answers! He's developed easy to use kits to get you on the right track on your path to a happy and fulfilled life. See what Swami Ram has in store for you in a portable kit form! Healing has arrived.

Begin the process to living a richer... healthier... Clearer life...

Cleanse Your Surroundings...

Want to learn how to rid your life and home of bad energy and start leading a healthier more prosperous life? Swami Ram has the answers! He's developed easy to use kits to get you on the right track on your path to a happy and fulfilled life. See what Swami Ram has in store for you in a portable kit form! Healing has arrived.

Swami Ram
Presents
The Home Energy Cleansing Kit

A scientifically proven method of driving away negative energies from your home or business. By burning specially mixed aromas and elements in the home or business for at least one hour for one day. This packet will guarantee the user at least six months of peaceful existence in his or her home and larger profits at his or her business.

Swami Ram
Presents
The Ayurvedic Oil Healing Kit.

This special blend of natural oils helps to improve your overall circulation, digestive system and restore your skin to a better state while removing pains and ailments. It also eliminates internal blockages of progress and increases sexual energy for both men & women.

Begin the process to living a richer... healthier... Clearer life...

Cleanse Your Inner Self...

Want to learn how to rid your life and home of bad energy and start leading a healthier more prosperous life? Swami Ram has the answers! He's developed easy to use kits to get you on the right track on your path to a happy and fulfilled life. See what Swami Ram has in store for you in a portable kit form! Healing has arrived.

Begin the process to living a richer... healthier... Clearer life...

Cleanse Your Inner Self...

Want to learn how to rid your life and home of bad energy and start leading a healthier more prosperous life? Swami Ram has the answers! He's developed easy to use kits to get you on the right track on your path to a happy and fulfilled life. See what Swami Ram has in store for you in a portable kit form! Healing has arrived.

Printed in Great Britain
by Amazon

11004720R00092